The Character of God

Recent titles in

RELIGION IN AMERICA SERIES

Harry S. Stout, *General Editor*

MORMONS AND THE BIBLE
*The Place of the Latter-Day Saints in
American Religion*
Philip L. Barlow

THE SECULARIZATION OF THE ACADEMY
Edited by George M. Marsden and
Bradley J. Longfield

EPISCOPAL WOMEN
*Gender, Spirituality, and Commitment in
an American Mainline Denomination*
Edited by Catherine Prelinger

SUBMITTING TO FREEDOM
The Religious Vision of William James
Bennett Ramsey

OLD SHIP OF ZION
*The Afro-Baptist Ritual in
the African Diaspora*
Walter F. Pitts

AMERICAN TRANSCENDENTALISM AND
ASIAN RELIGIONS
Arthur Versluis

CHURCH PEOPLE IN THE STRUGGLE
*The National Council of Churches
and the Black Freedom Movement,
1950–1970*
James F. Findlay, Jr.

CONJURING CULTURE
Biblical Formations in Black America
Theophus Smith

REIMAGINING DENOMINATIONALISM
Interpretive Essays
Edited by Robert Bruce Mullin and
Russell E. Richey

KEEPERS OF THE COVENANT
*Frontier Missions and the Decline of
Congregationalism, 1774–1818*
James R. Rohrer

SAINTS IN EXILE
*The Holiness-Pentecostal Experience in
African American Religion and Culture*
Cheryl J. Sanders

DEMOCRATIC RELIGION
*Freedom, Authority, and Church Discipline
in the Baptist South, 1785–1900*
Gregory A. Wills

THE SOUL OF DEVELOPMENT
*Biblical Christianity and Economic
Transformation in Guatemala*
Amy L. Sherman

THE VIPER ON THE HEARTH
*Mormons, Myths, and the Construction
of Heresy*
Terryl L. Givens

SACRED COMPANIES
*Organizational Aspects of Religion and
Religious Aspects of Organizations*
Edited by N. J. Demerath III,
Peter Dobkin Hall, Terry Schmitt, and
Rhys H. Williams

MARY LYON AND THE MOUNT HOLYOKE
MISSIONARIES
Amanda Porterfield

BEING THERE
*Culture and Formation in Two
Theological Schools*
Jackson W. Carroll, Barbara G. Wheeler,
Daniel O. Aleshire, and
Penny Long Marler

THE CHARACTER OF GOD
*Recovering the Lost Literary Power of
American Protestantism*
Thomas E. Jenkins

The Character of God

Recovering the Lost Literary Power of American Protestantism

THOMAS E. JENKINS

New York Oxford
Oxford University Press
1997

Oxford University Press

Oxford   New York

Athens   Auckland   Bangkok   Bogota   Bombay   Buenos Aires
Calcutta   Cape Town   Dar es Salaam   Delhi   Florence   Hong Kong
Istanbul   Karachi   Kuala Lumpur   Madras   Madrid   Melbourne
Mexico City   Nairobi   Paris   Singapore   Taipei   Tokyo   Toronto   Warsaw

and associated companies in
Berlin   Ibadan

Copyright © 1997 by Thomas E. Jenkins

Published by Oxford University Press, Inc.
198 Madison Avenue, New York, New York 10016

Oxford is a registered trademark of Oxford University Press

Library of Congress Cataloging-in-Publication Data
Jenkins, Thomas E., 1962–
The character of God : recovering the lost literary power of
American Protestantism / Thomas E. Jenkins.
p.   cm. — (Religion in America series)
Includes bibliographical references and index.
ISBN 0-19-511202-4
1. God—Attributes—History of doctrines—19th century.
2. Christianity and literature—United States—History—19th
century.   3. Protestant churches—United States—Doctrines—
History—19th century.   4. God—Attributes—History of
doctrines—20th century.   5. Christianity and literature—United
States—History—20th century.   6. Protestant churches—United
States—Doctrines—History—20th century.   I. Title.   II. Series:
Religion in America series (Oxford University Press)
BT130.J46   1997
230'.044'09034—dc21   96-45426

1 3 5 7 9 8 6 4 2

Printed in the United States of America
on acid-free paper

❧

For
Barbara R. Jenkins
Holman W. Jenkins

✧

Acknowledgments

I have benefited from the help of many kind people while I was researching and writing this book. Anne M. Boylan, Lawrence Buell, Jon Butler, David Brion Davis, Hans W. Frei, Eugene Genovese, Patricia Hill, E. Brooks Holifield, Jack Miles, and Harry S. Stout all offered valuable comments and I am very grateful to them. I am also grateful to everyone at Oxford University Press who worked on this book, especially Cynthia A. Read for her advice on shaping the final manuscript, and Paula Wald and David Severtson for improving its writing. My wife, Linda, helped me on all aspects of this book, and I owe her more than I can begin to tell.

West Newton, Massachusetts   T. E. J.
March 1997

Contents

1 Introduction: Character Styles   3

Part I   The Neoclassical and Sentimental God of the Nineteenth Century

2 The Problem of God's Anger   19

3 Serenity and Torment: William Ellery Channing, Edwards A. Park,
Charles Hodge, and Archibald Alexander Hodge   39

4 Sympathy and Alienation: Henry Ward Beecher
and Harriet Beecher Stowe   56

Part II   The Romantic God of the Nineteenth Century

5 Vitality and Anger: W. G. T. Shedd   79

6 Love in the Trinity: James Henley Thornwell,
George Griffin, and Samuel J. Baird   95

7 Desire and Disgust: Horace Bushnell   113

Part III   The Vague God of the Twentieth Century

8 Modernism and Literature: Theodore Munger
and Amos N. Wilder   137

9 The Social Gospel and Its Critics: Walter Rauschenbusch,
Reinhold Niebuhr, and J. Gresham Machen   160

10   The Limitations of Political Theology: Carl Henry,
Harvey Cox, and Martin Luther King, Jr.   180

11   Prospects   200

Notes   205

Index   263

The Character of God

CHAPTER ONE

✧

Introduction

Character Styles

*T*heology is so widely assumed to be boring that it is easy to take its dullness for granted. But why should this be? Why should the discourse that deals with one of the strangest characters imaginable—God—have become tedious? We can understand how this discourse might have become incredible, but how could it have become dull? How could God have become boring?

For American Protestant theology, a large part of the answer has to do with characterizations of God, especially God's emotions. Most American Protestant theologians have assumed that, strictly speaking, God does not have emotions, at least in a human sense. But most have also acknowledged that for the purposes of theological writing it is necessary to ascribe some feelings to God. The question is, which feelings? Here liberal and conservative theologians came to share similar assumptions beginning in the early nineteenth century. In general, they depicted God as an emotionally singular character, having one predominant feeling, such as a serene benevolence, holiness, or tender sympathy. The confinement of God's character to this emotional singularity, and these specific feelings, accounts in large measure for the dullness of modern Protestant theology.

Where did theologians get these notions about God's character in the early nineteenth century? The Bible might be a good guess, given that Protestants have traditionally claimed it as their chief authority. But we will see that theological characterizations of God were often at odds with the Bible. In fact, the effort to reconcile the two was at the center of Protestant theological writing in the nineteenth and twentieth centuries. So theological assumptions about God's character did not come straight from the Bible. Other influences on the depiction of God were doctrinal theories, biblical criticism, science, morality, and politics. But one of the most distinctive and persistent influences was literature. The impact of early nineteenth-century literature here was decisive and long lasting. Through the twentieth century, liberal and conservative theologians alike presented characterizations of God that derived from literary styles prominent in early nineteenth-century America. Although they may have been strong in the early nineteenth century, these styles lost a great deal of power

3

by the end of the century. The upshot was that during the twentieth century the character of God came to seem flat and vague.

Others have noted the dullness of twentieth-century theology, but few have pointed
to the literary reasons for it. In 1929, Walter Lippmann argued that the advance of
science "dissolves the concreteness" of theological imagery. "Modern religious writing," Lippmann observed, "at its best has the qualities of an impassioned argument
and more often it is intolerably flat and vague." In 1948, Whittaker Chambers pointed
to the aridity of theological writing and its failure to present a morally challenging
depiction of God. "Theology is jawbreakingly abstract and its mood is widely felt to
be about as bracing as an unaired vestry," noted Chambers; "God has become, at
best, a fairly furtive presence, a lurking luminosity, a cozy thought." In 1994, Stanley
Hauerwas, professor of theological ethics at Duke University, noted the isolation of
the theological community and its failure to make God interesting: "Theology is a
ghetto activity as insulated and uninteresting as the Saturday religion pages of the
local paper. God knows it's hard to make God boring, but American Christians, aided
and abetted by theologians, have accomplished that feat."[1]

What these commentators noted about twentieth-century Protestant theology—its
vagueness, obscurity, and dullness—certainly has complex causes. But some of it
stemmed from the efforts of twentieth-century theologians to sustain characterizations of God that derived from early nineteenth-century literature, and resonated with
nineteenth-century American culture but had lost much of their power by the twentieth century. This is not to say that Lippmann's point about science and Chambers's
and Hauerwas's points about the ethical dimensions of theology were not also important. They were very important; but we can better understand the relationship of
theology to science and ethics if we appreciate the literary influences on the character of God. Central to this study will be an exploration of the close connections between the literary and ethical assumptions of theologians. Likewise, we will see that
certain literary assumptions about God's character were associated with certain scientific views of nature. Indeed, one reason late nineteenth- and twentieth-century
theologians, both liberal and conservative, had such difficulty coming to grips with
Darwinism was that they clung to characterizations of God that derived from a literary style grounded in the enlightenment vision of nature. For our purposes, however,
an examination of the relationship between the natural sciences and theology cannot
be pursued in detail here.

Other limitations of this book need to be noted. I am only concerned with American theology written at the most prestigious level. I use the word "cosmopolitan" as
a synonym for "highbrow" to distinguish these theologians and their cultural milieu
from popular theologians and their culture. The worldly, trans-Atlantic connotations
of "cosmopolitan" are significant, for in theological and literary matters cosmopolitan Americans followed Europeans. Again, due to size constraints, I outline but do
not discuss in detail the European background of the relevant theological and literary trends. Nor, for the same reasons, do I delve into the similarities and differences
between cosmopolitan and popular theology in America.

There is, however, one significant similarity that is worth noting here, for it helps
to explain why cosmopolitan theologians embraced literature in the first place in the
early nineteenth century. They did so for some of the same reasons that popular clergy

took up popular literary styles at the same time. Both cosmopolitan and popular clergy were trying to keep up with the rapidly expanding secular print culture, which had emerged in America in the eighteenth century and took off in the early nineteenth century, propelled by the growing capitalist market and the invention of stereotype printing and the steam press. "Keeping up" for ministers meant, to some extent, appropriating popular and cosmopolitan literary styles for religious purposes. In all of this, there emerged social divisions between denominations. As Nathan Hatch, Jon Butler, R. Laurence Moore, and others have shown, Baptists and Methodists took the lead in evangelizing American society at large. They tailored their message to the idioms of America's popular culture on the frontier, in the countryside and new industrial towns. They congregated outdoors, sung their message to the tunes of popular songs, and preached and wrote in accessible, vernacular styles. Congregationalists, Presbyterians, Unitarians, and Episcopalians led the way in analogous efforts to reach cosmopolitan Americans. As Richard Bushman has shown, they topped their churches with spires, rebuilt churches following the fashions of Greek and Gothic revival, made the interiors more ornate with brass railings, carpeted aisles, and seat cushions, and set the pulpit out from a backdrop of scarlet drapery. Organs and choirs livened up the service, as did efforts to achieve some literary effect in sermons. Snobbery broke out on both sides of this divide (as did imitation in some instances). Popular revivalists denounced the cosmopolitan clergy for lacking in spirit, and cosmopolitan clergy reproached the revivalists for lacking in literary eloquence.[2]

But if status anxiety provided incentives for theologians to make use of literature, the central motive was more profound and went to the heart of theological writing. Many theologians themselves had become fascinated with secular literature. As we will see, this involved a substantial change from the days of the Puritans. During the eighteenth century, not only had a widespread secular print culture emerged in America making fiction more available, but a revolution in literary criticism had occurred making fiction more acceptable to theologians. The frequent denunciations of popular novels by nineteenth-century theologians should not obscure the fact that they made exceptions for their own tastes. And they took these tastes seriously. Many considered literature as worthy of serious study as science and philosophy. An indication of this is the subjects covered in the *New Englander*, the scholarly journal of Connecticut Congregationalists. Between 1843 and 1861, forty-one articles were devoted to science, forty to literature.[3]

But even this example is misleading because articles on science blended into literary discussions and vice versa. Boundaries between fiction and nonfiction were often blurred. If theologians invoked these boundaries when dismissing popular literature, they just as readily overlooked them when promoting their favorite authors. The fictitious was not necessarily considered unreal. Nor was it considered unscriptural, for the artfulness and poetry of biblical language was often noted. Historians have long studied the efforts of eighteenth- and nineteenth-century theologians to come to grips with the enlightenment and Darwinian science and to reconcile faith with reason.[4] With the emergence of a secular literary culture, there were analogous efforts to reconcile faith with the imagination. In 1870, Noah Porter, Congregationalist theologian and president of Yale, thought this was vitally important to the future of theology: "It is because the imagination is so nearly allied to faith that her power to hinder or help is so unlimited, and that literature itself becomes to religion either the dead-liest foe or the most potent ally."[5]

Theologians believed that literature was most "potent" in the depiction of charac-ter. In the exploration of character, literature had something of the status of moral philosophy and psychology. This view was widespread in American cosmopolitan culture. The distinguished American political economist Francis Lieber, in his 1833 treatise on prison reform, cited long passages from Satan's monologues in Milton's *Paradise Lost* in order to illustrate the kind of recalcitrance that wardens could ex-pect from newly admitted inmates. So it was natural that this use of literature carried over into doctrinal theology. The conservative Calvinist W. G. T. Shedd, in his 1859 essay "The Atonement: A Satisfaction for the Ethical Nature of Both God and Man," considered the nature of sin as revealed in the criminal mind. To back up his specu-lations, he cited Johann Heinroth's *Criminal Psychologie* but primarily relied on scenes and lines from Samuel Coleridge's play *Remorse*.[6]

It was recognized, of course, that literature could convey many things—scenery, customs, and so on—but character was the crucial test of a writer's skill. In 1849, the conservative Southern Presbyterian Robert Lewis Dabney, in an article denouncing popular novelists but praising Shakespeare, Milton, and Sir Walter Scott, declared, "To draw an imaginary man, like nature in his feelings and conduct, is the hardest task of literary genius." It was also the task that promised the biggest impact. For it was widely assumed that literature not only was a guide to character but also could influence character. Solon Bush, a Unitarian minister, exclaimed, "Character has great influence whether bodied forth in ideal creations or exhibited in actual life."[7]

Another Unitarian writer went even further in his 1863 essay in the *Christian Examiner* entitled "The Reality of Fiction." The ostensible purpose of the article was to review the novels of Charles Dickens. But its deeper purpose was to argue for the spiritual importance of literature. The reviewer did this by asserting the reality of literary characters: "These brain children of the tale-wright are no mere shadows, myths or phantoms. The spiritual vision rivals the bodily vision." For the purposes of deep thought and feeling, "the personages of romance are real personages." Indeed, reading and reality so overlapped that they came to much the same thing. "Let us read society as we read a novel," the reviewer declared, for "reading is simply another way of living." Noah Porter agreed: literary characters had something of the influence of real people. He confessed that a few writers—Shakespeare, Milton, Scott, and Robert Burns—had influenced him to this extent. "The characters and scenes described and depicted by each have become to us as real and as permanent as are the sun and the stars, or the faces of our familiar friends. We never behold them but they quicken our thoughts and give new life to our feel-ings. They are a part, and not the least important of the actual world, ever exerting upon our characters and lives a powerful and constant influence." Porter counseled people to choose their books as carefully as they choose their friends. Almost as influential on a young person as "falling in love," according to Porter, was "the reading of the first really good novel or poem which takes a strong and permanent hold of heart and character."[8]

The presumed influence of literary characterization was, thus, a major reason it could be such an important tool for theologians. Noah Porter believed that an entire "theory of moral culture" could be organized around literature. Literature, he argued, was already having great influence on people; "the private history" of many testified to it. Why not devise a complete method of character formation using literature? "Were a wise man to have the complete control over the mind and heart of a young person of either sex, and to seek to form him or her after the ideal of generous, affectionate, and heroic character which would be ready to labor, to suffer, and if need be, to die for man or for God, he would freely avail himself, at proper intervals and in a due proportion, of the writings of men of imaginative genius."[9]

What kind of "heroic character" is the crucial question. One comes to mind—one who was "ready to labor, to suffer, and if need be, to die for man [and] for God." This was obviously Jesus. But the question is, how was Jesus to be characterized? What emotions drove him to labor, suffer, and die? What did he feel while he was doing this?

Here is where different literary styles began to matter. In the middle of the nineteenth century, theologians were straddling a period of transition between literary styles. On one side was neoclassicism and sentimentalism, and on the other, romanticism. Literary trends, of course, cannot be dated with any precision, but some generalizations can be made. British neoclassicism, led by John Dryden, arose in the late seventeenth century but did not become assimilated into American cosmopolitan culture until the Federalist period in the late eighteenth and early nineteenth century. This style was exemplified by such American writers as Timothy Dwight and the critic James Kirk Paulding, who in 1818 could still confidently call Dryden the best modern critic. The sentimental novel arose in the eighteenth century and achieved an unprecedented success in both popular and cosmopolitan America in the mid-nineteenth century in the works of Susan Warner and Harriet Beecher Stowe. Romanticism emerged in Britain in the early nineteenth century, led by Wordsworth, Coleridge, Byron, Shelley, and Keats, and surfaced a generation later in the work of Emerson, Hawthorne, Melville, and Whitman during the "American renaissance" of the 1850s. Romanticism in Britain and America, however, did not entirely displace neoclassicism and sentimentalism at midcentury. Rather, they all mixed together as British and American cosmopolitan culture assimilated and tempered this initial expression of romanticism. In Britain, this period of settling in produced the Victorian poets Tennyson, Arnold, and the Brownings. In America, it produced the "genteel tradition" of Bryant, Whittier, Holmes, Longfellow, and Lowell, in whom neoclassical, sentimental, and romantic trends are all evident. The meaning of these trends for characterization also resists precise definition, but again we can outline some general patterns.[10]

There are differences between neoclassicism and sentimentalism, but when it comes to characterization, they have key points in common. Both emphasize a certain emotional singularity. The tendency in neoclassical and sentimental characterization is to polarize contrary feelings and traits—such as love and hate, honesty and deceitfulness, generosity and jealousy. In fact, contrary emotions sometimes become mutually exclusive to the point where they have to be set in different characters. Neoclassical and sentimental characters, thus, often come to be defined by one leading trait with subsidiary traits complementing it. Walter Jackson Bate has pointed to the precept in neoclassicism of the "ruling passion." "A character," John Dryden wrote in 1679, "is a composition of qualities which are not contrary to one another in the same person; thus, the same man may be liberal and valiant, but not liberal and covetous. . . . One virtue, vice, or passion, ought to be shown in every man as predominant over all the rest."[11]

The great appeal of neoclassical and sentimental characters is their ethical clarity. The polarization of emotions clears the ground morally. Good and bad characters are as distinct as their "predominant" feelings. "Confused passions," noted John Dryden, "make indistinguishable characters."[12] In the eighteenth century, benevolence became the leading trait of the neoclassical hero. Benevolence is a special kind of love; it is love purged of irrationality, eroticism, passion, and jealousy. It is an altruistic, rational love whose signature is serenity. The sentimental hero (and often heroine) is also altruistic but more impulsive and expressive, the characteristic trait being a tearful sympathy. Evil characters, by contrast, are self-absorbed and betray themselves by their lack of self-control, manifest in an escalating range of bodily agitation, from nervous tics to manic rage.

In addition to being prominent literary styles, neoclassical and sentimental characterizations had substantial intellectual and social support in antebellum America. The neoclassical ideal of a character harmonious in reason and love resonated with the enlightenment vision of nature as an orderly, divine design in which every life form was perfectly adapted to its environment. Both styles of characterization also informed the ideals and role models for humanitarian reformers such as temperance and antislavery activists. More generally still, these characterizations were widely accepted as civic ideals, for their emergence coincided with the breakdown of traditional, hereditary social hierarchies brought on by the expansion of the capitalist market and democratic politics. In recommending self-restraint and commitment to community and family, these characterizations provided reassurance that capitalism and democracy would not atomize society into a war of all against all. Some of the moral authority of these styles continued through the twentieth century. The unambiguous moral heroes in movies draw on them, as do our of ideals of parents, political leaders, and social activists. The familiar image of the politician—the self-effacing war hero kissing babies—draws on the lingering moral power of neoclassical and sentimental characterization. But this being said, much of the literary, intellectual, and social support for these styles of characterization collapsed by the early twentieth century. This meant that, notwithstanding their continuing moral appeal, they could easily seem hackneyed, nostalgic, or corny. For more profound characterization, twentieth-century cosmopolitan Americans followed another literary style: romanticism.

Our depiction of emotional depth owes a great deal to romanticism. This does not mean that we idealize nature and young love. These are popular misconceptions of romanticism. As a literary movement, of course, romanticism and its continuing permutations through our culture are varied and the subject of continual academic debate. But when it comes to the depiction of character, romanticism is distinctive in this respect: there is a fascination with emotional ambivalence. In this, romantic characterization differs from the emphasis in neoclassicism and sentimentalism on one predominant feeling. Romantic characters typically struggle with contradictory feelings. The same person may attract and repel them. And this is the challenge they face: not overcoming exterior obstacles but seeing through their own inner complexity. "The story of ambivalent love is a characteristic one of the nineteenth century," observed Lionel Trilling; "poets tell of lovers separated not by difficult circumstances but the inability of man to know the true tendency of his heart."[13]

In many respects, this remains characteristic of cosmopolitan literature. "Contemporary people, it seems, like split personalities, just as much as their romantic predecessors did," wrote Adam Gopnik in the *New Yorker* in 1995. He was right, but we would put it differently. We do not just like personalities that are neatly "split." We want a mixture of contradictory feelings. And we have taken romantic characterization into ourselves. Stormy love affairs, poignant conflict and reconciliation with parents: this is what we have come to expect from fictional and real characters. We have had nearly a century of Freudian psychology to sanction such feelings as normal if kept in bounds. Harold Bloom, one of the most prominent American literary critics, confesses his obsession with "Freudian conflicts of heightened emotional ambivalence." But before Freud, as Bloom and many critics have noted, the romantics of the early nineteenth century first made such conflicted emotional states the center of attention. Romantics, of course, were not the first to find drama in this, but they did bring these states to the fore and celebrate them. The conflicted character became not simply confused but profound; ambivalence became the threshold of insight into the depths of character.[14]

A lot, of course, has happened in literature since the romantic movement of the early nineteenth century. "Realism" and "aestheticism" in the late nineteenth century, "modernism" in the early twentieth century, and "postmodernism" in the late twentieth century are just some of the terms literary critics use to designate important trends since romanticism. These trends have changed many things in literature. Among them, realism brought in a Darwinian vision of human nature; aestheticism celebrated the artificial; modernism, influenced by archaeology and psychology, assembled narratives that seemed to be derived from the unearthed fragments of the primitive and the unconscious; and postmodernism blended the human with the technological. But in large measure these movements have not changed the fundamental romantic fascination with emotional ambivalence. If anything, they have added to it. Thomas Pynchon's 1973 novel, *Gravity's Rainbow*, is a showpiece of postmodern tendencies. Yet its paranoid, sadomasochistic vision of behavioral conditioning gone awry acts out the central romantic problem of characters conflicted in their attraction and repulsion. In Toni Morrison's 1987 historical novel, *Beloved*, a mother kills her infant daughter to prevent her from being returned to slavery. The ghost of that child then becomes a focal point for the longings and apprehensions of characters. The sister of the dead infant feels this toward the ghost keenly: "Now it held for her all the anger, love and fear she didn't know what to do with."[15]

Why such characters have a hold over us is difficult to say. But one thing seems certain: it is how we have come to depict emotional depth. The assumption is that the deeper you go into yourself the more conflicted your feelings will be. The more conflicted your feelings are, the more intensely will you feel; conflict and intensity feed off each other. This is why romantic characters, despite their near paralysis from ambivalence, also have tremendous energy. The abbot who attends Byron's romantic hero Manfred does not understand this:

> He hath all the energy which would have made
> A goodly frame of glorious elements
> Had they been wisely mingled; as it is
> It is an awful chaos—light and darkness
> and mind and dust, and passions and pure thoughts
> Mixed, and contending without end or order.[16]

What the abbott does not see is that Manfred's wild energy comes from his "mixed" nature.

But this is difficult to accept. Like the abbot, we often want what attracts us without the danger. Romantic characters are dangerous and disruptive; they cannot be role models like neoclassical and sentimental characters. Morse Peckham has called the romantic hero an "anti-role." From the early nineteenth through the twentieth century, there have been a number of variations on this character. Peckham traced the development from the Byronic hero to the bohemian, the virtuoso, the dandy, and the late twentieth-century celebrity writer who creates a persona that becomes his own greatest fiction.[17] It is true that these characterizations became more socially acceptable in the twentieth century. A certain virtue was found in artistic provocation, and the romantic impulse was celebrated as an expression of authenticity. There are numerous intellectual and social reasons for this. Darwinism and Freudianism injected a measure of normal conflict into the harmonious visions of enlightenment nature and the humanitarian family that had once supported neoclassicism and sentimentalism. Also playing a part here was the emergence of a consumer culture in the late nineteenth century, encouraging some relaxation of the earlier capitalist emphasis on self-restraint. Twentieth-century bohemians might be in revolt against American society, but they provided the entertainer, the designer, and the adman with new angles into old markets. Romantic idiosyncrasies were packaged in accessible forms, such as sex appeal. But this greater acceptance of romantic characterization never became total. Romantic characters did not become adult role models. What is being acted out by the romantic character is something that we should recognize in ourselves but not entirely want to act out—usually for good reason. Romantic characters remain proxies we send out to suffer passions that are normally best kept under wraps.[18]

So, in the end, we remain ambivalent about romantic characters. But this only intensifies our fascination with them. They are unforgettable, which makes their psychological states infectious because romantic characters typically strive to forget something that torments and yet tantalizes them. So what haunts us is a character who is haunted; an unforgettable character who cannot forget; an ambivalent character about whom we remain ambivalent. Our entire relationship with such a character becomes a kind of echo chamber for how we have come to depict our own emotional depth. Once again Byron provides a ready example of this. If not the most subtle of romantic writers, he is for this reason the most quotable.

> None knew nor how, nor why, but he entwined
> Himself perforce around the hearer's mind;
> There he was stamp'd, in liking or in hate,
> If greeted once; however brief the date

That friendship, pity, or aversion knew,
Still there within the inmost thought he grew.
You could not penetrate his soul, but found,
Despite your wonder, to your own he wound;
His presence haunted still; and from the breast
He forced an all unwilling interest:
Vain as the struggle in the mental net,
His spirit seem'd to dare you to forget![19]

Can such a character be ascribed to God? It would mean ascribing to him some ambivalence—God feeling anger as well as love toward humans. It might mean that God seeks relief in forgetfulness as well as forgiveness. In the nineteenth century, a few maverick theologians ascribed such traits to God. The vast majority of theologians, however, dismissed this as immoral and ascribed neoclassical and sentimental traits to him. It is easy to see why: a God of serene benevolence or tender sympathy was certainly more reassuring and easier to understand morally. Yet we also need to understand why a few nineteenth-century theologians drew on romanticism to depict God. They did so in spite of the moral ambiguity of romanticism. In 1861, for instance, the *Presbyterian Quarterly Review* acknowledged Byron's "immorality" but recognized the "vitality" of his style, likened it to Milton's, and found the source for both in the Bible.[20] Indeed, here was the justification for romantic characterization: the Bible ascribed a complex and visceral mixture of love and anger to God and Jesus. The morality of these depictions of God is hard to understand. But must God's morality always be understandable? Must he be seen only as a moral role model? These were difficult questions in the nineteenth century and remain so today. If the vast majority of theologians in the nineteenth and twentieth centuries were confident in their neoclassical and sentimental characterizations of God, they still had to wrestle with the complex depictions of him in the Bible.

To understand how theologians could read the Bible according to neoclassical, sentimental, or romantic styles, we need to grasp one major point. The same text can be read according to different literary styles. What matters is the eye of the beholder: the literary assumptions the reader brings to the text. For instance, though we speak of Byron as a romantic poet writing in a romantic era, many nineteenth-century Americans read him with neoclassical assumptions. Noah Porter admired much romantic literature but still tended to evaluate romantic characters by neoclassical criteria. He was not wrong to do this. There is no right or wrong here; neoclassicism, sentimentalism, and romanticism are all ways to appreciate literary characterization however an author has come to be classified by literary critics. Moreover, the authors that American theologians most admired in the nineteenth century, Shakespeare and Milton, wrote before any of these styles of characterization had crystallized in Britain. So, properly speaking, one cannot classify characters from Shakespeare and Milton as neoclassical, sentimental, or romantic—any more than one can classify God in the Bible as neoclassical, sentimental, or romantic. But theologians, like everyone else, still interpreted literary and biblical characters according to neoclassical, sentimental, and romantic styles. This could lead to very different interpretations of literature and the Bible.

To get a sense of how different, consider how neoclassical and romantic critics and theologians reacted to the famous scene in *Hamlet*, in which Hamlet finds his stepfather and nemesis, Claudius, at prayer. Hamlet considers seizing the moment and killing Claudius. But then Hamlet reasons with himself: if he killed Claudius now, Claudius's soul might go to heaven. Better to wait, Hamlet figures, and kill Claudius while he is drunk, or committing some other sin, so his soul will go to hell. To neoclassical critics, such impious conniving seemed unworthy of a heroic character. "This speech, in which Hamlet, represented as a virtuous character, is not content with taking blood for blood, but contrives damnation for the man that he would punish, is too horrible to be read or to be uttered," declared Samuel Johnson in 1765. In fact, this and other troublesome aspects of Hamlet were sometimes smoothed out by neoclassical dramatists when they performed the play. "The hero needed to be made as straightforward, godly and admirable as possible," wrote Gary Taylor; "this reshaping of *Hamlet* satisfies a neoclassical preference for unambiguous heroes and villains, for moral as well as structural clarity and contrast."[21]

By the early nineteenth century, however, romantic critics such as Johann Wolfgang von Goethe, Samuel Taylor Coleridge, and William Hazlitt saw Hamlet's character differently. The supposed inconsistencies in his character were taken as symptoms of deeper, emotional complexity. Hamlet's delay in killing the king, Hazlitt argued in 1817, did not really have to do with the exterior circumstance that Claudius was at his prayers but rather with the inner confusion that plagued Hamlet himself. That Hamlet "refuses to kill the King when he is at his prayers," Hazlitt acknowledged, could be seen as a "refinement of malice," but on a deeper level it was "in truth only an excuse for his own want of resolution." This reversed the neoclassical reading. Rather than showing a fiendish determination to send Claudius to hell, Hamlet lacked the decisiveness to carry out his revenge. This is because Hamlet does not know whether to trust the ghost who claims to be his murdered father; he does not know whether to see his stepfather as king or usurper, his mother as queen or whore. Here is the romantic emphasis on inner ambivalence rather than exterior circumstance. Exterior complications mainly provide the occasion to draw out latent emotional conflicts.[22]

Romanticism thus makes the writer more of a psychologist than a moralist. Coleridge saw Shakespeare as an investigator of the human psyche. "The seeming inconsistencies in the conduct and character of Hamlet," Coleridge declared, "may be traced to Shakespeare's deep and accurate science in mental philosophy." The overlap between literature and life here was obvious. Shakespeare's "mental philosophy," as Coleridge wrote about it, was a kind of psychology. Indeed, Coleridge coined the word "psycho-analytical." And Coleridge never hesitated to apply the lessons of literature to life. "It [is] essential to the understanding Hamlet's character," Coleridge argued, "that we should reflect on the constitution of our own minds." "I have a smack of Hamlet myself, if I may say so," remarked Coleridge.[23]

By the fourth decade of the century, a few American writers were beginning to feel the same way. "Our age is bewailed as the age of Introversion," declared Ralph Waldo Emerson in 1837; "the time is infected with Hamlet's unhappiness." This was not such a bad thing, according to Emerson: "I look upon the discontent of the literary class as a mere announcement of the fact that they find themselves not in the state of mind of their fathers, and regret the coming state as untried." The assimilation of romantic characterization into American cosmopolitan culture, however, was a long process. Not many Americans would claim to have a "smack of Hamlet" until Freudianism became assimilated into cosmopolitan culture in the 1920s. By then, however, they would be saying they had a "smack of Oedipus." But a few American theologians in the nineteenth century did have a romantic view of Shakespeare. Horace Bushnell was intrigued by Hamlet's inner complexity and, like Coleridge, personified his own feelings with characters from Shakespeare (as well as from Goethe). Indeed, this was Bushnell's recommendation to divinity students in 1866. He told them to look into themselves when they wrote their sermons: "Here in the soul's secret chambers are Fausts more subtle than Faust, Hamlets more mysterious than Hamlet, Lears more distracted and desolate than Lear." The historian Daniel Walker Howe has seen in this passage an anticipation of the Freudian unconscious. Bushnell did rely on romantic characterization to sound his own depth. This appears to have been increasingly common over the course of the nineteenth century and prepared the way for the reception of Freud.[24]

In the second half of the nineteenth century, however, most American theologians were still closer to Samuel Johnson's view of Hamlet. This did not mean that they had no appreciation of romanticism. In 1870, Noah Porter praised Goethe for calling attention to Hamlet's "conflicting emotions" and making sense of "incidents and sayings that would otherwise be unintelligible, if not offensive." But still Porter suggested that critics such as Goethe and Coleridge may have been a bit too ingenious in their interpretations of Hamlet. Porter saw Hamlet as a relatively straightforward character, at least compared to such romantic characters as Byron's Manfred. Both Hamlet and Manfred, Porter pointed out, suffer from great guilt. But Manfred's guilt is mixed with inexplicable pride, which leads him to fear no punishment after death. To Porter's eyes this simply made Manfred into a "stupid Atheist"—stupid because he does not realize that his guilt should temper his pride. Hamlet, by contrast, Porter argued, was the more profound character; at least Hamlet, according to Porter, still has the sense to recognize that a guilty conscience might be a foreboding of future punishment (as suggested to Porter in Hamlet's famous "to be or not to be" soliloquy). This is not to say that Porter dismissed Byron as a bad poet, just not a profound one when it came to characterization. Porter admired Byron's writing for its vigorous diction, but Byron's romantic characterizations—mixing the contrary feelings of pride and guilt—came across as simple confusion.[25]

Of course, the characters that really concerned theologians were God and Jesus and their depictions in the Bible. But there were similarities between the ways in which nineteenth-century theologians interpreted God and Jesus and the way they interpreted literary characters such as Hamlet. The vast majority of theologians, liberal and conservative alike, followed neoclassical and sentimental styles of characterization. They highlighted biblical passages that helped them to ascribe a serene benevolence or a tender sympathy to God and Jesus. But, similar to *Hamlet*, the Bible contained depictions of God and Jesus that theologians found troublesome. Especially difficult were Old Testament depictions of God's visceral anger and the suggestion in the Gospels that Jesus had been irritated with his mother or that he was unnerved in the Garden of Gethsemane or on the cross. Liberals and conservatives handled these

problems differently. Liberals drew on new methods of biblical criticism to marginalize Old Testament depictions of God's anger. But they still had to wrestle with
the characterizations of Jesus in the Gospels. Their effort here, and that of conservatives, is most evident in their expositions of the doctrine of the atonement, the doctrine that theologians believed revealed the most about God's character. And just as
Noah Porter acknowledged that aspects of Hamlet's character seemed "unintelligible,
if not offensive," some theologians admitted that they were baffled, even disappointed,
in the gospel depictions of Jesus. But sometimes theologians allowed his depiction
to stretch their neoclassical and sentimental assumptions about his character.

In a few instances, this led theologians to romanticism, for romantic characterization helped them to make sense of biblical depictions of God and Jesus feeling a
mixture of love and anger. Of the few theologians who developed romantic characterizations of God, most were conservatives. Though this goes against common historical notions that associate romanticism with liberal theology, the conservative
interest in romanticism makes sense once one delves into the details of doctrinal
theology and biblical exegesis.[26] Calvinist interpretations of the atonement and the
Bible had emphasized God's wrath as well as his love. It is true that during the early
part of the nineteenth century most conservatives, while defending Calvinism, adopted
a neoclassical characterization of God, despite the fact that this did not always con-
form with their doctrinal and biblical views. So strong was the cultural pressure to
adopt a neoclassical characterization of God that few conservatives resisted. A few
did, however—the most prominent one being W. G. T. Shedd, who drew support for
his work from romanticism. At least one prominent liberal, Horace Bushnell (in part
influenced by Shedd), also developed romantic characterizations of God. These romantic theologians, however, were mavericks in nineteenth-century America. The
vast majority of theologians depicted God and Jesus as neoclassical and sentimental
characters.

If theological characterization merely followed the fortunes of literary styles, then
we would expect more romantic characterizations of God in twentieth-century theology. But this did not happen. Indeed, I have not discovered any examples of this.
Moreover, the nineteenth-century examples were largely forgotten in the twentieth
century. Shedd's work was almost entirely neglected, and Bushnell's romantic characterizations of God were often ignored, despite the fact that Bushnell became the
most studied and celebrated American theologian of the nineteenth century. The
reason for this seems to be that for most of the twentieth century neoclassical and
sentimental characterizations of God came to be taken for granted as the only ways
to depict God.

When historians have considered the relationship between American Protestantism and literature, they have mainly focused on how Protestantism influenced secular literature or how Protestantism promoted popular religious forms of literature.[27]
The impact of literature on cosmopolitan theology has received little attention.[28] Only
nineteenth-century sentimentalism has received some sustained historical examination here. But treated in isolation from the impact of neoclassicism and romanticism
on theology, the influence of sentimentalism has sometimes appeared more peculiar
than it actually was.[29] The important point to understand here is that the penetration
of theology by literature was deep, widespread, and long lasting. In the nineteenth

century, liberals and conservatives alike were influenced by neoclassicism; sentimentalism was mostly taken up by liberals, while the few theologians who developed romantic characterizations of God were mainly conservatives. In the twentieth century, theologians appear to have relied exclusively on neoclassical and sentimental characterizations of God.

This continued reliance on neoclassical and sentimental styles helps to account for two features of Protestant theology in the twentieth century: God's vagueness and his political orientation. God became vague because by the late nineteenth century many of the intellectual and social supports for neoclassicism and sentimentalism had collapsed. One that remained was politics. Taken on its own, the moral authority of a neoclassical and sentimental God risked seeming narrow or nostalgic by the late nineteenth century. But God's neoclassical and sentimental character could still convey some wider moral power by being attached to prominent political movements. The liberal social gospel theologians of the late nineteenth century were the first to recognize this. Conservative theologians during the first half of the twentieth century criticized this politicization of God's character. But by the late twentieth century even they were drawn to this. This politicization of theology, though in some respects an innovation, was more of a holding operation when it came to the character of God. It propped up neoclassical and sentimental characterizations of God long after these had lost their nineteenth-century foundations.

By the middle of the twentieth century, a few theologians were lamenting the gap that had grown between theology and literature. In 1964, the liberal Harvard theologian Amos Wilder chided his fellow theologians, observing that modern art, beginning with romanticism, had developed "paradigms of man in depth" that "rebuke [the] conventionality" and "shrunken outlook" of the theological community.[30] But Wilder could offer little in the way of a solution because he did not question his own neoclassical and sentimental assumptions about God's character. In this, he was like liberal, theological "modernists" going back to the turn of the century. They maintained a commitment to literature in theory but in practice found ways to dismiss much of modern literature for failing to support their assumptions about God's character. Conservatives, for their part, largely gave up on modern literature in the twentieth century. They denounced it as necessarily decadent and forgot that in the nineteenth century some of the most daring theological uses of romanticism had come from conservatives. The irony here is that the difficulties liberals and conservatives both had with romantic characterization were related to the difficulties they had had since the early nineteenth century in reconciling their neoclassical and sentimental characterizations of God with the Bible.

❧

PART ONE

The Neoclassical and Sentimental God of the Nineteenth Century

✧

CHAPTER TWO

The Problem of God's Anger

*F*or nineteenth- and twentieth-century theologians, the great problem with the biblical depiction of God and Jesus is that they sometimes seem to feel a visceral anger. Moreover, this anger may occur in complex combinations with their love. There is no neat polarization of emotions here. For theologians intent on depicting God as a neoclassical or sentimental character, these biblical passages have presented a real difficulty. Indeed, this may be the chief problem underlying efforts to depict God in nineteenth- and twentieth-century Protestant theology. Liberal theologians found help here in new forms of biblical criticism and doctrinal interpretation. But this did not solve the problem entirely and in some instances aggravated it. Conservatives, for their part, while maintaining allegiance in theory to traditional Protestant doctrines that had recognized God's anger, still developed neoclassical characterizations of God. Conservatives, like liberals here, were influenced by neoclassicism and sentimentalism because of the extraordinary authority of these styles in the nineteenth century.

The Prestige of Neoclassicism and Sentimentalism

Neoclassicism made it possible for the first time in the history of the West to think of great literature as distinctly Christian. The critical revolution here was remarkable. For the first 1,700 years of Christianity, it had been almost axiomatic that the great writers came from ancient Greece and Rome. This meant that they were pagan. Of course, Christians faced similar problems with classical philosophy. But at least Plato and Aristotle had been suspicious about the pagan gods. But in the works of Homer, Aeschylus, Sophocles, Virgil, Ovid, and others, the pagan deities played major roles. This left Christians with a real problem. They could see the stylistic power of these writers, but they distrusted the pagan content. In late antiquity, Augustine set the pattern that carried through the Reformation: the classics were to be studied for their style rather than their content. This, however, could go a long way. Martin Luther, for example, was devoted to classical literature. When as a young man he entered a monastery, he discarded all of his books except for his copies of Virgil and Plautus. The rallying cry of the Reformation was *sola scriptura*, but this did not mean that the Bible was the only book to be read. It meant that the Bible was the final authority for the church, but in the exposition of the Bible classical rhetoric could help. Luther even called the Bible the "divine Aeneid" and recommended the study of classical literature for theologians: "By these studies, as by no other means, people are wonderfully fitted for the grasping of sacred truth and handling it skillfully."[1]

The American Puritans inherited these attitudes. Their image as cultural curmudgeons here is often overdone. "The cultivated Puritan was in no sense an implacable foe to the arts," noted Perry Miller. They read classical authors and even a few moderns, such as Spenser, Sidney, and Milton, and produced a few poets of their own, such as Edward Taylor, Michael Wigglesworth, and Anne Bradstreet. Yet into the early eighteenth century, Puritan theologians still remained leery of literature. Cotton Mather, in his 1726 handbook for divinity students, cautiously suggested that some profit as well as pleasure might be gained from studying Homer, Horace, and Virgil. But again the old division between style and content had to be observed. "As to the moral part of Homer," Mather warned, "by first exhibiting their gods as no better than rogues, he set open the flood gates for a prodigious inundation of wickedness to break upon the nations, and was one of the greatest apostles the devil ever had in the world." This was mild, however, compared to Mather's sweeping condemnation of most modern literature. The "muses" were "harlots" and books were their allures. "The powers of darkness have a library among us, whereof the poets have been the most numerous and venomous authors," he declared. "Most of the modern plays, as well as the romances, novels and fictions, which are a sort of poems, belong to the catalogue of this cursed library."[2]

Neoclassicism relieved theologians of a great deal of their worries about both ancient and modern literature. Neoclassical critics downplayed the paganism in classical literature and dwelt instead on philosophical and moral matters, especially stoicism, which, with its emphasis on moderation and emotional reserve, was seen as refined and compatible with Christian ethics. But more important in the long run was the changing evaluation of modern literature. Neoclassical writers were not so much devoted to the past as they were interested in finding the merits of the ancient authors in modern times. Crucial here was the work of such critics as Dryden, Joseph Addison, and Samuel Johnson. They ranked Shakespeare and Milton as high, or higher, than classical authors. This raised the prospect that not just the style but the content of literature could be embraced by theologians. Moreover, the idea took hold that great literature could be not only acceptable to Christians but actually Christian. Some believed that a distinguished Protestant literature was emerging in Europe. Milton was the obvious example of this (though some questioned his doctrinal soundness). But even Shakespeare came to be considered a distinctly Christian author.[3]

American theologians absorbed this in the late eighteenth century during the Federalist era. The crucial figure here was Timothy Dwight. Poet, critic, theologian, and president of Yale, he inaugurated a tradition of clerical use of literature. From his 1772 Yale commencement address, "On the History, Eloquence, and Poetry of the Bible," to his 1785 epic, *The Conquest of Canaan*, he treated the Bible according to neoclassical norms.[4] His successor in the mid-nineteenth century was Noah Porter, also a critic, theologian, and president of Yale. This is not to say that there was no difference between Dwight's taste and Porter's. Porter found Alexander Pope's language stilted and much of Samuel Johnson's criticism fractious. Porter, like many of his American contemporaries of the "genteel tradition," preferred a more natural diction if not strikingly more complex characterization. Porter's favorite writers, besides Shakespeare and Milton, were Scott and those poets ranging from Thomas Gray to William Wordsworth who had reacted against the arch urbanity of official English neoclassicism and developed a more natural and expressive style. But Porter still recognized what American theologians owed to urbane neoclassicism. It had prodded the American clergy from provincialism to cosmopolitanism. In 1883, Porter counseled his readers not to be too severe in judging their Puritan forefathers. "We should remember as we drag through the old sermons, and the books of ghostly counsel, and the poetry of doubtful inspiration, that the first preachers of New England were two generations earlier than Locke, three before Addison and five before Johnson."[5]

Significant in Porter's remark is the effortless grouping of Johnson and Addison with the enlightenment philosopher John Locke. Literature, philosophy, science, and morality all seemed of a piece in neoclassicism. The style had such prestige among theologians because it did not seem merely a literary style but the most refined and intelligent way to take in the world. A major reason for this was the support neoclassicism found in the enlightenment.

The enlightenment provided important supports for both neoclassical characterization and setting. For characterization, there was an emphasis on emotional restraint and rationality. This came from the enlightenment celebration of ancient stoicism and modern science. And, as in neoclassicism, this centered on one trait in particular: benevolence. Benevolence was the key emotion emulated by people and ascribed to God. As the historian James Turner put it: "As the archetype of morality, God expressed the most elevated human ethics. He thus above all had to be—perhaps the favorite adjective of enlightenment divines—benevolent: disinterestedly willing the happiness of all His creatures."[6]

The enlightenment also provided settings in which neoclassical characters could display their benevolence. The study of history and nature was key here—in particular, the meditation on the course of human empires and the solar system. The latter was seen as God's empire, compared to which human empires seemed necessarily fitful and faulty. The neoclassical reflection on historical empires was flexible enough to suit a variety of agendas. In *Absalom and Achitophel*, Dryden told the story of a ruinous rebellion in ancient Israel from an Anglican and royalist perspective; Dwight, the American Congregationalist, in *The Conquest of Canaan*, told the story of the founding of Israel from a perspective suiting the newly independent and expansive United States; and the skeptical Edward Gibbon, in *The Decline and Fall of the Roman Empire*, told the story of how a great cosmopolitan empire was undermined by ancient Christian fanatics. The example of Gibbon is a reminder that some of the most brilliant enlightenment writers turned against Christianity. But it was far more common for British and American writers to use the enlightenment to recommend Christianity.[7]

Here they often pointed to nature as a reflection on God's character. As one English theologian put it: "The universe is reasonable and ordered because God is prompted by his feelings—the original and eternal benevolence of his nature—to exercise his power in a rational manner." But, unlike the religious radicals of the enlightenment, the Deists, the vast majority of neoclassical Christian writers did not depict God as a distant watchmaker. They saw him governing nature as an empire. Like the Deists, neoclassical theologians drew their metaphors for God's power from Newtonian astronomy, which described the orbits of the planets according to relatively simple laws of gravitation. Especially impressive here was the combination of power and restraint; despite the awesome size of the planets and their tremendous velocities, they remained bound to their prescribed orbits. Such imagery also provided metaphors for aesthetic and moral laws in neoclassical literature. "Nature, like liberty, is but restrained / By the same laws which herself first ordained," declared Alexander Pope. God's rule over nature, however, was always the measure against which human rule fell short. "Instruct the planets in what orbs to run," Pope taunted the ambitions of science in his satire on human vanity.[8]

But God was able to do just this—govern the orbits of the planets. For well over a century, this provided the common image for God's character in neoclassical theology. Unlike the Deists, who used the economy of natural laws to suggest that after God had created nature he no longer needed to intervene, neoclassical theologians argued that God needed to intervene for moral reasons—as in the atonement; and when he did so, he demonstrated the deepest aspects of his character. But even these aspects of his character could still be expressed in Newtonian metaphors. Theologians were quite aware of their reliance on this symbolism. "I may say that love to God is the gravitating principle of the moral universe," noted Horace Bushnell in 1839, "and challenge anyone to express the same thought in language older than the Newtonian system." Through the end of the nineteenth century—despite the emergence of Darwinism—American theologians still relied on this enlightenment vision to provide concrete imagery for their neoclassical characterizations of God. Astronomy demonstrated the "benevolence of Jehovah," Edwards Park declared in an essay published in 1885. "The planetary system we admire for the simple force which controls its movements," Park explained. "All of the works of the great Architect afford a symbol of the unity which exists in himself. One great principle permeates the phenomena of the suns and the stars, just as a single moral feeling is expressed in the countless acts of Him who develops his unity in the material creation."[9]

The fact that this essay was published in 1885 reminds us of how long the enlightenment vision of nature persisted in American theology. It also suggests one reason the neoclassical characterization of God became so vulnerable. A neoclassical God might make sense with an enlightenment vision of nature as basically a fixed, benevolent order. But such a characterization of God did not make much sense in Darwinism, for Darwinian nature gave much play to chance and violence. How could theologians depict an orderly, benevolent God presiding over the Darwinian vision of nature in which some species prospered while others became extinct, all as part of the normal struggle for existence determined by apparently chance variations in heredity and environment? The answer is that theologians could not do this—at least not in any detail. This is one reason theology became so vague in the late nineteenth and twentieth century. In order to sustain God's neoclassical character, theologians needed to distance it from Darwinian nature or temper this vision of nature and make it so vague that it did not seem to contradict God's neoclassical character. What propped up these characterizations of God through the twentieth century, however, was not scientific but moral support. This had its roots in humanitarianism.

Humanitarianism roughly paralleled the rise of the enlightenment in Britain during the eighteenth century and spread through American cosmopolitan culture in the early nineteenth century. In many respects, humanitarianism was the social analogue to the enlightenment. Humanitarianism urged human beings to carry out in society what God had done in nature. The English philosopher Samuel Clarke, a disciple of Newton, argued for this in his 1705 tract, *The Great Duty of Universal Love.* The purpose of religion, Clarke claimed, was to make men "imitate God; to cause them to extend their love and goodness and charity to all their fellow creatures, each in their several stations . . . in like manner as the universal goodness of God extends itself over all his works through the whole creation."[10]

Like the enlightenment, humanitarianism could be used by those opposed to Christianity to deny the depth of human sin and hence the need for a redeemer. But such opinions were confined to the radical few. The majority of British and American Christians embraced humanitarianism in the same way they did the enlightenment—as an opportunity. The enlightenment supported the neoclassical benevolence of God, and humanitarianism supported the Christian benevolence of man. Depending on how conservative or liberal a theologian was, this might lead to a reassessment of the nature of human sin. The late seventeenth-century Anglican John Tillotson went quite far here. "Nothing is more unnatural than sin," declared Tillotson; "'tis not according to our original nature and frame, but it is the corruption and depravation of it, a second nature, superimposed upon us by custom." But this did not mean that Tillotson denied the need for supernatural grace; rather, grace was needed to liberate man's original capacity for benevolence. Likewise, it was the duty of Christians to remove sinful customs that corrupted society. On this, many conservative and liberal theologians could agree. There was an area of sin that humans could do something about: they could reform society.[11]

Here is where humanitarianism was most visible. By the early nineteenth century, it had spawned reform movements such as the temperance and antislavery crusades, new forms of child rearing, and improvements in prisons, schools, the military, and mental asylums. A great and exciting vision of historical progress was contained in humanitarian reform. But there was also a conservative note, for the "several stations" of society that Clarke had mentioned in 1705 were breaking down in the Anglo-American world by the end of the eighteenth century. Champions of the capitalist market and democratic politics welcomed this. But even the most enthusiastic worried that this breakdown of the traditional order might destroy any sense of social responsibility. Society might become atomized into a war of all against all. Individualism, in short, had to have its limits.[12]

Humanitarianism provided a sense of limits, and one expression of this was neoclassical benevolence. Particularly important here was the emphasis on stoical moderation and restraint. This became particularly prominent for men in their roles as civic leaders and eventually politicians. Yet within humanitarianism there was also a partial reaction against this. Already in the late seventeenth century, some had found this stoical restraint cold and un-Christian. More emotional engagement was wanted. This led to the growth of sentimentalism in Britain during the eighteenth century.[13]

In sentimentalism, love became more emotionally expressive. Sympathy, not benevolence, became the distinguishing feeling. Where neoclassical benevolence was serene and rational, sentimental sympathy prompted characters to worry and weep for others. With this shift in characterization, there was a shift in setting. Neoclassical characters were pictured against a panoramic landscape, such as the vast order of the Newtonian universe, or the sweep of history. Sentimental characters were usually found in the home. The scene might not be David leading his army to crush the rebellion instigated by his son in Dryden's *Absalom and Achitophel*, but it could be the everyday trials of parents in disciplining their children. This discipline was not simply a matter of making children behave. It involved going to the roots of their behavior. It was a matter of molding their character. One of the central concerns of sentimentalism was how to make children control their anger for here, the polarization of emotions remained in place. Sentimental sympathy, like neoclassical benevolence, was altruistic. Both stood in sharp contrast with the feverish self-centeredness ascribed to anger.[14]

A good example of this can be found in a popular sentimental novel of 1841, *Home*, by the American writer Catharine Sedgwick. Early in the novel, she told the story of how a father teaches his unruly boy to control his temper—or, as Sedgwick called it, his "passion." Little Wallace, upset with his sister, flings her kitten into a pot of boiling water. For this, he is confined to his room when not in school. After several weeks of this confinement, Wallace asks to see his father. The point of the meeting is not for the boy to confess his crime and ask forgiveness (he has done this long ago) but to tell his father that he has learned to control his temper. His father asks him for proof. So Wallace tells his father of an incident at school that day. A bully had ruined Wallace's homework. Wallace was about to strike back when he remembered to control himself. This involved an inner struggle. But Wallace proved successful, as he told his father: "There was a horrid choking feeling in my throat, and angry words seemed crowding out. . . . I had to bite my lips, though, so that the blood ran." The father immediately interjects, "God bless you my son."[15]

Thus, neoclassical and sentimental characters might express their love differently; but neoclassical benevolence and sentimental sympathy both stood in sharp contrast to anger. This polarization of emotions informed a vast array of cultural characterizations separating the good from the bad in humanitarian reform writing. The diligent wage laborer, the paternal employer, the earnest father, the tender mother, and the well-behaved child exhibited a mixture of neoclassical benevolence and sentimental sympathy. The slaveholder, the drunkard, and the unruly child all were possessed with anger and its primitive passion. Evidence suggests that American men, women, and children in the nineteenth century took these emotional norms to heart. Karen Lystra has found evidence of them in the most personal of documents—love letters. "Ideas about men and women," Lystra observed, "were translated into actual relationships." These ideas were overwhelmingly sentimental. James Hague, in a letter to his beloved, struck the sentimental pose of an unruly but endearing child; he hoped that his betrothed would "continue to love your old boy even when he is grouty."

Common also was the sentimental pose where one (or both) lover claims to be spiritually lost and declares the other the angel of salvation.[16]

The opposite of such stylized self-deprecation, of course, was anger. Assertive, agitated, it broke the bounds of self-control and imposed itself on others. "Shows of anger concerned writers most," noted John Kasson in his study of nineteenth-century advice books; "of all emotions, anger most violently betrayed a loss of self possession and irreparably shattered the spirit of civility." Proper behavior, in turn, conformed to neoclassical norms about serenity and sentimental norms about sympathy. "An admirable method of controlling feeling is to maintain by effort, the serenity and suavity of the countenance," counseled the 1839 *Advice to a Young Gentleman.* "It is impossible for a man to have rage in his breast who has a smile on his countenance." For a woman, anger was not only rude but repulsive. *The Young Lady's Own Book* of 1833 minced no words about it: "An enraged woman . . . is one of the most disgusting sights in nature." Given this, we can appreciate some of the power of Frederick Douglass's portrayal of how slavery corrupted whites such as Sophia Auld. In Douglass's portrayal, she had been an exemplary sentimental wife and mother. But when she became a slaveholder, the lure of absolute power ruined her character: "That cheerful eye, under the influence of slavery, soon reduced her to rage; that voice, made all of sweet accord, changed to one of harsh and horrid discord and that angelic face gave place to that of a demon."[17]

Given all of this, it is not hard to see why Americans found romanticism difficult to appreciate. Romanticism made anger a sign of vitality and love distinctly erotic, and it mixed the two together into the agitated intensity of ambivalence. To American readers raised on neoclassical and sentimental norms—with all of their supports in matters of taste, science, and morality—romantic characters necessarily seemed rude, irrational, and immoral. And yet were also intriguing. By the early twentieth century, cosmopolitan Americans had learned to split the difference: they allowed themselves the fascinating depth of romantic characterization but still maintained neoclassical and sentimental norms in their roles as professionals and parents. But by then the character of God had been refashioned to reflect neoclassical and sentimental norms. This refashioning is most evident in two areas: the doctrine of the atonement and biblical criticism.

The Atonement

Many theologians took the atonement as the central and defining doctrine of Christianity.[18] This was because they believed that here was the deepest revelation of God's character. Of course, there were other ways to get at God's character even outside revelation. "Scientific truth," as one minister put it in 1853, "makes us acquainted with the character of God." But many theologians believed that the atonement opened up the deepest, most mysterious aspects of God's character. This is because the doctrine concerned such an extraordinary and unfathomable act that no one could have expected it of God or deduced it from his other works alone. Theologians speculated that even the angels were amazed by the atonement (and they were supposed to have the most scientific minds in creation). Angels, rational beings on other planets, the human saints in heaven, sinners and devils in hell—everyone would contemplate the cross in wonder for all eternity. No other act of God said so much about who he really was—his inner being, his attributes, his emotions. American theologians across the doctrinal spectrum would have agreed with the Presbyterian Gardiner Spring when he declared in 1846: "No where is the character of God so fully revealed as in the cross."[19]

Yet a massive shift in how theologians understood this revelation of God's character was occurring. This was the shift from the juristic tradition to philanthropism. It is one of the major changes that distinguish traditional from modern Protestant theology.[20]

In the juristic tradition, God was an emotionally complex character. This was because his primary trait was his justice. Because of this, theologians could depict God as feeling both love and wrath as he rewarded the righteous and punished the guilty. Nowhere was this more evident than in the crucifixion. In the juristic theory of the atonement, there was an amazing mixture of love and anger in God. God, in this theory, felt tremendous anger at human sin; but God also felt great love for humankind as the pinnacle of the earthly creation. "In a marvelous and divine way he loved us even when he hated us," wrote Calvin, citing Augustine.[21] In order to spare people his wrath, God diverted it onto Jesus, his beloved son. So both humans and Jesus experienced a mixture of love and anger in God. On the cross, Jesus absorbed God's wrath against human sin, exhausted it, and satisfied God's justice. Thus, Jesus was the penal substitute for people; as such, he enabled God to offer salvation to sinful humans. Aspects of the juristic theory of the atonement, also called the penal substitute theory, had been a part of Christian theology since late antiquity. But it did not emerge as the central formulation of the doctrine of the atonement until the work of Anselm in the eleventh century. From then on it dominated Western theology for nearly 800 years. Through the Reformation, this was the major characterization of God. It was the theology of Calvin and the Puritans. Well into the middle of the eighteenth century, it remained at the center of American theology.[22]

But in European Protestantism, a more emotionally singular characterization of God was emerging in philanthropism. Not God's judicial anger and love but love above all else characterized God in philanthropism. Roots of the philanthropic characterization of God also go back to late antiquity. But it did not begin to displace the juristic tradition in Europe until the seventeenth century. The modern critique began with Faustus Socinus in his 1578 treatise *Of Jesus Christ the Savior*. Socinus argued that God, out of his love for human beings, had waived the penalty against sin and sent Jesus to proclaim this free pardon. What of God's duty to uphold the law? Socinus argued that it was God's prerogative as sovereign to overrule the law when he saw fit. What of the crucifixion? Socinus argued that it was not God's work but that of evil people who refused to hear Christ's message and tried to silence him. But instead of thwarting God, their actions threw into relief God's boundless love, for the cross showed that despite the worst people could do, God still forgave them.

This critique proved deeply compelling. In order to refute it, some Protestant theologians made major concessions. The most important came from Hugo Grotius in his 1617 treatise *The Defence of the Catholic Faith concerning the Satisfaction of Christ against Faustus Socinus*. Grotius granted Socinus's major point: that the atonement revealed the priority of God's love over his justice and that it was God's prerogative as sovereign to waive the penalty of the law and pardon humankind. But here is where Grotius drew the line. God as governor of the universe still had the duty to uphold the honor, if not the letter, of the law. God also had the duty to ensure that the deterrent force of the law still remained in effect. God might forgive humanity, but he might not forgive offenders in the future (such as creatures on other planets). So because God did not execute the law against the human race, he needed to make a demonstration of the power of the law. This was the purpose of the crucifixion. It was not simply the work of people; it was still the work of God. But now Christ was not the literal substitute for humans, as in the juristic theory, but only the symbolic substitute. That is, he did not suffer the full measure of the penalty against sin, only an expression of this penalty. In the Grotian theory, God sent Jesus to the cross to provide a demonstration of the price of sin.

By the early years of the nineteenth century, variations on the Socinian and Grotian theories had entered the mainstream of American theology.[23] Socinianism was taken up by Unitarians and liberal Congregationalists under the general name of the moral influence theory. This theory got its name from the suggestion that men could be redeemed by the influence or example of God's love manifested in the life of Jesus. The Grotian theory spread widely through American theology during the early nineteenth century. In large measure, it had always been the doctrine of Arminians following Grotius and was taken up by American Methodists and Baptists with little controversy.

The real controversy came when Congregationalists and liberal Presbyterians began to abandon their traditional theology of juristic Calvinism for the Grotian theory. Jonathan Edwards, in the middle of the eighteenth century, was an important transitional figure here. He was a key conduit for making elements of the Grotian theory respectable to Congregationalists and Presbyterians. Edwards, while famous for systematically refuting Arminianism in its bearing on the doctrine of original sin, more casually adopted features of the Grotian theory in his discussions of the atonement. His successors in the late eighteenth century, the New Divinity theologians, Samuel Hopkins and Joseph Bellamy, passed the Grotian theory into mainstream Congregationalism.[24] From there it spread to the Presbyterians, contributing to the 1837 division of the denomination into Old and New School factions.[25] By this time, the Grotian theory became known as the governmental theory. The name came from the idea that despite the fact that God's essential nature was love, it was still his duty as governor of the universe to uphold respect for the law.

The moral and governmental theories of the atonement defined two-thirds of the theological spectrum in America. The remaining third was left to defenders of the juristic tradition. These included some conservative New England Congregationalists, but most were Old School Presbyterians in the middle Atlantic and southern states. These conservatives upheld the penal substitute theory, so called because it emphasized that Jesus bore the full punishment due humanity, not the symbolic punishment of the governmental theory.

The rise of the governmental and moral theories of the atonement at the expense of the penal theory generated much theological debate during the nineteenth century. As late as 1900, Theodore Munger declared that along with the controversy over evolution, American Presbyterians were torn over the interpretation of the atonement. But the middle of the nineteenth century was the crucial era of debate about this doctrine. As one writer for the *New Englander* put it in 1862, "at present" the doctrine of the atonement "is almost the only vital and really contested battleground in the domain of theology."[26]

The coincidence of this with the controversy over slavery and the Civil War intensified this debate. Imagery of the cross was central to all kinds of discourses—political, social, and, of course, theological. Commenting on the Christlike imagery in Harriet Beecher Stowe's 1852 novel, *Uncle Tom's Cabin*, Jane Tompkins called the crucifixion America's "central religious myth" in the nineteenth century. She was right about its centrality. The awful bloodshed and sacrifice of the Civil War gave even more urgency to the discussion of the penalty for human sin and how it related to God's character—a point raised by Abraham Lincoln in his second inaugural address. But the war was not the cause of the theological debate about the atonement. This debate had been raging in America for decades and in Europe for centuries. American theologians often took a long view of the controversy. Doing so sometimes made the immediate events of the war pale by comparison, for the atonement was about God's character, and in the long run nothing was more important than this.[27]

This explains why, in the summer of 1863, the conservative theologian W. G. T. Shedd denounced "the over-refinement of the age." It might seem perverse to make such a statement during the summer of the battles of Vicksburg and Gettysburg. It might seem an especially unfortunate comment for a theologian like Shedd based in New York City, for that July the city was convulsed by the worst riots in American history—the New York City draft riots. For a week the city was in mayhem; over 100 people were killed. Union troops straight from the battle of Gettysburg were sent to restore order. But Shedd was concerned about something else when he condemned "the over-refinement of the age." The traditional Protestant and biblical characterization of God was being lost. Theologians had come to emphasize God's love and downplay his wrath. Shedd traced this back two and a half centuries to the work of Grotius.

American theology had become penetrated to its core by philanthropism. Indeed, it was so prevalent in 1859 that Shedd remarked that it had become nearly impossible to ascribe anger to God without people thinking of "an enraged and ugly demon." Shedd was right. At the cutting edge of philanthropism was just such a caricature of the juristic God.[28]

As we have seen, the neoclassical and sentimental polarization of emotions informed a vast array of cultural characterizations separating the good from the bad. In reform literature, the slaveholder (or in proslavery tracts, the abolitionist), the drunkard, and the unruly child were possessed with anger and its primitive passion. This polarization of emotions played an important part in theological polemics as well. The liberal champions of philanthropism used this polarization to caricature the juristic tradition as putting forth a God of wrath in contrast to philanthropism's God of love.

It is easy to see why this polemic was so effective. In its most basic sense, the polarization of emotions denied the possibility of the juristic God. In the neoclassical and sentimental ideal of character, no one, much less God (a perfect being), could simultaneously be wrathful and loving. What had been the dramatic potential at the heart of the juristic tradition, therefore, was no longer credible. It simply seemed crude. This, in turn, exposed the juristic God to easy caricature. Because philanthropism characterized God primarily by his love, the juristic tradition could easily be caricatured as the opposite: that is, as characterizing God primarily by his anger. In this way, the real character of the juristic God—an emotionally complex God of love and wrath—was buried under polemical attacks and forgotten. The choice between the juristic tradition and philanthropism seemed easy and self-evident: a God of wrath or a God of love?

All of this gave the champions of philanthropism a great deal of confidence. Many felt they were riding the tide of historical progress. They could dismiss the juristic God as a primitive God of passionate anger. In doing this, they might not even be conscious that they were relying on a caricature. It came to seem axiomatic that passionate anger could not legitimately be ascribed to God, and certainly not on an equal footing with God's love. So prevalent did these assumptions become that even conservatives adopted them. While maintaining the penal theory of the atonement in the abstract, conservatives toned down their depictions of God's anger. If they did not, they suffered the withering polemic of liberals who caricatured their God as a vicious God of wrath.

The supreme confidence of this polemic can be seen in an 1829 tract written by the Unitarian theologian Noah Worcester, *The Atoning Sacrifice: A Display of Love Not of Wrath*. The very title takes the polemical distinction between philanthropism and the juristic tradition for granted: God is either a God of love or a God of wrath. It would be a mistake, however, to think of Worcester as a polemicist conniving to misrepresent the juristic God. Misrepresenting it he was; but in American cosmopolitan culture in the early nineteenth century it was difficult not to. It was hard for Worcester to see how a loving God could really feel anger. So the caricature of the juristic God came easily.

Worcester was entirely sincere; he was what we would call a true humanitarian. A veteran of the American Revolution, he had seen the misery of war firsthand and worked for its eradication. Along with William Ellery Channing, he helped form the Massachusetts Peace Society in 1815. He thought a congress of nations could come together and abolish war. His hopes for humanity, however, were pinned on his assumptions about God's character. If God did not resort to wrath, then neither should people. Worcester felt confident that other theologians were coming to agree with him, even conservatives. "With real pleasure," Worcester noted eagerly, "I have observed that many modern writers in favor of substituted sufferings [the juristic theory of the atonement] have avoided the use of such harsh language and revolting representations, as were common at a former period in describing the manner in which God treated his Son while on the cross."[29]

Worcester was basically correct. His terms are not that of a modern historian, but he was observing the impact of neoclassicism and sentimentalism on theology. But there was more to it than this. Why was it that even conservatives now were toning down their characterizations of God, Worcester asked. He supposed that it was due to "something more than a mere advance in literary taste." He continued: "I am inclined to impute it to a progress of light and a growing conviction that there is something in the doctrine of penal suffering too shocking to be expressed in bold emphatic language." Again he was basically right. "Literary taste"—neoclassicism and sentimentalism—was certainly a part of this change in theology. But what gave these styles of characterization such cultural power was what Worcester called "a progress of light"—what we now call the enlightenment and humanitarianism.[30]

So the juristic characterization of God was either abandoned or muffled. But one problem remained. The Bible contained many depictions of God that theologians with Worcester's neoclassical sensibility found "shocking." This proved a real difficulty for the champions of philanthropism. Could theologians dismiss the Bible as they had the juristic tradition? In part, yes; they did discredit much of the Old Testament depiction of God. It was more difficult, however, to dismiss the depictions of Jesus in the Gospels.

The Bible

In the Old Testament, God was clearly depicted as feeling both love and anger. For this reason, juristic theologians had put the Old Testament at the center of their theology. For the same reason, the liberal champions of philanthropism tried to marginalize the Old Testament. Their strategy can be simply stated: they distanced the Old Testament from the New and then said that the Old Testament was basically a primitive revelation, much of it irrelevant for modern Christians.

Cutting off the Old Testament from the New meant undoing a system of interpretation called typology. This had been used by juristic theologians to knit the Old and New Testaments together into a seamless whole. In this system of interpretation, events, characters, and religious practices—almost everything in the Old Testament— were taken in one way or another as a foreshadowing of the life and death of Jesus. Central to this entire scheme of interpretation was the Mosaic system of sacrifices. In the Old Testament, God had demanded that an animal, usually a lamb, be sacrificed for human sins. Juristic theologians interpreted the lamb as a foreshadowing of Jesus, who was the real penal substitute for human beings. Liberal biblical critics questioned the whole orientation of this interpretation. They argued that ancient Hebrew practices should be seen not as harbingers of the future but as historical artifacts to be understood mainly in terms of their own time. For instance, some liberals argued that the ancient Hebrew practices were just what they appeared to be: animal sacrifices. In 1855, the Harvard biblical scholar George Rapall Noyes argued that the Hebraic sacrifices were essentially the same as the animal sacrifices of the ancient Egyptians and Aztecs. Such a view of the Bible, of course, may be seen as an advance in historical understanding. But Noyes also had a clear theological agenda for his biblical criticism. A "false view" of ancient Hebraic animal sacrifices, he declared, "continues to uphold one of the most irrational doctrines which ever prevailed in the church"—namely, the juristic theory of the atonement.[31]

It was more difficult, however, to primitivize the Old Testament depiction of God. Ancient religious practices were one thing, but how could Christian theologians say that the Bible did not depict God accurately? The problem here was not simply the characterization of God but the kind of language used in the Bible. It was not easy to explain, as one theologian put it in 1862, "the very strong anthropopathic language, so abundant in scripture, such as 'vengeance is mine'; 'ah, I will ease me of my adversaries and avenge me of mine enemies'; 'my wrath shall wax hot' etc." For, the theologian continued, "if we take avenging justice in a sense which allows a disconnection of it from the rule of love, and suppose its inflictions to be for their own sake without any reference to ulterior good, and apply such language as that cited above to God as having such an attribute, this were not only to undeify him, but to make him an object of infinite horror."[32]

The point here was remarkable. This theologian was urging his colleagues to be careful not to write about God as the Old Testament did lest they give the impression that God is some kind of monster. How could this writer so easily toss off the notion that the Old Testament was crude in its depiction of God? The answer is in the author's phrase, "anthropopathic language."

Anthropomorphism is a way of picturing God that ascribes to him human traits, from a body with arms and legs, to the full array of human emotions. In contrast to this, we can use the term "theism" to denote a more abstract way of picturing God. Here God is described as a disembodied spirit with abstract attributes such as omnipotence, omniscience, and immutability. Throughout the history of Christian theology, there has been a great deal of overlap between theistic and anthropomorphic characterizations of God, but theism has been the more prestigious way to write about God. Theistic characterizations of God have been taken as scholarly and intellectual. Anthropomorphism has been considered more artistic and emotional. Yet there is a great deal of anthropomorphism in the Bible. So although anthropomorphism has traditionally taken a back seat to theism, it was by no means ignored or dismissed.[33]

For instance, juristic theologians, while honoring theism as the more intellectual characterization of God, reserved a place for biblical anthropomorphism. John Owen, in his 1626 *Dissertation on Divine Justice*, developed a theistic characterization of God by citing Seneca and Aquinas to the effect that God, a perfect being, could not experience passions such as anger. But having said this, Owen also acknowledged the importance of biblical anthropomorphism. "However this matter be," Owen reflected, "certain it is, that God himself assumed no affection of our nature so often to himself in Scripture [as anger] in words, which, for the most part, denote the greatest commotion of mind . . . in words too, which among the Hebrews express the parts of the body affected by such commotions." Owen went on to list these anthropomorphic expressions—God's "nostrils inflamed" with wrath and so on.[34] If God used such language to describe himself, how could we criticize it?

This was the crucial question. However much juristic theologians might cite scholarly authorities to build up a theistic characterization of God, they never allowed themselves to feel superior to the Bible. Nor did they allow themselves to feel substantially superior to the ancient Hebrews, to whom this revelation had been given. Sadly, however, this theological honoring of the ancient Hebrews could exist side by side with Christian persecution of contemporary Jews. Indeed, this persecution and honoring could go together, for, in the minds of some Christians, Jews were guilty of rejecting the redeemer whom their ancestors supposedly had anticipated. The point here is that juristic theologians did feel close to the ancient Hebrews. At issue was a vision of history. Medieval and Reformation theologians might consider themselves further along in history than the ancient Hebrews, but not significantly so when it came to understanding God's character. Calvin, for instance, likened the ancient Hebrews to "children" and Christians to "young men." By this, Calvin meant no disparagement of the ancient Hebrews. If Christians had been able to grow in their faith beyond the ancient Hebrews, it was only because Christians had the good fortune of being born after, rather than before, the incarnation. This meant that Christians could have a fuller understanding of Christ than the ancient Hebrews. But being "young men" did not mean that Christians had outgrown everything from their spiritual childhood. Before God, the historical differences between individuals shrank to very little. All people, in short, were children before God. And God, in some measure, treated all people accordingly. "For who even of slight intelligence does not understand," Calvin wrote, "that, as Nurses commonly do with infants, God is wont in a measure to 'lisp' when speaking to us?"—which is to say, reveal himself in anthropomorphic language.[35]

Here was a key difference between the juristic tradition and philanthropism. The champions of philanthropism still felt they were but infants compared to God, but they no longer felt that they were the same sort of children before God as were the ancient Hebrews. Their view was grounded in the humanitarian vision of historical progress and found easy analogies with sentimental notions about child rearing. The argument went like this: to primitive people, as to unruly children, God needed to be very stern and express his concern for them as anger. But among modern people, as among generally well-behaved children, God needed only to encourage their disciplined instincts with tender offerings of his love. It was this basic assumption that allowed nineteenth-century liberal biblical critics to primitivize Old Testament anthropomorphism and make it seem crude and unfit for educated audiences. Theism, in turn, became almost the only authoritative way to depict God in theology. As we will see, the abstract nature of theism blended smoothly with the emphasis on serenity and rationality in neoclassicism.

But first theologians had to put anthropomorphism behind them. In order to primitivize anthropomorphism, American liberals drew on some of the latest biblical criticism from Britain and Germany.[36] By importing this European scholarship, liberals substantially improved American biblical criticism. But it must not be forgotten that biblical criticism was serving the needs of theology. Liberal biblical critics primitivized anthropomorphism as part of their effort to discredit the juristic tradition. Taking the case of the Old Testament, American theologians increasingly sought to understand these writings in the historical context in which they were written rather than as harbingers of Christianity. This certainly was a scholarly advance. The effort is always liberating for the historian to try to see the past in its own terms. But this effort may also serve polemical purposes. By making the past distinct from the present, you also create a dumping ground for getting rid of what you do not like in the present.

This is exactly what the liberal champions of philanthropism did with the Old Testament. First, they claimed to understand the Old Testament in terms of its own time, and then they declared that these times were primitive indeed and thus not immediately relevant to modern Christians. There was a corollary to this: because the Old Testament anthropomorphism provided a foundation for the juristic characterization of God, it was also primitive and unsuited to the needs of modern people.

But liberals still needed to explain why anthropomorphism had been appropriate in the past, though not in the present. A large part of their argument was that God had revealed himself in anthropomorphic form not as a concession to human beings in general but as a concession to the ancient Hebrews in particular. In other words, specific historical circumstances in ancient times had made it appropriate for God to reveal himself in anthropomorphic form. What were these circumstances? They had to do with the prevalence of idol worship in ancient times: because the ancient Hebrews had been surrounded by idol worshipers, God occasionally took on the guise of these idols to prove his power against them. "Without the least irreverence it may be said that a sort of necessity was laid upon the true God," the biblical critic E. C. Wines wrote in 1850; "how could he check the propensity to idolatry [in ancient times] but by doing in reality what the false Gods pretended to do?"[37]

That same year Edwards Park put it even more strongly in a famous and controversial sermon given to the annual meeting of Congregationalist ministers. The title of the sermon was "The Theology of the Intellect and That of the Feelings." The sermon had a number of layers, but its basic gist was that "the theology of the intellect" was theistic, scientific, and refined and used precise literal language, whereas the "theology of the feelings" was anthropomorphic and crude and used bold, figurative language. Much of the Bible, according to Park, was given in the language of the "feelings"—that is, anthropomorphism. This, Park explained, suited the ancient Hebrews, given their primitive level of culture. Therefore, when one reads the Bible, Park counseled, the historical context of the ancient Hebrews must be kept in mind. Readers, in short, must not take biblical anthropomorphism too seriously as a representation of God, for it was a representation suited to the specific historical circumstances of a primitive people—for instance, it frightened them away from idol worship. As Park explained: "In order to hold the Jews back from the foul, cruel vices of their neighbors . . . in order to stop their degrading worship of Moloch, Dagon, Baal, Tammuz, they were plied with a stern theology, well fitted by its terrible denunciations to save them from the crime which was still more terrible. . . . This fearful anthropomorphism estamped a truth upon their hearts."[38]

Park did grant some biblical anthropomorphism a larger, spiritual significance. For instance, imagery of God as a loving shepherd, according to Park, transcended the ages. But this showed Park's agenda. His point was not so much to primitivize anthropomorphism per se but to primitivize anthropomorphic imagery of God's anger. Thus, imagery of God as a good shepherd provided Park with the occasion to acclaim the common humanity of God's people across the ages. Anthropomorphic imagery of God's anger, on the other hand, could only be understood in terms of the specific historical context of the ancient Hebrews. God's love, in short, was unproblematic, whether represented anthropomorphically or theistically. It was God's anger that needed to be explained away. One reason for this was to discredit the juristic tradition.

Park suggested that anthropomorphic language survived in theology out of "antique fashion." He likened it to the way in which astronomers continued to use mythological names for planets and constellations. If modern astronomy had its "dragon" and "great bear," theology still had its primitive, Old Testament terms for God. But Park was not satisfied with this. He was most likely aware that at this very time astronomers were debating whether to stop naming stars and planets after mythological figures. The worry was that this practice gave the public the impression that astronomy was not thoroughly scientific. Park shared similar fears for theology. "We mourn over the ruinous impression" caused by the phrase "vindictive justice."[39] Here was Park's polemical jab. "Vindictive justice" was the common name for God's punitive wrath in the juristic tradition. Park was reducing it to a mythological carryover.

To a large extent, conservatives collapsed before this polemic against Old Testament anthropomorphism. Most folded just as they had done when confronted with the caricature of the juristic God. The two were of a piece; the juristic God and anthropomorphism went down together. Conservatives adapted to the new norms set by the liberals. They abstracted their depictions of God's wrath and, like liberals, drove anthropomorphism out of their theology. In short, conservatives assumed a posture of defensive accommodation with liberalism.

Charles Hodge led the way. He defended the juristic tradition against the liberal polemic, while making his own characterization of God neoclassical and theistic so as to be invulnerable to this polemic. As part of this, Hodge engaged Park in a lengthy and sometimes vitriolic debate over Park's sermon, "The Theology of the Intellect and That of the Feelings."[40] Hodge deftly demonstrated that much of Park's argument was a sham. It was impossible to draw sharp distinctions between the "intellect" and the "feelings" or, for that matter, "literal" and "figurative" language. Likewise, in the Bible, anthropomorphic and theistic characterizations of God were often combined with each other. So it was useless to try to draw sharp distinctions between them. Park had only done so for polemical purposes, Hodge charged. Hodge clearly saw that this was the purpose of Park's sermon. By reducing the juristic theology to a primitive "theology of the feelings," Park was undermining its intellectual authority.[41] But Hodge still went along with an important assumption in Park's sermon: that the theological depiction of God should be theistic and neoclassical.

The difference was that Hodge argued that the ancient Hebrews had seen God this way too. This was one way of preserving the Old Testament, something that Hodge as a penal theologian needed to do. Hodge argued that true religious feelings were essentially the same throughout history. Therefore, when God condescended to reveal himself to the ancient Hebrews, he had not been forced to appeal to them in ways that were now dated. Hodge was not saying that modern Christians should embrace the vivid anthropomorphism of the Old Testament; rather, he was suggesting that the ancient Hebrews were basically neoclassical theists. In other words, Hodge shared many of Park's basic assumptions about God's character. Hodge assumed along with Park that extravagant, figurative language about God was primitive, but he downplayed the fact that this language was in the Bible. He did not deny Park's point that the ancient Hebrews were given to emotion. But their emotion was mainly sober and calm—in short, it suited neoclassicism. This was a sign, according to Hodge, that their faith was as sophisticated as his own. "Our author," Hodge wrote of Park, "represents the feelings as expressing themselves in figures, and demanding 'visible and tangible images.' We question the correctness of this statement. The highest language of emotion is generally simple."[42]

The word "highest" was the crucial qualifier. But what about what Park had called the "fearful anthropomorphism" of the Old Testament? With typical aplomb, Hodge steered around the issue. "The emotions of terror and sublimity," Hodge acknowledged, "as they are commonly excited through the imagination, naturally clothe themselves in imaginative language. But the moral, religious and social affections, when strongly moved, commonly demand the simplest form of utterance." For Hodge, then, religious emotion had little to do with "terror and sublimity." In this way, Hodge dismissed the issue of God's wrath. Instead, he kept the focus on feelings that suited a neoclassical sensibility. Hodge listed some examples of these in the Old Testament, such as David's lament over Absalom.[43]

Of course, it was questionable whether this example could be described as a simple utterance, not given to bold figures of speech. Perhaps in choosing the example of David mourning Absalom, Hodge had been influenced by Dryden's *Absalom and Achitophel*. But others drew on different literary authorities. A writer for the Unitarian *Christian Examiner*, reviewing the debate between Park and Hodge, was surprised that Hodge characterized David's outcries as simple and straightforward. "John Milton," the reviewer remarked, "who has been supposed to know something of emotional language and figurative style, pronounces [David's lament] as highly figurative."[44]

Whatever one decided to label as "emotional" and "figurative" or "literal" and "intellectual," the important point was what one did with these categories. And here most conservatives went along with the tide of philanthropism. It was just as Worcester had observed in 1829: conservatives were toning down their depictions of God. By the 1850s, the process had spread throughout cosmopolitan theology. Following Hodge, the majority of conservative theologians went along with this.

It was difficult not to, for liberals had positioned themselves to appear both learned and fair-minded. For conservatives to reject this was to risk appearing obscurantist and narrow-minded. Did not liberals have prestigious European biblical criticism on their side? Were not liberals fair-minded in not demanding too much of such an ancient book as the Old Testament? Again, it was a matter of historical perspective. Calvin had likened the difference between the ancient Hebrews and modern Christians to that between children and young men. Nineteenth-century liberals drew the same comparison, but for different purposes. Now the object was to amplify the sense of historical distance. This came across as good sense and good taste. "Let us not be guilty of the folly, the injustice, we may say," Wines intoned, "of measuring the intellectual wants and religious wants of a comparatively rude and infant state of society, by those of our own more cultivated, more enlightened, more spiritual, more manly and Christian age of the world."[45]

This became the received wisdom. It caused the conservative biblical scholar and classical critic Lewis Taylor to remark ruefully in 1850: "[It] is one of the most noticeable signs of the times that the Old Testament is rapidly becoming, if it has not already become, obsolete in respect to us and our age,—that for the present Christian church it possesses chiefly an antiquarian value."[46]

But the Old Testament was not just left for antiquarians. Liberals played it up to sustain their polemic against the juristic tradition. They even found a positive use for the Old Testament: if no longer helpful in addressing sophisticated audiences, it did speak to the masses, children, and savages. Its very primitive nature made the Old Testament good for some kinds of popular evangelism and missionary work. This was one reason Park maintained that the modern world still needed a "theology of the feelings." It might be the best way to get the Christian message across to criminals or unruly children.[47] In 1874, the celebrated Brooklyn minister Henry Ward Beecher tied these notions together into a vision of human progress. The very primitiveness of the Bible was its recommendation, he declared to the students of the Yale Divinity School. "The Old Testament," Beecher exclaimed, "is wonderfully adapted to the wants of the mind in childhood and in the savage state, and the preparation of mind, all through the different stages of civilization, for the higher condition of culture."[48]

There was one problem with all of this, however. In primitivizing the Old Testament, theologians assumed that the penultimate revelation of God was to be found in the New Testament. Here, supposedly, was a revelation appropriate for modern, sophisticated audiences. Here should be a God of love, not of wrath. In the New Testament should be depictions of God that conformed with the neoclassical and sentimental assumptions of theologians. But this was not always the case.

On a superficial level, the champions of philanthropism found it easier to deal with the New Testament than with the Old. The New Testament Epistles were cryptic enough that liberals and conservatives alike could interpret them to their advantage. The Gospels, however, were another story. There were two issues here: the depiction of God and the depiction of Jesus. The depiction of God was easiest to handle. The reason was that God (the Father, as a distinct character from Jesus) appears in the Gospels only two times—at the baptism and the transfiguration of Jesus. In both instances, God speaks from behind a cloud, declaring roughly the same thing: "This is my beloved Son in whom I am well pleased."[49] This seemed to support the image of the benevolent God of philanthropism.

Juristic theologians, of course, had plenty of explanations for this. But the point is that the Gospels themselves did not give juristic theologians much to work with when it came to depicting God diverting his wrath from humanity onto Jesus. From the first emergence of philanthropism, Socinians had pointed this out to the juristic theologians. If God was such a strict judge, willing even to send his son to the cross, then why, at his only appearances in the Gospels, did God simply declare his love for his son? Sometimes juristic theologians just ploughed through the difficulties here. For instance, in the seventeenth century, John Owen responded to Socinian queries this way: "The Lord Christ (if I may so say,) was sued by his Father's justice into an execution [and] if it be excepted (as it is) that God was always well-pleased with His Son [I reply] It is true, He was always well-pleased with Him, yet it pleased Him to bruise Him and put Him to grief."[50]

By the nineteenth century, such assertions had come to seem rather crude. This sort of writing may have been what Worcester had in mind when he objected to the "harsh language and revolting representations [that] were common at a former period in describing the manner in which God treated his Son while on the cross." So the liberal champions of philanthropism had some reason to feel confident in their command over the Bible. Old Testament imagery of God's anger could be primitivized; the New Testament Epistles were open to various interpretations; and the characterization of God in the Gospels seemed to support philanthropism. Only one major problem remained: Jesus.

He, of course, was key. All leading American theologians assumed that, in one way or another, Jesus was the manifestation of God (though Unitarians, not believing in a Trinity, did not think that Christ was co-equal with God). The gospel depictions of Jesus, however, were not always easy to square with neoclassical and sentimental assumptions about his character and did not always mesh easily with philanthropism. In fact, much of Jesus' behavior made more sense with the juristic theory. Although God did not actually appear in the Gospels prosecuting Jesus, Jesus sometimes acted as if he was being prosecuted by God. In Matthew, Mark, and Luke, Jesus was portrayed as physically trembling and overcome by the events leading to his death. In the Garden of Gethsemane, he agonized over his fate and prayed for God to "remove the cup of suffering" from him, but he added that if it was God's will he would submit. After being beaten by the Roman soldiers, Jesus was made to carry his cross to Golgotha, but he stumbled under the weight of it, and it was given to Simon of Cyrene to carry. And on the cross Jesus had cried out: "My God, my God, why have you forsaken me?" None of this made immediate sense in the characterization of God in philanthropism: that God was chiefly a God of love.[51]

Of course, it could be said that Jesus had been unnerved by his human persecutors, but this raised other problems. Why did he address God as if he was the one who was sending him to the cross? In the seventeenth century, the juristic theologians had not hesitated to point this out to the early Socinians and Grotians. If God had not been bearing down on Jesus in the Garden of Gethsemane and on the cross, juristic theologians asked, then why would Jesus cry out to God at these two moments and not others, such as when he was arrested by the Roman soldiers? "Surely it was a strong and close trial and that immediately from the Father," Owen argued, "for how meekly and cheerfully doth he submit without any regret or trouble of spirit to all the cruelty of men."[52] Owen was overplaying his hand in saying Jesus submitted himself for arrest "cheerfully." But the force of the argument still rung from the seventeenth century down to the nineteenth century.

The problem became worse when Jesus was compared with martyrs. Even if the liberal point was granted—that people, not God, were tormenting Jesus—then why had Jesus become so unnerved? Could mere humans frighten the Son of God? Even if Jesus was not taken to be the Son of God, but only an inspired man, this still did not explain why he became so unnerved. Thousands of martyrs, including women and children, had suffered worse torments than Jesus, yet some of them had not only shown resilience but suffered joyfully and praised God throughout their trials. Why had Jesus not shown similar fortitude and faith? Was Jesus "of more feeble mind and possessed of less heroic firmness than innumerable martyrs?," François Turretin asked Socinians in the seventeenth century. Nearly two centuries later the question still troubled Moses Stuart, one of America's leading liberal biblical critics. Thousands of martyrs, "thousands even of the more delicate sex," Stuart acknowledged in 1828, had suffered prolonged and horrifying deaths "with a dauntless, nay a triumphant spirit." Compared to them, Jesus appeared to be "wanting in calmness and fortitude of soul." Stuart confessed that this baffled him.[53]

Neoclassicism had made the problem even more troubling, for the most celebrated traits in neoclassicism were serenity and self-control. Neoclassical characters were not to show anger, nor were they to show anxiety or suffering. Virtuous characters should be self-possessed and face adversity calmly. Anything less might be cause for censure. Thus, when Edward Gibbon in *The Decline and Fall of the Roman Empire* mentioned that Augustus received news of a military setback, he felt compelled to remark in a footnote: "Augustus did not receive the melancholy news with all the temper and firmness that might have been expected from his character."[54] Neoclassical theologians expected even more firmness from Jesus. Only weak-willed and shallow characters gave passionate vent to their troubles. Therefore, even if Jesus was suffering greatly (and even if he was only a man, as some Unitarians believed), he should have remained self-possessed throughout his ordeal.

This was a real challenge for neoclassical theologians. Over and over again in their writing, they wrestled with the gospel accounts of Jesus in the Garden of Gethsemane and on the cross. Their effort to square the Gospels with their neoclassical expectations drew from them some of their most ingenious writing.

Sentimental theologians also faced challenges in the Gospels. Jesus' anxiety and outcries raised problems for them too, but sentimentalism allowed more physical expression than neoclassicism. So to some extent sentimentalists could attribute Jesus' outbursts to his sympathetic identification with human suffering. Still, they had their own problems with Jesus' behavior. These concerned his treatment of his family. If he did not have to be serene, as in neoclassicism, Jesus did have to be a good son, for the heart of sentimentalism was family bonding. The problem was that Jesus did not always appear to be the best of sons. As a boy, Jesus had wandered off from his parents; when they found him in the temple, he appeared unmindful of their concern. As a young man, he attended a wedding in Cana with his mother; when the party ran out of wine, she suggested that he miraculously provide more, but he seemed to rebuke her. Later in his ministry, when he was addressing a crowd, his mother and other members of his family had tried to reach him by pressing through the throng. When told of their presence, he seemed to disavow them and declared that his family was made up of those who followed God. These incidents were as troublesome for sentimental writers as some of the scenes in the Garden of Gethsemane and at the cross were for neoclassical theologians.

Close attention to the Gospels, however, did push some neoclassical and sentimental religious writers to generate ingenious characterizations of God. Neoclassical and sentimental theologians had largely cut themselves off from the power of Old Testament anthropomorphism. But they still had the Gospels to challenge them.

✌

CHAPTER THREE

Serenity and Torment

William Ellery Channing, Edwards A. Park, Charles Hodge, and Archibald Alexander Hodge

Serenity is the distinguishing trait of the God of neoclassical theism. He is serene because he experiences no inner conflict or complexity. All of his attributes, even his judgment of sin, are brought into harmony by his one encompassing trait—his love. And this love makes him serene because it is neoclassical love or, more precisely, benevolence—a harmonious fusion of feeling and reason. The classic statement of this is Edwards Park's sermon "All the Moral Attributes of God Are Comprehended in His Love." There, Park alluded to God's declaration to Moses in the Book of Exodus, "I am that I am." Park used this declaration to contrast the human mind with God's. "We rejoice that there is a mind free from the complexities and discrepancies that mar our character; having no inward strife to quell, no intestine contradictions to reconcile, no disparities nor inaptitudes to subdue. We are calmed by the announcement, 'I am that I am,' for this indicates an elevation above all inward fears."[1]

If the neoclassical God was serene, it was a masterful serenity, for the setting in which he operated was immense. When theologians thought of him, they thought on a big scale. The universe and the sweep of human history were his domains. His serenity was reflected in the natural and moral order. This was the creator God of the Newtonian universe who set the planets moving in their majestic orbits and designed the precise adaptation between each life form and its environment. Given the wonder of such natural design, it was easy for nineteenth-century theologians to think that there must be other rational creatures on other planets. God could not have created all of this simply for humankind. Yet this did not mean that humans were simply one among many rational creatures, for if logic suggested that the benevolence of the natural order extended through the universe, it also suggested that something unique in God's moral order had occurred on earth. This was the atonement. It could not be imagined that this was a routine event for God. He had sent his beloved son (or representative), Jesus, to his death. It must have occurred only on earth. And if so, this must have been the wonder of the universe.

Neoclassical theists thus considered the atonement from a panoramic view. Some imagined the angels and creatures on other planets becoming fascinated by what was happening on earth after the fall. They would wonder why God had not sent Adam and Eve straightaway to hell following their sin, for this departed from precedent. In the punishment of the fallen angels, God had sent them straight to hell. Now in his different treatment of humanity, God must be planning to reveal something deeper about himself. When the mystery was uncovered in the cross, the entire universe was amazed. God could save sinners. God's love was paramount over his justice—though not at the cost of justice, for God had harmonized the demands of his justice with the greater prerogative of his love. Nothing like this had been seen in the universe before. "The light of God's glory, reflected from the face of His Son, darted its rays from heaven, earth and hell," declared the Presbyterian theologian James Henley Thornwell in 1845. "The cross became the center of universal attraction, displayed the perfections of the Deity in singular and rare combination, and was the source at once of rapture to angels, of terror to the lost and of hope to men."[2]

This was a majestic vision, but the problem, as always, was the Bible. To begin with, the fact that God had declared "I am that I am" to Moses from a burning bush did not exactly convey a feeling of serenity. Park, however, could easily overlook this, as he could overlook much of the Old Testament depiction of God. What he could not overlook, however, were the Gospels. This left neoclassical theists with a real problem. Inside himself, God might be serene, and to the universe at large, the atonement might be majestic, but in God's relationship with his own son, Jesus, serenity was sometimes wanting. The problem was Jesus' behavior. Particularly troubling was that twice—in the Garden of Gethsemane and on the cross—Jesus appeared to lose control. Given the assumptions of neoclassical theologians about how characters should conduct themselves, Jesus' displays of anxiety were disturbing. One way or another they had to deal with these displays. Some chose to write over these passages, in effect denying that Jesus showed any anxiety; some chose to deal with these passages up front. Either way, this all took some effort and ingenuity. So it is in the treatment of Jesus in the garden and on the cross that the neoclassical theists were tested and that we discover their most creative writing.

Three of the most important of these theologians were William Ellery Channing, Edwards A. Park, and Charles Hodge. In the world of cosmopolitan theology, all of them were what we would call establishment-types, though they had different constituencies. They all dominated their respective faiths for a long time. On the left wing of American theology, Channing was the premier spokesman for Unitarianism. For nearly forty years, from 1803 to 1842, he presided over the Federal Street Church in Boston. Although Unitarianism was ensconced in the Harvard Divinity School, no theologian there had greater prominence or influence than Channing. Many of the enduring traits of the liberal neoclassical depiction of Jesus can be found in his writing. Park, in the middle of the theological spectrum, reigned at Andover Seminary from 1836 to 1881. He helped delineate the neoclassical characterization of God for doctrinal moderates. On the right, Hodge presided over Princeton Seminary from 1822 to 1878 and then passed the torch to his son, Archibald Alexander Hodge, who succeeded his father in his chair of systematic theology at Princeton from 1878 to

1885. These two developed the conservative characterization of God that would persist through the twentieth century.

William Ellery Channing

The Transcendentalist Ralph Waldo Emerson called Channing "our bishop," and this is how he has come down to us.[3] As a young man, Channing had made a great change in his theological outlook. He was brought up under the tutelage of Samuel Hopkins, a disciple of Jonathan Edwards, in Newport, Rhode Island. But Channing, after attending Harvard, saw his way to Unitarianism. The generation that grew up under his influence in Boston tried to go even further. But it was not clear where to go. Two directions seemed open: social reform and romanticism.[4] But they never sat well together. Social reform was inspired by the humanitarian ethic, which was expressed through altruistic neoclassical and sentimental ideals of character; but the romantic character was more isolated and ambivalent. Emerson felt the difficulty in his own work and began to sour on the social reformers. But even here he ran into a problem: he could romanticize the religious character of human beings, but he never dared to romanticize the character of God. So Emerson's God evaporated into a series of abstractions and moral laws; he had to be absorbed into humanity for Emerson to make anything out of him.[5]

The problem was already evident in Channing's writing. He could ascribe a powerful, romantic evil to humans, but his depiction of God remained confined to neoclassicism.[6] The two existed in different literary worlds, and God came out the worse for it. Given that Channing's God did not punish sin (nature did it automatically) and did not send Christ to the cross (people did), there was little for Channing's God to do. He remained available as a vague but stimulating presence that human beings could draw on should they decide to rescue themselves from their own titanic, sinful characters. The only nearly divine character of any drama in Channing's writing was Jesus. And his drama was mostly to preserve his neoclassical serenity in face of the mobs who persecuted him. This was not easy; it involved some struggle. In this, however, Channing was as much struggling against the gospel depictions of Jesus as anything else.

Channing handled the Gospels as creatively as any theologian of his day. His effort, like so many of his colleagues, was to maintain a neoclassical characterization of Jesus despite the Gospels' awkward details about Jesus' behavior in the Garden of Gethsemane and on the cross. In doing this, Channing worked within the framework of the moral theory of the atonement. For Channing, then, Jesus' sufferings were the work of people. This relieved Channing from the burden that fell on the governmental and penal theologians of representing a God of benevolence prosecuting his own Son. But relieved of this burden in representing God, Channing picked up a new burden in depicting Christ: how could mere humans upset Christ so?

Now, it might be thought that this need not trouble Channing, given his theological understanding of Christ. As a Unitarian, Channing did not believe that Christ was a person of the Trinitarian Godhead; therefore, Channing did not have to impose on

Jesus the serenity that, as a neoclassical theist, he expected of God. And some Unitarians did make use of Christ's less-than-divine status to account for his less-than-serene behavior. For instance, Channing's colleague Noah Worcester, perplexed at Jesus' anxiety in the Garden of Gethsemane, suggested some quite un-neoclassical interpretations for Jesus' behavior—even noting that fortitude was not necessarily a sign of virtue.[7] This sort of speculation, in turn, opened the door for wider interest in Jesus' emotional displays and physical suffering. And this partly explains why so many of the early sentimental incarnationalists came from the ranks of the moral theologians.

But Channing would have none of this. Channing was committed to neoclassical theism and representing the power of this in Christ. What Christ lacked in divinity he made up for in dignity. He might not be a direct descendent of God's, but there was still a family resemblance. What Jesus did have from God, according to Channing, was what every rational creature had: "mind." This contained a "spark of infinity" that gave all people the potential to be in touch with God. Channing's God was the "Almighty renewer," and what made Jesus special was that he never lost consciousness of his own "spark of divinity" and thus stayed in touch with God, who, in turn, kept Jesus filled with God's own renewing influence. God's influence was displayed in Jesus in typical neoclassical form: Jesus' mind remained focused and unperturbed, and this was reflected in the serenity of his body.[8]

How did Channing square this characterization of Jesus with the gospel accounts of his suffering? The brief answer is that he did not; he simply denied that the Gospels depicted Jesus as anxious or upset by his sufferings. He blamed Catholic and Protestant tradition for representing Christ as having a "low character," weighed down by his trials. Channing was not entirely consistent on this point; sometimes he charged that the doctrine of the Trinity diminished the significance of Christ's trial by making him incapable (because of his divine impassivity) of suffering. But few theologians were entirely consistent in these complex matters. Channing also scorned sentimentalism for its suggestion that Christ had been agitated because of his sympathy for the suffering of humans. Channing declared that Christ was not swayed by "pity" or "any other passion." Rather, Channing's Christ was the exemplar of the neoclassical ideal of the rational, resilient, and benevolent character who remained unfazed through his trials. "To know Jesus Christ," Channing declared, "is to understand this attribute of mind, to understand the strength and triumph of benevolent principle in the severest trial, to understand the energy with which he held fast the virtue he had enjoined."[9]

In order to show the "strength and triumph" of Christ's "mind," Channing had to brush by some incidents in the Gospels. What of Christ's anxiety in the Garden of Gethsemane? "He distinctly foresaw the violent death towards which he was fast approaching," Channing declared, "yet he possessed his soul in peace." What of his prayer in the garden that the "cup of suffering" be removed from him? And what of the fact that he could not bear the weight of his cross on the way to Golgotha? Channing turned these incidents into rallying points. "Expect nothing from the cross," Channing charged, "unless a power comes from it strengthening you to 'bear his cross,' or 'drink his cup,' with his own unconquerable love." In the moral theology, it was not God but a mob who threatened Christ, and Channing had only scorn for the mob's efforts. "The malignity of Christ's foes, though never surpassed, never robbed him of his self-possession, roused no passion and threw no vehemence or precipitation into his exertions."[10]

The resilience of Christ was a sign that he had remained connected to God. This set him off from all others before or since. "I say then," Channing declared in his sermon "The Character of Christ," "that serenity and self-possession were peculiarly the attributes of Christ." This statement might be taken as the apothegm of nineteenth-century neoclassical theology. Layers of cultural, literary, and theological mandates on the depiction of character backed up Channing in his forceful characterization of Christ.[11]

Edwards A. Park

Emily Dickinson said that when Edwards A. Park preached in Amherst the congregation was so quiet you could hear the bees buzzing outside the church window. This gives an accurate impression of the man and his influence. If Channing inadvertently ushered in the "flowering of New England" in the early decades of the nineteenth century, Park presided over its more prosaic summer during the middle of the century. Channing's children, the romantics of the "American renaissance," bloomed, then they faded, were pressed between moldy books, and were not revived until the twentieth century. In the meantime, clergymen like Park preached to quiet audiences.

Park stressed the literary importance of the clergy. He rebutted the charge that the ministry was less demanding than the law or politics by saying that the clergy had great literary influence. This influence, in Park's conception, extended to two different groups: society at large and writers themselves. Such power stemmed from the fact that ministers dealt with the archetype of all beauty, goodness, and truth: God. "The preacher holds before his congregation the choicest models of all that can please the taste," Park declared, "of that spiritual comeliness which is the archetype of all that is graceful and refined in nature and art." Fed on divine beauty, congregations would be more apt to appreciate human beauty. "By winning his hearer to what is beautiful and grand in religious truth, he fosters the love of those lower excellencies," Park continued; "in many minds he cherishes a taste for the elegances of Addison and Gray and Cowper and Wordsworth, and encourages that sense of honor, that interest in heroic deeds, that reverence for genius and worth, in fine all those amiable sentiments which are allied with a due appreciation of the beauties of nature and art."[12]

Here we see Park's taste in 1845: it spanned the neoclassicism of the early eighteenth century and blended into the early romanticism of Wordsworth. Like Porter, Park admired Gray, Cowper, and Wordsworth primarily for their poetic style, which was more natural and straightforward than the sometimes abstruse syntax of Pope. Beyond the issue of style, however, there still remained the emphasis on neoclassical heroism, reverence, and "amiable sentiments." When Park considered the influence of the clergy on literature, his examples were even more distinctly neoclassical. John Tillotson, the late seventeenth-century Anglican minister, was one of Park's chief examples. Park cited Dryden's and Addison's praise for Tillotson's style.

It was difficult, however, to find more recent examples. "Literary journalists" in Britain, according to Park, had lately taken a "supercilious tone" toward the ministry partly because British religious writing had become mediocre and predictable. The decline of British religious writing, Park suggested, was due to the fact that the Anglican church was supported by the state. Clergy in the United States, by contrast, had to earn their status, and this would spur them on to higher literary accomplishment—"for the high character of our clergy is the only 'national establishment' that our church has to rest on. We cannot maintain the authority of religious truth, unless it is preached by men to whom all others shall have reason to look *up*."[13]

Like Channing, Park had undergone a transition in his life. "I was," he wrote, "at ten years of age somewhat of a theologian and a rigid Calvinist." In later life, he became a moderate Calvinist. He attended Andover Seminary (formed by a coalition of moderates and conservatives in 1808 when Harvard became Unitarian) and was pastor for three years until his health declined. But then he received the call to a professorship at Andover. His health was restored and he thrived at Andover for forty-five years, becoming one of America's leading theologians.[14]

His theological development was told in the name of his father, Calvin Park, and his own name, Edwards Park (his wife was also the great granddaughter of both Jonathan Edwards and Benjamin Franklin). Park, in short, liberalized Calvinism by relying on the work and authority of Jonathan Edwards. He was Edwards's champion and documented his influence in the theologians that succeeded him, the New Divinity theologians of the late eighteenth century, such as Samuel Hopkins (who had tutored Channing before his lapse into Unitarianism).

Edwards, according to Park, had glimpsed the crucial issue: that God's character was love. Now all that remained to be done was to make the necessary adjustments in Calvinism that followed from this change in God's character. As such, much of this work involved tinkering. Even here sometimes there seemed little to do. Park devoted much of his time to writing histories and biographical sketches of his predecessors. Park's student Frank Hugh Foster carried on the tradition. In 1907, he wrote one of the best histories of American theology, the aptly named *Genetic History of New England Theology*, taking the story from Edwards up to Edwards Park.[15]

Park's theological position, however, was more difficult than it appears. He was a moderate, but this was why his job was so hard. Rather than taking one side or the other, he had moved just enough to straddle two positions: the juristic tradition and philanthropism. Therefore, though Park's work was something of a holding operation, it should be remembered that Park was trying to hold together two disparate views of God. It would have been easier if, like Channing, Park had gone to the extreme and emphasized God's love to the near exclusion of his justice. But Park, like most cosmopolitan Americans, could not go this far. "Herein is love,—justice also, but justice involving the moral element of love," Park declared of God; he spent the rest of his career trying to smooth this statement out.[16]

Of course, he did have a theological formula for doing this—the governmental theory of the atonement. Grotius had steered down the middle between the juristic tradition and philanthropism, and this was also Park's position. So, unlike Channing, Park did not see the crucifixion as merely the work of people. It remained the work of God. But now this was not an expression of God's love and wrath equally, as in the juristic tradition, but primarily an expression of God's love and only secondarily an expression of God's wrath—or, more politely stated, his opposition to sin. In the governmental theology the major message was that God had pardoned sinners without a strict accounting of the law; this showed his love. But as governor of the universe, it was his duty to maintain respect for the law despite this reprieve of mankind. So God sent Christ to the cross as a token, or symbolic expression, of what sin deserved, thus honoring the law and sustaining its power to deter future would-be sinners. In the abstract, this Grotian, or governmental, formula made sense. It did what Park needed to do: emphasize God's love while reserving a secondary place for his justice.

But the problem once again was the Gospels. Christ did not act as if he was going to the cross simply to suffer a symbolic punishment. This exposed governmental theologians to two charges. One was that Jesus had not really been suffering and had faked it. The other was that Jesus had actually been unnerved by his symbolic punishment. Both charges had hounded governmental theologians for centuries. Calvin had mocked early proponents of the theory, asking whether Christ had writhed in agony out of "sport." By the nineteenth century, governmental theologians got it from both sides. Both Unitarians and conservative Calvinists charged that the governmental theology reduced the crucifixion to a "fiction." What were governmental theologians to say? Some, like Park's predecessor at Andover, James Murdock, admitted that God and Christ were, in some sense, "actors." Most governmental theologians, however, rejected this. Jesus had really been suffering, they claimed. But the question was, why? If he was not suffering the full penalty of the law, but only a symbolic punishment, then why had he become so unnerved?

The question perplexed Park. He was clearly bothered by Jesus' displays of anxiety and agony. Unlike Channing, Park could not simply write these off as the product of a false tradition. Park was too much of a biblical scholar for this. Besides, the crucifixion was central to the governmental theology. Unlike Channing, Park could not avoid it and focus on Jesus' life. In the governmental theology, the cross stood as a symbol of the law. The problem was that its effect on Jesus seemed more than symbolic.

Park turned the problem over in a sermon entitled "The Sorrow of the Redeemer in Anticipation of His Death." Park admitted his surprise and even disappointment in Jesus' behavior. "Judging from his nature alone," Park declared, "we should be surprised to hear him exclaiming [in the Garden of Gethsemane], 'My soul is exceedingly sorrowful, so that I feel as if I should die under my grief.'" What Park assumed to be Jesus' "nature" was that of a neoclassical character. Jesus, according to Park, was normally serene. He was in harmony with himself: "All his powers and emotions were so happily adjusted to each other." This was why Jesus' anxiety and his outcries were so baffling. Park walked his audience through the problem: given Jesus' "constitution," his "intellectual and moral elevation," and his "kindly thoughts," there was no reason for his trial to have unnerved him. Even the nature of his sufferings did not account for his behavior; the fact that his sufferings were but a prelude to his "entry into paradise"; the fact of the "publicity of [his] agonies," as those of martyrs—some of whom were "even children" who had borne their trial with dignity and praise for God—all of these facts, Park concluded, "would lead us to suppose that when his death drew near he would meet it with composure." Frankly, Park admitted, "we are disappointed."[17]

In this sermon, Park did not resolve the mystery. He reviewed some solutions that had been put forth. Jesus' outcry, "My God, my God, why have you forsaken me?" was taken from a passage in the Psalms, so perhaps Jesus was showing how Bible verses could be cited as a way to express deep feelings. No, there was more to his outcry than that. Perhaps, given the gross miscarriage of justice in his trial and execution, Jesus, who had "a peculiar regard for the decorum and propriety of things," was especially grieved. These and other suggestions were offered by Park but then rejected as unsatisfactory.[18]

Park thought it best to leave the matter a mystery. This was permissible in such a popular forum as a sermon (being an example of what Park would call "the theology of the feelings"). So he concluded with the sort of confounding biblical anthropomorphism that John Owen had used two centuries earlier. "We do not dare to imagine," Park intoned, "the peculiarities of expression with which the Father's eye looked upon the Son, or the Son's eye looked upon the Father, when 'it pleased the Lord to bruise him.'"[19]

In a more intellectual forum, however, Park was willing to "imagine" a solution to the problem. This solution was even hinted at in the sermon. Some secret visual exchange had occurred between God and Jesus. Only now, it did not involve them seeing each other but Jesus being given a vision of something that horrified him. Perhaps God had given Jesus a vision of hell, Park speculated. It was not entirely original. Park's colleague at Andover, Moses Stuart, had suggested something close to this. Two centuries earlier, juristic theologians such as Owen and Turretin had accounted for Jesus' apparent despair by arguing that God had placed on Jesus some secret mental affliction. But Park took this reasoning further than most. He wanted to account for the matter more philosophically, more in line with what he saw as the scientific nature of the governmental theory of the atonement.[20]

Park's way of doing this was to claim that God was causing Jesus to suffer mentally rather than physically. Emphasizing the mental side of Jesus' suffering helped Park to deflect attention away from his physical agitation. This did not mean that Park was dropping the neoclassical ideal of a character whose mind perfectly controlled his body. But Park was reversing the dynamic somewhat. Rather than the serenity of the body being simply an expression of the rational, benevolent mind, the body hid as much—or more—than it revealed. All of this helped Park to deal with the question of why Jesus had been so agitated. Park could say that Jesus' passion was only a dim expression of the vast mental torment he experienced but had largely kept hidden. Jesus hid more than he showed, in short. And this returned some measure of neoclassical resilience to him.

This was a tried and true way to represent strong feelings in a neoclassical character. Dryden's declaration, "Beware the fury of a patient man," was neoclassical in its suggestion that great men had such bodily control that they could contain tumultuous feelings with little physical expression. As we have seen, such notions were in keeping with the 1839 *Advice to a Young Gentleman*, which counseled, "An admirable method of controlling feeling is to maintain by effort, the serenity and suavity of the countenance."[21] If Jesus had not entirely maintained a serene countenance, this suggested all the more how horrible his vision of sin had been. So Park's explanation of Jesus' behavior was that his physical suffering was nothing compared to what he had suffered in his mind. In other words, it was as if Park had turned Dryden's dictum around: not "beware the fury of a patient man" but "beware the suffering of a patient man"—or, given that Jesus had not been entirely "patient," then at least "beware—for what he suffered inside was far greater than he showed and this secret suffering was what awaits mankind in hell."

Park tried to explain all of this in his 1859 essay "The Rise of the Edwardean Theory of the Atonement." He picked through Edwards's epistemological reflections. From these, Park concluded that Edwards had argued that ideas and sympathy functioned as substitutes for actual experience. That is, by the power of thought and sympathy one could, as it were, put oneself in another's place. This was what happened to Jesus, Park concluded; and it was in this philosophical sense that Jesus could be called a "substitute" for sinners. That is, in his mind, Jesus grasped what sinners suffered in hell. How did Jesus achieve this extraordinary mental feat of perception?

This was Park's answer: God must have given Jesus an astoundingly clear vision of hell. To make this especially powerful, God had erased from Jesus' mind any "counterbalancing" ideas of God's goodness or the purpose of Jesus' own mission. So Jesus had momentarily been left alone with his vision of hell. His vivid intelligence and sympathy had entered into the vision, so that he felt as if he was actually in hell, suffering what the damned felt. What was the purpose of all of this? Though humans could not see hell, Jesus' reaction to his perception of hell stood as a warning to them. Park approvingly cited a remark by Edwards: "If then, the Son of God was in such amazement in expectation of what he was to suffer for a few hours, how sottish are you who are continually exposed to sufferings immensely more dreadful."[22]

This shows the ingenuity of Park in turning a great difficulty into a kind of advantage. Rather than Jesus' anxiety showing a lack of fortitude, it was a credit to his intelligence. And, as the statement by Edwards suggested, people, who could suffer death calmly, were at fault, not Jesus. Of course, it was a big stretch to say that any of this was suggested in the Gospels. It was Edwards's and Park's creativity as theologians that enabled them to read these meanings into the Gospels.

But stepping back from Park's ingenious scenario, we can see that his overall picture of the atonement had become rather unwieldy. Because the crucifixion in itself was not enough to unnerve Jesus, the cross became a visual manifestation of a special vision of hell that only Jesus could see. There were layers of spectacles here, visions of people seeing visions. All of this had a kind of visual linearity that may have pleased a neoclassical imagination. But the question arises, why have a crucifixion at all? Why not just see Jesus seeing hell? Does not the crucifixion, by suggesting a physical source for Jesus' suffering, obscure the point that Jesus was suffering because he was seeing a vision of hell—a vision that humanity must heed?

These questions could not be answered without saying, in effect, that the Gospels were ineffective or at least had been rendered obsolete by the ingenuity of theologians. Liberal theologians in the mid-nineteenth century were not prepared to primitivize the Gospels as they had the Old Testament. It would not be until the late nineteenth century that liberals would be emboldened by the so-called German higher criticism to primitivize portions of the New Testament that did not agree with their expectations about Jesus' character. So Park, like Channing, was stuck with the gospel accounts of Jesus. To square these with their assumptions about Jesus' character, they had to rely on the force of their writing and their ingenuity.

Charles Hodge and Archibald Alexander Hodge

Conservatives had one up on liberals and moderates here. Accounting for Jesus' anxiety was relatively easy for Calvinists. For in the penal substitute theory of the atonement, Jesus suffered the literal punishment that was due all humankind in hell for all eternity. It had been Jesus' infinite, divine, and perfect nature that had allowed him to bear this. Of course, it might also be said that such a nature should have made him bear it with more composure. But given the extraordinary circumstances, few conservatives felt apologetic about Jesus' behavior. "It was not the death of one that he was about to endure," Gardiner Spring wrote in 1846, "but the concentrated wrath of God which his violated law denounces upon millions. It is no marvel he was afraid."[23]

This, in turn, allowed conservatives to get their licks in against liberals and moderates for all of their hand-wringing over Jesus' behavior. "As to objections which are mere matters of taste or sensibility, or due to soft Unitarian culture, they need no statement or refutation," declared the *Princeton Review* in 1857. "The tenderest affections of the Church have ever gathered around Him, who then became a curse for us, and in 'most grievous torments immediately from God upon his soul,' exclaimed, 'My God, my God, why has thou forsaken me!'"[24]

But relieved of one problem, conservatives were saddled with another: how to account for God's behavior. How could God subject his own son to the concentrated punishment due all people—those "most grievous torments immediately from God"? If the penal theologians were simple defenders of the juristic tradition, this question would not have posed significant problems. They could have answered in one of the many ways their juristic predecessors had answered: that God and Christ, for instance, had made a pact in which Christ had agreed to bear the penalty of the law; or, like Owen, conservatives simply could have dismissed the question as impertinent and cited scripture to the effect that it "pleased" God to "bruise" his son. To some degree, the penal theologians did rely on these sorts of answers.

But the answers of the past were no longer enough. The penal theologians were men of their time, however much they might dismiss "soft Unitarian culture." In fact, conservatives were indeed influenced by "matters of taste [and] sensibility," as the Unitarian Noah Worcester had pointed out in 1829. As Worcester had observed, "Writers in favor of substituted sufferings have avoided the use of such harsh language and revolting representations as were common at a former period in describing the manner in which God treated his Son while on the cross." The problem was, it was difficult to use gentle and reassuring language to describe God subjecting his son to the concentrated torment due all of humanity for eternity in hell.

The problem conservatives faced was similar to that of moderates like Park. Like the governmental theologians, conservatives insisted on retaining justice as a distinctive attribute of God's character. Unlike the governmental theologians, however, the conservatives had to give justice more prominence. It could not be just a secondary trait, always subordinate to God's larger designs of love, for if this were the case, then why did Jesus have to suffer the full punishment against people? Why could God not lessen this punishment into a symbolic display of the law as he transferred it to Jesus? Surely, God's judicial attribute must be a central part of his character for God to demand that Jesus suffer the full penalty of the law.

How could conservatives ascribe justice and benevolence to God in equal measure? All of the major currents in American cosmopolitan culture—the enlightenment, humanitarianism, neoclassicism, and sentimentalism—put pressure on conservatives to simplify God's character and make love his distinctive attribute. The vast majority of conservatives rejected sentimentalism as going too far here, but most gave in to neoclassicism. Again this created problems. How could a serene, benevolent, neoclassical God be depicted unleashing the accumulated wrath of eternity onto his son? To develop such language was not easy. The successors of Jonathan Edwards, the New Divinity theologians of the late eighteenth century such as Samuel Hopkins, were major pioneers. Moderates such as Park picked up their language and developed it in ways that suited the governmental theology. Conservatives used such language in ways that suited the penal theology.

It was Charles Hodge who developed this style with the most authority for conservatives. Hodge was around a long time. Channing was at the Federal Street Church for thirty-nine years, Park at Andover Seminary for forty-five years, but Hodge presided over Princeton Seminary for fifty-six years.[25] He was a major influence on cosmopolitan conservative theology through the twentieth century. Outside of conservative theological circles, however, Hodge does not have a good reputation among historians. He is most remembered for a remark he made in 1872 at the celebration for his fiftieth year of teaching at Princeton. "A new idea never originated in this seminary," Hodge proudly proclaimed. For many historians, this has been enough to clinch the case against him.[26] Hodge and Princeton Seminary easily seem closedminded. If Channing and Park have about them the air of mandarins, Hodge has the air of mausoleums.

But if this was all there was to him, his influence would not have been so great. Hodge was a shrewd writer and polemicist. When he declared that "a new idea never originated" at Princeton, he was saying that he had never bowed to the bogus claims of innovation or fashion. He had kept Princeton—alone among America's distinguished seminaries—to conservative Calvinism, which Hodge considered the theology of Augustine, Paul, and the Bible. He was saying that the meaning of the revealed word of God had been preserved at Princeton.

If there was a combination of humility and pride in Hodge's remark, there was also a mixture of deference and dynasty. By saying that "a new idea never originated" at Princeton, Hodge was implying that he had kept faith with his Princeton mentor, Archibald Alexander. Their relationship had been intense. Hodge's father had died when Hodge was an infant, and Alexander became a second father to him. Just before Alexander's death in 1851, he called Hodge to his bedside. After praying together, Alexander gave Hodge a carved walking stick that Alexander had been given years before by a Samoan chief. Pressing the patriarchal staff into Hodge's hand, the dying Alexander whispered, "You must hand this to your successor in office, that it may be handed down as a kind of symbol of orthodoxy." Whether Hodge carried on this patriarchal rite with his successor is unknown; but he did honor his mentor by naming his son after him. And Archibald Alexander Hodge, following his father's death in 1878, assumed his father's chair of theology.[27]

Charles Hodge developed a style and tone that would be used by conservative theologians through the twentieth century. Hodge preserved the authority of major aspects of the juristic tradition while accommodating it to the neoclassicism that had such prestige in nineteenth-century America. Hodge's prose, despite being dense, was remarkably fluid. Logic was occasionally relieved with concise and memorable anecdotes. His colleagues appreciated this. Hodge's misunderstood remark at his semicentennial celebration needs to be balanced with another one made there. Professor Vermilye, of the Theological Institute of Connecticut, stood up to toast the man of the hour. Hodge's three-volume *Systematic Theology* had just been published. "I have read it with almost the same interest with which I should read a novel," Vermilye quipped, "well, I will say with almost the same interest with which I should read a novel (laughter); with more interest than ever a novel is read by persons who read novels. I was fascinated and carried on, page by page, by the logic, the learning, the simplicity, the power, the spirituality."[28]

The combination of "simplicity" and "power" was key here. Anxiety about the popularity of novels is evident in Vermilye's remark, but so is the sense of relief in finding an appealing authority in Hodge. In this, Hodge's style owed much to neoclassicism. For Hodge, as for Channing and Park, however, this was not just a literary style but part of an intellectual framework embracing literature, science, philosophy, and theology. Neoclassicism provided a dignified diction for all disciplines. This allowed neoclassical theologians to dismiss other literary styles as "merely" literary. This was how Hodge dismissed Bushnell's romantic work of 1849, *God in Christ*. There Bushnell had argued that in order to depict God's character, theologians had to use highly figurative, even contradictory, language and that this was sanctioned by the Bible, which also used such language for God. But to Hodge's mind, Bushnell had given up on reason and consistency and withdrawn into poetic self-indulgence. In making his point, Hodge relied on the familiar Newtonian metaphors of neoclassicism. "Dr. Bushnell," Hodge declared, "is a poet and neither a philosopher nor a theologian; a bright star which has wandered from its orbit, and which must continue to wander, unless it return and obey the attraction of the great central orb— God's everlasting word."[29]

Part of the authority of neoclassicism was its air of comprehensiveness. It was a style well suited to conveying the tone of having seen it all and having the good sense to eschew fashions and respect human limitations. This tone was key for Hodge's authority. He gave the impression that the conservative case was not hard to make because it really faced no new challenges. This undercut the claims of liberals that they were riding a tide of historical progress. And this reassured conservatives, many of whom felt embattled by liberalism—and for good reason. Despite the apparent success of liberalism, Hodge offered a reassuring long-range perspective. He argued that in spite of the decline of the juristic tradition in Europe, the near extinction of conservative Calvinism in the former Puritan churches of New England Congregationalism, and the 1837 breakup of the Presbyterian church into New School and Old

School factions (standing for the governmental and penal theology, respectively), the juristic theology would ultimately prevail over its liberal competitors. The reason for this, according to Hodge, was not only because the juristic theology was true but also because it had weathered similar storms before. Hodge maintained that all of the varieties of liberal theology were really ancient exploded heresies repackaged and exported from Europe to America as the latest fashion. They would not last; they had all been seen before.

And, after a time, Hodge had seen them all before too. He edited the *Princeton Review* for decades. The more he repeated his criticism of moderates and liberals, the more he could sustain his argument that there was nothing new. Reviewing a governmental interpretation of the atonement by the New School Presbyterian Albert Barnes in 1858, Hodge reflected: "It is a weary business to have to answer the same objections, correct the same misrepresentations, day after day and year after year."[30]

Hodge saw an end to this foolishness if not in human history, then at least in individual lives. Old age and a sense of mortality would sober people up. He considered himself lucky; he had recognized this early. At the age of twenty, while still a student at Princeton, he wrote his mother and informed her that he recognized his life might be half over and that he welcomed old age. He deployed the same tone effectively for the next sixty years. He confidently predicted that whatever fashionable liberal doctrines theologians had espoused during their careers, they would return in old age to "the doctrines of nursery"—the doctrines of Calvinism (which, for instance, Channing and Park had been reared on but abandoned). This tone served Hodge and his successors well in their debate with liberals.[31]

But, in fact, Hodge had his work cut out for him. In order to preserve Calvinism, he was driven to create a neoclassical character for the God of the penal theology. What Hodge did was blend the God of the juristic tradition with the God of philanthropism—not as far as the governmental theologians did, but far enough to preserve his depiction of God from caricature as a God of wrath. The blending occurred in what essentially was a compromise between the juristic conception of God and philanthropism. Neither justice nor benevolence completely characterized God in Hodge's theology. Rather, both justice and benevolence were comprehended in an even more general trait: holiness.

Emphasis on God holiness in itself was not new in theology. What was new was how Hodge and other conservatives used the concept of holiness to create a neoclassical character for God. They used holiness not only to comprehend justice and benevolence but also to abstract them. Holiness, in short, could not easily be personified. Thus, descriptions of the delivery of this holiness, whether in the form of a punishment or a blessing, could be written impersonally. This impersonality, in turn, could be used to distance God from his acts—especially his acts of punishment. This, in turn, helped to safeguard the conservative characterization of God from the caricature that had undermined the juristic God. Finally, the concept of holiness made God's actions seem not only impersonal but also automatic. This further distanced God from his acts of punishment, thus preserving his neoclassical serenity.

Hodge developed a complex scheme to account for the blessings and punishments that issued from God. In this scheme, little reference was made to the character of God (which was always one of invariable holiness) or, for that matter, to the recipient's character (which helped Hodge explain why Christ could receive punishment). But, if it was neither God's character nor the recipient's character that determined the nature of God's specific acts (whether he blessed or punished them), then what was it? It was the nature of the relationship that existed between God and the recipient. The language that Hodge developed to explain the varying relationships between God and humanity was sometimes tendentious, but it did serve to reconcile a neoclassical characterization of God with the penal theory of the atonement.

Hodge was not the first to develop this language of relationships to account for the delivery of punishments and blessings from God. American theologians had been using it for a while to finesse the difference between philanthropism and the juristic tradition. Samuel Hopkins had been key here. "Justice or righteousness in the divine Being," Hopkins had declared in 1792, "is nothing but universal, infinite benevolence considered with relation to particular objects, and as acted out in particular circumstances."[32] Hodge also relied on the terminology of sixteenth- and seventeenth-century Calvinist scholasticism, particularly for the concepts of imputation and federal headship. Calvin had elaborated on the idea of imputation to account for God's predestination of some sinners for salvation and others for damnation. Turretin further elaborated on it through the notion of federal headship: that Adam and Christ were the federal heads, or representatives, of the human race, and therefore because of their actions, sin and grace, respectively, could be imputed to all or some of the human race.[33] Hodge took these terms and placed them center stage in depicting God's interaction with human beings.

But Hodge tended to use these terms selectively to describe God's love and his anger. When it came to God's love, Hodge tended to write about God expressing himself in immediate and direct ways. But when it came to God's anger, Hodge often relied on the intermediary relationships of federal headship and imputation that linked God and humans. This meant that Hodge could write about God punishing sinners in impersonal and automatic ways that did not disturb the sense of God's serenity.

Hodge developed this in his commentary on the New Testament book of Romans. This was his first major work. It was dedicated to his mentor, Archibald Alexander. Hodge later expanded this work, and it became the touchstone of his theological vision through nearly fifty years of writing. The key to Hodge's entire system can be found in his often repeated interpretation of the fifth chapter of Romans. There the Apostle Paul drew a parallel between Adam's and Christ's relationships to the human race. Sin came through Adam and salvation through Christ, whom theologians, in interpreting this passage, came to call the "second Adam." In contrast to many earlier and contemporary conservative theologians, Hodge declared that the analogy between Adam and Christ was not just a passing comparison but a strict parallel. Paul, according to Hodge, had been suggesting that just as God imputed sin to a person not because of the individual's personal failing but because of Adam's fall, so God imputed righteousness to a person not because of that individual's merit but because of Christ's sacrifice (the parallel was not perfect, Hodge admitted, because Adam's sin was imputed to all people, while Christ's righteousness was imputed only to the elect).[34]

This being said, however, Hodge still tended to write of God's saving grace as a direct and immediate expression of God's love. Hodge emphasized the role of imputation in communicating God's grace mainly to reinforce the idea that sinners could do nothing on their own to merit redemption. But otherwise, Hodge emphasized the personal nature of God's love. Indeed, this was part of his polemic against the liberals. They claimed that God loved everyone and would save anyone who came to him. Conservatives, by contrast, argued that sin was so disabling that no one would voluntarily come to God. God had to elect people to salvation. But this (conservatives argued) showed how powerful God's love was: he chose specific people and drew them irresistibly to him (the question of how God felt toward those not elected was a difficult question for conservatives).[35] As a polemic against liberals, this conservative charge could be effective. Conservatives could claim that they depicted God's love as powerful and personal while liberals made it weak and indiscriminate. God's saving love, Hodge declared in 1865, was not mere "philanthropy," it was "mysterious," "wonderful," and excited "the amazement of the angels." The following year, Archibald Alexander Hodge echoed the claim: God's love was like that of a husband for his wife; it was not "a mere general philanthropy, but the highest most peculiar and personal love."[36]

Both Hodges, however, made God's anger into something impersonal. This was the point: to emphasize the personal nature of God's love and the impersonal nature of his anger. The major function of the concepts of imputation and federal headship, therefore, was to carry the burden of God's wrath to the sinner. This enabled Charles Hodge and Archibald Alexander Hodge to depict God's wrathful relationship to human beings as having a prearranged, automatic, and impersonal character.

Much of the power of this was in Hodge's language itself rather than in any explicit theory. This can be seen in Hodge's treatise on the Book of Romans. "The word 'enemies' is applied to God," Hodge explained in his exegesis of Romans 5:10, "not only as descriptive of [sinners'] moral character, but also of the relationship in which they stand to God as objects of his displeasure. There is not only a wicked opposition of the sinner to God, but a holy opposition of God to the sinner." This language of "holiness" and "relationships" enabled Hodge to depict sin as animating human character while distancing God from his "displeasure" at sin. It is true that this "displeasure" was still ascribed to God. But the suggestion of actual anger in God was muted. The "displeasure" was spread out over the entire "relationship in which [sinners] stand to God as objects of his displeasure."[37] God's "opposition" to sin, moreover, was qualified as "holy," meaning expressive of his love for the righteous as well as his condemnation of sinners.

But what of those passages in Romans where Paul ascribed "wrath" to God? Once again, Hodge explained that this word did not really suggest something animating God's character. Rather, what was meant was the nature of God's relationship with sinners. "The word 'wrath,'" Hodge asserted in his exegesis of Romans 5:9, "of course, means the effects of wrath or punishment, those sufferings with which the divine displeasure visits sin." So God did not feel wrath so much as sinners felt the "effects" of his holiness as wrath. In Hodge's writing, "wrath" became a kind of free-floating trait, the "divine displeasure." And this "displeasure" did not really attack the sinner but simply came into contact with him; it "visits sin," was Hodge's phrase.[38]

In all of this, the language itself was as important as the ideas conveyed by it. It was not that Hodge so often claimed that God remained serene in his "holy opposition" to sin; it was that he wrote of God in such a way that did not allow his neoclassical serenity to be questioned. This language protected Hodge's God from the caricature that had undermined the juristic God.

Archibald Alexander Hodge, however, made this more explicit. "The scripture teaches us very plainly," he asserted in his 1867 treatise *The Atonement*, "that this infinite moral perfection, or holiness of God, stands to sin as immutable hatred or vindicatory justice." "Stands" is the key word here, suggesting a variability in the relationship between God and humans but not in God's character. Whether "scripture teaches" this "very plainly" was debatable. But Archibald Alexander Hodge had learned from his father how to give a neoclassical gloss to the most vivid biblical anthropomorphism. "Although the heart of God remains eternally calm as it is deep," Archibald Alexander Hodge wrote, "the 'egress of his wrath is terrible.'" Thus, the sinner might perceive a God of passionate wrath while God's "heart" remained "eternally calm." The reason was simple: what God experienced of himself was his own serene holiness, regardless of how this holiness manifested itself to creatures in their varying relationships to God. "From eternity to eternity he abides the same without change of state or affection," Archibald Alexander Hodge declared. "His holiness, therefore, is one infinite perfection of moral excellence, varied only in outward excesses and manifestations as it operates upon different objects in different relations."[39]

What about God's relationship to Christ at the atonement? How could God's "holiness" turn to wrath as it descended onto Christ? Christ was perfect; so, presumably, God's holiness would descend upon him in the form of blessing. But, of course, the opposite happened in the penal theory of the atonement. How could this occur unless God overrode the automatic network of relationships that bound him to humans? Archibald Alexander Hodge explained that the network remained in place; all that mattered was that the concentration of punishment be adjusted. Finite humans could never exhaust God's infinite wrath, so it needed to be spread out over eternity; but Christ, a perfect, infinite being, was able to absorb God's infinite wrath all at once on the cross. How the law calibrated punishment to suit the nature of the victim could be described quite impersonally. Hodge's tone was like that of a general manager in a shipping department explaining how a mechanism adjusted the shipments of orders to different people. He explained that at the crucifixion the law automatically concentrated the punishment that all of humanity deserved onto the single person of Christ: "The person upon whom the penalty is to be inflicted—one divine person being substituted for many human persons—the Law itself, on principles of essential justice, spontaneously adjusts the quality of suffering constituting the penalty to the quality of the victim."[40] Given the pressures on conservatives in nineteenth-century American cosmopolitan culture, this language did what it needed to do. It distanced God from his punishment and brought the juristic God within the bounds of neoclassical theism.

Thus, the vast majority of conservative as well as liberal theologians developed neoclassical characterizations of God. Hodge's vision of God's holiness was as serene as Channing's vision of a mentally empowered Christ. A high level of abstraction was inherently a part of this. The need to reconcile a neoclassical characterization of God with the behavior of Jesus in the Gospels, however, pushed theologians to write even more abstractly. Theologians had two options. They could either downplay the suggestion that Jesus felt any "passion," as Channing did, or find suitably abstract ways of tormenting Jesus, as Park and Hodge did. Yet, in spite of this, we should take Park at his word when he declared: "We rejoice that there is a mind free from the complexities and discrepancies that mar our character." There was reason to rejoice in such a vision of God, given neoclassical assumptions about his character. This only seemed cold and lifeless when other views of character were admitted as suitable for God, ones that valued some "complexities and discrepancies."

❧

CHAPTER FOUR

Sympathy and Alienation

Henry Ward Beecher and Harriet Beecher Stowe

Where neoclassical theists pictured God as having a mind (in Park's words) "free from the complexities and discrepancies that mar our character," sentimental incarnationalists brought God down to earth in the form of Christ and made him more accessible. And this, at its most dramatic, led to some tension in Christ's mind. The tension involved the mixing of high and low, God and human; it involved a drama of an eternal, perfect being allowing himself to become involved in the plight of sinful beings. Harriet Beecher Stowe took this dramatic element of sentimental incarnationalism very far. Whereas Park used God's statement to Moses, "I am that I am," as evidence of God's uniquely calm mind, Stowe used Jesus' allusion to this same statement, "Before Abraham was I am," as a glimpse into Jesus' complex perspective as God and man. According to Stowe, Jesus had allowed this remark to slip from him "in a moment of high excitement"; he had expressed himself "unconsciously, as it were . . . in his native language"—the language of God. The drama of incarnationalism was in this: the astonishing mystery and tension of God on earth, incarnate.

Sentimental incarnationalism emerged in the 1840s as an effort to make God more emotional and expressive.[1] The emphasis on the incarnation was in part a reaction against theism. Whereas theists abstracted God, incarnationalists brought him down to earth—literally. They emphasized that what people needed to know about God was revealed in Jesus. At issue between theists and incarnationalists was rarely a matter of doctrinal debate over the Trinity or Christ's divinity but more an issue of representing God in theological and religious writing. How best could God be depicted? Incarnationalists granted many of the justifications for theism: that anthropomorphic representations of God in the Old Testament were primitive; or that God's real nature could be grasped only in highly abstract terms. But given all of this (the argument of the incarnationalists went), ordinary people still needed some immediate characterization of God. God had used Jesus for this purpose, so why should not theologians?

James Coolidge raised this argument in his 1848 tract *Jesus the Manifestation of the Father.* Coolidge was a Unitarian but reacted against Channing's brand of neoclassical theism. Coolidge acknowledged the significance of "mind" in Channing's

sense—that it was the "spark of infinity" that signified human immortality and allied humans with God. But people also needed to grasp the emotional side of God,
Coolidge argued. "You tell me of the Infinite Mind, to which mine own is allied,"
Coolidge exclaimed, "but I need,—yes, to save me from the most bitter anguish of
spirit—I need to know and realize an infinite love, which shelters me while it bruises
me, which heals while it wounds, which gently wipes away the tears itself causes to
flow. Is there such a love?"[2]

Yes: in sentimentalism. Much as incarnationalism was a theological reaction against
theism, sentimentalism was a literary reaction against neoclassicism. Their scenarios
were different. Neoclassical scenarios were vast, often encompassing the Newtonian
cosmos and the rise and fall of empires. Sentimental scenarios were situated in the
trials of the middle-class family (though in the sentimental novel these trials might
reflect, in microcosm, issues of national destiny, such as the abolition of slavery).
As part of this, female characters took on more heroic roles in sentimentalism. Mothers, in particular, rose to prominence. Jesus' mother, Mary, came to the fore. But
male as well as female characters could be sentimental. The basic difference between
neoclassical and sentimental characterization turned not on gender but on the depiction of love. Neoclassical benevolence was a fusion of reason with love; sentimental
sympathy was a fusion of pity with love. Characters expressed these emotions differently. Serenity was the mark of the neoclassical character; the mark of the sentimental character was asympathetic shedding of tears. Sentimentalism thus allowed
more expressiveness to the body.

In religious writing, this marked a significant departure from neoclassical theism.
It was not a return to anthropomorphism, however: in sentimentalism, Jesus' body
was emphasized, not God's. Still, sentimental incarnationalism seemed to bring God
nearer. Coolidge imagined a God who, through Christ's earthly ministry, removed
the distance the neoclassical theists had set between God and human beings. Coolidge
exclaimed, "No longer need man feel estranged by the immensity of the Ruler of
heaven and earth, for also God was in Christ." In Christ was revealed "the urgency
of [God's] affection"; God, through Christ, came close to humans in a very tactile
way—"not casting the humblest penitent away, but pressing him to his bosom." This
was not the distant God of theism, nor a God of neoclassical bodily reserve. This
was a God of physical contact—which contact, in turn, released a flood of emotions:
"not condemning the weeping sinner, but suffering her whose touch was deemed
pollution to cling to his feet and bedew him with tears—tears, not of bitterness, but
of gushing joy."[3]

In sentimentalism, Jesus became a kind of magnet for emotional release, as if breaking the damn of the pent-up emotions of neoclassicism. Physical contact was always
a part of this emotional expressiveness. This was a far cry from Channing's Christ,
unique in his physical reserve and power to preserve his dignity in the face of the
mobs who thronged him. Coolidge, by contrast, was developing the sentimental
emphasis on Jesus "pressing" into crowds, pressing flesh, it might be said, and over-
turning conventional norms about physical contact—"suffering her whose touch was
deemed pollution to cling to his feet."

This emphasis on the physical agitation of sentimental love signified a partial disruption of the polarization of emotions. Love could now have some of the physical

expressiveness of anger. But when it came to the emotions themselves, the polarization remained in place. That is to say, there could be no ambivalence. Moreover, the general humanitarian emphasis on love as altruistic and contributing to social stability still held for both neoclassicism and sentimentalism.

Because of this, both camps could get along. Theism was for the theologians in their speculative moods, incarnationalism for everyone in their emotional moments, according to the accepted division of labor. Park relied on this division to outline the difference between the "theology of the intellect" and the "theology of the feelings" (or the "thinking few" and the "feeling many," as the Unitarian James Freeman Clarke had put it). This division, moreover, could be easily comprehended within the nineteenth-century notion of separate spheres for men and women. Neoclassicism could be thought of as manly and sentimentalism as feminine. Both styles could be seen as complementing each other within the same person. As Park wrote in "The Theology of the Intellect and That of the Feelings," a learned and sensitive minister must combine both traits to reach his congregation. "Large minded, then, and large hearted must be the minister," Park intoned, "having all the sensibility of a woman without being womanish, and all the perspicacity of the logician without being merely logical."[4]

Despite this accepted division between neoclassical theism and sentimental incarnationalism, conflict did break out. Most often it occurred in the ranks of Congregationalists and liberal Presbyterians, many of whom were torn between the neoclassical theism of the governmental theology and the more liberal moral theory of the atonement surfacing in sentimental incarnationalism. And, like most theological conflicts, this one often degenerated into polemics. The "logician" became "merely logical"; the "woman" became merely "womanish."

Neoclassical theologians sometimes ridiculed sentimentalists as effeminate, literary dilettantes who reduced God's principled love to a mindless gush. This polemic had a long history in Protestantism. In the seventeenth century, juristic theologians such as John Owen had sneered at Socinians as "these fashionable and dainty gentlemen [who] talk of nothing in their discourses, but of the goodness of God." By the nineteenth century, neoclassical theologians from all along the doctrinal spectrum leveled these charges at sentimentalists. The governmental theologian Joseph Thompson, in his trenchantly named treatise of 1859, *Love and Penalty*, on the one hand scorned Calvinism as "a chilly invention" and on the other hand dismissed those sentimentalists, "of celebrity in the circles of literature and philanthropy," who ascribed to God a "woman's heart."[5]

The association of the words "literary," "effeminate," and "trivial" in this polemic should not mislead us into thinking that neoclassical theologians were opposed to all kinds of literature. Rather, they championed what Noah Porter called "manly thinking and the diction which is common to all literature"—that is, the neoclassical idiom found in enlightenment science, philosophy, history, and fiction.[6] To neoclassical theologians, sentimentalism seemed "merely literary" because it did not have these strong links with other disciplines (though sentimentalism did have support in humanitarian social reform and phrenology). Moreover, the fact that some of the most successful sentimental novelists were women made it suspect in the eyes of theologians and other male writers. Their attacks could be particularly testy. Nathaniel

Hawthorne caustically referred to the "damned mob of scribbling women." Theologians added their sneers. In 1866, James Freeman Clarke recommended recent treatises on the atonement by Edwards Park and Horace Bushnell in contrast to the more popular expressions of the doctrine "propagated" in the novels of Susan Warner.[7]

Sentimentalists, in turn, had a ready way to defend themselves. They directed the polemic against the juristic tradition at neoclassical theologians. The charge was that if the neoclassical theists did not put forth a tyrannical God of wrath (as in the juristic tradition), they still put forth an abstract, distant "monarchical" God of inflexible order. Against this, sentimentalists appealed to an intimate, familial God who, they claimed, resonated with their "experience," which they construed in sentimental terms.[8]

As we have seen with the charges against the juristic tradition, the historian must take religious polemics with a grain of salt. They obscure as much as they reveal. Still, if they are not accurate depictions of an opponent, they do show us some of the values espoused by the combatant who launches the charges. But even here we must be careful not to let the self-advertisements of theologians obscure what they have in common with their opponents.

Neoclassical theists and sentimental incarnationalists were both champions of philanthropism. So both tried to outdo each other when it came to celebrating the power of God's love. Henry Ward Beecher, the most celebrated sentimental preacher of the mid-nineteenth century, emphasized the personal power of love in his attack on the governmental theology. "No one can love a governor," Beecher intoned in 1863. "Governor is an official title, and not a personal one." God should be thought of as a father, Beecher declared. Moreover (Beecher argued), the fatherhood of God exhibited his power even more than the title of governor, for so great was God's love that he could even make the universe feel intimate. "God is able to do towards the race what the father in the family is able to do towards a few persons," Beecher declared; "God is able to carry his mind so that love shall be predominant, and justice shall be but a modification of love."[9]

Edwards Park was not so sure. "The government of our Heavenly Father is more extended than that of a family on earth, it reaches the bounds of the universe," Park gently sought to correct the sentimentalists. Therefore (Park concluded more sharply), God's government "is not to be debased by accommodating it to the superficial, outward, ephemeral policy of a narrow household, or of a nation." And what God ruled, in turn, reflected the sort of character he was. It was because of his love for his vast creation that God ruled according to consistent principles of justice: "It is not the mere *sentiment* of love [in God]," Park declared; "it is the love which comprehends justice and proves the necessity of it."[10]

So both Beecher and Park awarded love priority over justice. For Beecher, justice was a "modification" of love; for Park, love "comprehends" justice. Stated in these abstract terms, the points of debate seem minor. They mattered a lot, however, when people tried to imagine God in some detail. Yet the positions were never so far apart that the different sides could not talk to each other.

Harriet Beecher Stowe even invited Park to tea to share her views on the matter with him. This was in 1859, seven years after publication of *Uncle Tom's Cabin*, a best-seller in America and Europe. While Stowe was in Europe in 1853 basking in the positive reception of her novel, her husband, Calvin Stowe, was appointed to the faculty of Andover Seminary. Over the next couple of years, the Stowes had their differences with Park, who also taught at Andover. But in 1859 Stowe invited Park to her house to read to him from her new novel, *The Minister's Wooing*. One of its major characters (the "minister" of the title) was the late eighteenth-century neoclassical theist Samuel Hopkins. As we have seen, he was a major figure in the development of neoclassical theism. He had been a disciple of Jonathan Edwards and Channing's tutor. Hopkins had developed characterizations of God remaining serene in his holiness and variable in his manifestations; Hodge would adapt these manifestations to the penal theology. And Edwards Park had taken Hopkins as a major contributor to the governmental theology. In 1852 (the same year as the publication of *Uncle Tom's Cabin*), Park published a long "Memoir of the Life and Character of Samuel Hopkins." Stowe used this as a source for her novelistic depiction of the man in *The Minister's Wooing*. Park accepted the invitation to the reading, scrawling a note, "I will go if I can get away at 8 o'clock."[11]

In *The Minister's Wooing*, Stowe depicted Hopkins as an elderly pedant clumsily but endearingly courting a young woman named Mary. But Mary, while accepting his proposal, is unconsciously pining away for young James, whom she fears has been lost at sea. The relation between Hopkins and Mary is much like that between Mr. Casaubon and Dorothea in George Eliot's *Middlemarch* (written twelve years later). Stowe's novel, however, has a happier ending. James returns and a servant discretely informs Hopkins to withdraw his proposal, thus allowing James and Mary to wed. In all of this, Hopkins does not come off as a bad fellow (and Stowe especially commended him for his opposition to slavery); but Stowe's Hopkins is clearly out of touch with affairs of the heart.

So was much of his theology, according to Stowe. In her depiction of Hopkins, his mind was on the infinite works of God rather the intimate needs of men and women. Moreover, by assuming such a cosmic view, Hopkins (and theologians of his ilk), Stowe suggested, ran the risk of distorting God's character. This is because any small error in their system, projected onto the backdrop of the universe, would be magnified to a vast scale. Far from honoring God by trying to imagine the immensity of his rule, therefore, these theologians sometimes distorted his character out of all proportion. "The smallest speck of earth's dust, in the focus of an infinite lens," Stowe cautioned, "appears magnified among the heavenly orbs as a frightful monster." So much for the harmony of the Newtonian universe. The lesson for theologians was clear: it was safer to imagine God in the intimate terms of sentimental incarnationalism than in the terms of neoclassical theism.[12]

The Beechers

The Beechers were formidable champions of sentimentalism. They were the first family of American Protestantism in the mid-nineteenth century, analogous to what the Kennedys were to the Democratic party in the mid-twentieth century. The father, Lyman Beecher, was a prominent evangelist in the Presbyterian church who preached a popular version of the governmental theology. Widowed once, he married again and from the two marriages raised twelve children. The majority of the boys grew up to be ministers. Once, while listening to Park preaching at Andover, Harriet Beecher Stowe had daydreamed about her brothers forming their own seminary. The daughters of Lyman Beecher, despite the fact that the profession of the ministry was closed to them, were forces in their own right.[13]

The eldest, Catharine Beecher, was a prominent educator and writer of advice manuals. Her 1841 *Treatise on Domestic Economy* (housekeeping) was reprinted sixteen times in as many years. The third child, Edward Beecher, wrote a learned and idiosyncratic treatise entitled *The Conflict of Ages*, which accounted for original sin by the prebirth activity of the soul. Harriet and Henry, the sixth and seventh children (who were extremely close to each other throughout their lives), became the most famous of the Beechers. From 1847 to 1887, Henry Ward Beecher was pastor of the Plymouth Church in Brooklyn Heights, then a fashionable suburb of Manhattan. It was estimated that there were twenty millionaires in his congregation. Harriet Beecher Stowe also enjoyed great success but could not reap the rewards as early as her brother. In addition to writing some of the most popular novels in nineteenth-century America, she raised six children and had to cope with the genteel poverty of her husband's academic life. Between their two incomes, they finally enjoyed some security at Andover. In 1863, when Calvin retired, Stowe became the sole breadwinner and moved the family to Hartford. After 1867, they spent winters at their Florida home, Mandarin.[14]

Their father had been a champion of social causes. In the early nineteenth century, he was one of the national leaders against dueling, alcohol, Sunday mail delivery, Catholicism, and theatergoing. He was also opposed to slavery, but the split in the antislavery movement in the 1830s between radicals and moderates confused him. He was of an earlier generation, and the issues were changing. Nor did he think the issues through deeply. The pattern would repeat itself in his children. They had an instinct for dramatizing social issues. *Uncle Tom's Cabin* was a great success in portraying the horrors of slavery and celebrating the piety and humanity of African Americans. But many abolitionists were dismayed by Stowe's sometimes patronizing views of blacks and her suggestion that colonization, or the return of blacks to Africa, was the best solution to America's racial problems. Henry Ward Beecher also was given to dramatic support for antislavery. "Beecher's Bible" became the sobriquet for the Sharpe's rifle after Beecher declared it would have greater "moral agency" than the Bible in Kansas during the terrorist war erupting there in the late 1850s. At his parish in Brooklyn, Beecher brought enslaved African Americans, mostly women and children, in front of his congregation and held auctions to purchase their freedom.

Following the Civil War, the issue became women's rights. Like their father's experience with antislavery, the radicalization of this movement confused the Beechers. Their sentimentalism only took them so far. It was also a problem of generations; the Beecher children were products of the early nineteenth century. Tensions surfaced among them. Catharine, the eldest, had always held back from women's suffrage, endorsing a strict separate-spheres ideology (however much her own life testified against it). But Isabella, the youngest of Lyman Beecher's daughters, claimed that this was her issue. She declared that just as Harriet had spoken for antislavery, she would speak for women's rights.[15]

Harriet and Henry also got involved, but more circumspectly. Like their father, they distrusted radicals. Harriet began to incorporate women's rights themes in her novels and in 1869 wrote "The True Story of Lady Byron's Life." This detailed the alleged wrongs that Lady Byron had suffered in her marriage to the notorious romantic poet Lord Byron. It caused a sensation but was denounced by conservatives as slanderous and was not warmly embraced by feminists because of its sentimental idealization of Lady Byron. Stowe refused an invitation to join Elizabeth Cady Stanton's journal *Revolution*. Also in 1869 the American Woman Suffrage Association, the conservative rival to Stanton's organization, elected Henry Ward Beecher president. In 1872, partly through the lobbying of the AWSA, the Republican party mentioned woman's suffrage in its platform. The same year, Stanton's organization nominated Victoria Woodhull for the U.S. presidency.

Things degenerated from there. Woodhull charged Beecher with having had an adulterous affair with one of his parishioners, Elizabeth Tilton. "I cast a thunderbolt in the very centre of the socio-religio-moral camp of the enemy," Woodhull declared, "and struck their chieftain, and the world trembled at the blow." Liberal cosmopolitan America at least trembled; the charges caused a sensation. Besides, there was something to them. Harriet rose to her brother's defense and called Woodhull a "witch" (and said she had cast a spell on Isabella, who was stunned into silence by the whole affair). Mr. Tilton, a former business partner and friend of Beecher's, brought a lawsuit against him. The jury acquitted Beecher nine to three. Public opinion turned against his accusers; the hapless Mr. Tilton exiled himself to Paris, and Woodhull emigrated to England. Beecher's reputation survived, and many, like Harriet, chose not to mention the charges again.[16]

What gave Henry and Harriet such moral authority was their sentimental incarnationalism. They could use it to dramatize political issues (making Christ figures out of Uncle Tom or Lady Byron, for instance), but it was founded on their sentimental interpretations of the Gospels. This was the foundation for their work. In Beecher's case, this is clear because he mostly wrote sermons. But Stowe also wrote some religious meditations. Whether she would have liked to preach or write theology instead of writing novels is not clear. As a woman in the nineteenth century, she did not have that option open to her. Despite this, Stowe was an extraordinary religious writer. Though justly famous for the power of *Uncle Tom's Cabin*, Stowe's religious writings have not been widely appreciated. But her depictions of Mary and Jesus are among the most striking in American theology.[17]

Harriet and Henry learned how to combine theology and literature at an early age. In their father's library, they mainly had access to theological treatises. Lyman Beecher disapproved of novels and would not let them in his house. But Uncle Samuel Foote (their mother's brother) did provide the children with reading—Byron and Scott in particular. The children were captivated. At Amherst, Henry, though not a successful student, buried himself in English literature (as well as the popular science of phrenology). When Stowe owned her own house, she had a special "Walter Scott bookcase." Even Lyman was not immune to these temptations. About Scott's novels, he said, "I have always disapproved of novels as trash, but in these is real genius and real culture." Harriet remembered her father reading aloud from *Paradise Lost*, evidently with great sympathy for Satan's indomitable but tragic will. Still, this powerful characterization had to be kept in an appropriate moral framework. Lyman Beecher fantasized about converting Byron, the leader of the so-called satanic school of poetry. Stowe set up a sentimental image of Byron's wife as his victim but also his suffering savior. Stowe, in short, contained romanticism within sentimentalism. The real challenge for her and Henry as religious writers, however, was to square the Gospels with their sentimental ideals of character.[18]

The Problem of the Gospels Again

Sentimentalists faced some of the same problems here as neoclassical theists. Both could, if they wanted, dismiss Old Testament characterizations of God as primitive and largely irrelevant for modern, refined people. But neither group could dismiss the Gospels. We have seen the problems that neoclassical theists faced. They wrestled with the gospel depictions of Jesus in the Garden of Gethsemane and on the cross. Sentimental incarnationalists also found these passages troubling. But they faced another set of problems as well. These came from passages concerning Jesus' birth, childhood, and early ministry. It made sense that sentimental incarnationalists should be forced to confront these passages because sentimental incarnationalists followed the moral theology and thus emphasized Christ's life as much as his death. More important, because they conceived of God's relation to human beings as that of a father in relation to his children, sentimental writers focused on Jesus' family. If God was the exemplary father, Jesus should be the model son. But they did not always appear that way in the Gospels.

To begin with, the timing of Christ's conception put Mary in an awkward position—she was engaged but apparently not yet married to Joseph. As a child, Jesus did not always seem to obey his parents. In the second chapter of Luke, it is recounted that when he was only twelve he wandered away from them on a trip to Jerusalem and, when they finally found him in the temple, expressed surprise at their concern. This attitude, bordering on disrespect, became even more marked as he began his ministry. When he returned from his baptism and his forty days in the desert, he attended a wedding with his mother (his father now presumably deceased) in Cana. The party having run out of wine, Mary seemed to suggest that he miraculously produce more, to which he replied, as told in the second chapter of John, "Woman, what have I do to with you?" Still later, after his ministry was in full swing, Mary, accompanied by other family members, tried to press through a crowd of his followers to see him. On being told of their presence, he seemed to discount them, saying in Mark 3: "Who is my mother, who are my brethren? My mother and brethren are these that hear the word of God and do it."[19]

Sentimental incarnationalists worked through these difficult passages in the genre they developed during the nineteenth century, the life of Christ. These gospel-based biographies of Christ served as a kind of accessible, sentimental biblical criticism. As a form of criticism, of course, this genre could be very radical. But during the nineteenth century this use was largely confined to Europe. The lives of Christ by the German D. F. Strauss and the French Ernest Renan were generally viewed in America as dangerous examples of European skepticism. Americans tended to use the genre to support their faith. They also used the genre to make the Bible accessible in a sentimental vein at a time when theistic theologians were increasingly historicizing the Bible and removing it from the general reader.[20]

The sentimental life of Christ has a common plot that turns on how and when Christ's followers realize that his kingdom is not of this world. Given sentimentalism's emphasis on the family, the key players in this plot tend to be his family members, especially his mother. Typically, the royal ancestry of Joseph and Mary is stressed. Despite their poverty and simplicity they retain a dignity that distinguishes them from their more common neighbors. This royal lineage makes them the natural leaders against the Roman occupation. The astonishing birth and boyhood of Jesus convince people that Jesus will lead an insurrection against the Romans and restore the line of David to power. But incidents in Jesus' early life, particularly with his mother—from the annunciation of his birth, to his straying from his parents as a boy in the temple, to the rebuke of his mother at the wedding at Cana and his further disassociation from her and his siblings while preaching to the crowd—all suggest the difficult truth that the reader knows but that Mary and others will not fully understand until the crucifixion and resurrection. This is the truth that his kingdom is not of this world; that he has come not to liberate the Jews from the Romans but to save humankind from its sin.

The dramatic power of this plot depends in large measure on how much the sentimental writer was willing to play up the misunderstanding between Jesus and his mother and other intimates. Few writers played it up very far. This is why most sentimental portraits of Jesus are so flat. Most sentimental writers saw it as their job to resolve difficulties in Christ's behavior quickly and easily. We can appreciate, however, their ingenuity in finding ways to explain away Christ's conduct, say, toward his mother, and make it seem pious or normal. Henry Ward Beecher was the premier nineteenth-century writer in this form of sentimental incarnationalism. Harriet Beecher Stowe, however, represents sentimentalism at its most dramatic. Whereas her brother sought a way around difficult passages in the Gospels, she delved into them. Whereas her brother's work demonstrates a facile ingenuity, her work shows some dramatic profundity. By contrasting their writing, we can take a measure of the shallows and depths of the character of God in sentimental incarnationalism.

Henry Ward Beecher

Beecher wrote hundreds of sermons, scores of lectures, and a novel, but his great work was to be his life of Christ. Beecher began *The Life of Jesus, the Christ* in 1869 and issued the first volume in 1871. This took the story of Jesus' life from his birth up to the zenith of his ministry. Throughout the work, Beecher scorned what he called the "ingenuity" of expositors,[21] by which he meant those critics who had seen discordances in Jesus' life and racked their brains to explain them. Beecher had a point:

attempting to make sense of Jesus' life had led theologians to some far-fetched rationalizations. But in trying to prove that all discordances in Jesus' life were merely apparent and not substantial, Beecher's own ingenuity was tested. Indeed, the range of Beecher's imagination is nowhere more evident than in his reasoning about why the character of Jesus was actually so unproblematic.

Beginning with the annunciation and the virgin birth, Beecher had ready explanations for why these events were really quite normal. Of course the virgin birth was a miracle, Beecher admitted, but as modern, enlightened people, we should not focus on the miraculous nature of the birth. Miracles, Beecher asserted, were really God's concessions to ancient people's lack of spiritual understanding. Beecher's manner of reasoning here resembled the biblical critics of his generation who dismissed Old Testament anthropomorphism as God's concession to primitive people, a concession that modern, educated people no longer needed. Miracles were needed in ancient times, Beecher explained, because the "moral sense" had not advanced to the stage where it could be led by "the ministry of reason." Miracles then were not a revelation of something unusual. To the contrary, God had used them to direct people's attention to his presence in the ordinary, which, because it was ordinary, thay had overlooked. But as their "moral sense" progressed, Beecher argued, people needed fewer miracles because their sensibilities became refined. They could detect the presence of God in everyday events around them. Much of Beecher's effort in interpreting the Gospels sought to show just this: that the miracles of the Gospels really demonstrated the spiritual significance of everyday life.

One such everyday event was pregnancy. Ancient people, Beecher surmised, occasionally required sensational displays of the divine in relation to pregnancy so they could appreciate its astonishing nature. One such occasion was the birth of Jesus. Mary, however, Beecher suggested, did appreciate the wonder of pregnancy even without the supernatural events surrounding the birth of Jesus. Beecher thus asserted that the "Magnificat," Mary's song celebrating her conception, was not inspired by the angel or the supernatural progeny she was carrying; rather, she was inspired simply because she was pregnant. This is what led her to break into song. "Well, she might!," Beecher exclaimed. "What other mystery of human life is so profound as the bearing of life?" An appreciation of pregnancy even demystified the mysterious union of God and Mary. Pregnancy, Beecher declared, made every woman feel as if she was visited by God. So it is no wonder that Mary felt "more sacred than the most sacred temple; and to herself, she must seem as if overshadowed by the Holy Ghost."[22]

In this, Beecher was not disputing the miraculous nature of the virgin birth. He was only suggesting that, though this really happened to Mary, any mother could feel as she had. Beecher did commend Mary's "childlike faith" in the angel. But Beecher's treatment of her and the virgin birth was designed to show something else—that modern people, who no longer needed miracles to appreciate God's works, could find a more constant source of joy in the contemplation of ordinary motherhood.[23]

This effort to make Mary's experience seem normal extended to her relationship with Jesus. Mary's relationship to her child, in short, replicated the experience of all true mothers and children down through history. This began from the moment of conception. Pregnancy was a kind of "double life," according to Beecher. It bound mother and child. Rather than this tie becoming a source of tension as the child grew, Beecher insisted that, on the contrary, mothers and their children must always be in harmony. Thus, there could be no tension between Jesus and Mary.

Once Beecher began to deal with the details of the Gospels, however, it was not easy for him to maintain this ideal of perfect harmony between mother and son. What of the wedding at Cana, when, in response to her request that he miraculously produce more wine, Jesus asked, "Woman, what have I to do with thee?" And what of the scene when Mary, at the edge of the crowd, tried to approach Jesus, and he responded, "Who is my mother, who are my brethren?"

Beecher handled each of these. He denied that there was any rebuke at Cana. The only possible question for the expositor to consider was the propriety of serving alcoholic beverages. As for the incident in the crowd, "while this was unquestionably a rebuke," Beecher conceded, "it presents an admirable illustration of the way in which Jesus looked upon all the social relationships of life": Jesus saw the whole world as his family.[24]

This brings us back to Beecher's agenda as a biblical expositor. For him, the point of interpreting the Gospels was to show that there were no difficulties in the text and no discordances in Christ's character. Given this, he found it easy to scorn the work of scholars who found the Gospels to be challenging. For instance, he noted that Theodore Dwight Woolsey, professor of ancient Greek and, later, president of Yale, had seen difficulties in Mary's relationship with her son. "It is thus remarkable," Woolsey wrote in his 1871 work *Religion of the Past and of the Future*, "that in the only two instances until the crucifixion, where Mary figures in the Gospel—the marriage at Cana and the passage before us [the crowd scene]—she appears in order to be reproved by the Savior." Woolsey struggled with these passages and in the end fell back on a common Protestant explanation for them: they were "protests laid up in store" against the "heathenish eminence" that the Roman church assigned to Mary.[25] We can appreciate Beecher's dissatisfaction with such rationalizations. But Beecher, for his part, often did little more than cover over difficulties in the text. He continually reiterated that Christ's life and his relationships with friends and family had been exemplary and reassuringly normal.

But what of the crucifixion, the most discordant event in Christ's life? Beecher had intended to deal with it in the second volume of *The Life of Jesus, the Christ*. Soon after issuing the first volume, however, Beecher was charged with adultery. He survived this ordeal and went on to write many more popular sermons, but he never finished his life of Christ. He struggled with the final volume for the rest of his life but died before completing it.

The sticking point for Beecher in finishing his *Life of Jesus* may well have been the crucifixion. Beecher's sentimentalism simply did not equip him to deal with such a difficult issue. After Beecher's death, his editors drew together what he had written of the second volume and filled in the gaps with passages from Beecher's sermons. Yet, after combing through hundreds of Beecher's sermons, these editors could not find a single, sustained description of the crucifixion. "The most marked omission is the narrative of the crucifixion," wrote the editors in the introduction to the posthumous second volume; "we cannot find, after an examination of many hundreds of sermons, published and unpublished, that Mr. Beecher ever preached directly on that subject." Why had America's most popular minister not preached directly on the crucifixion? His editors (one of whom was Beecher's son) concluded, "He often said that it was impossible: the subject was too awful and sublime."[26]

Without being uncharitable to Beecher, we might also suggest that the material of the crucifixion may have been too much for him. Despite his ingenuity, even Beecher may not have been able to make the crucifixion seem an uncomplicated event.

Harriet Beecher Stowe

By contrast, Harriet Beecher Stowe's imagination latched on to the crucifixion. Moreover, she focused on all of the difficulties in the sentimental account of Christ's life. Combined, her two discussions of Christ's life were a fraction of the length of her brother's *Life of Jesus, the Christ*. But, unlike his work, hers has dramatic power. In each work, she interpreted the crucifixion from a different angle. In *Woman in Sacred History* (1873; reissued as *Bible Heroines* in 1878), a chapter was given to Mary. As Henry Ward Beecher had called pregnancy a "double life" that forever binds mother and child, so Harriet Beecher Stowe explored the merged identities of Mary and Jesus. But for Stowe this confluence of identities was a source of pain as well as joy. Mary must suffer the alliance to be broken, and yet it cannot be broken because her sympathetic love remains tied to her son. In all of this, Mary's sufferings become as dramatic as Christ's. In *Footsteps of the Master* (1877), Stowe entirely changed the drama. Now mother and son are perfectly merged and Mary almost contributes to the Godhead. The drama lay not in the bodily incarnation but in the process by which Christ allows himself to be drawn down into the world. Yet his sympathetic love for human beings, forcing him to suffer what they suffer, draws him down into an astonishing alienation from himself.[27]

In both of these works, Stowe's approach to the Bible resembled that of her husband, the biblical critic Calvin Stowe. His appreciation of the Bible differed markedly from that of his Andover colleague Edwards Park. Calvin Stowe's interest was less in historicizing the supposedly primitive portions of the Bible than in drawing out the complexity of the biblical writing. He was, of course, still interested in the historical and philological study of the Bible. But he was also concerned to bring out the Bible's artistic side, what he called its "Shakespearean power." This meant that he did not shy away from passages attributing difficult emotions to God or to other biblical characters. Calvin Stowe's sensibility in this was almost romantic. In the sermon he gave at his induction ceremony at Andover, he declared that the beauty of the Bible was more like that of a "mountain range" than the "crystal palace." A hardy imagination, therefore, was needed to enter into the depths of the Bible: "It has its hard places and rough places and dark places, such as the cultivated man in his fastidiousness seeks to avoid." For sentimentalists, these difficult passages were to be found in the situation of Christ's mother at his birth, the wedding at Cana, the crowd scenes, and ultimately the crucifixion.[28]

These were the places that Henry Ward Beecher had steered around. Though Beecher sometimes claimed to agree with his brother-in-law's scholarly views of the Bible, Beecher actually shared little of Calvin Stowe's sensibility on the matter.

Beecher's attitude toward the Bible was summed up in his *Yale Lectures on Preaching* when he suggested that the Bible might not meet the "poetical" or "philosophical" tastes of men "in this later civilization" but was still useful for instructing uneducated people and savages. Calvin Stowe had a different attitude. Though the Bible is "not at all genteel," he told his Andover audience, "[it is] always in exact keeping and abounding in heights of sublimity and depths of pathos." "It has given occasion," he continued, "to probably more than half of all the literary labor which has been performed in the world; and the very highest and happiest efforts of the human mind have been put forth under its influence." This was also the way in which Harriet Beecher Stowe saw the Bible.[29]

In *Woman in Sacred History*, Harriet Beecher Stowe traced a succession of characters through the Old Testament culminating in the character of Mary, the mother of Jesus. Stowe's intention was to show the continuity and fulfillment of the Old Testament in the New. In this effort, there is some echo of the typological scheme of the juristic tradition and a rejection of the tendency in philanthropism to primitivize the Old Testament in relation to the New. Stowe emphasized not Christ's descent from heaven but Mary's Old Testament lineage and her readiness to bear and educate Christ.

Physically, spiritually, and even artistically, Mary was prepared for her task. In physique, she exemplified what Stowe considered a unique trait of the Jewish people. Citing contemporary statistics from the French Ministry of Commerce, Stowe argued that even today the Jewish people showed extraordinary physical "vitality." This was a result of God's original blessing of the "patriarchal stock." This blessing endowed them with the physical ability to bear and raise strong children. They were also endowed emotionally with a solemn sense of the responsibilities of parents. That the ancient Hebrews had been polygamous did give Stowe some pause. This did not fit with her sentimental ideal of the two-parent household. But Stowe went on to insist that ancient Hebrew men had always shown a special respect for a single wife and mother of their children. So, in practice, the ancient Hebrews did meet the sentimental ideal.[30]

Stowe also claimed that Hebrew women had a strong religious and artistic role in ancient times. Sentimentalism generally honored the religious nature of women, but usually not to the extent of suggesting that they should have public roles. Stowe may have been pressing against a narrow interpretation of the separate-spheres ideology, which allowed women few public occupations outside the home. Moses' wife, Miriam, Stowe declared, had been a poet and prophetess. Mary, Miriam's namesake, inherited these poetic and prophetic talents. What equipped Mary, then, to be the mother of Christ was not just her purity in some general sense but quite literally the qualities of her body and mind. The latter was especially important, for, according to Stowe, God had selected Mary not just to bear Christ but educate him as well.[31]

Mary's refinement was evident in her calm reception of the angel at the annunciation. Mary's song, the "Magnificat," along with her good sense and resilience in managing her pregnancy while remaining unwed, all testified to her superior character. In this, Stowe's portrait of Mary stands in contrast to Henry's depiction of Mary and her "childlike faith." Stowe's Mary was no child. As Stowe remarked, "That the Divine Being, in choosing a woman to be the Mother, the Educator, and for thirty years the intimate Friend, of his Son should have selected one of rare and peculiar excellencies seems of probability."[32]

Mary's authority, however, was also a source of dramatic tension. This arose out of the competing influences of Mary and God on their son. This took some daring on Stowe's part. She had to build up Mary's character to the point where the reader could feel she should have almost equal authority with God over Jesus. Moreover, the drama was heightened by the inevitable decline of Mary's influence when Jesus was called to the cross. All of this served to heighten the dramatic tension of the narrative. Though Stowe relied on the common sentimental plot line for the life of Christ, she got more drama out of this plot than most writers. "The great truth that the kingdom was not of this world," Stowe wrote, "was as much hidden from the eyes of Mary, as from those of the whole nation." What makes Stowe's handling of this common plot so striking is that, despite the fact that Mary cannot fully understand what is happening (her prophetic powers notwithstanding), the reader's sympathy stays with her rather than with Christ or even with God. Her "anguish of disappointed hopes," as Stowe put it, "was to increase from year to year, till it culminated in the cross." So the cross became as much a culmination of Mary's life as Christ's.[33]

From Christ's childhood on, the tension between Jesus and Mary grows. The first intimation of this comes when Jesus is twelve. On a trip to Jerusalem with his parents, he separates himself from them, and when his mother finds him and scolds him, he replies that he has been about his father's business. Mary, not understanding, ponders these cryptic comments. Apparently, however, even Jesus does not fully understand what is moving him. Stowe brings this point out in her interpretation of the wedding at Cana. Jesus has reached adulthood, been baptized by John, been announced by God, and fasted in the wilderness, where he was confronted and tempted by Satan. Now he is ready to begin his ministry and returns home to see his mother. While at home, he attends the wedding at Cana; the company runs out of wine and Mary turns to Jesus for help, implying that he should miraculously produce more wine. "Immediately from him, usually so tender and yielding," Stowe wrote, "comes an abrupt repulse."[34]

According to Stowe, the repulse comes from the fact that Mary and Jesus no longer understand their relationship anymore. Both are at the point of overreaching their powers with each other; hence the irritability. Why had Mary's request seemed so inappropriate to Christ, Stowe asked: "What sacred vital spot has she touched unaware with her maternal hand?" Christ's confusion, in fact, was understandable. He had come out of the desert, where the devil had tempted him to perform miracles. How could Christ know for sure now whether the temptation to perform miracles came from Satan or Mary? It took him a moment to realize that Mary's suggestion was in accord with God's will, "some inward voice or call by which he felt the divine will moving with his own." This explained the odd fact that, after rebuking his mother, he went ahead and miraculously made more wine, just as his mother had asked.[35]

But now the coincidence between his mother and God could no longer be taken for granted. Their voices were no longer in sync. "What he might not do from partial affection, he might do at divine motion," Stowe wrote. This problem occupied the remainder of Stowe's account of Mary's life. Her relationship with her son was falling by the wayside as God's plan for Jesus led him in directions that Mary did not understand.[36]

As Mary's influence with Jesus recedes, she begins a descent into her own exemplary sufferings. These parallel Christ's own. Mary's suffering becomes for Stowe a lens through which to understand and even magnify Christ's passion. To shore up this linkage between Christ and Mary, Stowe recalled the prophecy of Simeon in the Book of Luke. When Christ was only a child, Simeon had cryptically declared to Mary that her son was destined to fall and "a sword shall pass through thine own soul also."[37]

Alarmed and searching for the meaning of this prophecy, Mary follows Jesus on his ministry. Standing at the edge of the crowd, Mary, according to Stowe, hears whispers of plots against him and tries to push forward to warn him, but Christ ignores her. Like Woolsey, Stowe suggested that this passage may have been recorded, in part, as a warning against the Roman Catholic veneration of Mary. But Stowe made more of it than this. Simeon had also prophesied to Mary that, in her suffering, "the thoughts of many hearts may be revealed." Stowe used this prophecy to universalize Mary's loss. "In this hour of her life," Stowe wrote (again echoing the typological style of juristic theologians), "Mary is the type of the trial through which all mothers must pass at the time when they are called to resign a son to his destiny in the world, and to feel that he is theirs no more."[38]

The climax of Mary's trial comes at the crucifixion. Here Stowe gave the plot an extraordinary twist. Instead of just signifying the fulfillment of God's will and the final breakdown of Mary's will, the crucifixion is made to glorify the resilience of Mary's love despite the fact that her mother's love has led her to misunderstand God's mission for Christ. In all of this, Stowe gives what must be one of the most extraordinary glosses on the passage that had continually exercised the best theological minds in America during the nineteenth century. This passage was Christ's outcry from the cross: "My God, my God why hast thou forsaken me?"

Astonishingly, Stowe suggested that Christ's outcry was against God for abandoning him and contained the implicit recognition that Mary had not abandoned him. It was thus an outcry as much addressed to God as to Mary standing at the foot of the cross. This interpretation even suggests that, for a moment at least, Jesus suddenly thought that he had made an enormous mistake; perhaps he should have followed his mother's advice rather than God's. Or at least, perhaps, he should have given his mother's warnings more heed and not been so sharp with her. Stowe's skill in interpolating her meaning into the biblical text is evident in the way in which she suggested this by putting into italics one little word in Christ's outcry. "After years of waiting and hope deferred," Stowe wrote of Mary standing under the cross, and "such evident tokens of God's approval, she sees her son forsaken by God and man. To hers as to no other mortal ears must have sounded the death-cry, 'My God, my God, why hast *thou* forsaken me?'" Why have *you*, God, forsaken me, while my mother continues to stand by me?[39]

But in her suffering Mary has vindicated herself. The audacity of this interpretation is that Stowe has Mary vindicate herself at the expense of God. Strictly speaking, Mary is wrong. Even Jesus, for that matter, is wrong. He has not been abandoned by God; in his death, Jesus is fulfilling God's mission. But Stowe has made the logic of these points pale beside her characterization of Mary.

Moreover, Stowe seems even to rebuke the church (and through it, theologians) for missing what must have seemed to Stowe the truth of Christianity in the truth of Mary's character. Three times in two paragraphs (twice in italics), Stowe reiterated that Mary "stood" by the cross as if to emphasize the contrast with Peter, who three times denied Christ yet went on to found the church. "But through all, Mary *stood*," Stowe wrote, "she did not faint or fall,—she was resolved to drink of HIS cup to the last bitter dregs. Though the whole world turn against him, though God himself seems to forsake him, she will stand by him, she will love him, she will adore him till death, and after, and forever!"[40]

In this, Mary not only has outdone the disciples and the future church but also for a moment seems to outdo God himself. The Mother has momentarily replaced the Father in a coequal union with the Son. Of course, Stowe was not actually saying that Mary was divine. As a matter of Protestant principle, Stowe objected to the Roman Catholic veneration of Mary (though Stowe felt an ambivalent attraction toward Catholicism).[41] But at the very least Stowe allowed her characterization of Mary great imaginative leeway in rich and supercharged language. And this occasionally out-ran the boundaries of established doctrine.

Despite all of the attention to Mary, however, Stowe tried to return the spotlight to Christ. Her sufferings, in paralleling his, were a kind of human mirror for his divine sufferings. "If any mortal creature might be said to have entered into the suffering of the atonement of Jesus, it was his mother," Stowe concluded.[42] This was an extraordinary and daring new take on incarnationalism.

It shows the remarkable range of Stowe's imagination that, four years after publishing *Woman in Sacred History*, she could publish a different interpretation of the incarnation with a different, though just as compelling, explanation for Christ's outcry, "My God, my God, why has thou forsaken me?" In her 1877 work *Footsteps of the Master*, Stowe asserted that there was never any misunderstanding between Jesus and his mother. He had not rebuked her at Cana, Stowe now asserted, falling back on the most common and banal gloss on this passage—the one used by Theodore Woolsey. That is, Jesus was not rebuking Mary but making a public statement intended to warn future generations against idolizing her. Like her brother, Stowe insisted that there could be no tension between Jesus and Mary. Their closeness made this impossible. Their "souls," Stowe wrote, were "so perfectly allied to each other" that they always shared an "exact understanding and sympathy." This continued all the way to the crucifixion. At the cross, Stowe wrote, "it is all told in one word, 'Now there *stood* by the cross of Jesus his mother.'"[43]

What had happened to Stowe's characterizations of Jesus and Mary? Four years earlier, Stowe had drawn out a triangular conflict between Mary, Jesus, and God by emphasizing this one word, "stood." Now, by putting the same word in italics again, she used it to argue that there was no misunderstanding; there was nothing to be explained; she could say it "all . . . in one word." Four years earlier Mary's fidelity to Christ, the fact that she stood by the cross, pressed home the dramatic climax of the crucifixion as the center of tragic misunderstanding. Now, by standing beside the cross, Mary establishes the crucifixion as a foreseen and unproblematic event in Mary and Christ's relationship. Was Stowe embracing the banal criticism of her brother and admitting no family problems into the divine circle? Was she, like her brother, now writing a blandly sentimental account of Christ's life in which Mary becomes indistinct and fades into the character of Christ?

Far from it. Rather, in Stowe's account, Christ's character has begun to fade into Mary's. Mary has so thoroughly worked her character into his that she and Jesus emerge, in Stowe's narrative, as almost a new kind of being. They reverse the biblical gender roles that theologians had used to interpret the atonement. Traditionally, Christ was called the second Adam and Mary the second Eve. But Stowe switched the genders here. It is Mary who functions like a "second Adam" and Christ emerges from her like a second Eve. "He was bone of her bone and flesh of her flesh," Stowe wrote of Christ alluding to the Genesis account of how Eve came from Adam; and then, amazingly, Stowe added, "his life grew out of her immortal nature."[44]

"*Her* immortal nature"? This almost suggests that it is she who made Christ the Son of God. What Stowe meant by this she did not pause to say. She dropped it and moved on to claim that, because "he had no mortal father," Jesus had a peculiar kind of femininity. This made Jesus unique among men. In fact, Mary gives this femininity not only to Jesus but also, through his divine nature, to God, suggesting the creation of a new kind of divinity. "All that was human in him was her nature," Stowe declared; "it was the union of the divine nature with the nature of a pure woman. Hence there was in Jesus more of the pure feminine element than in any other man. It was the feminine element exalted and taken in union with divinity."[45]

But what of God in all of this? If Christ did not have "a mortal father," what can be said about God the Father here?

This is the key to the whole work and explains why it differs so much from *Woman in Sacred History*. In that work, God was a real presence and in competition with Mary. Now, in *Footsteps of the Master*, God the Father is almost entirely absent. Why this is so Stowe did not explain. It is as if she was studiously avoiding the subject. This vagueness about the Father allowed her to give such power to Mary, allowed her to refer to "her immortal nature" and write of "divinity" with a small "d" as if it was some kind of divine stuff that Christ was bearing. But there is a problem with this. Where does Christ come from before the incarnation? What of the Old Testament?

Here Stowe declared that all appearances of Jehovah in the Old Testament were really "preappearances" of Christ. This was a remarkable strategy. It allowed her to assimilate her incarnationalism with Old Testament anthropomorphism, creating a mixture of extraordinary dramatic power. This was a power that most incarnationalists, like theists, denied themselves by distancing their characterizations of God from the Old Testament. Thus, Henry Ward Beecher had exclaimed, "O, take away my Jehovah, but do not take away my Jesus." Stowe combined the two. She did not linger on substantiating her claim, however. Rather, she brusquely declared that the identification of Christ with Jehovah "has been the approved sentiment of sound theologians." To back this up, she listed Jonathan Edwards in his *History of the Work of Redemption*, Isaac Watts in his *True Glory of Christ*, and John Milton in *Paradise Lost*—a motley group to call "sound theologians." Stowe tried to cover herself further by bringing in the common incarnationalist justification for not representing God—Christ's assertion that whoever has seen him has seen the Father. But all of this resort to proof was beside the point. Stowe's skill was in characterization, not documentation.[46]

This is evident in her depiction of Christ. She turned the ambiguity of Jesus' status as God into a character trait that made him even more intriguing. Jesus had not made it plain that he was God, Stowe surmised, because of his "divine reticence and composure." Yet at one point he forgot himself. We have seen how Stowe handled this scene. Jesus is surrounded by skeptics who balk at him for implying that he has greater authority than Abraham. Allowing himself to be goaded, Jesus momentarily "rose into the language of heaven, and spoke for a moment unconsciously, as it were, in the style of a higher world," when he declared, "before Abraham was, I AM."[47]

Stowe's most compelling characterization of this "reticent" Jesus, however, occurs before his incarnation. This opened up to Stowe a rich field for dramatic interpretation. She imagined Jesus appearing here and there on earth in anticipation of his complete incarnation. Given the importance that Stowe attached to Mary's contribution to Jesus' character, Stowe might have described Jesus looking forward to his bodily birth and the infusion of femininity into his character. This would have made a fascinating spectacle, but perhaps it was too rich even for Stowe's imagination. Instead, what she describes is the way in which Christ allows himself to descend again and again to the earth during the Old Testament until he finally gives way to his actual birth. In these prebirth, preincarnate appearances, Christ is mournfully relenting to the human needs drawing him to earth. Stowe referred to him as "a voluntary exile, from a higher and purer life." In what sense he is an "exile" from heaven, however, is never pursued.[48]

If anything, he is an exile on earth prior to his intense bond with Mary. In describing his character during his intermittent, preincarnate descents to earth, Stowe achieved something astonishing in American theology. As we have noted, it is a feature of incarnationalism to play on the contrast of high and low, God in his majestic isolation and sinful humans in dusty crowds. Stowe took this theme to new heights and depths. Coolidge wrote of the crowds pressing on the incarnate Christ. Stowe wrote of men grappling with the preincarnate Christ. Throughout the Old Testament, Jesus-Jehovah allowed himself to be touched by ancient people. The Genesis account of the mysterious angel who wrestled at night with the ambitious and anxious patriarch Jacob was really Jesus. He had come down to comfort Jacob and embolden him; but Jacob clung to him and Jesus sorrowfully and reluctantly allowed himself to be detained until the last possible moment. The sun coming up, Jesus, for some reason, had to ascend to heaven. As he left, he struck a blow to Jacob but also blessed him. Why he did this could not be explained. All that could be grasped was something about the character of Christ in this:

> He reveals himself not as a fixed Fate—a mighty, crushing, inexorable Power—but as a Being relenting, tender, yearning towards the race of man with infinite tenderness. He suffers himself to be importuned: he hides himself that he may be sought, and, although he is omnipotent, though with one touch he might weaken and paralyze human strength, yet he suffers human arms to detain and human importunity to conquer him, and blesses the man that will not let him go except he bless.[49]

This God "suffers himself to be importuned," detained, and even conquered all the way to the cross. Yet throughout, it is this God's mournful sense of resignation, as much as his "tenderness," that gives him a compelling character and saves him from becoming simply the gentle Jesus of sentimental stereotype. It is the fact that Jesus has seen it all before and accepts humanity's fate over his own that makes it possible for him to reach a powerful self-perspective. Paradoxically, his very sympathy for man, which allows him to be drawn down to earth, alienates Jesus from himself.

It is along these lines that Stowe comes up with her second astonishing gloss on Christ's outcry, "My God, My God, why hast thou forsaken me?" How could these words make sense in *Footsteps of the Master*? What alienation is Christ experiencing? His mother, as Stowe asserted, "stood" by him, and there was no confusion or complication in this. Nor was there any confusion or complication in Christ's understanding of his own mission. Who was he even crying to? Christ was Jehovah after all. So who could he be crying to but himself?

The answer was in the question; Christ was crying to himself. He had forgotten himself again, as he had when Stowe described him slipping "unconsciously" back "into the language of heaven" and uttering, "Before Abraham was: I AM." Only now he is looking back in wonder on his descent from heaven into human history. The perspective is reversed—not going up but tracing his way down to this final depth of degradation. The words Christ spoke from the cross, in which he addressed God as a being separate from himself, Stowe pointed out, were from the Twenty-second Psalm. Christ was quoting this. Other commentators had pointed this out to try to relieve the impression that Christ was distracted or in despair in his suffering. If he was quoting scripture, the banal gloss went, then he must have been composed and was illustrating the proper way to deport oneself while suffering. With remarkable ingenuity and control of tone, Stowe gave a different interpretation of why Christ recalled the Psalm:

> In this Psalm, written more than a thousand years before he came into the world, our Lord beheld ever before him the scenes of his own crucifixion; he could see the heartless stare of idle, malignant curiosity around his cross; he could hear the very words of the taunts and revilings, and a part of the language of this Psalm was among his last utterances. While the shadows of the great darkness were gathering around his cross he cried, "My God, my God, why hast thou forsaken me?" It would seem as if the words so bitterly fulfilled passed through his mind, as one by one the agonies and indignities followed each other, till at last he bowed his head and said, "It is finished."[50]

"It would seem as if the words so bitterly fulfilled passed through his mind, as one by one the agonies and indignities followed each other"—with this sentence, Stowe transforms the tone of the whole scene. In his expectation fulfilled, Christ is almost absent from himself. Just for having "passed through his mind," the ancient words of his expectation are articulated on his lips.

In this, Stowe had found the "Shakespearean power" in the Bible. Her Christ resembles no other character so much as Macbeth. Both are great victims of expectation and eventual self-alienation. Both are characters who have lost themselves in the wonder of prophecy fulfilled. And in those moments of fulfillment, both characters gain an uncanny perspective on time. "She should have died hereafter," said Macbeth on hearing news of his wife's death. In sure anticipation of his own demise, he gives his most famous speech; "All our yesterdays have lighted the way of fools to dusty death." *Footsteps of the Master* seems a reverse image of this, showing the way not for fools but for the blessed. But Stowe entertained no sentimental optimism that following Christ would make this life any easier. "We are born to die," she declared in her introduction to the book. Following "the footsteps of the master" was all "that a human being needs in this transitory, perplexing and dangerous pilgrimage of life."[51] Shakespeare may have had his image of the fool playing out his part in life, and Stowe may have had her image of Jesus—two very different characters indeed, but the image of life itself was not that different. In all of this, Stowe had reached the heights of sentimental incarnationalism. Indeed, she was almost working in a romantic mode by suggesting a strange ambivalence in her tender though alienated Christ.

❧

PART TWO

The Romantic God
of the Nineteenth Century

CHAPTER FIVE

Vitality and Anger

W. G. T. Shedd

The God of romantic anthropomorphism was very different from the God of sentimental incarnationalism and neoclassical theism. The differences among these styles can be seen by referring again to God's statement in Exodus, "I am that I am." Park, the neoclassical theist, found in this a declaration of God's serenity: "We rejoice that there is a mind free from the complexities and discrepancies that mar our character. . . . We are calmed by the announcement, 'I am that I am.'" Stowe, the sentimental incarnationalist, found in Jesus' version of this statement, "before Abraham was I am," a clue to the mysterious mixing of God and humanity in the incarnation; Jesus had given his true nature away "in a moment of high excitement" and let slip from himself an utterance "unconsciously, as it were . . . in his native language."

The romantic anthropomorphist W. G. T. Shedd, by contrast, found neither the serenity of the neoclassical theists nor the mysterious condescension of the sentimental incarnationalists in God's statement, "I am that I am." Rather, Shedd read God's declaration as a statement of the irresistible vitality of God's presence. Man was neither calmed nor intrigued but shaken and infected with this energy. "Aware that the intelligent and emotional I AM is penetrating his innermost soul," Shedd wrote, "[man] is, if ever upon earth, a roused man, an earnest, energized creature." The reason for this was the power of God's character. Picking up on the fact that in Exodus God declared himself to Moses from a burning bush, Shedd wrote: "The human mind thrills to its innermost fibre . . . when God's personal character darts its dazzling rays into the darkness" of sinful man.[1]

Romantic anthropomorphism emerged in the 1850s and 1860s as a reaction against neoclassical theism. In this sense, romantic anthropomorphism resembles sentimental incarnationalism. In both styles, theologians sought to make God's character more emotional and dramatic. But there was also this difference. Where sentimental incarnationalists largely came from the left and center of the theological spectrum, romantic anthropomorphists (with the one great exception of Horace Bushnell) came from the right wing of the theological spectrum; that is, from the ranks of Old School Calvinists.

Conservative theologians turned to anthropomorphism for much the same reason that liberal theologians turned to incarnationalism. Both felt that the prevailing theistic manner of characterizing God made him too abstract and too distant. Where incarnationalists brought God down to earth in the form of the Son of God, anthropomorphists brought God the Father down to earth. They wanted to imagine humanity being confronted by God as God (as opposed to God as Jesus in incarnate form). How God, as God, could appear to humans, of course, was a problem. It meant restoring authority to anthropomorphism. This, in turn, meant restoring authority to the Old Testament and finding new ways to connect it with the New Testament.

Romanticism could help them here, for theologians could use romanticism to celebrate the Old Testament precisely for being an ancient text. Some romantics questioned the visions of historical progress inscribed into the enlightenment celebration of rationality and the humanitarian celebration of refinement. They celebrated the passionate and primitive. This romantic vision of history involved rediscovering lost, original capacities in human beings. History was not progressive. The human race was not becoming more capable with the development of civilization. Rationality and gentility repressed its native instincts. To recover these, people had to try to restore in themselves ancient imaginative capacities. This celebration of the primitive made romanticism a key element in the attempt to restore legitimacy to Old Testament anthropomorphism.

Romanticism was also key in the effort to restore legitimacy to God's anger. In neoclassicism and sentimentalism, anger typically signified a loss of self-control, an embarrassing capitulation to bodily agitation and passion, making such a character forfeit any claims to legitimate authority. In romanticism, by contrast, anger could become a sign of vitality. By the same token, so could guilt. Guilt deepened experience, threw off artificiality, and brought humanity face to face with its essential self. All of this helped theologians to throw off the caricature of the juristic God. What Worcester, from his neoclassical perspective, had deemed "harsh and revolting" in the juristic God now could seem energizing and profound from a romantic perspective.

The romantic anthropomorphists, however, remain virtually unknown. There are a number of reasons for this. Though they were among the leading theologians of their era, considered as a group they were tiny; furthermore, they had no self-consciousness of themselves as a group. In the case of Bushnell, this is understandable, for he was the lone prominent liberal to take up romantic characterization. But in the case of the conservatives, such as Shedd, Griffin, and Baird, their isolation and neglect is harder to understand. Romantic characterization offered conservatives a way to throw off liberal attacks and promote a powerful depiction of the Calvinist God. It might be thought that this would be attractive to conservatives and a movement would gather around romantic anthropomorphism. We can only speculate why this did not happen. But a major reason seems to be the prestige of Charles Hodge and his brand of neoclassical theism.

For a conservative to take up romantic anthropomorphism meant not just a rejection of liberalism but (at least implicitly) a rejection of Hodge's brand of neoclassical theism. As we have seen, Hodge was not interested in "the emotions of terror and sublimity" in the Old Testament, so he had little use for anthropomorphism or romanticism.[2] As we have also seen, Hodge had tremendous prestige among Old School

Presbyterians. Much of this came from the perception that he was providing the last solid line of defense against liberalism. This was a defense that many conservatives assumed it was best not to tamper with. In the early nineteenth century, many conservative Presbyterians feared that a wave of liberalism was sweeping over American cosmopolitan culture. The prominence of Unitarians and Transcendentalists was only the most obvious manifestation of this. It was also apparent among the Congregationalists (former Calvinist allies of the Presbyterians) and even within the ranks of the Presbyterians themselves. In 1837, the denomination split into New School and Old School factions, the New School largely adopting the governmental theology.[3]

Against this wave of liberalism Hodge erected what appeared to be a solid bulwark. He provided an authoritative and consistent defense of the penal theology of Old School Calvinism. He reassured his fellow conservatives by claiming that the liberal positions were simply rehatched ancient heresies or the exotic but ultimately ephemeral fancies of German idealism and pantheism. Through his editorship of the *Princeton Review*, and his oversight of Princeton Seminary, he eloquently upheld Calvinist doctrines while deftly picking holes in the reasoning of governmental and moral theologians. Criticism of Hodge from his Old School colleagues, therefore, may well have been muted for the sake of unity against what seemed an ascending foe.

And because conservatives locked themselves into a defensive posture behind Hodge, this may have limited the development of romantic anthropomorphism. Romantic anthropomorphism, if it jarred with Hodge's theism, was also an aggressive counteroffensive against liberalism. But apparently most conservatives preferred a strategy of defense with Hodge rather than one of offense. So, because many Old School Presbyterians lined up behind Hodge, contemporaries (and historians after them) easily assumed that Hodge's neoclassical theism was the last word in nineteenth-century American conservative theology. Therefore, the romantic anthropomorphism of Shedd, Baird, and Griffin was forgotten.

Also, romantic anthropomorphism was a short-lived phenomenon. It emerged in the 1850s and declined in the 1860s. In the postwar climate of Northern Presbyterianism, the maverick theological impulse disappeared. The war helped to unify the Northern Presbyterian church (the Old and New Schools reuniting in 1869), and a more ecumenical spirit reigned, at least between penal and governmental theologians. They both retreated into increasingly abstract and defensive forms of neoclassical theism in order to sustain the idea of a transcendent God in contrast to the liberal effort in the late nineteenth century to picture God as immanent in nature and human history.

The maverick efforts of the romantic anthropomorphists were obscured in another way by the defensiveness of conservative theology. It became easy to assume that nothing new—and certainly nothing literary—was to come from the right wing of American theology. This assumption was part of the common stereotype of theological conservativism, which even most conservatives, such as Hodge, upheld. The use of literature in religious writing was associated with liberalism, particularly with the moral theology and sentimental incarnationalism. Conservatives called this liberal use of literature dilettantish, while liberals called it cosmopolitan; but they agreed on the basic distinction: liberals were imaginative and literary, conservatives were hardheaded and philosophical.

This basic distinction has come down to us in history and literary criticism. Much of the critical tradition celebrating the "American renaissance" of the 1850s relied on this common liberal caricature of conservative religious writing. In this caricature, conservative theology is little more than dry-as-dust metaphysics. Calvinism, declared the Unitarian theologian and literary critic James Freeman Clarke in 1866, is "dry, cold, hard [and] very logical."[4] Only in the late twentieth century have critics broken out of this stereotype.[5] Conservative theologians (and historians sympathetic to them) did not help their case much, for they were also trapped by the polemical terms of the old theological debate. While denying that Calvinism is dull, they still insisted that it is rigorously logical. Of course, it can be this, but it can also be more literary. But given the stereotyped dichotomy between liberals and conservatives, the last place we would expect to find romantic characterizations of God emerging in the 1850s would be among the Presbyterian Calvinists.[6]

We can delineate two parts in this development of American romantic anthropomorphism: one dealing with God's anger, the other with God's love. It should be noted, however, that this division mainly helps our purposes of exposition. It does not imply a rigid sequence of development. Nor should this division itself be taken too strictly; after all, central to romantic characterization is the mixture of love and anger. Still, however, the second part, concerning God's love, may best be understood by approaching it through the first part: the romantic rehabilitation of God's anger. One theologian more than any other worked through this first part: W. G. T. Shedd.

After Charles Hodge, William Greenough Thayer Shedd was the leading penal theologian in the North during the middle decades of the nineteenth century. Educated at the University of Vermont and Andover Seminary, he briefly served as a Congregationalist pastor before returning to Vermont to teach English literature for seven years under the auspices of the university's president, James Marsh. Marsh was a keen follower of European romanticism, from Immanuel Kant's epistemology and Friedrich von Schiller's aesthetics to their permutations through English literature, especially in the works of Samuel Coleridge. Shedd followed Marsh's interest and, in fact, edited the first American edition of the complete works of Coleridge. But Shedd's main work was in theology. After teaching at the University of Vermont, he held brief posts at Auburn and Andover Seminaries before settling down at Union Seminary in New York City in 1863, where he remained until 1890; he died in 1894.[7]

While at Union, he wrote large volumes on theology and the history of theology. But his most important writing came earlier when his youthful interest in literature still had its spark. "We live in an age when theology has become entirely divorced from literature, and when supernatural science forms no part of the studies of the cultivated class," Shedd declared in a lecture to the Literary Society of the University of Vermont in 1845. Shedd was overstating the case, but his interest in European romanticism made him more sensitive than others to the growing gap between literature and theology and the effect this was having on cosmopolitan readers.[8] In a series of essays in the 1850s and 1860s, Shedd addressed this problem. He combined

Calvinism and romanticism and experimented with new ways to depict God's anger. Shedd's romantic rehabilitation of God's anger was based on one major claim: that God's anger had an energizing effect on sinners.

Anger and Energy

This claim had much in common with arguments made by juristic theologians. Calvin, for instance, had suggested that God used his anger to motivate people. There was a suggestion of a division of labor in this between the Old Testament Jehovah and the New Testament Christ—a sort of good cop, bad cop routine. As Calvin had put it, "Since our hearts cannot, in God's mercy, either seize upon life ardently enough or accept it with the gratefulness we owe, unless our minds are first struck and overwhelmed by fear of God's wrath and by dread of eternal death, we are taught by Scripture to perceive that apart from Christ, God is, so to speak, hostile to us, and his hand is armed for our destruction; to embrace his benevolence and fatherly love in Christ alone."[9]

Neoclassical and sentimental writers also recognized the dramatic potential of anger. This, of course, had caused them some problems, for they could not approve of this anger, yet its dramatic power was attractive. Alexander Pope compared the merits of the *Iliad* and *Aeneid* on this point. He believed the *Iliad* was the greatest epic poem, yet its driving force, he acknowledged, was Achilles, whose ruling passion was anger. Aeneas, by contrast, was more restrained but for this reason was less interesting. Leading characters reflected the styles of their authors. "Homer, boundless and irresistible, as Achilles, bears all before him," Pope observed; "Virgil, calmly daring like Aeneas, appears undisturbed in the midst of action." Aeneas met the neoclassical ideal, but Achilles was more compelling. This could have implications for theology. Pope raised the issue only in terms of the pagan gods: "Homer seems like his own Jupiter in his terrors, shaking Olympus, scattering the lightenings and firing the heavens; Virgil, like the same power in his benevolence, counseling with the gods, laying plans for empires, and regularly ordering his whole creation." A similar comparison might be made between the juristic tradition and philanthropism.[10]

Dryden allowed some of these theological issues to surface in *Absalom and Achitophel*. This recounted the story from Second Samuel of how Achitophel tempts Absalom, King David's son, to lead a rebellion against his father. Dryden, while remaining squarely on the side of "the godlike David," aired the thought that David's aversion to violence had encouraged the rebels. David's tenderness seemed peculiar for a true king. This gives the demonic tempter in the poem, Achitophel, his opening to David's son, Absalom. "Not that your father's mildness I condemn," Achitophel whispers, "but manly force becomes the diadem." Absalom wonders, "If mildness ill with stubborn Israel suit / His crime is God's beloved attribute." Could "God's beloved attribute" be wrong? David spends the latter part of the poem justifying his "mildness" as really neoclassical reserve: "They call my tenderness of blood, my fear / Though manly tempers can the longest bear." In the end, however, David is forced to act. But he remains reluctant, for he is acting against his inner nature; what eventually decides the issue is his duty to uphold the law and its deterrent value. This, of course, was exactly the same reasoning used by governmental theologians in their interpretation of the atonement:

Oh, that my power to saving were confin'd;
Why am I forced, like Heaven, against my mind
To make examples of another kind?
Must I at length the sword of justice draw?
Oh, curst effects of necessary law!
How ill my fear they by my mercy scan
Beware the fury of a patient man.[11]

Even sentimental writers left some opening for the dramatic, if not moral, merits of anger. Literary critics make an important point when they say that sentimental novels inculcated an "ethic of submission." The sentimental novel was certainly didactic, particularly in teaching the restraint of anger. But to read the sentimental novel as only didactic underestimates it. For the sentimental novel was not just an advice book but a dramatic story. And drama was sustained in the sentimental novel partly by allowing eruptions of anger to have some play. For instance, in her best-selling 1850 novel, *The Wide, Wide World*, Susan Warner told the story of how little Ellen Montgomery learns to control her temper. But Ellen keeps on getting provoked and loses her self-control. One of her aptly named provocateurs, Aunt Fortune, remarks, "I don't believe in this jumping into goodness all at once." It was a good thing; for if Ellen had "jumped into goodness all at once," Warner would not have had much of a story. So the struggle to attain self-control was at the dramatic core of many of these novels. Moreover, this struggle can duplicate the dramatic expression of anger, but in a more socially respectable way. For instance, recall that little Wallace in Catharine Sedgwick's *Home* reproduced the very symptoms of rage in struggling to suppress it: "There was a horrid choking feeling in my throat, and angry words seemed crowding out. . . . I had to bite my lips, though, so that the blood ran." His father sanctions this with, "God bless you my son."[12]

It would not take much to flip this condemnation of anger around into a celebration of its power. Indeed, some critics have suggested that sentimental novelists played both sides at once: a condemnation of violence and a more surreptitious, sometimes prurient, fascination with it. Some critics have also suggested that the play given to anger in sentimental novels written by women was a covert, or unconscious, expression of their authors' frustration with the limited opportunities open to women in nineteenth-century America. The challenge may also be to emotional norms more generally. If some passages in the sentimental novel seem protofeminist, some also seem protoromantic. Little Ellen and Wallace were a few steps away from assuming the traits of Catherine and Heathcliff in *Wuthering Heights*.

Thus, writers pushed the boundaries of characterization. Most theologians, however, stuck with stricter delineations of neoclassicism and sentimentalism in their depictions of God. Shedd was one of the rare theologians who recognized the potential of romanticism to celebrate God's anger as energizing.[13]

Most theologians, however, were suspicious of romantic characterization. Primed by neoclassicism and sentimentalism to polarize emotions, some theologians saw romantic characterization as a celebration of violence and, thus, irresponsible, juvenile, and sensationalist. Moreover, given the support of the enlightenment and humanitarian reform for neoclassicism and sentimentalism, romanticism could seem self-indulgent and immoral. This is how a writer for the *Presbyterian Quarterly Review* took romanticism in 1855. "Is Effective Writing Necessarily 'Volcanic'?," the anonymous author asked in the title. The answer was definitely not. There were two ways of portraying power, the author argued. One was by depicting serenity and order, the other by depicting turbulence and agitation. One way stood for neoclassicism, and the other stood for romanticism. "It was the fashion after the time of Byron," the author wrote, "to connect turbulence with power and wickedness with strength." This had momentarily captured the public imagination. It was easy to see why: "[We] are so much more struck by violence than the calm on-going of real power." Here was the neoclassical ideal of serene control. To illustrate it, the author drew on the typical Newtonian imagery. Despite the "inconceivable velocity" of the planets, those "worlds of God" remained "true to their orbits." Likewise, all liberty needed to be regulated. Nearly paraphrasing Alexander Pope's famous line from a century and a half earlier—"Nature, like liberty, is but restrained / By the same laws which herself first ordained"—the Presbyterian author declared that freedom "is not licence, but liberty under law."[14]

In 1855, it still looked to this Presbyterian reviewer as if romanticism was a passing fashion. He had some reason to think so. The author acknowledged that "there are undoubtedly some painful signs of the failure of calm and sobered thought among our people" and many American writers were busy "straining after eloquence in words, when they have no eloquent thought." The reviewer regretted that in prose writing the dignified styles of George Washington, Alexander Hamilton, and Washington Irving were no longer so prominent. But at least American poetry was holding to high standards. The author pointed to Holmes, Lowell, and Longfellow, the poets of the "genteel tradition." Indeed, these writers would remain the major, celebrated American poets into the early twentieth century.[15]

Given all of this, we see the difficulty for theologians in endorsing romanticism, much less ascribing romantic traits to God. Everything seemed to be against this except one thing: biblical anthropomorphism. But this was a weakened ally in the nineteenth century, for, as we have seen, biblical anthropomorphism had been undermined and marginalized by the champions of a neoclassical and sentimental God. Romanticism, however, could help here too; it could be used to restore legitimacy to Old Testament anthropomorphism.

The Revival of Anthropomorphism

Romanticism could be used to celebrate the antiquity of the Old Testament. Evoking the ancient and (according to the cultural paradigms of the time) unprogressive Eastern character of the Old Testament was a way to throw off the accoutrements of a genteel and scientific civilization and return to a profoundly primitive human state. In romantic literary criticism, the idea took hold that the primitive was the poetic. Such thoughts had been sounded before romanticism in the early and mid-eighteenth-century writings of Joseph Addison on Milton and the Psalms and of Richard Lowth on ancient Hebrew poetry. But in the early nineteenth century, Thomas Macaulay and Samuel Coleridge, among others, made it a staple of romantic criticism. Thus, whereas neoclassicists imitated Augustan styles, which were notably urbane, the romantics made a point of mining the supposedly more primitive Old Testament (Homer and the ancient Greeks being fair game for both).[16]

A few American theologians began to pick up on these trends. In an 1861 essay in the *Presbyterian Quarterly Review* entitled "Hebrew Language and Literature," the anonymous author took a very different view of romantic power from the author of "Is Effective Writing Necessarily 'Volcanic'?" The author of "Hebrew Language and Literature" asserted: "In proportion as poets are acknowledged to be vast and sublime in their genius, they approach the spirit of Hebrew poetry." Notice that it is they who "approach," not the Hebrew poets who "approach" them. Inspiration is found by going back in time, not forward.[17]

The poets the Presbyterian author had in mind were Milton and Byron. And by the "vast and sublime," the author did not mean a vision of the heavens informed by astronomy but rather a vision of psychological space. This was a psychological vision of character torn by ambition and guilt. The landscape reflecting these mental states was not a vista of planets keeping to their orbits but flitting "moonbeams" on a "heaving ocean." Such characters do not exemplify "the calm on-going of real power." Rather, they are energized by a vivid restlessness characteristic of the very style of the ancient Hebrew writers: "The narrator's mind is full of the verb—the moment—the situation—in a word, will or causality."[18]

The author acknowledged that this was not the dominant literary style in contemporary culture. But he questioned whether this showed a lack in the modern sensibility rather than in the ancient. "The Hebrew poetry is anything but rude," he wrote; "it is bold, sometimes too highly figurative for the occidental taste and too rough for our ideas of refinement, which are, perhaps, as much a proof of corruption as of purity."[19]

But could theologians really represent God in anthropomorphic form to an educated audience? Was appreciation of the literary merit of the ancient Hebrew writers enough to bridge the gap between antiquity and the modern age? Even romantics admitted that the gap existed. These were difficult questions.

As so often in Christian reflection on anthropomorphism, the question came down to one of assigning the labels "literal" and "figurative" to theistic and anthropomorphic depictions of God. Even in the juristic tradition anthropomorphism was considered to be figurative, or metaphorical, and so, in one sense or another, a less authoritative characterization of God than a more literal one, which they assumed must be theistic. But now with the emergence of romanticism it could be asked, why must theologians assume that anthropomorphism was any more metaphorical than a theistic view of God? Or even, could there be a literal sense in which God was truly conceived in anthropomorphic form?

Taylor Lewis raised these questions in an article he wrote in 1850 for the *Biblical Repository and Classical Review* entitled "The Spirit of the Old Testament." Lewis was a professor of classics at Union College in upstate New York (not to be confused with Union Seminary in New York City, where Shedd taught). Lewis was a keen commentator on the state of biblical criticism and theology in America. As a

scholar of the classics, perhaps he was more comfortable than many of his generation with vivid depictions of the divine. Whatever the reason, he strongly objected to
the increasing emphasis on theistic characterizations of God and the corresponding
primitivization of Old Testament anthropomorphism. Writing in the same year as
Park's "Theology of the Intellect and That of the Feelings," Lewis scorned what he
called the "barren negatives" of modern theism. Particularly irksome to Lewis was
the tendency of liberal biblical critics to reduce Old Testament images of God to the
"grossest anthropomorphism." What bothered Lewis was the assumption that anthropomorphism was gross and simplistic.

Indeed, this was the assumption behind much liberal biblical criticism in the nineteenth century. As we have seen, Park and other neoclassical theists reduced Old
Testament anthropomorphism to gross images of wrath and simple images of love,
in Park's case the "fearful anthropomorphism" of God as a warrior or the "soothing"
image of God as a shepherd. Park and others could easily isolate and exaggerate these
images of God in the Old Testament because they assumed that love and anger must
be contradictory states—that is, not only opposite emotions but emotions that could
not truly coexist in the same kind of character.

This was precisely the sort of "gross" simplification to which Taylor objected. He
pointed out that Old Testament anthropomorphism did not separate God's love from
his anger. There was a complex fusion of these emotions. This was part of their power.
"We find," Lewis declared, "the awful equilibrium of the divine character maintained,
and apparently opposing attributes set forth in the same passage." Old Testament
anthropomorphism thus did not reflect the neoclassical and sentimental polarization
of emotions. But for Taylor this did not make Old Testament anthropomorphism
"gross." Rather, it was complex. And if it was complex, it might have something
important to say about God.[20]

This, in turn, led Lewis to ask whether there was any reason to assume that theism
was necessarily superior to anthropomorphism. Was one inherently more true of God
than another? Both were necessarily imperfect, as humans were imperfect. If the two
ways of representing God seemed at odds with each other, perhaps this was a reflection of human limitation, not a limitation of anthropomorphism. Perhaps both
anthropomorphism and theism presented aspects of God that were equally true and
from which human beings equally needed to learn. Perhaps theism conveyed God's
distance from people but anthropomorphism conveyed his nearness. Lewis groped
to express his idea here: "In other words, [God] would not be perfect and infinite, if
he could not in truth and reality, present to us the other side of Deity (to use the strange
expression with all reverence) which he truly and actually, and not merely by way of
metaphorical accommodation, 'comes down to see the children of men.'"[21]

With such thoughts, American theologians might have awarded anthropomorphism
a higher status than it had even achieved in the juristic tradition. The romantic
anthropomorphists were imagining that God really came "down to see the children
of men." But it was not as children that he came to see them. Calvin had offered a
standard juristic apology for anthropomorphism: "For who even of slight intelligence
does not understand that, as Nurses commonly do with infants, God is wont in a
measure to lisp with us." By the nineteenth century, Calvin's analogy no longer
worked. Nurses were no longer allowed to "lisp" the sorts of frightening images to

their wards that they had used in Calvin's day. Humanitarian reforms in child rearing had seen to that. Joseph Thompson in his 1860 work *Love and Penalty* rejected
the common claim that the Old Testament had been written for humanity in a childlike state. We would fire a nanny today, he pointed out, who threatened our children
the way Jehovah threatened the Hebrews. As a governmental theologian, Thompson
made his point to support the idea that God's threats were real.[22] Romantic anthropomorphists, however, went even further and claimed—along the lines of Taylor
Lewis—that God was not only real in his anthropomorphic anger but also strangely
appealing.

Where Taylor left off, Shedd began in an extraordinary essay published anonymously in Hodge's *Princeton Review* in 1863 entitled "The True Tone in Preaching
and the True Temper in Hearing." The essay reads as a point-by-point rebuttal of
Park's "Theology of the Intellect and That of the Feelings" from thirteen years earlier. That had been an essay intended to provide ministers with basic working principles of liberal biblical criticism. So was Shedd's, but he came at it from a radical,
conservative perspective. Their agendas were exactly opposite. Whereas Park elevated
theism, Shedd elevated anthropomorphism. Whereas Park celebrated the progress
of culture, which underlay his theistic view of God, Shedd condemned the cultural
movement that led to the decline of anthropomorphism—the "increasing civilization and over-refinement of the age." Since the time of Grotius—the founder of the
governmental theology—Shedd charged, Protestant theologians had turned away from
representing God in his emotional complexity and power.

In other words, they had turned away from anthropomorphism, what Shedd called
"the biblical representation of God," God as "an emotional person, or in Scripture
phrase, the 'living God.'" Through their biblical criticism, liberal theologians in the
previous 300 years had stripped God of half his character. The effort had been "to
literalize and emphasize the love, but convert the wrath into metaphor and hyper-
bole." Confident that they were historically progressive, these liberal theologians
imagined that they had advanced beyond the biblical characterization of God. They
imagined that they could contemplate God with the "serene spirit of angels," not the
mixture of reverence and fear with which the "children of Israel" looked to God. Shedd
drove the point home with the vigor of an Old Testament prophet: "Let, then, these
two specific personal qualities—the divine wrath and the divine love," Shedd
exclaimed, "be smitten, driven, hurled, like javelins into the consciousness of the
nations."[23]

There was a startling vision of history in this. As we have seen, receptivity to anthropomorphism has turned on views of history. Juristic theologians stressed their
historical continuity with the ancient Hebrews and saw the fortunes of Israel as a
paradigm for their own history. Such a historical perspective helped legitimate the
use of anthropomorphism in theological writing. The champions of philanthropism,
on the other hand, stressed their difference from the ancient Hebrews and primitivized
the Old Testament. Hodge had tried to sustain some historical continuity with the
ancient Hebrews by ascribing to them refined, neoclassical sensibilities. Shedd also
stressed historical continuity but ascribed to the ancient Hebrews a very different
character. For him their supposed primitiveness was what made them attractive.

Astonishingly, Shedd even speculated on the "educational" benefits of restoring "the mosaic system of sacrifices" in modern society. By contrast, liberal biblical critics in Shedd's day were at best making apologies for the practice even in primitive times. As we have seen, the Harvard biblical scholar and Unitarian George Noyes had likened the ancient Hebrews to the ancient Egyptians and Aztecs and dismissed the practice of "animal sacrifices" as "abhorrent to the feelings of enlightened nations." He added that "a false view" of the ancient rites of animal sacrifice "continues to uphold one of the most irrational doctrines which ever prevailed in the church"—the penal theory of the atonement.[24]

Even as a penal theologian, however, Shedd's flirtation with the idea of reinstating animal sacrifices was peculiar. The juristic theologians believed that the death of Jesus had ended the need for sacrifices. Shedd acknowledged all of this. His suggestion for restoring them was couched in hypothetical terms. The point, however, still held: people needed to be reminded of the punitive side of God's character, and what could do this better than confronting them, as the Hebrews of old, with a "frequent bleeding victim"?[25]

Short of reinstituting animal sacrifices, however, Shedd's serious proposal was that a full representation of God's character—his anger as well as his love—depended on the ministry. Ministers must convey the complex character of God to their congregations. Ministers should insist on doing this, and their congregations, in turn, should not ask for anything but this. This was the point of the title of Shedd's essay, "The True Tone in Preaching and the True Temper in Hearing." Shedd acknowledged that this would not be popular at first. The problem was not only that theologians had turned away from the biblical character of God. More insidiously, congregations, Shedd charged, had pressured ministers not to remind them of the wrathful side of God's character. Shedd suggested that there had grown up a kind of collusion between ministers and their congregations to avoid mention of God's anger and to speak only of his love. This was as irresponsible of ministers as it was of lay people. They should not shy away from God's anger. Rather, they should say with David, "Let the righteous smite me, and it will be a kindness."

Moreover, it will be exciting. This is where Shedd's romanticism came in. He argued that God's anger was awful and wonderful to behold. Shedd's romantic association of vitality with anger and guilt figured into his argument here. Once the members of a congregation allowed themselves to contemplate God's wrath against their sins, they would find the effect to be energizing. If this seemed counterintuitive, Shedd drew an analogy with the artistic effect of tragedy. If one had never seen a tragic play, one might suppose that it would be depressing. But the opposite was the case. Why exactly people enjoyed tragedies, however, was a difficult question. Indeed, this had been a key concern for eighteenth- and nineteenth-century literary critics, especially when trying to account for Shakespeare's power. Shedd briefly articulated a theory of tragedy similar to one developed by the eighteenth-century Scottish philosopher David Hume. The excitement of tragedy, Shedd argued, resulted from identification with the guilty protagonist. The protagonist's rising level of fear infects the audience. As the protagonist tries to escape his fate, the audience, in turn, feels a rising sense of "energy" in themselves to escape danger. But, of course, the audience does not leave the theater. Instead, their rising "energy" is channeled into their absorption in the play. With the climax, the audience is released from the grip of this absorption and feels a sense of peace.

Like an audience in their seats, the congregants in their pews would feel the rising excitement and release as they became convicted of their sins. One of Shakespeare's most famous characters served to illustrate the heightened awareness that comes from guilt. Let the man in the pew, like the man in the theater, restrain his natural energy to avoid pain, Shedd declared, and "compel his ear to doctrinal statements . . . that weigh like night upon his feelings, and that say to him, as did the voice that cried in the tormented soul of Macbeth, 'Sleep no more; rest and peace for thy present state are gone forever.'"[26]

The Vitality of God's Anger

All of this fit into Shedd's larger romantic vision of the vitality of God's anger. In "The True Tone in Preaching and the True Temper in Hearing," Shedd had claimed that the Hebrew mind had remained "vivid" while other ancient peoples, such as Persians and Hindus, had become "sluggish." The reason for this was that the Hebrews had a punitive God. And this was what gave Christian civilization its vigor. "This doctrine of expiation," Shedd wrote, "is like a ganglion in the human frame; it is a knot of nerves; it is the oscillating centre where several primal and vital truths meet in unity." Note here the romantic association between "primal" and "vital." Modern Christians in their "over-refinement" risked losing these "primal and vital truths." The solution was to forsake the prevalent fashions in theology and go back to the base of Christianity in ancient Judaism. "For the God of the selfish heart is the deity of sentimentalism," Shedd declared in another essay; "the God of the imagination and the taste is the beautiful Grecian Apollo; the God of the understanding merely is the cold and unemotional abstraction of the deist and the pantheist; but the God of the conscience is the living and holy God of Israel—the God of punishments and atonements."[27]

Key for Shedd in all of this was the romantic fascination with guilt as leading to a profound and electrifying sensitivity. As part of this, Shedd followed the romantics in portraying criminals and sinners as craving punishment on some deep psychological level. Similar notions had existed in the juristic tradition, whose theologians had used the term "satisfaction" in a legal sense to denote the meeting of God's judicial demands. But they also let the emotional connotations of the word "satisfaction" have play in their writing and even wrote of the conscience of the sinner gaining "satisfaction" (in both a legal and an emotional sense) in receiving a just punishment. Shedd drew on romantic imagery to express these notions of the pleasure of punishment in startling new ways.

All of this was common in romantic characterization. The eroticism of punishment was a major way in which romantics evoked emotional ambivalence and isolation. Romantic critics focused on Shakespearean characters, particularly Macbeth and Lear, to bring out this idea of a character achieving a kind of profound mental energy through his guilty conscience. Such characters populated the works of romantic poetry and became some of the most famous characters of romanticism, such as Coleridge's Ancient Mariner, Byron's Manfred, and Shelley's Alastor. Shedd himself drew on imagery from Shakespeare and Coleridge in this regard.[28]

This can be seen in his 1859 essay "The Atonement: A Satisfaction for the Ethical Nature of Both God and Man." Shedd portrayed sinners as craving punishment on a deep psychological level. For some scientific grounding, Shedd made a passing reference to Johann Heinroth's *Criminal-Psychologie*. But Shedd's primary evidence came from romantic literature. He summed up the conclusion to Samuel Coleridge's play *Remorse*. In this play, a wife avenged the murder of her husband by killing the murderer. The criminal actually welcomed this vengeance and felt the relief of an atonement for his crimes in his own lush death. "The guilty and guilt-smitten Ordonio is stabbed by Alhadra, the wife of the murdered Isidore," Shedd declared; "as the steel drinks his own heart's blood, he utters the one single word, 'Atonement!'" Not even forgiveness, Shedd added, had been able to "soothe" the guilty conscience of Ordonio. Stabbed by the wife of his victim, he felt released from the pain of his own conscience: "His self-accusing spirit actually feels its first gush of relief only as the avenging knife enters, and crime meets penalty."[29]

The atonement provided by Christ, in turn, enabled sinners to feel this compelling "gush" of vindicatory justice without being destroyed by it. The atonement thus gave sinners the best of both worlds. They could appreciate God's compelling anger and yet be sustained by his love. So God's anger at sin still served to excite sinners and raise them to a higher level of consciousness; but now they were preserved through this experience. Moreover, because of the atonement, sinners could also experience God's love, a love thrown into even greater relief by the atonement because it is experienced against the backdrop of God's anger.

Shedd spelled this out in his essay "The Uses of Fear in Religion." Here, in contrast to Park's aspersions against the "fearful anthropomorphism" of the Old Testament, Shedd argued that fear of God was a legitimate and profound religious emotion. It was also sublime. Shedd imagined a bewildering and awesome mixture of love and anger in God. It was this mixture that sinners experienced when God came to them. God's anger at sin, evident in an awakened conscience, was the first step in the sinner's encounter with God. "I am brought by this chapter in my experience into very close contact with my Maker," Shedd wrote in measured tones. Then the pace of his prose builds: God's anger suddenly crashes down upon the sinner and is about to overcome him when, through a quick series of transitions, the sinner recognizes that this anger is at once appropriate, given his sin, and yet has already been borne for him by Christ; so the sinner suddenly realizes that he can accept the awesome spectacle of God's anger, which is directed at his sin but does not destroy him because of the atonement. "Suddenly, he [the sinner] gives way, acknowledges that it is a good and just anger"; so the sinner "lets the billows roll over while he casts himself on the divine pity." The atonement, as it were, lets the sinner ride the vitality of God's anger but does not let it destroy him. More so, the sinner can see God's love best when it is thrown into relief against his anger: "For, paradoxical as it sounds," Shedd asserted, "God's love is best seen in the light of his displeasure."[30]

The imagery is even stronger in "The Atonement: A Satisfaction for the Ethical Nature of Both God and Man." In this essay, the conscience serves as the conduit for

God to come down to humankind. Shedd called the conscience a "relic" from man's state before the fall. He did not mean a relic in an antiquarian sense but almost in a medieval sense: the conscience was an object through which heaven and earth met. The conscience, Shedd wrote, was "the finite contacting point in man which corresponds with the infinite surface in God." The conscience shrunk time back to zero and put every man in the place of Adam in direct contact with God. Only now, because of sin, man did not walk with God in the cool of the evening but faced the fiery enormity of God's wrath. "Like hot lava down a mountain gorge," Shedd wrote of God in his anger bursting into the finite channel of man's mind. But because of the atonement, this volcanic downpour was suddenly not destructive but constructive. "Like Darien," Shedd wrote of the absolved conscience as the Panamanian strip of land, "the isthmus of volcanic fire that both divides and joins the oceans."[31]

The language of opposites—infinite and finite, fire and water—and their sudden reconciliation were common elements of the romantic encounter. Shedd's imagery also recalls the essay from four years earlier, "Is Effective Writing Necessarily 'Volcanic'?" Whether this was conscious or not we do not know. But Shedd's imagery does seem designed to recall a poem Shedd knew well. This was John Keats's famous sonnet, "On First Looking into Chapman's Homer." Keats had described the sublime awe of the Spanish explorer Cortes and his men "silent, upon a peak in Darien," when they suddenly discovered the object of their quest, the Pacific Ocean.[32]

The vigor that benevolence lacked in neoclassical theism and that sympathy lacked in sentimental incarnationalism God's anger gave to his love in romantic anthropomorphism. This was a vigor, however, that humanity, as the object of God's emotions, felt more than God himself felt, for Shedd only went so far with his romantic anthropomorphism.

Shedd mostly confined his use of anthropomorphism to depict how human beings experienced God, not how God experienced himself. There was a real difference between the two, not so much worked out explicitly but implied in Shedd's writing. It most likely reflects Shedd's basic acceptance of the neoclassical assumptions of the day, which were so important in guiding the depiction of God in American theology. It was one thing to say that because of sin people needed to experience God's anger as a passionate outburst; it was another thing to say that God—a perfect being—experienced his anger in this way.

Shedd tried to account for the difference in "The Atonement: A Satisfaction for the Ethical Nature of Both God and Man." In this essay, Shedd used the word "satisfaction" in the particular legal sense used by penal theologians. But inevitably the word also carried emotional connotations. And it was on this level that God's and man's experiences of God's anger at the atonement differed so much. This difference corresponded to different literary styles. In brief, whereas people got romantic satisfaction from the atonement, God got a neoclassical satisfaction. There was thus no outburst in God as he unleashed his anger. Rather, God felt serene from having directed his anger at a fit object. Thus, despite Shedd's romantic depictions of God from the perspective of the guilty sinner, when Shedd tried to imagine how God experienced himself, he edged back toward neoclassical theism.

One reason for this is pretty clear. Like Hodge, Shedd ensconced his characterization of God in neoclassical theism in order to shield his depiction of God from the liberal caricature of the juristic tradition. Shedd acknowledged the problem. He faced the caricature of the juristic God head-on. The effort was not so much to reject it, however, as to contain the damage. Shedd noted that the ascription of anger to God had become associated in the popular mind with making God into "an enraged and ugly demon." This was a caricature, Shedd pointed out. But he also admitted that there was a real point here: God and humans experienced anger differently. To explain this, Shedd relied on the polarization of emotions. There was nothing noble in people's experience of anger. "Anger and hatred," Shedd declared, "are indissolubly connected in our minds with mental wretchedness." But not so with God. Human beings found anger distressing, Shedd explained, because they often confused what they should hate with what they should love. God experienced no such confusion. This meant that he experienced no such turbulence in his anger. In fact, the contrary was the case. God was as serene in his anger as in his love. The reason was that God's anger and love were directed at their proper objects. "The deity is blessed in his displacency at that which is hateful," Shedd summed the matter up, "for pleasure is the coincidence between a feeling and its correlated object."[33]

This comes close to how Charles Hodge and Archibald Alexander Hodge had described God's holiness. How this holiness was distributed as anger and love depended on a series of object relations and thus had little bearing on how God experienced his feelings. Shedd, in short, was following the same tactic as the Hodges to preserve God's neoclassical serenity.

There was always a problem with this line of thought, however. What about when God expressed his anger at that which was loveable—such as Jesus? Would not this cause some turbulence, mixing up God's emotions like humans? This question had forced Archibald Alexander Hodge into some ingenious theological constructions. Shedd had gotten himself into the same corner. The difference was that Shedd handled this question in ways that pointed toward a romantic characterization of God's love.

How did God direct his anger onto his beloved son? And why did God not feel confusion or at least ambivalence when he prosecuted Jesus on the cross? To answer these questions, Shedd turned to the doctrine of the Trinity. In his essay on the atonement, Shedd used the Trinity as a forum for separating conflicting emotions in God. By a kind of psychological division of labor, the Son took on the Father's anger against sin, freeing the Father to express his love for the human race. There was no conflict in this, Shedd maintained, because in having the Son bear his anger, the Father was really bearing it himself. "Side by side in the Godhead," Shedd explained, "there dwells the impulse to punish and the desire to pardon; but the desire to pardon is realized in act, by carrying out the impulse to punish, not indeed upon the person of the criminal, but on that of the substitute. And the substitute is the punisher himself!"[34]

This use of the Trinity, however, took Shedd only so far. It might account for the internal dynamic of God's feelings, but how could it account for Jesus' very visible suffering when hanging on the cross? In his late work of 1888, *Dogmatic Theology*, Shedd wrestled with this question. He seems to have been as confounded as Park had been over how to account for Jesus' agony. Like Park, Shedd attributed a serene character to Jesus, but this only made the problem worse. Why, Shedd asked, would the "patient and mighty heart" of Jesus utter the cry, "My God, my God why hast thou forsaken me?"

Shedd remained cagey on the issue. Jesus' outcry "cannot be explained by natural laws"—no natural or human force could make Jesus cry out like this. So there was only one option. But, again, Shedd could barely bring himself to admit it. All he could say was that Jesus must have received "a stroke delivered by a divine person." Presumably this was God, but this is as far as Shedd would take it. How did Shedd manage to avoid the issue? Like Park, Shedd assumed that the "stroke" must have been a blow to Jesus' mind, and this prohibited further investigation. "Suffering is a form of consciousness," Shedd intoned, "and consciousness can only be known by the possessor of it."[35]

Despite this obfuscatory language, Shedd had arrived at an important point. If the physical evidence of Jesus' sufferings on the cross somehow made his mental sufferings impenetrable, this helped Shedd to shift attention back to the Trinity. This centering of the drama in the Trinity was the crucial new element, for it led Shedd to consider that the atonement was not the moment of greatest suffering for God. Instead, the moment of greatest suffering was the breakup of the Trinity at the incarnation. Shedd edged his way toward these conclusions. If Jesus bore God's anger, he also opened up God to express his love—not only for humanity but for Jesus himself. Though God acted out of wrath at the atonement, he actually "felt" love.[36] Ultimately, this meant that the crucifixion was not a scene of rupture between God and Jesus but a scene of reunion. It was the anger in God that had divided him and that had caused Christ to be sent out from the Trinity to bear this anger. Now, because God's anger was exhausted on Jesus, God's love could come out more fully, allowing for the integration of his emotions and the reintegration of the Trinity.

Bringing this thought around full circle meant that it was not the crucifixion but the incarnation that was the real moment of suffering for God and Jesus. The real pain was at the beginning of the incarnation, when the Father and the Son separated from each other, not at the end, when they reunited. Shedd imagined the moment in heaven when the Son accepted the Father's mission and departed for earth; that was the real moment of grief. That "transaction in the depths of the Trinity," Shedd declared, "cost the infinite and adorable Trinity an effort, a sacrifice that is inconceivable and unutterable."[37]

At the end of his career, Shedd had touched upon the romantic potential of the Trinity. It was key for ascribing romantic love, as well as wrath, to God. The breakup of the Trinity—the Father sending the Son down into the world—could be pictured as a moment of suffering, as Shedd did. Also, it could be pictured as a moment of birth, or even erotic release. Samuel J. Baird developed the first option, Horace Bushnell the second.

⚶

CHAPTER SIX

Love in the Trinity

James Henley Thornwell, George Griffin, and Samuel J. Baird

*T*he great problem with romantic love is that it makes a character look weak and confused. In neoclassicism, love blends with reason into a serene benevolence. Even in sentimentalism, where love is more properly a passion, one mainly suffers for others, not for oneself. But in romantic love you long for someone else and suffer for yourself. This is why in the end it was almost easier to ascribe romantic anger rather than romantic love to God. If anger in humanitarianism had been associated with weakness, in romanticism it could be associated with strength. Romanticism, in a sense, reverses the neoclassical and sentimental polarization of emotions, making love now look weak and anger strong. Romanticism also can shatter this polarization. Then you get the romantic emotional state par excellence: ambivalence. A character weakened by love may seek to assert himself through anger—at the person loved. Short of hating the beloved, the character moves from a longing love to paralysis and sometimes derangement. "To be wroth with one we love / Doth work like madness in the brain," wrote Coleridge. Yet in romanticism ambivalence need not be a disaster. It can be the threshold leading to a deeper understanding of the self and reconciliation with others.[1]

How could theologians ascribe such emotions to God? The weakness and frustration aside, with whom could God have this kind of romantic relationship? Neoclassical benevolence and sentimental love could easily be ascribed to God because both kinds of love did not have to be directed at equals. In fact, they worked better if there was an element of condescension. But there must be some level of parity between romantic lovers. They must be able to affect each other. How can this occur in monotheism? How can the Christian God have an equal to love?

The answer is that he always has equals in the Trinity. Christianity may be monotheistic, meaning one God, but this God is made up of three persons, Father, Son, and Holy Ghost. For this reason, the Trinity became important for some romantic anthropomorphists. James Henley Thornwell, George Griffin, and Samuel J. Baird— all conservative Calvinists—used the Trinity to imagine God in the company of equals with whom he could interact, thus bringing out different sides of his character. Two

aspects of this were particularly significant: the use of the Trinity to ascribe something analogous to sexual desire in God and the use of the Trinity to ascribe emotional complexity to him.

The Trinity and God's Desire

Key to the concept of the Trinity in the juristic tradition was the idea that God's character was parental. This was not just a metaphorical way of talking about God's relationship to humans as their creator. God's very nature was parental, and this was
shown in the Trinity. God the Father was in some literal way the parent of his Son.
There was an ongoing procreative tie between them (in some way the Father and the
Son also generated the Holy Ghost). The idea was that the Father perpetually generated the Son, even while the Son shared equal status with God the Father and the
Holy Ghost in the triune Godhead. These notions fed into the juristic theology of the
atonement, for it was because Christ was equal with God that he was able to bear the
full measure of God's concentrated wrath against the human race in the short time of
the crucifixion.

With the emergence of philanthropism, however, things began to change. Theologians questioned whether it was necessary for Christ to absorb God's entire judgment against the human race. Theologians also asked whether Christ really was the
equal of God. Unitarianism, coming out of Socinianism, of course, took these tendencies to their logical conclusion. But even where there was not an open rejection
of the Trinity in philanthropism, such as in the governmental theology, the significance of the Trinity began to diminish. One reason for this was that the decline of
anthropomorphism made it more difficult to depict the different members of the
Trinity as distinct persons.

Here is where the romantic anthropomorphists entered the picture. Their restoration of anthropomorphism and their interest in attributing complex feelings to God
all led them back to the Trinity. We have seen how this occurred in Shedd's case.
And we have seen how his use of the Trinity led him to emphasize God's parental
nature. Sentimental writers, of course, also relied on parental imagery for God. But
there was a difference: sentimentalists used parental imagery mainly to emphasize
God's sympathy with humanity. Romantics did this too, but they also ascribed anguish, frustration, wrath, and even disgust to God. This followed from the visceral
way in which the romantics depicted God's parental nature. It was in some sense
distinctly propagative or parental in a sexual sense. In this, romantic theologians were
drawing not only on traditional Christian notions of the Trinity but on Victorian
notions about sexuality.

This may sound strange, for we tend to think of the middle decades of the nineteenth century as "Victorian," meaning prudish. The reputation of Victorians here,
however, has often been exaggerated. A large part of it was created by turn-of-the-
century devotees of aestheticism, realism, and, later, Freudianism. In the late twentieth century, historians began uncovering the Victorian discussion of sexuality. And
there was, it turns out, quite a lot of it. Sexuality, of course, can be understood in
different ways. And this is the point. Victorians thought of sexuality differently from

the modern view, which emerged in the late nineteenth century. A key difference between Victorians and moderns turns on the perceived relationship between sexuality and reproduction. Moderns tend to assume that sexuality and reproduction are different considerations. Thus, they assume that what makes for good sex, as opposed to bad, has little to do with reproduction. Victorians, by contrast, at least in their formal discourse, tended to equate sexuality with reproduction. In their minds, that was what sex was for. That was what made it meaningful, enjoyable, and healthy. Therefore, it is really more accurate to write of Victorian ideas about propagation rather than sex per se. Good sex, in theory, was understood in terms of the family for the production of children; bad sex, often associated with prostitution, was seen to undermine the family.

This was not only pious sentiment. These views were supported by the science of the day, from phrenology in the first half of the nineteenth century to eugenics in the second half. Thinkers from across the spectrum—from conservative theologians to liberal feminists—picked up on these notions. And by all appearances, there was a substantial middle-class market for them. During the middle decades of the nineteenth century, dozens of advice books and marriage manuals for men and women went through numerous printings. These contained explicit and detailed instructions on how to care for one's body; how to resist temptation; how to select physical and temperamental characteristics in a mate for marriage; and how to engage in specific kinds of intercourse to produce desired traits in children.[2]

It is therefore not strange to find these views informing characterizations of God. Some theologians, such as the conservative Presbyterian Samuel Baird, emphasized the divine analogue of human propagation in the Trinity. Other theologians emphasized the human side of propagation. For instance, the liberal Congregationalist Henry Clarke Wright, who was trained at Andover Seminary in the early 1820s and later became a leading abolitionist, considered human propagation the key to salvation. "Marriage and parentage" (the title of one of Wright's works) were God's means of redemption.[3] Bushnell thought along similar lines. In his first major work, *Christian Nurture* (1847, revised in 1861), Bushnell imagined that parents might one day overcome original sin through what he called "propagated piety." In his late works, Bushnell (perhaps influenced by Baird) imagined God struggling to infuse new life into the human race. All of this helped theologians to ascribe desire to God in ways that made him into a romantic character.

The Trinity and God's Emotional Complexity

If the Trinity helped theologians to ascribe desire to God, it also helped theologians to ascribe emotional conflict, and even ambivalence, to him. This was the second important point about the Trinity for romantic anthropomorphism. What was significant about the Trinity is that it was an image of a perfectly harmonized being. But theologians could picture the incarnation and the atonement breaking up this harmony. We have seen how Shedd handled this and how it edged his characterization of God from neoclassical theism toward romantic anthropomorphism. By situating God in the Trinity, Shedd could ascribe suffering to him. Moreover, Shedd did not have to do this by depicting God tormenting Christ; Shedd could do it by writing about the breakup of the Trinity in the incarnation.

James Henley Thornwell and George Griffin took the breakup of the Trinity even further. Not only had the incarnation disrupted the Trinity, but Christ in his sufferings and death had been taken into the realm of Satan. A kind of reversal occurred here. From being bound to God in the Trinity, Christ became bound with Sin or Death (personified) in a kind of anti-Trinity. What could God's feelings toward Christ be now? How could God regard his son once he has gone over to the other side, as it were? In considering such scenes, Thornwell and Griffin suggested that God felt a mixture of love and hate as he regarded his Son overcome with evil.

In order to imagine such scenes, however, these theologians had to delve into some difficult areas of speculation. They had to suggest that at the atonement Christ had really been separated in some substantial way from God. To do this, they considered the atonement from unusual, but not unprecedented, angles. For instance, Griffin asserted that Christ had truly died, not only in his human nature but in his divine nature as well. Griffin also suggested that Satan had contributed to Christ's sufferings. This was not to say, however, that it was mainly Satan who tormented Christ (as in the ancient ransom theory of the atonement). God was still diverting his judicial wrath against sin onto Christ. But in exercising this wrath, God had opened the door for Satan to attack Christ. Indeed, Griffin suggested that Satan (or his forces) had been tracking Christ throughout his life. On the cross and during his death, Christ was almost swallowed up by the forces of evil.

There were some precedents for these scenarios. In fact, the notion that Christ had actually died and was in some sense given over to the devil was one way in which juristic theologians had accounted for Christ's distracted and anxious behavior. This was how Calvin had interpreted Christ's anxiety in the Garden of Gethsemane and his outcry on the cross, "My God, my God why hast thou forsaken me?" In these instances, Calvin explained, Christ was experiencing alienation from God, which was the result of death. To objections that Christ was behaving this way before he died, not after, Calvin replied that this was merely mincing words; the visible manifestations of Christ's sufferings recorded in the Gospels were not necessarily the same as the supernatural agony that Christ had suffered in his soul. "What Christ suffered in the sight of men," Calvin declared, was not the same as that "invisible and incomprehensible judgement which he underwent in the sight of God."[4] Park, as we have seen, drew a similar distinction between the hidden causes of Christ's sufferings and his visible behavior. But Park had used the distinction to forbid speculation into the secrets of Christ's passion.

Juristic theologians were not so inhibited. While noting the aura of mystery surrounding Christ's death, they pressed on with dramatic imagery to describe his torment. To be sure, they noted that a major cause of Christ's sufferings was God's wrath against the sins imputed to Christ. But juristic theologians also suggested that Satan and the devils had used the opportunity of Christ's vulnerability to attack him. And it was part of Christ's triumph that he resisted them. So, according to Calvin, Christ had to not only bear up under God's wrath but also "grapple hand to hand with the armies of hell." "All the powers of hell were let loose on him," John Owen declared. While on the cross, Christ saw Satan coming toward him. "He saw him coming with all his malice, fury and violence to set upon him, to ruin him if it were possible and that he had close contact with him on the cross is evident from the conquest that Christ there made of him," Owen asserted, adding, "which was not without wounds and blood; when he broke the serpent's head, the serpent bruised his heel, Genesis 3:15."[5]

Owen's reference to Genesis 3:15 was important, for it brought two aspects of the Trinity together: its propagative nature and its emotional complexity. Immediately following the account of Adam and Eve's fall came Genesis 3:15. In this verse, God declared that he would put "enmity" between the serpent and the "woman" and "between thy seed and her seed: it shall bruise thy head, and thou shalt bruise his heel." Juristic theologians had taken this as a prophecy of Christ. But more than this, they used the passage to imagine a struggle between two sorts of propagations: the devil's "seed" and the woman's "seed"; or, on another level, the human race, now taken over by sin, and God's generation of his son, who would enter the human race and redeem it. Juristic theologians also compared the offspring of these two tracks of propagation: one bred death, the other bred eternal life.

These notions led to some lavish speculation about the relationship between birth and death. Juristic theologians, and later romantic anthropomorphists, expounded on such paradoxical themes as Christ's death being a birth, the atonement bringing life out of death, and so on. Such discussion could easily become heady. But all of this had its logic. In the juristic doctrine of original sin, Satan could be pictured ruining Adam and Eve's power of propagation. Satan wrenches this power from God's purposes and uses it for his own. Rather than breeding offspring for eternal bliss as God had intended, humans now breed offspring in sin and therefore provide more victims for death. The only way to stop this chain of propagated sin might be for Christ to wrestle humankind's procreative power back from Satan. In this view, the atonement was a kind of rescue operation to save human sexuality. Samuel Baird imagined Christ, through his death, wrenching human beings' corrupted powers of propagation from sin and restoring their powers of generation by injecting some new divine element of grace into the human race.

Again, there were precedents for such rich imagery in the juristic tradition. John Owen expanded on the biblical imagery of Genesis 3:15 in his treatise *The Death of Death in the Death of Christ*. Owen declared that at the atonement the "seed of the woman" triumphed over "the seed of the serpent." The crucifixion, according to Owen, culminated not so much in Christ's death but in the death of death itself, thus canceling out, as a double negative would, Christ's death. This was why Christ's death was really a rebirth. It was both a new birth for humanity (a restoration of Eve's seed) and a second birth for Christ. Owen's contemporary John Howe (whom Shedd called the "loftiest of human spirits") made a similar argument. In his tract *The Redeemer's Dominion over the Invisible World, and the Entrance Thereinto by Death*, Howe called Christ the "only begotten Son" and "the first-begotten of the dead."[6]

In the middle of the nineteenth century, Griffin and Baird infused these scenes with romantic imagery. In this respect, they were like Shedd, who had updated juristic characterizations of God's anger with romantic vitality. There was, however, one substantial difference between the juristic theologians and the romantic anthropomorphists in their depictions of Christ's struggle with evil. In the juristic tradition, much of the drama came from imagining Christ battling Satan. But by the nineteenth century Satan had become a very indistinct character for theologians. The enlightenment, humanitarianism, and the effort to marginalize anthropomorphism had all contributed to this.[7] Once again, however, romanticism could help here. For, if the devil was out, romanticism introduced two other characters to take his place, Sin and Death.

As with so much nineteenth-century American theological writing, Milton was important here, especially the romantic take on Milton. Thornwell and Griffin drew on Milton's personifications of Sin and Death in *Paradise Lost*. Milton, of course, had also created a stunning character for Satan, which was celebrated by romantics. But Milton's Satan was not a great help to theologians. The problem was that Milton's Satan was so celebrated that he no longer seemed unambiguously evil; thus, a number of theologians demurred at the attractiveness of this character.[8] But if Milton's Satan had too much luster, Sin and Death were still suitably repellant. They were obscure and forbidding figures. Sin, in Milton's epic, was a female character whom Satan spontaneously generated and gave birth to out of his brain while still in heaven. He immediately has intercourse with his mental creation, which, he discovers later, has issued a progeny, Death. Death, in turn, rapes his mother, Sin, and keeps her on the borders of hell. Together, Satan, Sin, and Death form a kind of anti-Trinity, a Trinity bound together by rape and incest.[9]

All of this could be brought to bear on the atonement. There was a mirroring of the divine Trinity in the demonic threesome. In this demonic Trinity, Sin would correspond to Christ, the second person of the Trinity: Sin would provide the means to ruin humankind, Christ, the means to redeem it. James Henley Thornwell personified sin along these lines as the counterpart to Christ. But the imagery could be taken further. If Christ has to supplant his evil double, Sin, he also has to free humans from Death. It is Death, functioning as the third person of the demonic Trinity, who ultimately alienates the human race from God after the fall, just as from the opposite perspective the Holy Ghost, after the atonement, begins to sanctify the redeemed and prepare them to reunite with God. George Griffin used such imagery to depict the struggles that Christ underwent during his death.

It was shrewd of Griffin to draw on Milton's figure of Death. After Satan, Milton's Death was the character from *Paradise Lost* most celebrated by romantic critics. Edmund Burke and Samuel Coleridge singled out this character for special praise. Death, the biblical "king of terrors," was in Milton's formulation a giant, crowned, shapeless, shadowy mass. In Milton's epic, Satan mistakenly goes to battle with Death on the borders of hell before recognizing this monster as his own progeny. Death's very obscurity contributed to his sublime nature. Even such a neoclassical theologian as Park referred to the "king of terrors" in his popular sermons as a way to invoke the specter of death.[10] But, beyond this, Park did not do much with the figure of Death. George Griffin, however, vividly used Milton's image of Death to depict Christ's sufferings in hell.

Liberals and the Trinity

Conservatives were lucky to have the Trinity for all of this drama. Liberals, by contrast, had lost access to this drama of the Trinity, just as they had lost access to the dramatic anthropomorphism of the Old Testament. As a consequence, it became difficult for them to ascribe complex emotions to God, much less to ascribe any divine or demonic sufferings to Jesus. It took the highly idiosyncratic Bushnell to find a way to construct romantic anthropomorphism out of liberalism (albeit with some borrowings from conservativism). Most liberals could not come close to depicting God with this complexity.

For instance, Channing's characterization of God derived no drama from Channing's vision of hell. This was not just a theological point—that in Channing's theology sin punished itself and could never be turned directly against Christ—it was also a literary point. Channing's sense of good and evil existed in two different literary worlds. He depicted goodness according to neoclassical norms. But when it came to evil, Channing drew on romanticism. He even drew on a romantic appreciation of Milton's Satan. This is what made Channing's depiction of hell so compelling. According to Channing, those who persisted in sin and ignored God's benevolent powers of renewal condemned themselves to hell. This, in Channing's formulation, was a special kind of hell. In Channing's hell, the self-condemned would become almost perverse gods unto themselves. Each would fashion a unique world of horrors as befitted the condemned individual's sins. In depicting this, Channing ascribed to the self-condemned some of the perverse vitality of Milton's Satan. Channing did all of this, of course, not to glorify sinners. He did it to spare his neoclassical God from having to get mixed up in the sordid business of punishing sin. But for this very reason hell became the most dramatic place in Channing's theology. Distanced from this, Channing's God became more and more vague and his Christ more and more stolidly neoclassical.[11]

Channing could not see what he was missing. His neoclassical assumptions about God prevented him from appreciating the possibilities for drama in conservative theology. Of course, such possibilities may not have been foremost in his mind. But still it is remarkable how he applied his own neoclassical assumptions to Trinitarians. For instance, Channing assumed that Trinitarians must make Christ impassive because they believed he was God. This, Channing declared, "follows necessarily from the immutableness of the divine nature which they ascribe to Christ." Certainly this was logical. But Channing took it to an extreme for the purposes of caricature. Thus, he declared that Trinitarians really believed that Christ felt nothing on the cross. Indeed, Channing claimed that in conservative theology Christ hung on the cross without a care in the world: "The divine mind of Christ, that which was most properly himself, was infinitely happy at the very moment of the suffering of his humanity. Whilst hanging on the cross, he was the happiest being in the universe, as happy as the infinite father." "Not only does their doctrine," Channing continued, "when fully explained, reduce Christ's humiliation to a fiction, it almost wholly destroys the impressions with which his cross ought to be viewed."[12]

This was a clever polemic. But it may sound hypocritical coming from the theologian who argued that, by the power of his mind, Christ was moved by no passion—neither fear, nor anger, nor pity—in response to the mobs persecuting him. Rather, Channing's Christ always kept his mind on the high ideals of benevolence. But to call Channing hypocritical here is to miss an important point. Channing faulted Trinitarians not for holding Christ to a neoclassical ideal but for their supposed view that Christ's neoclassical fortitude took no effort, that it came easy to him because he was divine. If Christ remained serene simply because it was in his nature as God, then there was no reason to honor him for his resilience. Channing had a point. The problem was that it did not apply to many conservatives.

The reason was that Channing failed to take two things into account about the conservative scheme. First, if God was punishing Christ, then even if Christ was divine he might suffer and in some sense die. Second, Channing also neglected the fact that some conservatives had a more complex understanding of God's nature than the one Channing attributed to them. But this would have been difficult for Channing to appreciate because Channing's own characterization of God had become so simplified.

Channing did have a point, however, when he charged that some Trinitarians had reduced Christ's sufferings to a "fiction." This polemic found its mark against governmental theologians. In fact, this had been an old rebuttal against the argument that Christ had not really suffered on the cross. Calvin asked whether Christ had just been going through the motions, "as if in sport." This sort of criticism was turned against governmental theologians and dogged them for 300 years into the nineteenth century. From the right and the left, penal and moral theologians ganged up on the governmental moderates in the middle, accusing them of reducing Christ's sufferings to a fiction.[13] And governmental theologians did have a problem here. Unlike the Unitarians, they held onto the doctrine of the Trinity; but unlike the penal theologians, they did not believe that Christ had suffered the full measure of God's wrath against sin. Thus, they were always brought back to this problem: why had Christ, the Son of God, become so unnerved by a symbolic punishment? The Unitarian and penal positions both seemed to make more sense. Either Jesus was not God and, with some resilience, had withstood his human persecutors, or Jesus was the Son of God and bore the concentrated penalty of God's judgment against sin and suffered accordingly. To explain Christ's behavior, it helped to go one way or the other, not cut down the middle as the governmental theologians did. We have seen some of the expedients they resorted to in order to account for Christ's conduct—for instance, Park's notion that God had given Jesus a secret vision of hell, causing him to suffer as if he were actually there. But such expedients seemed to substantiate the charge that Christ's suffering was only a fiction.

One solution was simply to give in to the charge. To some extent, this is what the governmental theologian James Murdock did. His work is significant here, for it may have influenced Thornwell. Murdock blurred the difference between what was real and what was fictional when it came to God. The question Murdock posed was this: if Christ's sufferings were dramatic enough to move God, then who could criticize them for not being real?

James Murdock was a professor of sacred rhetoric and ecclesiastical history at Andover while Park was a student there. Four years before Park arrived, in 1823, Murdock delivered a sermon in the Andover chapel that subsequently achieved some notoriety (and controversy, for the seminary was not yet entirely committed to the governmental theology). The sermon was called simply "The Nature of the Atonement." A portion of the sermon was given to defending the governmental theology from the charge that it reduced Christ's sufferings to a "mere fiction." Murdock, being a governmental theologian, did not deny the symbolic aspect of Christ's sufferings.

But he tried to dislodge the notion that, because they were symbolic or dramatic, these sufferings were unworthy of attention. He did this by emphasizing that the atonement was a moving event to behold—moving not only for humans and the universe at large but also for God himself. It was this last point that made Murdock's view of the atonement striking. "The atonement was an exhibition or a display," he explained, "that is, it was a symbolical transaction. It was a transaction in which God and his Son were actors; and they acted in perfect harmony, though performing different parts in the august drama. The Son, in particular, passed voluntarily through various scenes of humiliation and sorrow and suffering; while the Father looked on with all that tenderness and deep concern which he—and none but he—could feel."[14]

Murdock never explicitly answered the criticism that by being "actors" God and Christ could not really be said to be suffering at the atonement. But if Christ's sufferings were dramatic, God's emotions in watching him seemed real enough. And if this was the case, then who could say that Christ's sufferings were not real enough? Besides, it could be asked, if God and Christ were the "actors," then who was to say what was "real" and what was "fiction"?

The question of the relationship between the real and the fictitious in Christ's sufferings was important for a number of romantic anthropomorphists. Thornwell and Griffin (both penal theologians) devised their theories of the atonement partly to argue against the governmental theology. Their point, in short, was that Christ's death was real, not a fiction. There is some irony in this, for in order to emphasize the reality of Christ's death, they had to draw on fiction. In particular, they argued for the reality of Christ's death through allusions to Milton's personifications of Sin and Death. By now, however, the irony of this should not surprise us, for it does not seem to have bothered Thornwell and Griffin. This shows again how little polemical language tells us about what theologians were really doing. Thornwell and Griffin denounced governmental theologians for making the atonement into a fiction. All the while, they drew on fiction to emphasize the reality of the atonement.

James Henley Thornwell

In the antebellum South, James Thornwell was the leading Presbyterian theologian. He was the closest that Southern Presbyterians came to producing a theologian with the prestige of Charles Hodge in the North.[15] Thornwell was the son of a plantation overseer in South Carolina. He went north for his seminary education because he wanted better training in languages. He studied German and Hebrew briefly at Harvard, and he attended classes at Andover Seminary, which he found "awfully New School," meaning governmental in its theology. This was in 1834, eleven years after Murdock had delivered his famous sermon, four years after Park had graduated from Andover, and two years before Park returned to begin his long reign at the seminary.[16]

When Thornwell returned to South Carolina, he took up the conservative penal theology, but he did not forget the governmental emphasis on the atonement as a display. Rather, like a number of penal theologians who had considered the governmental theology, he was intent on showing that the atonement was real and yet also a dramatic demonstration of God's justice and the evil of sin. This combination also may have come naturally to Thornwell, given that in his own career he had taught both literature and theology. Like Shedd at the University of Vermont, Thornwell began his career as a professor of "belles lettres" at South Carolina College. While there he delivered a sermon in the college chapel that was published in 1845 under the title "The Necessity of the Atonement." Like Murdock's "Nature of the Atonement," Thornwell's sermon emphasized that the atonement was indeed a display and one that involved God and Christ deeply. In fact, Thornwell attempted to show that the dramatic nature of the atonement stemmed necessarily from God's own nature; because God was constituted as a Trinity, he must display his virtue and contrast it with sin.

In "The Necessity of the Atonement," Thornwell argued that the Trinity was a social unit. He was particularly concerned with the "social relations of the Trinity." The fact that God existed as a Trinity, Thornwell argued, showed that God's character was fundamentally social. In this, God was like humans, Thornwell suggested, relying on Aristotle's definition of man as a social animal. But unlike human sociability, God's was perfect because his morality was perfect. His morality was also immutable; if this were not so, God's constitution as a Trinity must necessarily break up. In other words, if they were not perfect, the Father, Son, and Holy Ghost would not have been able to get along together. "It is certain that its social relations must have been the source of eternal confusion and disorder," Thornwell wrote of the Trinity, "unless they had been marked by the strictest integrity, fidelity and truth." The point was to make God's Trinitarian character a basis for explaining the atonement. In particular, three aspects of God's Trinitarian character determined the necessity and nature of the atonement: God's immutable opposition to sin; his interest in revealing himself to the creation—for as a social being, God must inevitably want to show himself; and his interest in contrasting himself with sin, which meant exposing the true nature of sin to mankind and all intelligent creatures in the universe.[17]

The third point was key. It was what made the atonement especially dramatic. In order to focus the attention of the entire universe onto the evil of sin, God had to take it upon himself. He had to wear it, as it were, if he wanted everyone to look at it. And here, for Thornwell, was the special ingenuity of the atonement: Christ not only revealed the heights of God's love but exposed the depths of sin's evil nature. This made the atonement an extraordinary showpiece of moral contrasts. In "the theatre of eternity," Thornwell exclaimed (revealing, perhaps, the influence of Andover's governmental theology), the cross became the "center of universal attraction." The angels gazed in "rapture" at the crucifixion of Christ. What an extraordinary moment this was, Thornwell exclaimed; it was the "sublimest" event in the "records of eternity." On the cross, Christ drank the "cup of suffering" to the "dregs" and exhausted the immutable penalty of the law. That he was able to do so showed his moral perfection and that he was a true member of the Trinity and so revealed God's true nature.[18]

But by bearing the penalty due sin, he also exposed sin's true nature. Unlike Park, who hypothesized that God implanted a private vision of sin in Christ's brain, Thornwell emphasized the visible nature of Christ's sufferings. This was an astonishing revelation. Thornwell pealed off the neoclassical serenity and immutability of the Trinity as Christ mutated into a personification of sin. This metamorphosis crossed the humanitarian polarization of emotions, from the serenity of neoclassical benevolence to the physical agitation of suffering. "What a commentary on its intrinsic demerit and turpitude is furnished in the groans, agony and anguish of the Son of God!," Thornwell exclaimed; "in the cross, it is proclaimed, in living characters, to be the thing which God hates."[19]

What were these "living characters," this hateful thing Christ had become? It was sin personified. "Learn the estimate to be put upon Sin," Thornwell declared to the young men of South Carolina College: "there, stripped of her blandishments, unmasked in her treachery, exposed in her seductions, she stands revealed in the hideous deformity of her nature, odious to God and deadly to man. Her steps lead down to death, and her feet take hold on hell."[20]

This was an extraordinary transformation of Christ. The exchange is almost a one-to-one correspondence of opposites. Christ—through his physical writhing—mutates from the character of God to the figure of Sin. Rather than posessing intrinsic integrity, Christ becomes the image of intrinsic evil. Rather than dwelling in the serene, theistic harmony of the Trinity, Christ takes on the "turpitude" of sin. Rather than exemplifying immutability, he becomes the traditional misogynist personification of mutability, a woman whose attractions are false and conceal her "hideous deformity." From the spirit of God that points to heaven, sights are lowered to the feet of the woman that lead to hell.

Thornwell's writing here was deft but creepy. His depiction of Sin has a prurient mixture of eroticism and disgust. There are resonances with the common scene in Juvenalian satire, as picked up by early eighteenth-century English poets such as Jonathan Swift, of an innocent suitor stumbling upon his lady, unmade-up, at her toilette. As the darker side of neoclassicism, this satiric sensibility could easily merge with romantic characterization once the tone of moral condemnation receded and a voice expressing ambivalence emerged.

The work also resonated with the contemporary religious discourse on prostitution. Moral condemnation here might be combined with prurient interest. The Princeton Seminary graduate turned social reformer, John McDowall, in his journal detailing the horrors of New York City prostitution, *Magdalen Facts*, made use of the same passage Thornwell used from the Old Testament Book of Proverbs: "Her house is the way of death, and her path lays hold to hell."[21] Similar to the way in which McDowall's warnings against prostitution are peppered with lascivious details, Thornwell's exposure of Sin seems designed (however unconsciously) to titillate as well as to repel. Moreover, the nature of her exhibition suggests a slave auction, a common sight in South Carolina in the 1840s and one undoubtedly familiar to the son of an overseer. The passage finally recalls Milton's famous personification of Sin in *Paradise Lost*. It was the allure of this figure that Thornwell sought to unmask.

Thornwell's theory of the atonement, however, was vulnerable on theological grounds to a common charge. The criticism that it reduced Christ's suffering to a fiction was not so much relevant here. But another charge could be laid against

Thornwell: his theory placed too much weight on the power of deterrence. In his sufferings on the cross, Christ revealed the nature of sin. But it could be asked of Thornwell, was it not a little late for this? Or, to put the question in terms of Thornwell's figures, was not more needed to save humankind than simply to unmask the allures of Sin? Had not Sin already fatally tempted humans and bound them over to her son, Death? What people needed now was to be rescued from Death and to have their powers of propagation cleansed from their embrace of Sin.

A vision along these lines was developed by George Griffin in 1846, a year after Thornwell's sermon appeared in print. The title of Griffin's work, *The Sufferings of Christ*, got right to the dramatic point at hand. Griffin used romantic imagery to depict Christ (and God above) wrestling with Sin and Death in an agonizing effort to free human life from their grip.

George Griffin

Griffin was a successful New York City lawyer, not a theologian. His brother, however, was. Edward Griffin had studied with Jonathan Edwards, Jr., had been professor of Rhetoric briefly at Andover Seminary and president of Williams College for fifteen years, and was a popular preacher whose collections of sermons sold widely. George Griffin, by contrast, initially published his book anonymously as a "Layman." The book proved successful, however, and he allowed his name to be printed in later editions. Reviews in the conservative theological press were enthusiastic, particularly praising the way in which Griffin denounced the "scholastic" theism of the governmental and moral theologians. Like Shedd, Griffin condemned theologians who thought the Bible was too harsh and preferred an "abstract" deity. Griffin's work thus gave conservative reviewers a chance to bash liberals.[22]

But many conservatives demurred at the extent of Griffin's anthropomorphism. Griffin's detailed depictions of Christ's suffering—and more so, the sufferings of the Father—were too heady for most conservatives. Reviewers thus made a point of noting that Griffin was only a "layman," and they dismissed much of his extraordinary anthropomorphism as simply intemperate language. His "highly colored phraseology," as one reviewer put it, was "reverent, but exceedingly bold and in some instances rather hazardous." Still, the book had fire. Taylor Lewis, who, as we have seen, urged a return to biblical anthropomorphism, had his doubts about Griffin's work but acknowledged its power. He also admitted that he had been prepared "to find fault with the style as too rhetorical and impassioned" but then concluded that just such a thing was needed "to arouse attention," to wake up the church from "lethargy." Almost like Park, these theologians were willing to allow a "theology of the feelings" some leeway if it gave a needed corrective to the "theology of the intellect." But these conservatives were willing to go much further than Park. The church, Lewis charged, needed to fasten on the image of a "divine, agonizing redeemer." "It is the intense contemplation of this central truth, of this *peculiarity* of Christianity," Lewis concluded, that can startle people out of their "fancied righteousness and resolutions of reform."[23]

In their discomfort with Griffin's anthropomorphism, however, these reviewers were making apologies for his writing that it is not likely Griffin himself would have made. Griffin did indeed insist on the peculiar nature of Christianity, but there is no reason to think that his rhetoric was designed simply to startle. This was his point: Christianity was strange. Indeed, to his mind, the awesome strangeness of the atonement testified to its reality. And the reality of the atonement, the reality of every aspect of it, including, and especially, the reality of Christ's death, was what Griffin wanted to emphasize. The target of his work was the governmental notion that Christ had not suffered the literal penalty of the law so had not really died. Griffin joined in the common ridicule of this as reducing Christ's death to a "mere fiction." Griffin's intention was to describe the real death of Christ. To do this, he drew on literature.

In particular, Griffin used literary allusion and imagery to describe the indescribableness of death. Literature, in fact, helped Griffin to get over a difficult point: that Christ had, in his divine nature, died at the atonement. Now, it could be asked, was it not a logical impossibility for Christ's divine nature to suffer death? If divinity meant anything, did it not mean immortality? Griffin's response to this was to change the question. The relevant question, according to him, was not about the nature of divinity but about the nature of death. How did we know what was possible or impossible when it came to death, he asked. We do not even know what death means for ourselves, he claimed, citing Hamlet's soliloquy on death as the "undiscovered country." So how did theologians know that it was impossible for Christ to die? Ignorance about death, however, did not mean that the only response was silence. Rather, there was a kind of negative language for death. Romantic invocations of death called up images of inscrutability, blindness, and terror. And yet despite the obscurity associated with death, romantics also found something uncanny and familiar about death, and this gave death its sublime quality. All of this came together in Milton's image of Satan meeting and at first not recognizing Death as his own illicit offspring.[24] It was this romantic sense of Milton's character Death that Griffin drew on to describe the experiences of Christ and God at the atonement.

Christ's descent into hell meant leaving the Trinity. For Griffin, however, both the Trinity and hell were much more tactile than for Thornwell. The Trinity was not just a "society" bound by the perfect exercise of principles of "integrity, fidelity and truth." Griffin's Trinity was closer. He wrote of the "conclave," the "brethren of the Trinity," "holding communion with their glorious selves." Then came the incarnation: "The second person of the Trinity 'emptied himself' of the glory and beatitude of his Godhead." He left all of this for his new companion, Death. Again, there was a tactile element to this relationship. From the "manger," to the "workshop of Joseph," through Christ's "terrestrial pilgrimage," Death stalked him, as a "shadow," as "a claw with a vulture's grasp [in his] bosom." Calvary, according to Griffin, was the "consummation" of Christ's lifelong communion with Death, "not its inception."[25]

In a sense, then, the incarnate Christ had never lived. There could be no "life of Christ," no incarnationalism, for Death had always been with him. His true birth came when he was finally released from Death. His birth was not in Bethlehem but when the stone was rolled from the tomb. What happened in between the cross and the tomb, when Christ had passed through hell, was obscure for then he had been in the realm of the "king of terrors." What happened there was barely revealed to us by "Inspiration." But Griffin did not hesitate to speculate.

> The viewless recess, in which were consummated the sufferings of the Prince of Life in his ethereal essence, witnessed throes and spasms sufficient to have dissolved the material universe, had it not been upheld by the power of its agonized creator. There, where the sword of hosts inflicted on God the Son, "the chastisement of our peace," was the scene of concentration and sublimation of unearthly agonies which Inspiration could but faintly intimate to our mortal vision even by the vague and shadowy and appalling figure of the king of terrors.[26]

This was an extraordinary passage. "Inspiration" here for "the vague and shadowy and appalling figure of the king of terrors" came as much from Milton as from the Bible. This, however, did not bother reviewers. Rather, they were shocked by Griffin's characterization of God. If Christ's death was "too highly colored" (as one reviewer put it), Griffin's depiction of God the Father went beyond bounds. "We are still more appalled," wrote an otherwise supportive reviewer, "when he speaks of the 'throes and spasms' of the suffering Godhead."[27]

Perhaps what made this passage so scandalous was that it (like so much else in Griffin's book) was so tactile. But this was powerful writing. It brought the sufferings of Christ closer than Thornwell had depicted them. Thornwell had used a standoffish vision of Sin, an exposure of her. Griffin, going with the logic of the inscrutability of Death, took readers into the obscurity and made them feel it. Even God does not seem to see what is happening. But he has to hold the creation together. He has to hold it through the death pangs of Christ, which radiate outward from the hidden scene through "throes and spasms," all the way up to the "agonized creator."

The language is so heady it brings us back to Milton. Sin, as part of her punishment, is condemned by God to bear the "hell hounds," dogs that wriggle out of her womb to gnaw on her then creep back inside where they (in Milton's words) "bark'd and howl'd within unseen."[28] Sin's punishment of continually bearing ravenous dogs was a foreboding of God's punishment of Eve (and all women) with labor pains and of all humanity with the propogation of sin through its offspring. The fact that in Griffin's vision Christ entered the "viewless recess" suggests that he was entering Sin. The "Prince of Life" was displacing there the offspring of Satan's son, the Prince of Death. In the "concentration and sublimation of unearthly agonies," Christ seems to have exhausted the propagation of sin and pain. More than suffering just death, Christ was suffering the cumulative pain of every birth of sinful humans. In Griffin's passage, Christ very viscerally had become, in John Howe's words, "the first begotten of the dead."

Did God have the propagative power in himself to save humankind? Samuel J. Baird argued that he did. Baird, unlike Thornwell and Griffin, emphasized God's own propagative power. God did not have to humiliate Sin or wrestle this power away from Death. Christ did not have to become "the first begotten of the dead" to restore human beings to life. Rather, as the "only begotten son" of God, Christ had it in himself to communicate a new life force to humans.

Samuel J. Baird

It is appropriate that Samuel John Baird developed the idea of God giving birth to Jesus. Baird's own birth—at least to his father—seemed nearly miraculous. Prior to Samuel's birth, his father had lost seven children. He desperately wanted a son. So when his eighth child was born, he named him Samuel John—asked of God, given of God. Baird followed an unusual path into the ministry for a conservative Northern Presbyterian. As with Shedd, this may have given Baird an independent strain of thought. He was raised in Ohio and partially educated in Pennsylvania but finished his education and spent much of his career in the South. Southern Presbyterianism (Thornwell's early education in the governmental theology notwithstanding) tended to be less accommodating of liberalism than Presbyterianism in the North. Whether this was the source of Baird's strong conservativism is not known, but when he came north and settled down as a Presbyterian pastor in Woodbury, New Jersey, in 1849, he took a more aggressive stance toward liberalism than the prevailing tone set at Princeton.

Baird remained on the watch against liberalism all of his life. Among other works by Baird was a history of the decline of Presbyterianism in England entitled *The Socinian Apostasy*. In 1869, the conservative Old School and liberal New School wings of the Northern Presbyterian church reunited. Baird vociferously opposed this and wrote a history of the 1837 breakup of the church to remind his fellow Old School Presbyterians of the issues that had led to the division. For this, he was increasingly written off as a controversialist and a crank. It was thus easy to forget his greatest work. It was not just an attack on liberalism; it was also an attack on Hodge's brand of conservativism.[29]

This was Baird's mammoth 700-page 1860 treatise entitled *The First Adam and the Second: The Elohim Revealed in the Creation and Redemption of Man*. In this work, Baird characterized God by his propagative nature. God's propagative power defined who he was in himself—that is, within the Trinity—and defined who he was in relationship to human beings. One point followed from the other. To understand God's relation to people, Baird argued, one had to begin with God's relationship to himself in the Trinity.

Baird made the Trinity particularly sexual in character. For Thornwell, it had been social; for Griffin, it had been tactile; but for Baird, it was intimate. Relying on long-standing Christian tradition, Baird described the Father as perpetually generating the Son. The word "Elohim" in Baird's title was an ancient Hebrew word for God. Because the word had a plural suffix, Christian theologians had long used this grammatical point to argue that the ancient Hebrews had known about the Trinity. Baird, however, took the significance of the word even further. He suggested that the "Elohim" referred to the propagative impulse of God the Father. This impulse had led God to generate the Son and, in a more general sense, to create the universe and everything in it. In the creation, however, God had fashioned two special beings. What made them special is that God had given them two traits in common with himself. They had immortal souls and the capacity to reason. These were the angels and humans.

Here again, however, Baird made sexuality significant. This was the difference between angels and humans. God had given humans a point of resemblance with himself that he had not given to the angels. This was a propagative power. The angels had immortal souls and could reason, but they could not reproduce. Reproduction, however, was not the only issue. Animals and plants could reproduce. But God had given to humans the power to generate a new, immortal, and rational soul through reproduction. In this, human sexuality was analogous to God's creative power. Human propagative power was an awesome, Godlike force. This power in humans, Baird argued, was what the Bible meant when it said that man was made in the image of God. Man was really made in the image of the Trinity: propagation being the image of the Father and the Son (breath being the image of the Holy Ghost). And, in a special sense, Adam's relation to the race was analogous to God the Father's relation to the Trinity. "He was the likeness of the Elohim, God the Father," Baird wrote of Adam, "as the representative of the Godhead, and head of the subsistence of the other persons. In Adam the generative function was designed as a means of revealing that mysterious generation which is in God."[30]

This was an astonishing statement. Baird paused to caution his readers not to imagine that God's mode of generation was "anything analogous to the mode of carnal generation." Still, Baird went on to assert that the propagative nature of humans was a unique exemplar of God's true nature. Anthropomorphism, then, was not some primitive form of revelation. Nor was it an erroneous projection of human nature onto God's. On the contrary, anthropomorphism was a legitimate way to understand God, for God himself had stamped his own nature on that of humans. This made man's most intimate understanding of himself a revelation of God. "Man's nature," Baird declared, "was in this respect constructed as it is, for the express purpose of shedding forth the likeness of God."[31]

This was a challenge to the common conservative theology (never mind liberalism). In particular, it ran against Hodge's theology. Baird made no secret of this. His book's title, *The First Adam and the Second*, announced that Baird was taking on Romans 5, the touchstone of Hodge's theology. In a lengthy consideration of Hodge's interpretation of these verses, Baird criticized Hodge's argument that Adam and Christ served as the federal heads, or representatives, of humanity. The mere fact of their representing humans, Baird complained, did not make it just for God to impute sin to all people because of Adam's sin, nor did it make it just for God to impute righteousness to the elect because of Christ's righteousness. Hodge's theory, Baird declared, came down to an "arbitrary transfer" of sin and righteousness. Only a deep, intimate, and sustained connection could make the "transfer" of sin and righteousness legitimate. Baird found this intimate connection in God's propagative nature and in the propagative nature he had given to Adam and Christ. All humans were sinners because all descended by propagation from Adam. But then how were people made righteous? It must also be through propagation. If Adam was the progenitor of the sinful human race, then Christ, in some sense, must be the progenitor of the redeemed race. This was the meaning of the second part of Baird's title: *The Elohim Revealed in the Creation and Redemption of Man.*[32]

God, Adam, and Christ, then, were all defined by their propagative nature. And, in a sense, they were all linked because of this. God's nature was revealed in the propagative capacity of all humans, but especially in Adam, for, as mentioned, Baird believed that Adam stood to the rest of the human race as God the Father stood to the Trinity. God, according to Baird, had given to Adam "a prolific constitution," analogous to God's own constitution. But, following the fall, this "constitution" became perverted. Rather than founding a race of blessed immortal souls, Adam's Godlike powers of reproduction founded a race of sinners destined for eternal misery. Adam's fall, therefore, according to Baird, required God to draw directly on his own propagative nature to save the race. He did this by sending out of the Trinity the "Second Adam," Christ. Christ would duplicate Adam's trial on earth, but this "Second Adam" would not fail. He would pass the test by successfully withstanding Satan's temptation. Having passed through this trial, he could proceed to take Adam's place and save the human race. By suffering and dying, he provided an atonement for human sin and become the progenitor of the new race of the redeemed.

How Christ actually did this is not clear in Baird's work. Baird did not spell out how the propagative transmission occurred between Christ and the redeemed. Baird's language here remained obscure. Though it was the climax of his book, it was understandably hard for Baird to depict this. At best, he drew on some traditional, juristic analogies and stretched them. For instance, Owen, in *The Death of Death in the Death of Christ*, had written: "By the seed of the woman is meant the whole body of the elect, Christ in the first place as the head, and all the rest as members."[33] It was this sort of language that Baird was reaching back to, and in doing so he was drawing on the anthropomorphic side of the juristic tradition. He wrote of the race "engrafting in [Christ] as his members."[34] It is not clear, however, whether Baird was using organic language as metaphors or to describe a literal process.

Whatever he actually thought (and he may not have known for sure himself), Baird was also struggling with a new sort of anthropomorphic language, one that was closer to romanticism. In this language, Christ was not just the legal head for the human "members" of his body. Rather, these organic metaphors allowed a fuller range of suggestive connotation. Christ was a propagative force entered into the human race. In some sense, God, in sending Christ to save the human race, was lending humans his own propagative nature. Christ was a kind of conduit for God to inject his vitality into the human race. Not the fifth chapter of Romans but the prophets provided Baird with his touchstone verses here. Baird cited Isaiah 53:10: "He shall see his seed. . . . He shall see the travail of his soul." God's wrath came down onto Christ as "the climax of exhausted patience and outpouring of wrath." Christ, in turn, struggled to give birth to new life: "His atoning sorrows were the birth pangs endured for his people as his seed—as the very fruit of his body."[35]

Understandably, this sort of writing did not sit well with neoclassical theists. Hodge considered Baird's work in a lengthy review but barely mentioned Baird's characterization of God. Instead, Hodge confined himself to examining Baird's characterization of humanity. To Hodge's mind, the whole theory stood or fell according to Baird's notion that the seed for the entire human race had been in Adam, a point that Hodge had no trouble demolishing. Having done this, Hodge, in turn, was left with plenty of room to take his readers through his familiar interpretation of Romans 5—that Adam and Christ had been appointed by God to serve as the legal representatives, or heads, of the human race. Baird also found little support for his work in the South. James Henley Thornwell did deign to note Baird's characterization of God. Thornwell, however, could only shake his head over it. "We regret," Thornwell wrote, "that the importance which Dr. Baird attaches to the propagative property of man has led him to rank this among the elements which enters into the biblical notion of the image of God." And with this, Baird's work was consigned to obscurity.[36]

❧

CHAPTER SEVEN

Desire and Disgust

Horace Bushnell

A year after the publication of Baird's 1860 treatise, *The First and Second Adam*, Horace Bushnell revised his 1847 work, *Christian Nurture*. Like Baird, Bushnell also gave Romans 5 an anthropomorphic gloss by characterizing God as a propagative force. Instead of drawing on the prophecy from Isaiah, however, Bushnell drew on the second chapter of Malachi, which also referred to God's "seed." The difference between the two verses was significant, for using the verse in Malachi made it easier for Bushnell to suggest that God the Father, rather than Christ, was involved with this "seed." This helped Bushnell to leave aside the Trinity as God's propagative sphere. In place of this, Bushnell imagined a more individuated characterization of God in a direct relationship with the human race. Applied to Romans 5, this did not mean that Christ, the "Second Adam," was replacing the first Adam; rather, it meant that the "Second Adam," Christ, was God's vehicle for inserting himself into the process of human generation. And imagining God in such intimate contact with human beings allowed Bushnell to characterize God by a powerful desire: "The Second Adam will get into power with the first, and be entered seminally into the same great process of propagated life," Bushnell declared. "This fulfills that primal desire of the world's creator and Father, of which the Prophet [Malachi] speaks, 'that he might have a godly seed.'"[1]

This was the center of Bushnell's romantic anthropomorphism: "the primal desire of the world's creator and Father." Anxious about his own language, Bushnell quickly added, "Let no one be offended by this."[2]

The revised 1861 edition of *Christian Nurture* was scarcely reviewed, so there was little opportunity for offense to be taken. But at the same time that Bushnell was adding to his old book, *Christian Nurture*, he had begun writing a new one, *The Vicarious Sacrifice*. In this work, Bushnell found an object for God's "primal desire" in the virgin Mary. This work was reviewed by a who's who of nineteenth-century American theology, including Charles Hodge, W. G. T. Shedd, Edwards Park, E. C. Towne, and the Swedenborgian Henry James, Sr. (the father of William and Henry James), for the largely secular *North American Review*. The reviewers who took the time to examine Bushnell's characterization of God did take offense.

The Vicarious Sacrifice, however, has largely been forgotten since. This is peculiar, for many twentieth-century historians have considered Bushnell the most important American theologian of the nineteenth century. Indeed, Bushnell may be the most studied American theologian after Jonathan Edwards. Yet *The Vicarious Sacrifice* and Bushnell's partial revision of it in 1874, *Forgiveness and Law*, have barely gotten any historical attention. Instead, historians have concentrated on Bushnell's earlier works. Why is this?

The answer was that historians followed the lead of liberal theologians. In the late nineteenth century, they interpreted Bushnell in ways that made him suit their own theological agenda. Foremost among them was Theodore Munger. What Munger and his generation of liberals did to Bushnell was analogous to what Park and his generation had done to Jonathan Edwards. They fashioned these past theologians in their own image. This was not always easy. Park had to treat much of Edwards's writing as a vague groping toward what Park himself was doing in theology; Munger and his colleagues treated Bushnell in the same way. They focused mainly on his earlier works: *Christian Nurture* (1847, 1861), *God in Christ* (1849), and *Nature and the Supernatural* (1858). These works show Bushnell's developing romantic anthropomorphism, but they also contain incarnationalist depictions of God that Bushnell's champions could latch onto. Not everything in Bushnell, however, could be brought around here. So Munger declared that Bushnell's romantic anthropomorphism was not an essential part of his work and dismissed it as an unfortunate throwback to the juristic tradition. Because of this effort by Munger and others, Bushnell has come down to us as a pioneering liberal incarnationalist anticipating such late nineteenth-century liberal developments as modernism, the social gospel, and progressive, evolutionary theism. The historian William Hutchison (borrowing Auden's line on Yeats) put the matter justly: "Bushnell became his admirers."[3]

Bushnell is far more interesting, however, if understood in his own right. He did indeed start out as a liberal. But he was never a typical one, and he quickly became something unique. Born in Connecticut in 1802, educated at Yale College and the Yale Divinity School, and securing a parish where he would remain all of his life in Hartford, Connecticut, Bushnell on the surface seemed marked for a career as a typical, liberal cosmopolitan Congregationalist. Indeed, he began his career in this mold and endorsed the moral theory of the atonement. It was thus natural that when he was young and wanted to find alternatives to neoclassical theism he tried out various forms of incarnationalism. It was also natural that from here he was drawn into sentimentalism and considered God in more personal terms as a parent. But he began to veer off in his own direction. Bushnell considered not only how God felt as a parent but also how he acted like one. Indeed, in *Christian Nurture* Bushnell suggested that God could be involved in the propagation of human children. This led Bushnell to ascribe a "primal desire" to God. In *The Vicarious Sacrifice* and *Forgiveness and Law*, Bushnell took his characterization of God one step further, ascribing frustration, disgust, and ambivalence to God's desire. How could Bushnell have devised such an extraordinary romantic anthropomorphism from a liberal position? And how could his later liberal champions have missed this? To understand this, we need to examine Bushnell's peculiar development as a theologian.

Bushnell's Liberal Anthropomorphism

Bushnell had strong views about women, which is not surprising, given his characterizations of God. There was a mixture of misogyny and acclaim for women in his writing. A lot of this was wrapped in the common sentimental idealization of women. But Bushnell simultaneously celebrated this ideal and lashed out against it. If his women were sentimental homemakers, his men were romantic individualists. He took a dim view of the emerging women's rights movement. In 1869, the year the American Woman Suffrage Association elected Henry Ward Beecher president, Bushnell published his booklet *Woman Suffrage: The Reform against Nature*. It was full of florid praise for women's place in the home. The young William James ridiculed it in one of his first published reviews. Shortly after Bushnell's death, Isabella Beecher Hooker (his Hartford neighbor) contacted Bushnell's spirit in a seance and got him to recant his opposition to suffrage. But despite this, Bushnell was no ordinary sentimentalist or sexist. A writer like Henry Ward Beecher extended his sentimentalism across the board to men and women. Bushnell never did. He can be faulted here for having a double standard, but in some cases this might be better than having a single bad standard. Bushnell's depictions of women were common for his time; it was his depiction of male characters—most of all God—that were so unusual.[4]

Yet the two were of a piece. In his theology, Bushnell relied on sentimental female figures (whether praising or blaming them) to throw into relief his romantic characterizations of God. It was as if he needed these female figures to knock against in order to establish the romantic masculinity of his God by contrast. If his method was not admirable, at least he produced some astonishing characterizations of God.

Bushnell's life had something of this pattern to it. The year of his death, 1876, he started a weird autobiographical essay linking his infancy with his old age. He had begun life in a "merely molusk and pulpy state of infancy" and broke into consciousness with a cry, "such a dismal figure did I make to myself; or perchance it was something prophetic, without inspiration, a foreshadow, dim and terrible, of the great battle of woe and sin I was sent hither to fight." Whichever it was, both his mother and God heard him. God came to him through his mother, but his care had been "deeper" and more "protracted" than hers: "Long years ago she vanished, but God stays by me still, embracing me in my gray hairs, as she did in my infancy."[5]

In fact, a network of women in his family had supported him all of his life. He seems to have cultivated this as well as chafed against it. But he owed them a lot. If Park had Frank Hugh Foster to perpetuate his reputation and Hodge had his son, Bushnell had his two daughters, Mary and Dotha. They were named for Bushnell's grandmother and mother and they lived up to their namesakes. Bushnell had credited his grandmother and mother with guiding him into the ministry. Following his death, he owed his growing reputation in part to the industry of his daughters.

Most of what we know of Bushnell's life comes from his daughter, Mary Bushnell Cheney. Her 1880 work, *Life and Letters of Horace Bushnell*, remains the major source on his life. Most of his private papers were destroyed in a fire following his death in 1876. So we are lucky that Mary reprinted so many letters in her biography of her father. She also included some intriguing asides about her father's character.

But still the work comes across (as one would expect) as a piece of filiopiety. Indeed, it is something right out of a nineteenth-century sentimental novel. Bushnell, during his life, and Mary, after his death, created a character for Bushnell that neatly fit with the contemporary vogue of New England regional literature, of which their Hartford neighbors, Harriet Beecher Stowe and Mark Twain, were among the leading practitioners. So Bushnell has come down to us as a stereotypical "Connecticut Yankee," a playful, indulgent father, sensitive to the little expressions of the spirit in everyday life, broad-minded, and optimistic; a boyish tinkerer with inventions; a civic booster; and an American patriot.[6]

There were other sides to him, however. For one thing, his entry into the ministry had not been easy. His grandmother, Mary, and his mother, Dotha, had selected him, the eldest son, for the ministry from an early age. He always gave them credit for this and attributed to them both spiritual and hereditary influences that carried through his life. Two years before his death, in 1874, Bushnell tried his hand at an autobiographical essay beginning with events before his infancy. He did not get very far with it. Following his death, Mary put this at the beginning of her biography of her father and called it "Sketches of His Grandmother and Mother." It began, "It has been my good fortune to be descended from two of the very best and noblest women." He only saw his grandmother twice (when he was six and twelve). But when she wrote to her son, Ensign Bushnell (Horace's father), the grandmother included snippets of her own poetry for Horace. Near the end of his own life, at the age of seventy-two, Bushnell wrote of her: "She has been almost visibly with me, and going, as it were through me by a kind of subtle waft, down to the present hour."[7]

He would say the same about his mother, a quiet but unmistakable influence. Everyday life with her made this influence more pronounced. His father was a clothmaker in Litchfield County, Connecticut, pressed by competition from imports and the emerging textile industry. His mother ran a shop for their goods in the front of the house. According to Bushnell, she ran things with the "exact order and time" of the "astronomic year." By the same drill and habit—"industry, order, time, fidelity, reverence, neatness, truth, intelligence, prayer"—she raised her children and conveyed to Horace that he was intended for the ministry. This meant he was to go to college. He was reluctant but finally acquiesced. "Perhaps she was ambitious, though I never saw the faintest token of it," Bushnell remembered; "it was her nature," he continued, "that lively and sharp as her excitabilities were, she could never help acting in the line of discretion."[8]

Bushnell tested this discretion when he went to Yale. His mother had instructed each family member on what he or she was to do and sacrifice so they could afford to send Horace to college. It took some time to get the money together. Bushnell did not enter Yale until the age of twenty-one (whereas some boys were entering in their mid-teens). At college, however, he began to express his literary ambitions. He wrote a college essay simply entitled "Ambition." "It is as natural for man to wish for an imperishable name as for an eternal existence," he declared. After four years at Yale, he returned home and told his mother that he had lost all religious feeling. "My mother felt the disappointment bitterly," he noted.[9]

Graduated at the late age of twenty-five, he spent his first year out of college in Norwich, Connecticut, halfheartedly working as a tutor and enjoying himself by reading old copies of the *Spectator* and smoking cigars. "In your next letter," his mother wrote to him, "let me know whether you take as much care to keep your heart right as to convert yourself into a gentleman." The following year, 1828, Bushnell strayed a little further, taking a job in Manhattan as a staff writer for Lewis Tappan's *Journal of Commerce*. Bushnell was invited to stay on and become the journal's literary and political editor.[10]

But he dithered. On his mother's advice, he tutored for a year at Yale. He attended law school classes there. He made plans to go to Ohio and make it big as a lawyer. But when he was set to leave, he suddenly became concerned about his soul. The ministry was for him after all. He dropped his plans to leave Connecticut and enrolled in the Yale Divinity School. Two years later, he was ordained and elected to the parish of the North Church in Hartford, where he remained for the rest of his life, not far from his boyhood home. Now, finally, at the age of thirty-one he had fulfilled his mother's ambitions for him.[11]

The same year he married Mary Apthorp. His marriage, however, was not easy. Bushnell loved to travel. He said he did it for his health. It also helped his writing. But it caused some friction with his wife. "You will soon see your guilty deserter return," he wrote to Mary in 1838, adding, "I can hardly understand how it has come to pass that I have turned my back on all that binds me to the earth." The compliment to Mary came across; but for Bushnell, who always praised poetry and his own writing with the Homeric phrase "winged words," likening marriage to being bound to the earth was not a ringing endorsement.[12]

His travels affected his family. Bushnell was rarely home while his children were growing up. During the 1830s through the 1850s, he lectured across New England, traveled to Europe, Cuba, and California, and made numerous trips through the American Midwest. On some of these trips, he was away for over a year at a time. His relationship with his wife became strained. He was away during the fatal illnesses of two of his children in 1836 and 1843. Still, he continued his lecture tours throughout New England and helped to organize the anti-Catholic Protestant League and spent a year in Europe. When he returned from Europe in 1845, Mary Bushnell Cheney later recorded that she, at the age of five, did not recognize her father. Shortly after Bushnell's return, his wife had a breakdown and he had to stay home and mind the children while she received care in New York City. He wrote to her and told her how much the children missed her. When she returned, he began his travels again.[13]

There were some good reasons for his wife's breakdown. In the twelve years of her marriage to 1845, she had borne six children, seen two of them die, and been left for long periods of time to care for them alone. There is the suggestion of a pattern here. Bushnell married a woman who shared some of his mother's weaknesses. Indeed, Bushnell's wife may have been disposed to repeat the anxious nature of his mother, for both Bushnell's mother and his wife had suffered as children from fathers who had abandoned their families.[14] Given this, one can imagine the poignancy when Bushnell wrote letters to Mary proclaiming himself her "guilty deserter."

At the same time, we can imagine his frustration in dealing with her anxieties. In 1858, he resigned his parish for reasons of health and began traveling again. The end of his adventures, however, came on a trip to Minnesota, where he was supposed to be resting but where he began writing *The Vicarious Sacrifice*. Hearing from friends there that he was working, Mary dashed off a letter scolding him. He wrote back to her: "The watch of a wife is a very close one and sublimely tireless. . . . God be thanked that my love for mine is worn so deep into me by her tender persecution."[15] Only the belief that he was near death brought him home to stay in 1860. Yet he lived for another sixteen years in the protection and confinement provided by his wife and daughters. They did everything to make it easy for him to write. In her recollection of his last days, Mary (who now had primary responsibility for her father) remembered him coming out of his study to sit down with them in the evening. "At the dinner-table, he came to us from the thought-world, from the writing of sermons and books," she recalled, "his very hair stood on end, electric with thought; his eyes had a fixed and absent look, and he forgot the name of a potato." She worried that these transports would give him indigestion.[16]

Bushnell conveyed some of this wild power in his writing. He was recognized as a poet-theologian. As a young writer, this had gotten him into trouble. His 1849 work, *God in Christ*, caused some controversy, and Bushnell's position at the North Church was threatened. But the majority of his congregation stood behind him, and he kept his pulpit. Understandably, Bushnell's writing elicited mixed reviews. But everyone agreed on one thing: he was a peculiar theologian. "Such madness excites nothing but commiseration," Hodge wrote of Bushnell. Noah Porter, Bushnell's friend, put it more gently. Bushnell was not a systematic thinker or a reliable biblical expositor; he was "scarcely a neophyte" in the sciences, but "he found himself possessed of a poet's imagery and a poet's fervor." For many, this was enough. Henry Goodwin in 1859 hailed Bushnell's "genius," "poetic insight," and "imaginative power." Bushnell held his reader spellbound: "Like [Coleridge's] Ancient Mariner, he holds him, if not with his 'glittering eye,' [then] with his vigorous and piercing thought." Reviewing *The Life and Letters of Horace Bushnell* two decades later, Goodwin declared that Bushnell's "style is a marvel and a model of condensed and visualized language." Goodwin went on to liken Bushnell to Shakespeare, Milton, Raphael, and Michelangelo. Goodwin concluded: "A grander intellect and a purer soul has not appeared on earth since Milton left it."[17]

Needless to say, we need to take these estimations of Bushnell, positive and negative, with a grain of salt. America's clergy were not the best literary critics. In keeping with the views of many in 1855, one minister pronounced Emerson "overrated" while declaring that "no sane person denies that Henry Ward Beecher is a man of genius."[18] This being said, however, Hodge, Porter, and Goodwin had a point. Bushnell was primarily a literary theologian. Of course, many theologians were interested in literature and drew on it in their works. But Bushnell did so to an unusual extent. Moreover, he did so often to the exclusion of other considerations—such as evidence and logic (which maddened his critics).

It took some time, however, for Bushnell to learn how to combine his literary ambitions with his career as a clergyman. Five years after he entered the ministry, in 1838, his mother died. It was during the summer, and Bushnell was vacationing on Long Island, away from his wife and their two young children. He was not able to attend his mother's funeral. Three years later, however, he returned to his boyhood home in Litchfield County and took stock of his life. He wrote to his wife that he had discovered that "Nature" was his "mother" and that she should not be surprised if he returned to her a "Poet."[19]

"Nature" was also a romantic literary conceit, and this was how Bushnell first came to justify his romantic anthropomorphism. He began working on this in 1839, in an unpublished essay simply entitled "Revelation."[20] But his views here did not fully come out until ten years later, in his 1849 essay, "A Preliminary Dissertation on Language as Related to Thought and Feeling." This served as the introductory essay to *God in Christ*. Three lectures given at Yale, Harvard, and Andover on the incarnation, atonement, and spirituality made up the body of the work. But the "Preliminary Dissertation," longer than any of the lectures, became the most famous part of *God in Christ*. In the twentieth century, Bushnell's liberal theological champions saw in it an anticipation of their own biblical criticism.[21] They were right, so far as taking biblical language metaphorically goes. But Bushnell and modern liberals took this in different directions. Whereas liberals read into the metaphorical language of the Bible neoclassical theism and sentimental incarnationalism, Bushnell read into it romantic anthropomorphism.

But coming from a liberal perspective, Bushnell could not easily justify romantic anthropomorphism. Liberals had cut themselves off from much of the Old Testament and the juristic tradition. Shedd had been able to draw on these to support his anthropomorphism. Bushnell, at least initially, could not do this. So he appealed to human nature. Science, he declared, could not explain the complexity of human character. Sin made humans a mystery that only a literary mind could fathom. "Poets, then," he declared, "are the true metaphysicians and if there be any complete science of man to come, they must bring it." His example for this was Shakespeare, "the universal poet of humanity." But what about grasping God's character? Here Bushnell appealed to nature. Metaphoric, poetic language, he asserted, was the language of the Bible and should be the language of theology for a good reason: this was the language of nature. God had designed nature as a vast analogy ("analogon," Bushnell called it) for the spiritual world. Therefore, words full of material imagery, rather than being an impediment to grasping nonmaterial, spiritual things, were really suited for just this purpose. Theologians, therefore, should follow the spiritual laws of language inscribed in nature to write about God. "The endeavor is," Bushnell declared, "by means of expression, and under the laws of expression, to set forth God—His providence, and His government, and what is more and higher than all, God's own feeling." Here was Bushnell's initial justification for romantic anthropomorphism.[22]

Bushnell's arguments here were riddled with contradictions, thin appeals to evidence, and half-digested linguistic theories and romantic notions about a natural language. Hostile commentators had no trouble toppling his arguments and had some fun at his expense.[23] But the "Preliminary Dissertation" does show us what Bushnell was reading. In addition to the authorities that Bushnell brushed by—Locke, Goethe, Friedrich von Schlegel, and Josiah Gibbs (one of America's leading philologists who had taught at the Yale Divinity School while Bushnell was there)—the work suggests the influence on Bushnell of Samuel Coleridge's *Aids to Reflection*, Percy Bysshe Shelley's *Defence of Poetry*, and Ralph Waldo Emerson's *Nature*. Bushnell's essay also shows how hard it was for a liberal to justify romantic anthropomorphism.

Conservatives could wrap themselves in the juristic tradition and appeal to the Old Testament. Liberals had cut the Old Testament out from under themselves. So Bushnell was forced to defend his effort by reaching for a grab bag of romantic theories about nature and language. If this offered Bushnell ways to justify romantic anthropomorphism, it still did not give his God much to do. Liberal doctrines did not provide much of a stage for God to demonstrate complex feelings.

So again Bushnell appealed to nature. He did this in his next major work, *Nature and the Supernatural*, written nearly ten years later in 1858. But now nature was no longer his benign, inspiring mother giving him natural laws for poetic language. Now she was the "angry motherhood of nature"; she was a dramatic, Gothic landscape wrecked by sin. For that matter, she was not even nature: "No[thing] more sufficient describes it unless we coin a name and call it a condition of 'unnature.'"[24]

But if unnatural, she was not unliterary. This was what Bushnell needed in order to give his theology some romantic drama. Now it was no longer a matter of justifying this drama but finding scenarios for it. Bushnell drew on current scientific theories about geological catastrophes in prehistory. But he subsumed all of this under his literary vision. "We may hear the grinding layers of rocks singing harshly: 'Of man's first disobedience and the fruit / of that forbidden tree,'" Bushnell intoned, citing *Paradise Lost*. These Miltonic chants, Bushnell went on, "are but the epic in stone of man's great history before his time." Along these lines, Bushnell explained the extinction of the giant prehistoric animals. The revolt in heaven might have had some impact on the prehistoric earth, Bushnell speculated. Perhaps the banished spirits visited earth and corrupted the early creatures. This could account for the presence of "extinctions and deformities" during the prehistoric era. Bushnell imagined the "audacity" of the evil spirits during the early age, "hovering it may be in the smoke and steam or watching for congenial sounds and sights among the crashing masses and grinding layers even before the huge monsters began to wallow in the ooze of the waters, or the giant birds to stalk along the hardening shores."[25]

But humankind was even more dramatic than nature, for humans had some element of the supernatural. Channing had seen this as the human "mind" and wrote about it in terms of neoclassical serenity. Bushnell found the supernatural element in the human will and wrote about it in terms of romantic vitality. What made the will supernatural in Bushnell's estimation was that it was an originating power. His will was not simply a link in the chain of causal sequences that bound natural events together. The will of heroes in tragedies and novels captured Bushnell's imagination in *Nature and the Supernatural*. "In every hero," Bushnell exclaimed, "we discern a majestic spirit transcending the merely necessary acts of animal and vegetable life." He cited Shakespeare's Coriolanus, who declared, "I'll n'ere be such a gosling as to obey instinct, but stand as if man was author of himself." This famous defiance of natural necessity would be echoed by Milton's Satan in his more famous defiance of God. This perverse will made humans dramatic (never mind the morality of it), and Bushnell even implied that the tragic will was inherently ennobling. This was why the human will was always more awful to ponder than the greatest of natural phenomena. Nature acted out of necessity, whereas human actions had a perverse, supernatural element: "We regard in him a power—a bad will doing battle with God

... be it a Macbeth, an Othello, a Richard, a Faust, a Napoleon, or only the Jew Fagin."[26]

Bushnell, however, faced a problem: how to get God into the act. How could God battle nature or battle himself? In *Nature and the Supernatural*, Bushnell wrote vaguely of the ennobling struggle of tragedy, "that which imparts an interest so profound to human history, to the novel and the drama, and even to the crucifixion of Christ."[27] But how could God act with the dramatic power of a Napoleon, a Macbeth, or even a Fagin from *Oliver Twist*?

In *Nature and the Supernatural*, Bushnell could not say. The problem for Bushnell was how to bring God down into the world of dramatic conflict. In *God in Christ*, hints of a romantic depiction of God were weakly justified as a result of the natural "laws of expression"; in *Nature and the Supernatural*, God was Milton's God, presiding over but not participating in the spectacle of evil. By 1861, however, with the beginning of the Civil War and Bushnell returning home to stay, he found a way to ascribe dramatic conflict to God: it was to be found in his "primal desire" to redeem humanity through propagation. So in 1861, Bushnell took up again his old work from 1847, *Christian Nurture*.

Christian Nurture

It is easy to see why Bushnell's liberal champions found something that looked familiar in *Christian Nurture*. The title seemed to say it all. By "Christian nurture," Bushnell meant rearing children as Christians. He advocated this approach in contrast to revivalism. In itself, this was not unusual. Cosmopolitan theologians across the doctrinal spectrum in the early nineteenth century, from Channing to Hodge, had expressed reservations about revivalism. This is one reason that in 1847 Hodge gave the first edition of *Christian Nurture* such a positive review. But as the century went on, the book began to seem more distinctly liberal. The word "nurture" seemed sentimental. Moreover, Bushnell's book was a kind of instruction manual. It told people how to become Christian parents. Bushnell emphasized early child care. Infants, he explained, were sensitive to the slightest impressions. "A mother teaches by words only? No!," Bushnell declared, "but more, a great deal more, by the atmosphere and patience she breathes."[28]

By the twentieth century, liberals began to claim that this was scientific, not sentimental. Liberal theologians declared that Bushnell had anticipated twentieth-century sociology and child psychology. Such claims were important for liberals in the twentieth century, who wanted to throw off the accusation that they were "sentimental" (in a pejorative sense) and wanted their theology to seem scientific. So many embraced sociology and psychology but claimed that some of the insights of these disciplines could be found in Bushnell's work. This made Bushnell attractive for another reason. The theological use of sociology and psychology had been first developed by Europeans (especially Germans). So it was particularly gratifying for American liberals to claim in Bushnell an American precursor for their interests.[29] This view of *Christian Nurture* was institutionalized in 1916 when Dotha Bushnell Hillyer saw into publication another edition of her father's work. She also provided the endowment for the Horace Bushnell Professorship of Christian Nurture at the Yale Divinity School. In 1966, Luther Weigle, Sterling Professor of Religious Education at Yale, wrote a new introduction for the work. He declared: "Horace Bushnell's *Christian Nurture* is as significant today as when it was published a hundred years ago. Modern psychology and sociology have confirmed its insights, and the best modern education is in its spirit."[30]

There was something to this assertion, but it also left something out. Weigle, like most of Bushnell's liberal champions, concentrated on what Bushnell called "postnatal" nurture. This was care for the infant and child after birth. But Bushnell also wrote about "ante-natal" nurture. This concerned hereditary influences on the child and how parents could influence it through regimens of health and piety. Weigle made a passing reference to this as "a doctrine of Christian eugenics, long before the term came into use."[31] Indeed, Bushnell developed his theory about thirty years before Francis Galton coined the term "eugenics." But this did not mean that Bushnell anticipated eugenics any more than he anticipated twentieth-century sociology or psychology, for Bushnell was relying on the common notions of mid-nineteenth-century phrenology.

Phrenology had some intellectual authority, but it was basically the pop psychology of the day. Cosmopolitan Americans, from Walt Whitman to Henry Ward Beecher, were keen on it. Bushnell, as usual, took what he could use from it but, when it no longer served his purposes, dropped it and even criticized it (as he did in *God in Christ*).[32] It is not surprising that Bushnell borrowed from phrenology to lay out his ideas about propagation and child rearing. As we have seen, there was a market for quite explicit phrenological marriage manuals in the mid-nineteenth century. These explained in detail how parents could have some influence on the religious nature, mental aptitude, and emotional temperament of their future child. Prior to conception, parents could do this by carefully cultivating their tastes, monitoring their diet, and engaging in exercise, religious devotion, and, finally, a proper act of intercourse. So Bushnell's emphasis on the receptivity of the infant to nonverbal impressions was not unusual. According to phrenology, people could be seriously affected by the slightest stimulants. Tea, tobacco, or mustards, for instance, could affect the level and orientation of sexual desire. *Christian Nurture*, in short, was very much a book of Victorian America.[33]

Its anti-Catholicism and racism were also products of Victorian America. Like many American Protestants, Bushnell was alarmed by the increasing number of Catholic immigrants in America. Among other things, he feared that American Catholics were producing more children than Protestants. Indeed, middle-class Protestant birth rates were declining. This was one reason that phrenology books were so popular. If Protestants were having fewer children, at least they could ensure that the children they had were up to the mark. This more-bang-for-the-buck theory of propagation was considered an advance in refinement. It was all part of the process of humanitarian progress that American Protestants assumed they were heading. Humanitarian notions of historical progress dovetailed with notions about child rearing. The logical step was to take these notions into child making. So Bushnell imagined that his regimen of "Christian nurture" represented a higher stage of Christianity. Evangelism might be the first stage. It was still necessary for the masses and primitive people around the world. But it was not necessary for the future children of America's middle class. Bushnell speculated that through "propagated piety" a "regenerated stock" of Christians could be produced. Even original sin might be overcome.[34]

There was, however, a troubling implication to this. Other "stocks" might be left behind. Bushnell, like many of his contemporaries, thought of different cultures as different races. For this reason, his regimen of Christian propagation could be a very effective selection process. Those who used it would be starting out on the high road of hereditary righteousness; others would continue to propagate sinful offspring. It is true that Bushnell acknowledged the possibility that God intended all races to become regenerate. But Bushnell also raised the other possibility: "What if it should be God's plan to people the world with better and finer material?" Some races might be destined for extinction. In articles in the 1840s prior to *Christian Nurture*, Bushnell showed that he clearly believed that "Anglo-Saxons" were God's chosen people. Bushnell believed that God was allowing them to "live down" other people, such as Irish, Italians, Spaniards, Africans, and Native Americans. In *Christian Nurture*, however, Bushnell cautioned his readers: "It is for God to say what races are to be finally submerged and lost, and not for us."[35]

This led Bushnell to conclude that Anglo-Saxons should still try to convert the world. The thought that they might spread their piety through interbreeding with other people was not considered. So the old-fashioned method of evangelism would have to do. For that matter, it would have to do for many Anglo-Saxons. Bushnell cautioned against pride here. "What feebler and pitiful conceit could we fall into," Bushnell advised, "than to assume that we have the grand, overpopulating grace in our stock, and sit down thus to see it accomplished by mere propagation?"[36]

Still, "propagated piety" was the wave of the future. And it had an ancient precedent: the Jews of the Old Testament. Likening one's group to the ancient Jews was common in nineteenth-century America as a way to claim status as God's chosen people. But for a theologian coming from a liberal background, Bushnell put unusual stock in the Old Testament. He took it more seriously than many of his liberal colleagues and in some cases more literally (neglecting his own injunction in *God in Christ* to take the Bible metaphorically). Thus, in *Christian Nurture* Bushnell appealed to the example of the ancient Hebrews. According to Bushnell, God had given to Abraham a special propagative blessing: "God was to make his family fruitful, above others, by imparting Himself to it."[37] Bushnell thought that circumcision was the symbol of this. As we have seen, Harriet Beecher Stowe had similar ideas. She believed that God had given the Hebrew people an especially strong propagative nature. Stowe used this idea to unfold Mary's character. In *The Vicarious Sacrifice*, Bushnell used this idea to explore the character of the other partner at the annunciation, God the Father.

This brings us to an important point: God was involved in all of this. Even in *Christian Nurture*, God was part of the process of "propagated piety." This marked his character: he was driven by a "primal desire." This is what Bushnell's liberal champions have missed. By neglecting the "ante-natal" aspect of Bushnell's program, they have missed the role that Bushnell assigned to God. For this reason, they never understood Bushnell's characterization of God. For this reason also, Bushnell's work has been open to the charge of naturalism. The charge makes sense if one focuses mainly on the "post-natal" aspects of Christian nurture. But it must not be forgotten that there was always the other side to the equation—the "ante-natal" side. God's activity is to be found in this originating, "ante-natal" sphere. For Bushnell, as much as for Baird, God was the original force in the process of propagation. Thus, if there was some naturalism in this, there was also a lot of anthropomorphism. Bushnell was not just bringing God down into nature; he was bringing nature up into God. And for Bushnell, it was a measure of God's power that he could rescue the part of humanity most corrupted by sin, the organs of generation.

Look again at *Christian Nurture*. Immediately after saying that no one should be offended by his notion of God's "primal desire," Bushnell explained that he did not mean to suggest a process of "mere natural laws." "What higher ground of super-naturalism," he declared, "can be taken, than that which supposes a capacity in the Incarnate Word, and Sanctifying Spirit, to penetrate our fallen nature, at a point so deep as to cover the whole spread of the fall, and be a grace of life, traveling outward from the earliest, most latent germs of human development?" Again, he appealed to the Old Testament. He cited the Psalmist's celebration of being "curiously wrought in the lowest parts of the earth." Bushnell also mentioned the "sporadic cases of sanctification from the womb" in the Bible, such as in the cases of Samuel, Jeremiah, and John. These, Bushnell proclaimed, "are to become the ordinary and common fact of family development."[38]

Yet here we come to a discrepancy in Bushnell's work. In a sense, he was more optimistic about humanity than about God. That is, on one hand, Bushnell imagined that through Christian nurture human beings might weed out original sin. But, on the other hand, in *The Vicarious Sacrifice* and *Forgiveness and Law*, Bushnell imagined God's "primal desire" as frustrated and even disgusted by sin. If this did not stop the process of redemption, it still made it a rougher process than in *Christian Nurture*. To some degree, Bushnell kept both scenarios running at once. He was not a systematic thinker, and contradictions rarely bothered him. But there is more to it than this.

Bushnell was straddling the classic liberal dilemma between social reform and romanticism. Cosmopolitan liberals have been committed on one hand to social reform, founded on a humanitarian vision of historical progress and expressed through neoclassical and sentimental ideals of social harmony. But on the other hand they have been intrigued by the depth of conflicted and isolated romantic characters. Bushnell seems to have either accepted or ignored this division in his work. To humanitarianism, he offered the vision of "propagated piety" overcoming original sin. He imagined a harmonious society resting on the sure foundation of sentimental families. It is easy to see how Bushnell's liberal champions, focusing mainly on this part of his writing, could make him into their champion. But Bushnell also reserved a role for the romantic individualist. Ultimately, this was God. But there was still a problem here. Bushnell had accounted for emotional complexity by attributing it to sin. In *God in Christ* and *Nature and the Supernatural*, Bushnell had used sin to inject romantic complexity into his characters and had come close to glorifying sin. How, then, could he ascribe romantic feelings to God? It was not until *The Vicarious Sacrifice* and *Forgiveness and Law* that Bushnell found a way to do this.

The Vicarious Sacrifice

Bushnell wrote *The Vicarious Sacrifice* during the Civil War. The spectacle of the war fascinated him. It does not seem to have changed his thinking substantially, but it did give him some new imagery and help him to think about conflict as being normal. Good writing, after all, needed conflict; maybe life did too. One of the ways in which Bushnell saw the war was on this literary level. "Our Obligations to the Dead," he told a group of Yale alumni veterans in June 1865, were to celebrate the war in literature. Before the war, America did not have a dramatic history; but now it did. Bushnell had been looking for something similar in theology; some way to bring conflict up to God so to make theology dramatic.[39]

This was not easy for a liberal. But for the same reason, when Bushnell did it, he produced something astonishing: a highly individuated yet complex characterization of God. The complexity of Bushnell's God was not spread out over the Trinity, as it had been for conservatives such as Shedd, Thornwell, Griffin, and Baird. Indeed, when it came to the Trinity, Bushnell maintained a very liberal position, not far from Unitarianism. He had little use for the idea of Jesus as the coequal Son of God or God existing as three persons. In heaven, Bushnell suggested, the redeemed would look for Jesus but would not find him. This is because he was no longer needed; he had been subsumed back into the "All-Father, the original base, or fontal source." Bushnell's view of the Trinity (to the extent that he can be pinned down on the doctrine) was instrumental, or Sabellian, in the traditional theological nomenclature. Bushnell reduced Jesus to little more than a manifestation of God that God had found necessary to give to humans because of their limited ability to apprehend God. In this, Bushnell did to Jesus what liberals had done to Old Testament anthropomorphism. Indeed, Bushnell even wrote about Jesus in the same terms as liberals wrote about the Old Testament God. Park had said that the Old Testament was given to figurative, or metaphoric, depictions of God. Bushnell declared that Jesus was "God's last metaphor." As his "last metaphor," of course, he had some authority. But by the time of *The Vicarious Sacrifice*, Bushnell was preferring to concentrate on God's first metaphors for himself in the Old Testament.[40]

Here again, the Civil War may have helped Bushnell to appreciate the Old Testament, for the Old Testament gave him a way to sanction the war. After the first battle of Bull Run in 1861, he assumed the mantle of an Old Testament priest blessing the Israelites for battle. He approved of the passing of leadership from the aged Union general, Winfield Scott, to George McClellan. Bushnell pictured himself in the role of Samuel anointing the young David of McClellan. By 1864, Bushnell was intoning, "We thank God there was a Jonathan, if it was only that David might sing his death."[41] But in *The Vicarious Sacrifice* it was not so much the God of battles that Bushnell celebrated as the God of propagation. A little like Stowe imagining Christ on his lonely "preappearance" visits to the earth during Old Testament times, Bushnell imagined God longing for the annunciation.

In *The Vicarious Sacrifice*, Bushnell claimed that God's love for the world was sympathetic love. This was a common enough assertion, especially in sentimental characterizations of God. But Bushnell pushed beyond sentimentalism here. God's sympathetic love caused him to suffer, and this was normal. Love—all love, including God's—Bushnell declared, had a "doom of bleeding" on it.[42] Moreover, God's love included desire. God wanted to save humankind because he sympathized with its plight, but he also wanted to relieve himself from suffering for it. So he wanted to express his love for humanity, which meant expressing his sufferings, as part of the effort to redeem humanity and to relieve himself. In strikingly erotic terms, Bushnell described the annunciation as God's "outbirth" and his greatest moment of "relief."

Bushnell argued that the Old Testament described the long buildup in God as he withheld his love from the world. In this characterization of God, Bushnell integrated the Old and New Testaments in strange and new ways. The Old Testament, in Bushnell's vision, recorded the hardships that God had endured while withholding his love until humankind reached a level of civilization where it was able to appreciate God's full revelation. There were traces of liberal biblical criticism in this vision of progressive revelation. The Unitarian biblical critic George Noyes had written that the "age of definition [of God]" had not arrived during the Old Testament era. Bushnell echoed the thought, writing that "the day of ideas, thoughts, sentiments, words" had not yet been "quickened into a spiritual meaning."[43] But rather than treating the primitive level of the ancient Hebrews in a condescending fashion, Bushnell used their supposed limitations to amplify God's character. The fact that God had had to wait to reveal himself added drama to the Old Testament. Bushnell's use of the word "quickened" was also significant, for the waiting period was a kind of propagative buildup in God. Restraining himself became part of God's dramatic struggle. God's great frustration was like that of a suitor waiting for his young bride to reach the age of maturity.

Bushnell even made the astonishing claim that during the Old Testament waiting period God had suffered more than Christ. In this feat of retention during the Old Testament era, God had made the true sacrifice, of which Christ's crucifixion was only a reflection. This was a remarkable contrast to the liberal efforts to primitivize the "fearful anthropomorphism" (as Park had called it) of the Old Testament Jehovah. In contrast to this, Bushnell declared that Jehovah was the greatest characterization of God's suffering love in the Bible.

> Does he then, by condescending to the lowness of the barbarous mind [in the Old Testament], show that his character is equal to nothing higher? Ah, what struggles of suffering patience had he rather to endure, in these long ages of training under such narrow and meagre possibilities! Nowhere else, it seems to me, not even in the cross of Jesus itself, does he reveal more wonderfully the greatness and self-sacrificing patience of his feeling. And the fact breaks out, all along down the course of history—appearing and reappearing, by how many affecting declarations—that he is waiting for a better possibility, waiting to open his whole heart's love, and be known by what he can bear and do for mankind.[44]

The strain of this waiting reached its great moment of relief in the annunciation to Mary. Bushnell's description of God's "outbirth" through Mary is one of the most startling passages in nineteenth-century American theology. Whereas sentimental incarnationalists from Henry Ward Beecher to Harriet Beecher Stowe had sought to find the meaning of the annunciation in Mary's character, Bushnell made the moment all God's. It was his greatest moment of revelation and the beginning of the New Testament. But more important for Bushnell's characterization of God, it was the culmination of the Old Testament and the release of the Father's "primal desire."

> Nor was there any moment of relief to him so blessed as when he came to Mary with his "All Hail," and broke into the world as God with us; God now came at last to disburden his heart by sacrifice. The retention before was a greater burden on his feeling, we may well believe, than his glorious outbirth into loss and suffering now.[45]

The diminishment of Jesus here is astonishing. This was not just a consequence of the fact that Bushnell did not rely on the Trinity to depict God's emotions. Bushnell actively downplayed the significance of Christ compared to God. So if Bushnell steered clear of the conservative reliance on the Trinity, he also avoided the liberal emphasis on the incarnation. He kept his focus on his own complex, anthropomorphic characterization of God. This meant that the Old Testament began to take precedence over the New and the annunciation took precedence over the crucifixion. Look again at what Bushnell said about the cross. "Nowhere else, it seems to me," Bushnell wrote, "not even in the cross of Jesus itself, does he reveal more wonderfully the greatness and self-sacrificing patience of his feeling."

What, then, was the purpose of the cross? As in the moral theology generally, the cross in Bushnell's theology did not specifically accomplish anything. But it did show something. In this, Bushnell's interpretation of the crucifixion was like that in the governmental theology. But what the cross showed was different. In the governmental theology, it demonstrated God's opposition to sin. In Bushnell's theology, it showed God's anguish. This was remarkable enough, but what was even more striking was Bushnell's attitude toward the diminished role of the cross. Governmental theologians had wrestled with the charge that their view reduced the crucifixion to a showpiece or a fiction. Bushnell was untroubled by the implication that the cross was mainly a manifestation of suffering rather than the real thing. For Bushnell, the real thing was to be found in God's feelings.

Compared to God, Jesus was reduced to a secondary role. "Christ, in his vicarious sacrifice," Bushnell asserted, "only represents the feelings of God in all the preceding ages." Bushnell reduced Jesus' sufferings to a manifestation of God's. "What is his Gethsemane," Bushnell declared of Jesus, "but a revelation in time, of just that love that had been struggling always in God's bosom, watching wearily for the world and with inward groanings unheard by mortal ears?" Notice that Bushnell continually used the word "his" to distinguish and qualify Jesus' sufferings—"*his* vicarious sacrifice," "*his* Gethsemane." This reinforced the idea that the real suffering—the original suffering—had occurred prior to Jesus, in God himself.[46]

This was an astonishing assertion of anthropomorphism. It stepped around both the Trinity and the incarnation. It also broke down the barriers neoclassical theists and sentimental incarnationalists had erected around God. For instance, Park (and even Shedd) had counseled against speculating about Jesus' interior sufferings (presumably his divine sufferings) on the basis of his physical agitation. Even sentimentalists had maintained that Jesus' displays of emotion rarely reflected his own pain but rather signified his sympathy with the sufferings of others. But Bushnell focused on God's feelings. He lingered over the details of Christ's sufferings only to urge the reader to move beyond them and consider God's own feelings. "Let us come then not to the wood alone, not to the nails, not to the vinegar and the gall, not to the writhing body of Jesus, but to the very feeling of our God and there take shelter." In one of the most scandalous passages from *The Vicarious Sacrifice*, Bushnell suggested that theologians had erred in their concentration on Jesus. His sufferings were but a limited expression in time of God's ongoing sufferings in eternity: "Nay, there is a cross in God before the wood is seen upon Calvary; hid in God's own virtue itself, struggling on heavily in burdened feeling through all the previous ages, and struggling on now even in the throne of the worlds."[47]

So Christ suffered for a few hours to demonstrate what God suffered continually. God's struggle, therefore, was not just confined to the Old Testament buildup; nor was it permanently relieved in the annunciation (much less so by being made manifest in Christ). Rather, God suffered continuously. His love went out to sinners, and he longed for their salvation. Every time a sinner was saved, God gained a little relief. The model for each act of redemption thus remained the annunciation rather than the crucifixion. This was the case not only for "propagated piety" (as one might expect) but also for conversion. Bushnell depicted each conversion, or "new birth," in a sinner as a kind of propagative event in God.

The "new birth" of a sinner was a result of the interplay between God's justice and mercy. Relying on traditional, juristic imagery, Bushnell personified these two traits as antagonistic figures who came together and kissed each other at the atonement. Like most liberals here, however, Bushnell exteriorized God's justice. Rather than attributing it directly to God in the form of wrath, Bushnell wrote of "retributive forces" in nature that punished sin automatically. This being said, however, Bushnell still wrote of these natural forces as expressions of God's justice. More so, he depicted the relationship between God's justice and mercy in striking figures. The language he used for them not only was gendered but also suggested genitalia. Mercy was a limpid, dewy figure; justice was an "inflexible" "dread machine" carrying in tow a "caisson" (or artillery wagon) packed with explosive charges. Together, they both brought the sinner to his moment of truth—"that final crisis," Bushnell declared, "where he is either born, or never to be born of God."[48]

The image of a caisson obviously came from the Civil War, but it and other images also sustained some literary resonance. His personifications of justice as an iron, military man and mercy as a limpid, dewy female recalled two of literature's most famous and troubled couples, Hephaistos and Aphrodite and Othello and Desdemona. In the introduction to *The Vicarious Sacrifice*, Bushnell declared that the atonement was the "grand supernatural tragedy in the world"—even greater, he added, than Shakespeare's *Othello*.[49]

Beyond this, it was not just salvation that was dramatic. That is, when all sinners were saved, the drama would not end. If Bushnell was optimistic about "propagated piety" eradicating original sin, there was something more basic troubling the world. It was not simply sin that made for tragedy but the nature of creation. This, however, was a cause not for sadness but for celebration, for character was deepened and ennobled through struggle. "Our existence has been mixed with discord from the first," Bushnell declared, "and for ought we know, this rough element belongs inherent to the highest attainable state of good." God had not "swerved" from meeting the greatest evil. His love had impelled him into tragedy. Perhaps, Bushnell speculated, the "Kosmos" was such a dramatic theater, continually undergoing "shocks that will stir the tragic movement in feeling and keep off the tameness of any total elysium, or general peace-society state."[50]

Bushnell knew that he was flying in the face of liberalism, so he braced himself for the worst. He knew that he was exposing himself to the kinds of caricatures that conservative theologians were commonly tarred with. Thus, he anticipated that critics would call him a "man behind the age, a dark minded fanatic . . . representing God by the low severities of his morbid nature." But Bushnell threw caution to the wind. He scorned that "speculative philanthropism so much in fashion." "Do I love God," he mimicked; "how could I help loving him? God has never done anything bad to me and never wants to do anything but to make me happy."[51]

Reaction to The Vicarious Sacrifice

Reaction was more predictable than Bushnell expected. Bushnell was not caricatured as a conservative. Rather, because reviewers knew him by reputation as a liberal, they treated him as such. Conservatives and liberals, in short, both projected onto his work their expectations about liberalism. So most conservative and liberal reviewers misunderstood Bushnell. Shedd, at least, sensed that Bushnell was up to something strange. "'There is a cross in God before the wood is seen on Calvary; hid in God's own virtue itself, struggling on heavily in burdened feeling through all the previous ages, and struggling on heavily now even in the throne of the worlds,'" Shedd quoted with dismay. "This is a humanization of the Deity," he declared; it was a "vicious annihilation of the difference between the Infinite and the Finite"; "the Infinite is transmuted into the Finite, and appears clothed in the same feelings, affections [and] sympathies." This being said, however, Shedd did not move on to examine Bushnell's anthropomorphic imagery in detail. Instead, Shedd made his job as a reviewer easy. He shot from the hip, peppering Bushnell with the reflex conservative charge that Bushnell, the liberal, was given to sentimentalism. Needless to say, this last charge was off the mark.[52]

Hodge was further off the mark. In fact, he was so far off that he almost got it right. That is, he charged Bushnell with doing the very opposite of what he did. This is not to say that Hodge wanted a complex, anthropomorphic characterization of God. But Hodge did want a strong characterization of God's love—which for Hodge meant attributing to God the totally efficacious power of imputation. And to express his point Hodge drew on biblical imagery of God's love being like that of a bridegroom for his bride. But Hodge complained that Bushnell had done the opposite. This was one of Hodge's standard complaints about liberalism; it was "like changing a bridegroom's love for his bride into benevolence; or a mother's love for her child into philanthropy." This is just what Bushnell had not done. Bushnell's Old Testament God was very much like a bridegroom (and an eager one at that). But all of this was lost on Hodge.[53]

It was also lost on most liberals. Many of them simply assumed that because Bushnell was supposed to be a liberal, he was. They reasoned that Bushnell, in his own peculiar way, must have been advocating familiar liberal views. Thus, the Unitarian theologian and literary critic James Freeman Clarke, who was given to drawing summary distinctions between liberals and conservatives, pronounced Bushnell's work as basically liberal. Clarke even declared that *The Vicarious Sacrifice* was really just an amplification of Noah Worcester's 1829 Unitarian tract, *The Atoning Sacrifice: A Display of Love, Not of Wrath.* Edwards Park also weighed in. He acknowledged Bushnell's "gorgeousness of imagination" but then quickly moved on and encouraged Bushnell to review the finer points of the governmental theory of the atonement.[54]

Some liberals, however, did pause to examine Bushnell's imagery. And when they did they were appalled. E. C. Towne, reviewing the work for the Unitarian *Christian Examiner*, pointed out the problem here. "According to this view," wrote Towne, "the purpose of the incarnation was not to meet man's need, but God's." Towne was overstating the charge, but he had a point. Bushnell's conception of God's love was romantic rather than neoclassical or sentimental. This meant that God's love was neither serene nor selfless. It was turbulent and driven by desire; and to provide himself with some relief, God had come down to Mary. This was too much for Towne. "This theory hardly deserves to be criticized," Towne declared. He went on to scorn Bushnell's "wild fancies about God's burdened heart and wounded sensibility. 'More than mere human sensibility,' he says; as if this did not mean more than humanly weak." Towne, with his neoclassical sensibility, would allow no agitation to be ascribed to God's love. "Sympathy of the glad lover of men is one thing," Towne exclaimed, but "groaning sensibility is evident of human weakness."[55]

Towne had a point. The love that Bushnell ascribed to God made God vulnerable. But this was not the only problem. Partly because God was vulnerable, his love was also ambivalent. It was Henry James, Sr., the lapsed Presbyterian who had devoted himself to studying the eighteenth-century mystic Swedenborg, who pointed this out in a review of *The Vicarious Sacrifice* for the *North American Review*. "It is an outrage upon all love, divine as well as human," James declared, "to suppose that its subject is ever in normal discord, and not in fulness of accord with its object."[56]

In Towne and James spoke the voice of an essentially neoclassical and sentimental conception of love. In this, Towne and James held basically the same assumptions as the vast majority of liberal and conservative theologians across the doctrinal spectrum. The only difference was that other reviewers of Bushnell had been too quick to pigeonhole him. But Towne and James had taken the time to look closely at what Bushnell was actually doing. Then it became clear that Bushnell was no ordinary liberal. By ascribing to God's love such romantic traits as frustration and ambivalence, Bushnell had crossed a line. He had transgressed the assumptions about love that liberals and conservatives alike shared in the nineteenth century.

Forgiveness and Law

Bushnell pressed on, however. Two years after publishing *The Vicarious Sacrifice*, he delivered a lecture on homiletics at Andover Seminary called "Training for the Pulpit Manward." He told the students that ministers should not fear reaching down into themselves for their material. Within themselves, they would find "boundless capacities, never to be exhausted." "Here in the soul's secret chambers," Bushnell declared, "are Fausts more subtle than Faust, Hamlets more mysterious than Hamlet, Lears more distracted and desolate than Lear."[57] Perhaps by pursuing this method Bushnell himself was led to new ideas about the atonement. In 1874, he published *Forgiveness and Law*, a partial revision of *The Vicarious Sacrifice*. "Fresh light" onto the problem of the atonement, Bushnell wrote in the introduction, had impelled him to write the new work. What this new "light" was is not clear, but whatever it was, the new treatise was even more radical in its romantic anthropomorphism.[58]

Criticism of *The Vicarious Sacrifice* may also have influenced him. Bushnell may have been stung by Shedd's charge that his God was sentimental. This was unfair, for Bushnell had gone to great lengths in *The Vicarious Sacrifice* to show his scorn for sentimentalism ("God has never done anything bad to me and never wants to do anything but to make me happy"). In *Forgiveness and Law*, Bushnell went even further. God's attitude toward sinners was nothing like a mother's love for her children, Bushnell declared. "As if the mere maternity of natural instinct," he exclaimed, "could be cited as a match and parallel for the clear, everlastingly sealed acceptance and moral embrace of God. Just contrary to this, the wrath of offended holiness, the purer sensibilities shocked by disgust, the moral repugnances and displeasures, the immovable indignations must not hurry to clasp a wild and filthy reprobate."[59]

Forgiveness and Law marked another step to the right for Bushnell. As always, however, he made his moves on his own terms. He appropriated what he would from conservatives and made the rest his own. Thus, in the above statement, some of Bushnell's language sounds like the neoclassical theism of Hodge—"the clear, everlastingly sealed acceptance and moral embrace of God . . . the wrath of offended holiness." But then Bushnell's language took on more complex suggestions. If God's anger was not so much energizing and vitalizing (as Shedd had characterized it), it was paralyzing. And the crucial point was that it paralyzed God. Bushnell's God was "shocked by disgust, the moral repugnances and displeasures, the immovable indignations." In short, there was ambivalence in God.

To explain how God resolved these feelings, Bushnell endorsed Shedd's theory from his 1859 essay, "The Atonement: A Satisfaction for the Ethical Nature of Both God and Man." There Shedd had described how God used his constitution as a triune being to work out his simultaneous feelings of love and anger toward humanity. God exhausted his anger by punishing himself—that is, himself in his coequal Son. Bushnell picked up on this. This was quite a turnaround for him. Eight years earlier, in *The Vicarious Sacrifice*, he rarely commented on the work of other theologians, but he did pause to denounce Shedd's theory of God punishing himself. It made God into the "weakest of rulers," Bushnell had exclaimed. Now, in *Forgiveness and Law*, Bushnell changed his mind. "Shedd was right," Bushnell declared, "when he conceived of God as laying his wrath upon himself."[60] But once again Bushnell took only what he wanted from conservatives. Unlike Shedd, Bushnell did not rely on a division of labor in the Trinity to separate God's conflicted feelings. Bushnell packed these emotional conflicts into one complex, individuated romantic character. So Bushnell, unlike Shedd, did not withdraw God back into neoclassical serenity. Bushnell's God was a complex anthropomorphic figure whose feelings were in continual flux.

For Bushnell, God's greatness as a character depended on this flux. In *Nature and the Supernatural*, what made humans noble was their tragic resistance to nature. In *The Vicarious Sacrifice*, what made God's love great was its tragic suffering. So this is what made God's anger great in *Forgiveness and Law*. "Let us have tragedy and a strong mixture of it," Bushnell declared; "he is not less perfect because these antagonistic sentiments are in him." There was little trace of the neoclassical and sentimental polarization of emotions in this. Instead, God's emotions were mixed in a turbulent sea. For a neoclassical theist like Park, such imagery suggested what was wrong with human beings. "Our mind is like a sea, whose waters are restless even in their lowest depths," Park had declared in "All the Moral Attributes of God Are Comprehended in His Love." So Park had looked for something different in God; he had looked for a God who calmed this turbulence, as Jesus had calmed the Sea of Galilee. But Bushnell sought a God who shared his own complexities. An "impassable" God, Bushnell declared, cannot be "relational to my experience." "If his streams all ran one way, he would be too simply placid to be great, but he lives in everlasting countertides of struggle and victory—victory both over others without and violated good within."[61]

What did Bushnell mean by these "countertides"? It was difficult for him to say. Here there was an adjustment in Bushnell's justification for anthropomorphism. In *The Vicarious Sacrifice*, Bushnell had implied that he could describe how God experienced his love because it was essentially the same as human experience. This explained the subtitle to the work, *Grounded in Principles of Universal Obligation*. This is one of the points for which he was most severally criticized by Shedd and others. In his next work, Bushnell clarified his approach. The full title was *Forgiveness and Law: Grounded in Principles Interpreted by Human Analogies*. Three years later in a two-volume edition of both treatises, Bushnell dropped the first subtitle and used the second. In other words, he backed off the assertion that God and human beings felt the same things. Rather, Bushnell maintained the more modest idea that God's feelings could be interpreted by analogies with human feelings.

This was Bushnell's way of explaining God's disgust at sin. He relied on the classic romantic figure—the Ancient Mariner or the Byronic hero Manfred—who cannot forget a past crime. But now it was not his own crime but the sin of another that torments him. Yet his very inability to forgive and forget becomes almost a crime in itself. Writing analogously of God and humans, Bushnell described sin as wounding a good person; this wound forms a scar that the person can not simply forget by forgiving the offender. A man sinned against, Bushnell wrote, "is alienated, thrown off, thrust back into separation. . . . He is a wounded man whose damaged nature winces even in his prayers." The problem, however, did not stop there. Persons wounded in this way become caught up in irrepressibly repetitive feelings: "Their old mind returns upon them and their old animosities are rekindled. . . . They look on the faces and hear the voices of men they undertook to forgive and their disgusts come back upon them. The old wounds rattle as if in new offences, and there is no moral gong at hand by which they can be drowned."[62]

How could these repetitious feelings be stopped? By suffering in the service of the sinner, Bushnell answered. Such service caused the old scars to be softened and forgotten. Bushnell simply asserted this as a psychological fact. As such, it made some sense. But it had striking consequences when applied to God, for what it did was reverse the atonement. In most theories of the atonement from the juristic tradition to philanthropism, God had made a sacrifice on behalf of human beings—that is, to cover human sin. But in Bushnell's theory God made a sacrifice to free himself (and humankind) from God's own disgust at sin. That is, in order to forgive and forget in Bushnell's theory, God had to make a propitiation to sinners, not for them. This was an extraordinary twist on conservative and liberal theories of the atonement.

Of course, God's feelings here were not just selfless. Bushnell had given to God a self as complex as any human's. As much to free himself from his pain as to save humanity, God undertook the continual work of atonement. "In the eternal going on of God's interior nature," there was "an eternal going on of propitiation." "The beauty of the true conception is that God is not obliged," Bushnell wrote, "to be everlastingly disgusted." In the end, Bushnell's final theory of the atonement was premised on the idea that God's desire was to forget. And Bushnell raised forgetting to a continuous process in God. Expiatory forgetting was God's continual way of making a new future possible for himself and for people. Two years before his death, however, Bushnell did not have time to elaborate on this vision.[63]

Twenty-five years later, Bushnell's great liberal champion, Theodore Munger, struggled with the depiction of God in *Forgiveness and Law*. Munger tried to make it fit in with his own sentimentalism. "That God suffers with and for men in Christ rests on the broad analogy of Fatherhood, but that He suffers in order to become propitious, or rather by suffering *becomes* propitious,—for this point is guarded on page 53," Munger hedged, "is a doubtful feature of the analogy. It seems to detract from simple love, which needs nothing to complete itself, and certainly in God needs nothing to start it into exercise." Munger was right; Bushnell's depiction of God's love was not simple. It had never been. The romantic anthropomorphism of his earlier works had been mixed with enough sentimentalism that Munger had been able to construe them to suit his own theological agenda. But Munger could not do this with *Forgiveness and Law*. So Munger concluded that the work was a misguided throwback to the juristic tradition. Thus, it could be forgotten. And with this, Bushnell's real work was lost for most of the twentieth century.[64]

❧

PART THREE

The Vague God
of the Twentieth Century

✧

Modernism and Literature

Theodore Munger and Amos N. Wilder

By the late nineteenth century, the God of cosmopolitan theology was becoming vague. He was losing details and becoming a hollow God. Consider Exodus 3:14 again, the passage where God declares, "I am that I am." We have seen that Edwards Park, a neoclassical theist, used it to ascribe a magnificent serenity to God. Stowe, a sentimental incarnationalist, used an allusion to Exodus 3:14 in the Gospels to ascribe a poignant alienation to Jesus. And finally we have seen that Shedd, a romantic anthropomorphist, used Exodus 3:14 to ascribe an energizing vitality to God. Despite their different literary styles, each of these writers used the verse to get inside God. They used it to say something about his character. This was changing as God became vague. Look at how Theodore Munger used the verse in his 1883 work, *The Freedom of Faith*. "God," Munger exclaimed, "is not a power only, but also a person . . . the *I am*, the Personal Being!" Park, Stowe, and Shedd would have taken Munger's point for granted. Of course, God is a "personal being." The interesting question is, what is he like as a person?[1]

Why had it become enough for Munger vaguely to assert that God was a "Personal Being"? Part of the answer is that Munger was arguing against an impersonal definition of God devised by Matthew Arnold. But if Munger rejected Arnold's impersonality, he also seized upon Arnold's vagueness. Such vagueness had become increasingly necessary to sustain God's neoclassical and sentimental character in the late nineteenth century.

Arnold was a distinguished English Victorian poet, literary scholar, and social critic. In his 1873 work, *Literature and Dogma*, he laid out guidelines for studying the Bible (and by implication other texts) that would influence liberal theologians through the twentieth century. The distinction announced in the title of Arnold's work was crucial. "Dogma," Arnold asserted, was the effort to make religion into a precise science. This, he thought, was a mistake. It had strangled the life out of religion. Religious feeling, Arnold argued, was akin to morality and religious expression closer to literature than to science. Then Arnold went a step further. He suggested that the literary and moral nature of religion meant that religious writing should have a certain vagueness. This made for a neat contrast with the precision of dogma. It also changed the way one read a text for its religious import (in Arnold's case the Bible). Details were not to be "pressed," for this was "dogmatic." Religious language—taken in its profound moral and literary sense—Arnold claimed, was "language thrown out at objects of consciousness not fully grasped, which inspired emotion." And, of course, the most important object of religious language was God.

So God was to be vague. Arnold defined God as "a power not ourselves working for righteousness." "A power not ourselves" was key, for Arnold wanted to evoke (without being too dogmatic) the sense of influx from without that seemed typical of religious feeling. And he wanted to suggest the sense of moral duty, or altruism, that took people beyond themselves. Using this definition of God, Arnold went through the Old and New Testaments showing how vague the biblical God was. God's statement to Moses, "I am that I am," was not so much about God—for he was one of those "objects of consciousness not fully grasped." Rather, by saying, "I am," the notion conveyed here was "not you"—as in "a power not ourselves working for righteousness." What about passages where God was angry? Again, the important thing was not the characterization of God. "God," Arnold declared, "is here really, at bottom, a deeply moved way of saying conduct or righteousness." So imagery of a fearful God was "really, at bottom," a way of saying do not do bad—or do good. Arnold's sense of goodness was humanitarianism personified through neoclassicism and sentimentalism. So in the Old Testament, morality meant "the love of order, or righteousness." This, according to Arnold, reached its highest expression in Jesus. He had sustained the Old Testament commitment to righteousness but tempered and refreshed it with his "sweet reasonableness."[2]

American liberals made a point of dissenting from Arnold for the impersonality of his God, but they accepted his vagueness. So in *The Freedom of Faith* Munger declared, "The fault of Matthew Arnold's definition of God, is that it blurs the personality behind the righteousness, and so deprives it of motive."[3] This immediately preceded Munger's declaration about "the *I am*, the Personal Being!" Munger thus ascribed some personality to God—in particular, a "motive." What was this motive? God's sentimental love for humanity. This being said, Munger's God was still fairly vague. But now Munger could justify this vagueness. Details must not be dogmatically "pressed." Instead, theologians should look beneath the details of the Bible for the humanitarian morality that was "really, at bottom," here and so inevitably in accord with the neoclassical and sentimental character of God. Liberal theologians took the same approach to modern science, politics, and literature. Otherwise it was hard to find much support for a neoclassical and sentimental God in the twentieth century.

This was because the nineteenth-century cultural supports for these characterizations of God were collapsing. These characterizations had never been easy to reconcile with the Bible. But they did have the support of enlightenment science and humanitarian morality and the prestige of neoclassicism and sentimentalism as literary styles. Theologians had pictured the neoclassical God presiding over an orderly and benevolent universe, but now this vision of nature was shaken by Darwinism. The sentimental God had sanctioned the home as the foundation of society and the source of its moral renewal, but industrialization undermined this faith in the social power of the family. As literary styles, neoclassicism and sentimentalism had been sustained despite the emergence of romanticism by the popularity of the sentimental novel and the mixture of neoclassical, sentimental, and romantic styles in the English Victorian poets and the American "genteel tradition." But out of romanticism emerged two new literary movements, aestheticism and realism, that promoted a more emotionally charged and ambivalent characterization of men and women. In the face of all of these developments, the only way to sustain a neoclassical and sentimental characterization of God was to make him vague. On one hand, there were few credible or compelling details to picture such a God by; on the other hand, the only way to claim support for this God in any of these new movements was to overlook their details.

Liberals and conservatives made a virtue out of this vagueness in different ways. Little innovation came from the conservative side. Like Hodge, early twentieth-century conservatives continued to sustain their characterization of God by distancing him from the world. But whereas Hodge had mainly distanced God from his acts, conservatives came to distance God's whole being from the world. They emphasized his transcendence. The idea of God's transcendence, of course, had always had a place in traditional Christian theology. But rarely had this served so persistently to sustain such a vague characterization of God. As we will see in the next chapter, the conservative God became little more than a list of abstract traits with only the bare bones of a neoclassical character.

Liberal theologians developed nearly the opposite tack, and this led to some innovation in the late nineteenth and early twentieth century. Not God's transcendence but his immanence is what they emphasized. That is, they claimed God was, in some general sense, inside of and the driving force behind the evolution of nature, social progress, and even the development of literature. Of course, all of this was hard to sustain in any detail, for neither evolutionary science, nor the contemporary political struggles between business, labor, and agricultural interests, nor the bohemian world of modern literature made much sense with neoclassical and sentimental characterizations of God. But this was the advantage of the concept of God's immanence. It enabled liberal theologians to dismiss many details as surface phenomena and, following Arnold, claim that what was "really at bottom" of nature, politics, or literature was an expansive humanitarian morality in accord with God's neoclassical and sentimental character. The main development of liberal theology here was in the social gospel, which addressed political issues. We will examine this in the next chapter. Now let us consider the effort of liberal theologians to make sense of modern literature.[4]

Munger and Modernism

Modernism in American liberal theology (not to be confused with literary modernism) was a movement to reconcile theology with cosmopolitan culture that began in the late nineteenth century and continued in a variety of forms through the twentieth century. Theodore Munger was one of the American pioneers of this movement. Born in 1830, Munger was educated at Yale College and Yale Divinity School. After serving for twenty years in various parishes around New England, he returned to New

Haven in 1885, settling down at the prestigious United Congregational Church. This was two years after the publication of his most famous work, *The Freedom of Faith*.

This work was a manifesto of modernism, or the New Theology, as it was called at the time. It was "new" because it professed that theology could be new; it could be modern, which meant that theology could be reconciled with science and literature. The prospect seemed liberating, hence the title, *The Freedom of Faith*. Munger was saying that educated people no longer had to fear that modern culture would destroy their faith. Rather, they could let their faith out into the open air of modern culture. Some found it an intoxicating vision. The seventy-five-year-old John Greenleaf Whittier, one of America's senior poets of the "genteel tradition," called Munger's work as "refreshing and tonic as the north wind."[5]

With the publication of *The Freedom of Faith* and his return to New Haven, Munger's stature increased. In 1887, he became a member of the Yale Corporation. In 1905, he was elected to the American Institute of Arts and Letters. This last honor came around the time he published two other important works. One of these was his 1899 study, *Horace Bushnell: Preacher and Theologian*. This, more than any other work, established Bushnell's prominent liberal reputation in the twentieth century. The other work was Munger's 1904 collection of essays entitled *Essays for the Day*. This collection included another work on Bushnell entitled "The Secret of Horace Bushnell" and an important essay entitled "The Interplay of Christianity and Literature." This essay set out the basic views of the modernist approach to literature. The movement was carried on by Munger's New Haven colleague, Charles Allen Dinsmore, of the Yale Divinity School, who wrote such works as *Atonement in Literature and Life* (1906) and *The Great Poets and the Meaning of Life* (1937).

The liberal modernist characterization of God was much like the God of the social gospel, the wing of liberalism that dealt with politics. Both modernism and the social gospel had their roots in mid-nineteenth-century sentimental incarnationalism and neoclassical theism. Despite this, modernist and social gospel theologians often criticized these earlier depictions of God. They used the same polemic that mid-nineteenth-century neoclassical theists and sentimentalist incarnationalists had used against each other. Thus, modernist theologians denounced earlier neoclassical theists for making God cold and abstract, and they mocked earlier sentimental incarnationalists for making Jesus weak and effeminate. Some of this polemic was heartfelt, some bluster. But despite these charges, the God of modernism was still the God of neoclassical theism and the Jesus of sentimental incarnationalism. In fact, he was a merging of the two, which is one reason he seemed new.[6]

This merging of neoclassical and sentimental traits occurred in the more expansive nature of Jesus' humanitarian vision. If his primary emotion was sympathy, this was a sympathy that was no longer figured in familial terms but more broadly encompassed all of humanity. This broader vision, in the eyes of some liberals, served to toughen up Jesus and lend him an air of neoclassical fortitude. But still the connection with sentimentalism was there. In *The Freedom of Faith*, Munger laid out his expansive vision of Jesus. A person's natural sympathy was mainly limited to family members, Munger explained. The challenge was to expand this love to take in all of humanity. This is what Jesus had revealed. Munger walked the reader through this vision of expanding love. It began in the family, in childhood, and proceeded through adulthood to take in humanity at large. In the process, Munger downplayed Jesus' family ties, saying they were "obscured" in the Bible. This helped Munger to ascribe to Jesus a humanitarian vision that seemed larger than the mid-nineteenth-century emphasis on the family.

> At the threshold of life we are met by affections that check and call us off from inborn selfishness, the love of parents and of brother and sister, and then that fiery passion that ushers in a love that makes of twain one, and the diviner, downward-flowing love upon children; it is in such ways as these, all personal, that evil is kept or crowded out, and we become tender and generous and pure. But beyond lies the broader sphere of humanity, for which there is but small native passion, and hence but little inspiring force impelling us to its duties. Yet this is the field of our highest duties and widest relations. And it is here chiefly that Christ becomes an inspiration through the loyalty of love. Christ is humanity to us, He has hardly any other relation; He was not a father or husband, as son and brother his relation is obscured, his citizenship is not emphasized. . . . Hence Christ put himself solely and entirely into this relation, the Son of man, the Brother of all men, the Head of humanity, and there sets in play the divine forces of universal love and pity and sympathy.[7]

The kind of love that Munger validated here was significant for his characterization of God. In ascending order, each kind of love has its place and leads to the next, from children's love for their parents up to Jesus' love for humanity. But what did not fit neatly into this ascending scale was the love of the parents for each other, for this included erotic love, "that fiery passion that ushers in a love that makes of twain one." For Munger, this sort of love did not have much to do with either humanity's love for God or God's love for humanity. Two pages earlier Munger had made this point explicitly. In the past, he explained, erotic elements had been ascribed to God's love, but humankind had progressed beyond this. "The semi-erotic aspect it has sometimes been made to wear, and this still weakly cherished in some quarters, has largely passed," Munger declared; "in these latter days, it has the calm of thought, the sobriety of conviction." Here was the assertion of God's neoclassical traits. Yet these were also tempered with sentimental sympathy. In the passage above, Munger echoed this point in the manner in which he passed over the love between adults. It was succeeded by what Munger called the "diviner, downward-flowing love upon children."[8]

Why was parental love "diviner" than that between spouses? The reason was that parental love was more selfless. Parental love was not tainted by self-interest or desire. "There is depth even beyond love," he declared. Love always had some self-interest; "but pity or compassion has all the glory and power of love, but it forgets itself." Munger cited the obvious domestic example of such love: "A mother loves her child when it is well, but pities it when it is sick, and how much more is the pity than the love!"[9] So here was the link with nineteenth-century sentimental incarnationalism. But now this was lifted to a general level where theologians no longer had to wrestle with Jesus' apparent domestic difficulties and instead could claim that his feelings were directed toward humanity at large. Jesus was "the Head of humanity," and his chief traits were "Universal love and pity and sympathy."

This expanded sense of Jesus' sympathy rested on another new notion: God as immanent in history. Again, there was a merging of neoclassical and sentimental traits. This brought the neoclassical God down to earth and the sentimental Jesus up, out of his family; the two merged together in the middle ground of history. Whereas Park had imagined God presiding over the Newtonian universe, Munger imagined God within the world, driving history forward according to supposed laws of evolutionary progress. History thus became God's primary field of activity. This, in turn, changed the understanding of the incarnation, for if God was already in history, then the fact that he was in Jesus was not in itself entirely unique. Being in history, God was (in some sense) in everyone. The problem was to recognize God in oneself and in others. Otherwise, God was a diffuse presence in history. But in Jesus, God's character was focused in one person for people to behold. Jesus, in turn, conveyed to people the greater sense of God in humanity at large.

In practice, this emphasis on God's immanence tended to make the depiction of God and Jesus vague, but some liberals claimed that just the opposite was the case. They charged that past theologians had constructed artificial and abstract supernatural systems. Liberals now felt that, by declaring God's immanence in nature and history, they were grounding their characterization of God in the details of actual reality. "It builds not upon vague generalization, but upon actual experience," Munger's colleague Charles Allen Dinsmore declared in 1907. What was this "experience"? "The new theology in America rests upon the major premise that religion is to be interpreted in terms of [a] personal relationship between God and man, God being revealed through the aeonic movements of nature and the unfolding spiritual consciousness of man, culminating in the unique and authoritative life of Jesus."[10]

This might not seem the best rebuttal against a charge of vagueness. How could a distinctive characterization of God be "revealed through the aeonic movements of nature and the unfolding spiritual consciousness of man"? The notion of natural evolution that liberals championed was extremely vague, as it had to be, because it had little to do with the details of actual scientific theories. Likewise, the ideal of an "unfolding spiritual consciousness" was a vague humanitarianism that scarcely dealt with the difficult details of history or the contemporary social problems that liberals claimed to address.

The characterization of Jesus also suffered from vagueness. This was because it brushed aside the gospel details about Jesus' personal life. At least the sentimental characterization of Jesus had encouraged some attention to the details about his relationship with his mother. But liberals allowed themselves to ignore these details by making Christ's object of concern humanity at large. They began with historical generalizations about first-century Palestine and from there projected Jesus' character (as a reflection of God's) back and forth along progressive visions of human history and the evolution of the natural world. The upshot was that liberals took away from Jesus an intimate, dramatic setting and distinctive, individual characters to deal with, such as Mary.

The emphasis on God's immanence thus gave liberals greater freedom to depart from the Bible. If God was "revealed through the aeonic movements of nature and the unfolding spiritual consciousness of man," then less attention need be paid to the Bible. The notion that history was progressive also helped theologians to dismiss those portions of the Bible that did not suit their purposes. The primitivization of the Old Testament became unabashed. In *The Freedom of Faith*, Munger's declaration about "the I am" came boxed between two other statements: "Whatever significance there is in the Jewish Scriptures lies in the personality emblazoned on every page. . . . Cast this out, and they might have been burned with the books of Alexandria with little loss."[11] Calling the Old Testament "the Jewish Scriptures" was not a gesture of respect toward Judaism; rather, it was a way for liberal Christians to distance themselves from the Old Testament.

American liberals gained a great deal of confidence here, as they did earlier in the nineteenth century, by following trends in liberal European theology and biblical scholarship. Many of their ideas about Jesus' historical and humanitarian vision came from nineteenth-century German liberal theologians and church historians such as Albrecht Ritschl and Adolph von Harnack.[12] Having more direct contact with European liberals at the end of the century, the Americans became more confident and wanted more recognition for their own efforts. In 1900, Munger and other American liberals attended a symposium in London on the atonement. Distinguished European theologians and churchmen were there, such as Harnack, August Sabatier from France, and Frederic William Farrar from England. Munger's American colleague Lyman Abbott addressed the conference. Abbott was Henry Ward Beecher's biographer and successor to his Brooklyn parish. Before the distinguished liberal gathering, Abbott declared that the development from the Old Testament to the New marked the transition from "paganism" to "Christianity." "In the pagan conception God is wrathful," Abbott explained; "in the Christian conception God is love."[13]

Munger had his turn to address the symposium. In America, he said, the doctrine of the atonement still caused as much controversy as Darwinism. He praised the symposium for helping to resolve the debate. "This series of papers will add something to clearing the doctrine of its localism and provincialism and superstition," Munger declared, "but it will not be wholly clear until it undergoes the criticism of cultured and devout minds in all nations." Munger summed up what the future cosmopolitan view of the atonement would be: not a focus on Jesus' death but a focus on his life; not a struggle between God's love and wrath but a demonstration of the harmonious bond between parent and child. "Absolute Fatherhood and absolute Sonship, that is the good news of the Gospels," announced Munger; "it is the religion of humanity."[14]

American liberal theologians, however, did not want to appear entirely indebted to European liberal theology, so they looked for their own American precursors. Lyman Abbott correctly saw himself as continuing in the tradition of Henry Ward Beecher. More generally, the "New Theology" of liberal modernism owed a lot to earlier liberal forms of sentimental incarnationalism and neoclassical theism. Too much continuity with past American theology, of course, was not what liberal modernists were looking for. They wanted to see progress; they wanted to see sharp distinctions between liberals and conservatives; and they wanted to find an American original: that is, an American liberal who seemed to owe little to his American context or to influences from abroad but had anticipated the outlines of modernism and could be ranked beside the great German liberal theologians of the nineteenth century. Munger and others claimed to find this in Horace Bushnell. Through the twentieth century, liberals celebrated Bushnell as the American pioneer of modernism.

"Bushnell, outrunning his day, conceived of God as immanent in his works," Munger declared. Bushnell, according to Munger, had even anticipated an "evolutionary philosophy."[15]

These claims show how Munger's enthusiasm often got the better of his attention to detail. How could Bushnell have anticipated an "evolutionary philosophy" when in *Nature and the Supernatural* he had suggested that the fallen angels might have caused the extinction of prehistoric animals? Part of the answer is that Munger often overlooked textual details. The title of *Nature and the Supernatural* suggested to him the idea he was looking for—the immanence of God. Likewise, Munger pointed to the subtitle of Bushnell's treatise, *The Vicarious Sacrifice: Grounded in Principles of Universal Obligation*. The word "universal" to Munger's mind meant something like humanity, which Munger connected with God's immanence.[16] Yet Bushnell's emotionally complex anthropomorphic God hardly made sense with Munger's humanitarian Jesus. The details were unimportant, Munger declared: "Nor does it matter how he represented God in humanity; He is there because humanity exists eternally in God; and being there, He must appear in created humanity. Bushnell's pages overflow with this truth; it is the backbone of his doctrine of the atonement."[17]

Munger, however, had an explanation for Bushnell's failure to anticipate precisely what Munger himself was doing. Bushnell was a pioneer; he anticipated liberal modernism but did not complete it. This was the work of Munger's generation. Thus, in regards to Bushnell's "evolutionary philosophy," Munger explained: "If Bushnell did not work this out completely to its inevitable conclusion, he was always hovering near it. Indeed, it must be said of him that he was a theologian of the beginnings; he completed nothing."[18] So Munger completed a lot for Bushnell. Munger's approach to literature was similar.

Munger and Literature

Aestheticism and realism presented real challenges to theology. Both movements had roots in romanticism, became distinct in France in the middle of the century, and from there passed to Britain and became noteworthy in the United States by the 1870s. Realism rode the wave of Darwinism, which, in unadulterated form, shattered the enlightenment vision of a benevolent and orderly creation. Aestheticism uncoupled art from humanitarianism. "Art for art's sake" was the motto—implying that art was not to be bound by morality or religion and in some cases was to shake them up. In aestheticism and realism, the fascination with emotional ambivalence was more pronounced and prurient than in romanticism. Erotic desire and aggression were often fused; prostitutes and femmes fatales figured prominently in this literature. All of this was brought closer to home for middle-class readers. The romantic hero was often an alienated wanderer in the wilderness; in realism and aestheticism, characters slunk through society's urban depth below, clinked glasses with a decadent aristocratic class above, or, more alarmingly, were discovered in the unspoken hearts of middle-class men and women themselves.[19]

Both realism and aestheticism inaugurated a clash of artistic and religious cultures that resounded through the twentieth century. Of the two, theologians found it easiest to make accommodations with realism. This is because most cosmopolitan Americans preferred a tempered vision of evolution to the one Darwin had offered. Moreover, there was a humanitarian reform impulse in the realist novel that liberal theologians adapted to their own purposes in the social gospel. So, with some alterations, liberals were able to develop an evolutionary humanitarianism to sustain neoclassical and sentimental characterizations of God.

Aestheticism, however, was more of a challenge. The English aesthetes, such as Algernon Swinburne and Oscar Wilde, were shocking. Some American critics traced the immorality of aestheticism back to romanticism. Theodore Hunt, of Princeton College, suggested this in his 1882 article for the *Princeton Review* entitled "Modern Aestheticism." Hunt charged that the current generation of English writers, such as Swinburne and Wilde, had gone wrong by following the lead of Byron and Shelley rather than the more sober style of Wordsworth. Suggestive of the extent to which his own religious and literary views were bound together, Hunt called for a return to the "orthodox doctrine," by which he meant the style of John Milton.[20]

This became the attitude of most conservatives in the twentieth century. They often denounced modern literature as decadent and were done with it. This judgment is understandable, given the erotic and often anti-Christian agenda of this literature. But still the perfunctory nature of the conservative judgment against literature was often superficial and defensive, for not all modern literature was anti-Christian. In aestheticism and realism, there was a certain desire to shock Victorian piety, but these writers were also interested in Christian symbolism, if not doctrine. This interest was even more pronounced in modernism—which, as we will see, some liberals such as Amos Wilder picked up on. But most of this was lost on conservative theologians. In the twentieth century, they confined themselves to cultural parochialism. At its best, this enabled them to sound like Hodge in his disdain for fashion. But often they did this without Hodge's concern to know the opposition. Moreover, the very notion of a conservative theologian having an engaged, literary sensibility, such as Shedd's, was nearly forgotten in the twentieth century.[21]

Liberals in the late nineteenth century were also shocked by aestheticism. Particularly disturbing was the revival of the more lurid scenes of classical paganism. To some minds, this threatened to set the relationship between theology and literature back to the days of Cotton Mather, who had denounced the muses as "harlots." Noah Porter was driven close to this. He had been able to admire Byron's style, however disagreeable the content. But Porter could not grant the aesthetes even this. "Algernon Swinburne," Porter declared, was "a lecherous priest of Venus." "Let the imagination of such writers be ever so brilliant and their diction ever so enchanting," Porter warned, "the altar at which they serve is that of harlotry and pollution."[22] Munger, however, represented a new generation of liberals who were more confident in these matters. They pronounced aestheticism and realism as passing fashions that would have no lasting influence. One reason for this judgment was the immorality of this literature. But behind this was an objection to the depiction of character. Here we see how the neoclassical and sentimental assumptions of theologians clashed with the romantic characterization at the heart of modern literature.

In *The Freedom of Faith*, Munger denounced the depiction of character in aestheticism as puerile and selfish. Earlier theologians such as Porter had criticized Byron and other romantics for their pride. But Munger's criticism began to take on a more psychological idiom. What Munger declaimed as selfish in aestheticism would be called infantile or immature by later liberals, such as Amos Wilder and Harvey Cox, who drew on psychology. In Munger's scale of love in *The Freedom of Faith*, each person was born self-centered. But then love broke through and eventually opened up the child to other people: "We are met by affections that check and call us from inborn selfishness." Here was the problem with aestheticism, Munger implied. It represented a selfish and immature view of human nature. The notion of "art for art's sake" really meant pleasure for pleasure's sake. This was why, according to Munger, "the aesthetic school of the day" was confined to "small fancies and uncertain morality."[23]

In contrast to this superficial, puerile literature, Munger claimed to champion a deeper, more complex, and more literary view of character. This deeper literature would ultimately brush aestheticism aside. Or, as Munger put it, "a weak and false representative of this earnest age is this school with its brooding parade of self at the front, reminding one of the curtain of a theatre whereon is painted a careless youth touching the strings of a lute for listless girls amongst flowers and fountains, while behind it is Hamlet rehearsing his great question, 'To be, or not to be,' or Lear struggling with the tempest of his own heart."[24]

This might have been the beginning of a powerful critique—if only Munger had followed up on it. But despite what he said, Munger was not interested in the emotional depth of Hamlet or Lear. Munger was not following the romantic path of Bushnell, who in 1868 had recommended that seminary students look into themselves for their material, finding "Hamlets more mysterious than Hamlet, Lears more distracted and desolate than Lear." Munger, in fact, was not counseling theologians to look inward at all; rather, he was saying they should look outward. In altruism, beyond the self, they would find God. Thus, immediately following his declaration about Hamlet and Lear, Munger came upon his real material: "One of the main uses of God, so to speak, is to give us another consciousness than that of self,—a God consciousness."[25]

This was not a complex consciousness. Munger's notion of God as an altruistic alternative to the self was Matthew Arnold's notion of God as "a force not ourselves working for righteousness." In Munger's hands, of course, this was not just an impersonal "force" but the "Head of Humanity," atop Munger's ascending scale of love. But however noble in humanitarian sentiment, this was not a dramatic character.

The difficulty of aestheticism for theologians was therefore not just its apparent immorality but its depiction of character. Here lay the central problem for theologians in coming to grips with any kind of modern literature after romanticism. Modern literature need not be decadent or anti-Christian, but it does rely on depicting emotional depth through conflicted emotion. But this style of characterization simply did not make sense with the neoclassical and sentimental ideals of character that theologians had enshrined in God. At best, theologians interpreted complex literary characterization as a picture of human sin. But this missed the point that the complexity was a source of power and beauty. Still, liberal modernists such as Munger were prepared not only to dismiss aestheticism and realism as passing fashions but also to claim that modern literature inevitably supported their neoclassical and sentimental characterizations of God.

How could Munger do this? Only by the vague claim that Christianity and literature were both inevitably humanitarian. Here he had the example of how Arnold had read the Bible. Details must not be "pressed"; the critic instead must look for the humanitarian morality that was "really at bottom" of every profound piece of writing, sacred or secular. So Munger vaguely defined literature as an expression of humanitarianism, and this is where he found the overlap with liberal Christianity. He explained this in his 1904 essay, "The Interplay of Christianity and Literature." He listed the five points that Christianity and literature had in common. First, "both are keyed to the spirit." Second, "literature, with few exceptions, stands squarely upon humanity . . . and this is essential Christianity." Third, "literature in its highest form is unworldly." Fourth, "the great literature is prophetic and optimistic. Its keynote is 'All is well'" (which "accords" with Christianity). Fifth and finally, "literature is corrective of poor thinking"—by which Munger meant the theology of conservatives.[26]

Given the vagueness of these points, Munger could claim a great deal of literature for liberal theology. Key here was the emphasis on "humanity." This was so vague that details in an author's work did not really matter. "Take, for example, the plays of Shakespeare," Munger declared; "there is hardly anything in them that is obviously Christian. . . . Still they are Christian because they are so thoroughly on the side of humanity." Munger had more difficulty sustaining the contention that all great literature was optimistic ("Its keynote is 'All is well'"). He relied on some slim reeds. To prove that the keynote in Shakespeare was optimistic, Munger cited *Henry V*: "There is some soul of goodness in things evil / would men observingly distil it out." Two years later, Dinsmore in his 1906 work, *Atonement in Literature and Life*, repeatedly referred to this line and claimed some originality in applying it to the atonement.[27]

It was even more difficult to find this optimism in recent writers. Munger considered Robert Browning and Alfred, Lord Tennyson, both mid-nineteenth-century English poets. Both made the Victorian crisis of faith one of their themes, so both wrestled with the emerging evolutionary vision of nature and the historical criticism that undermined previous theological notions about the Bible. Munger could make the case that Browning had worked through some of his doubts here. But whether "all was well" in Browning's vision was questionable. It was even more questionable with Tennyson. In his long poem "In Memoriam," commemorating his deceased friend Arthur Hallam, Tennyson pondered the emerging vision of nature's brutality that would soon inform Darwin's evolutionary theory. Munger, however, leapt over these difficulties and simply asserted that Tennyson was a great Christian poet: "He turns evolution into faith and makes it a ground of hope."[28] Even Munger had to check himself here, however. He admitted that "In Memoriam" was not the best example of Tennyson's optimistic evolutionary faith. So Munger pointed to the death scene at the end of "Idylls of the King." There the dying King Arthur goes gracefully and calls for the prayers of his fellows. This, Munger declared, was the definitive statement of Tennyson's faith.[29]

Munger's case was not strong. His fallback position was to take a large historical perspective that allowed him to pin his hopes on the future. Rather than overlooking the details of a work for its basic humanity and optimism, Munger claimed to discern the tendencies of a work—tendencies that even the author might not have perceived but some future critic (such as Munger) could.

Munger traced his theological vision of literature back to the beginning of Christianity. Jesus, Munger declared, had made use of every means available to spread his word. It is true that Jesus was not a writer in the modern sense, but his use of parables showed his respect for imaginative literature. This made sense, Munger argued, for it was God's nature to make use of everything in creation. Therefore, because it was God who gives literary talent, he must make use of it to spread his message. If this was not entirely evident in history, Munger argued somewhat inconsistently, it is because Christianity got sidetracked in late antiquity. The spirit of Hellenism had been bringing Christianity closer to literature, but then the Latin spirit hijacked the religion and tried to make it legal, "formal," and "arbitrary"—thus taking it out of the literary realm. This, according to Munger, began with Augustine and lasted a thousand years (with the notable exception of Dante—whom Munger awkwardly classed as being neither Augustinian nor Latin in orientation).

Here we see Munger's reliance on the old polemic against the juristic tradition; but now it was also couched in terms that recalled Matthew Arnold's distinction between dogma (the Latin for Munger) and literature (the Hellenistic for Munger). "Both may have been necessary or inevitable in the evolution of Christianity," Munger asserted, "but the Roman form was fatal to literature. It is on this account that so long as the Augustinian theology held sway over the minds of men, literature held itself aloof from theology, or rather theology failed to produce literature. Hence there grew up a feeling that they are not good friends,—as Matthew Arnold indicates in his title, 'Literature and Dogma,'—setting over one against the other."[30]

Finally, the two began to come back together: "As the Renaissance and the Reformation prepared the field—one bringing back learning and the other liberty,—Christianity began to vest itself in literary forms. The relation has continued, and has gained in strength from century to century. The same process has been going on in each,—a gradual elimination of Pagan ideas."[31] This was an extraordinary argument. He was suggesting that the Renaissance rejected the "pagan" influence in Western literature and the Reformation repudiated Augustinianism and embraced art. But Munger did not linger over these historical assertions. He was concerned with the present and the future. But even here problems were pressing. According to his argument, literature had become more Christian with each century following the Renaissance. But this was hard to back up with evidence.

So he fell back on blaming conservatives. Christianity, he asserted, was finally poised to make literature its own. Why was this not more evident at the start of the twentieth century, four centuries after the Renaissance and Reformation? The answer is that conservatives (the heirs of Augustinian theology) got in the way. They impeded the flowering of Christian literature with their dry, abstract writing. This explained why so many writers seemed to be forsaking Christianity. Conservative theology was to blame. "Such a theology," Munger declared, "does not command the assent of those minds who express themselves in literature; the poet, the man of genius, the broad and universal thinker pass it by; they stand too near God to be deceived by such renderings of truth."[32]

Fortunately, this divorce between literature and theology was only temporary, Munger explained. God, working through history, was rapidly bringing about the day when literature and theology would come together. Then, theologians would also stand "near God," side by side with the great artists.

Much of Munger's case depended on the future. This is how he had made sense of Bushnell ("he was always hovering near it. . . . He was a theologian of the beginnings; he completed nothing").[33] This is also how he brought Goethe and Matthew Arnold over to his side. If neither of them was actually Christian in Munger's sense of the word, Munger at least felt confident picturing them as heading in the right direction. Though Goethe, Munger declared, "never fully mastered the secret of the cross, he reached the threshold of the great truth and stood facing the altar." Likewise for Arnold: "We picture him as one who stood on the threshold of the temple looking at the altar."[34]

Here was a real weakness of liberal modernism in general. Rather than wrestling with substantial divisions between theology and cosmopolitan culture, modernists devised ways to declare these divisions superficial and imagine that in the future everything would come out all right. So in Munger's writing everything depended on the future.

In the end, this was the only way he could make sense of the literature of his own day. If the greater part of nineteenth-century literature was hard to reconcile with his vision of literary history, late nineteenth-century literature was even more difficult. Indeed, in contrast with aestheticism, Arnold's Victorian crisis of faith seems practically pious. Late nineteenth-century aesthetes such as Algernon Swinburne were not just questioning Christianity, they were celebrating paganism. They conjured up the more racy stories of classical mythology. There were also the realists who turned their eye on the gritty details of everyday sexual life. Either way, the contemporary literary scene did not bode well for Munger's argument. Once again, he relied on the future to get himself around the evidence. This is how Munger dismissed the major trends of his day. "The novel of society and of naked realism, and the art-for-art's sake literature which lingering heathenism now and then strives to revive, have no deep and lasting regard," Munger intoned. "The time seems nearly to have come in when a Christian nation will accept and adopt as classic only the literature which is Christian. This is simply logical."[35]

Indeed, in Munger's theology it was "logical." His argument was (more or less) consistent. The problem was evidence. Only by defining literature and Christianity in the most vague, humanitarian terms could Munger claim any consistent overlap between them. And the closer he got to his own era, even this vague overlap could not be sustained. Indeed, for much of nineteenth-century literature, the logic of his argument forced him to dismiss the relevance of evidence. This made sense, for what he had to dismiss was much of romantic and postromantic literature. No matter how vaguely he defined Christianity and literature, he simply could not make theological sense of the emphasis on emotional complexity in modern literature. And things were getting worse, not better.

It was not that American writers gave themselves over to the abandon of Swinburne's neopaganism. But they did not shy away from such challenges. "The question was, where do we go from Swinburne?," wrote T. S. Eliot, reflecting on his generation's start at the beginning of the century. American writers went in many directions—and many went to Europe to escape American parochialism and immerse themselves in the new artistic currents. There they embraced modernism, which toned down the florid paganism of aestheticism and grim Darwinism of realism and relied more on the fragmented style of imagism in poetry and stream of consciousness in the novel to explore what modernists saw as the fundamental symbols of civilization and the unconscious.[36]

This was not necessarily incompatible with Christianity. Eliot, for instance, eventually landed on high-church Anglicanism—a perch upon which a number of the aesthetes before him had come to rest. And even where there was not a belief in Christianity, the modernist interest in myth and psychological complexity sometimes brought writers close to the sources of traditional Protestantism. In 1931, John Crowe Ransom wrote *God without Thunder: An Unorthodox Defence of Orthodoxy* in praise of the Old Testament characterization of God. The historian Ann Douglas called Freud "Calvin's heir" in describing how American modernists in the 1920s embraced Freudian psychology in order to throw off the legacy of the sentimental novel, recover Melville and the darker side of Hawthorne, and develop more complex characterizations of human beings. Certainly Freud, an atheist, was not "Calvin's heir" in theology; but Douglas did have a point that, on either side of the nineteenth century, Calvinism and Freudianism encouraged Americans to think of character as a labyrinth of complex and mysterious depth. And though this depth was often disturbing—a sign of sin or pathology—it could also be intriguing and might suggest redemptive and creative possibilities of an equally complex and mysterious nature.[37]

American theologians absorbed some of this but not enough to challenge their neoclassical and sentimental characterizations of God. As we will see, neo-orthodox liberals came to write respectfully about the "mythic paradoxes" of the Old Testament God but barely used this in their own depictions of him. Theologians alluded to Freudian psychology and the general emphasis on emotional complexity mostly to reinforce their notions of sin, immaturity, or primitive humans. Complexity, in short, became defined as a problem. It is no wonder that it seemed unsuitable for characterizing God. Thus, God's neoclassical and sentimental character was preserved. In contrast to the confusing depictions of humans in modernist literature, God still held up familiar moral ideals. In this too, theology and literature became estranged.

Twentieth-century writers no longer felt bound to teach a clear moral lesson. Literary characters no longer had to exemplify proper, everyday behavior. It was not just the aesthetes who sought to shock Victorian piety; modernists of all stripes often showed an exuberant disdain for moral conformity. Virginia Woolf compared the new impulse in literature to the impulses of "a boy staying with an aunt for the weekend [who] rolls in the geranium bed out of sheer desperation as the solemnities of the Sabbath wear on." If this led to some indecency, it was not because writers gave up on morality. They no longer saw it as their duty to write with the single-mindedness of the social reformer or to inculcate common decencies. These had their place, but the writer's task was to explore the depth of human character and provide this with some expression. This seemed a more pressing need than the reinforcement of role models. "You have gone to bed at night bewildered by the complexity of your feelings," wrote Woolf. "Thousands of emotions have met, collided, and disappeared in astonishing disorder. Nevertheless, you allow the writers to palm off upon you a [simplified] version of all this." Now times were changing. Woolf, with mock historical exactitude, gave it a date: "In or about December 1910, human character changed."[38]

It took some time for this to sink into American cosmopolitan culture. A measure here was the rising stock of the "American renaissance" writers and the decline of the "genteel tradition." Even in 1932, it was still news for Carl Van Doren to announce a "New Canon" in bold type in the pages of the *Nation*: "Thirty, even twenty years ago, it seemed to many observers that the end of a literary epoch had been reached and the elder classics were secure on solid thrones. Bearded and benevolent, the faces of Bryant, Longfellow, Whittier, Lowell, Holmes, and sometimes (rather oddly) Whitman looked down unchallenged from the walls of schoolrooms." Now all of these but Whitman were coming down. In place of them were Emerson and Hawthorne, who had always had some place in the canon but now were read for their romantic, psychological depth. More significant, the works of Melville and Dickinson received new consideration. Though these might seem like small changes, Van Doren did not think so. It showed the new literary sophistication of America. The United States, he declared, was "in the process of becoming aware of itself, of overcoming its hesitant, polite beginnings at self-expression, of admitting to the record the world of consciousness outside the genteel tradition, of engaging in violent critical debate between decorum and candor, of at last standing up among the literary nations of the earth."[39]

By the middle of the twentieth century, a new generation of liberal theologians recognized the importance of literary modernism and tried to throw off the "genteel" aspects of Munger's approach to literature. One of the most prominent of these theologians was Amos Wilder.

Amos N. Wilder

Wilder was born in Wisconsin in 1895, grew up in California, and spent two years at Oberlin University before transferring to Yale. Then the United States entered World War I and so did Wilder, serving ambulance and artillery duty. After the war ended, he studied briefly in France at Toulouse and Montauban Seminary, returned to finish his college education at Yale, and then went back to Europe to study at the University of Brussels and Oxford, where his subject was theology. He was also writing poetry. In 1923, on returning to America, he won the prestigious Yale Series of Younger Poets competition for his book, *Battle Retrospect and Other Poems*. This would be one of three books of verse he published (the other two in 1928 and 1943). Meanwhile, his younger brother, Thornton Wilder, was also writing and would publish his most famous novel, *The Bridge of San Luis Rey*, in 1927 and the play *Our Town* in 1938.

Theology, however, would be Amos Wilder's calling. After completing his divinity degree and doctorate in the New Testament at Yale, he served as professor of New Testament, first at Andover Newton Theological School from 1933 to 1943 and then at Chicago Theological Seminary from 1943 to 1954, until he made his last move to Harvard Theological Seminary. His publications were numerous. Though distinguished in his field of New Testament studies, his most influential works dealt with modern literature.[40]

Wilder distanced his work from the previous generation of modernists such as Munger and Dinsmore. At Yale College and Divinity School, Wilder may have come under Dinsmore's influence. In 1956, Wilder recalled Dinsmore's "contagious enthusiasm." But Wilder also referred to this earlier generation as "Christian idealists" and lumped them with nineteenth-century Victorians. Later he noted that in America the "genteel era of the post-Victorians" had persisted well into the twentieth century.[41] World War I had a large impact in driving Munger's sort of optimism from the scene. World War II and the early years of the Cold War, in turn, helped sustain a more somber mood in American liberal theology. There was an urgency and sense of crisis in the "theology and literature" school, as this phase of theological modernism came to be called. The problem seemed not just that theologians were falling behind cosmopolitan culture but that they were losing touch with how to express Christianity at all. As part of this, there was a new interest in the value of symbols and myths as permanent parts of culture. This echoed the concerns of literary modernists and made the theological interest in literature seem deeper than past efforts, which could be dismissed merely as attempts to seem refined. "It is no longer only a question of the Sacred Lyre and of the cultural formation of the clergy," Wilder declared in 1958. "More urgent today is the whole question of imaginative vehicles, of symbolization in religion."[42]

This resulted in some changes in American liberal theology. Wilder embraced contemporary writers to an extent that Munger never did. In 1940, in his first major theological work, *The Spiritual Aspects of the New Poetry*, Wilder declared that Tennyson and Browning "will always have telling power for the converted," but he acknowledged that a "social and aesthetic revolution" had occurred that raised new writers to the fore, whom theologians had to consider.[43] Also, more so than Munger, Wilder was interested in the darker side of literature. The neo-orthodox emphasis on the intractability of human sin was an important guide for Wilder here. So was the theology of the transplanted German Paul Tillich. Tillich developed a "method of correlation" between theology and culture. According to this theory, theologians must address the questions that culture puts to them and must strive to interpret the Christian message for the given cultural situation. Such notions led to a new respect for the profundity of modern culture. But this also meant that theologians tended to interpret modern culture as posing questions the theologians could answer. Worse, it meant that some took to interpreting modern culture in terms of their ready-made answers. Thus, it became easy for Wilder to assume that the emphasis on ambivalence arising out of romanticism was mainly a way to pose questions about sin, or, as liberal theologians liked to put it, "the human condition." This also marked some change in liberal theology. Gone was Munger's emphasis on the optimistic note in theology that "all is well."[44] Gone too was the effort to blame only conservatives for the declining stature of theology. Wilder, like the neo-orthodox critics of the social gospel, also blamed the earlier generation of liberals. They charged them with being "sentimental," in a polemical sense of the term, meaning superficial, unrealistic, and overly optimistic.

Here Wilder and his generation found some use for the complexity of romantic characterization at the heart of modern literature. "The hallmark . . . of modernist literature," Wilder declared in 1940, is "dissociation," by which he meant isolation and a fascination with the irrational and psychologically unstable. This had its negative aspects, but in some respects it provided a corrective to the "sentimentalism in Christianity." In a chapter of his 1940 work entitled "New Views of the Self," Wilder cautiously affirmed this aspect of modern literature: "As a matter of fact, should we not agree that true stability in personality is rare, and that we have here one field in which the new writers are truly more realistic than the old."[45] Throughout his career, Wilder continued to claim that this aspect of modern literature had lessons to teach theologians. "Our Christian habits of mind and heart," Wilder declared in 1962, "seem to inhibit, if not cripple, our resourcefulness, so that we are not able to communicate with the secular mystery of the age." Attention to literature could help. "It is good for Christians to have to make a place in their sometimes shrunken outlook for the formidable energies and realities evident in the arts. It represents a theological provocation that is good for us."[46] Modern writers, Wilder declared, "have restored to us an image of man, paradigms of man in depth, which rebuke our conventionality and expose the inadequacy of our speech."[47]

But this being said, Wilder mainly saw the "provocation" of literature here as pointing toward psychological and social problems that theology should address by offering a more harmonious vision of character. It is true that, to some extent, Wilder celebrated the emotional depth of the artist. But in this Wilder was much like Munger, who admired the aura and prestige of the writer, "the poet, the man of genius, the broad and universal thinker." Wilder also ascribed some of the power of modern literature to the participation of the artist in the political and social events of the day, whether fighting against totalitarianism in Europe or middle-class conformity in America. This was the context in which he made his statement about "paradigms of man in depth." Immediately preceding this he had declared, "We turn perforce to artists outside the camp who know modern man better than we know ourselves, men who have belonged to the resistance of our time, the anti-Fascist battalions, the anti-totalitarian cells, the anti-bourgeois insecure."[48]

There were a number of problems with this. For one thing, this political view of modern writers simply did not apply to all great literature. It did little to account for writers who lived in relative security, such as Wallace Stevens, who wrote modernist masterpieces while working for an insurance company in Hartford, Connecticut. There was another more basic problem. Wilder was relying on a dubious myth of the artist to account for the art. One reason for this may be that it allowed him to subsume romanticism under neoclassicism. The character of modern literature might be anguished, but the artist could be celebrated as a person of action. Such praise easily slid into paeans to neoclassical fortitude.

In those cases in which Wilder could not celebrate the political activity of the artist, he found much less to say for the complexity of character in modern literature. He mostly saw it as a provocative diagnosis of modern social and psychological ills that called for a Christian cure. This had been his approach to literature in his 1940 work, *The Spiritual Aspects of Modern Poetry*. There he had recommended Christianity as offering to writers "a full sense of selfhood, of mature responsible person-

ality," a more "disinterested" approach to "social reform," and a "universal tradition" to make their writing more coherent. Otherwise, Wilder suggested that the tradition of Proust and Joyce had "reached its dead end."[49]

Following the war, it was hard for Wilder to sustain this view. Instead, he saw the
Christian tradition as inevitably, if surreptitiously, at work in modernist literature.
Wilder's argument for this was much like Munger's. Both declared that historical
forces were at work that made Western literature inevitably Christian. Munger and
Wilder did differ on the nature of these forces. Whereas Munger attributed these forces
to the immanent, creative power of God in history, Wilder simply asserted that the
legacy of Christianity persisted in modern literature. The title to his 1952 work,
Modern Poetry and the Christian Tradition, stated Wilder's basic assumption. Modern poetry was carrying on the Christian tradition. It was "the most remarkable feature" of the twentieth century, Wilder asserted, that "custody" of the "Christian tradition" had passed from theology to the "arts and imaginative literature."[50]

There is much that was true in this statement. It was true if Wilder meant that theology had suffered a precipitous cultural decline in the twentieth century and that
cosmopolitan people were relying far more on literature than on theology to provide
them with insight into the meaning of life. The statement was also true if Wilder meant
that Western literature was permeated with Christian symbols, allusions, and references. It was also true if Wilder meant that some writers, such as T. S. Eliot, had
become Christians and made this part of their work. Finally, it was also true that a
number of leading literary critics at midcentury, such as Cleanth Brooks and William Wimsatt, maintained a low-level Christian apologetic in their criticism. So there
was some overlap between Christianity and literature in the middle of the twentieth
century.

But Wilder meant something more than this. Like Munger, Wilder suggested that
profound literature in the West almost inevitably held a Christian message. Like
Munger also, Wilder could sustain this point only by defining Christianity and literature so broadly that they must inevitably overlap. And the point of overlap was
the same for both men: "humanity." It was their touchstone. It was the bridge that
they imagined spanned the chasm between theology and literature. They tried to cross
this bridge, however, from different directions. This reflected their different theological perspectives. Munger came at it from an optimistic, modernist vision of history; Wilder came at it from a more somber, neo-orthodox vision of history. But these
differences in liberal theology did not translate into large differences in their appreciation of literature. Whether positive or negative, the spin was the same. Whereas
Munger declared that literature and Christianity celebrated humanity, Wilder claimed
that literature and Christianity protested against inhumanity.

All of this allowed them to overlook details in literary works and declare, as Arnold
did about the Old Testament, that "really, at bottom," these works were about humanitarian morality, so about Christianity. We have seen how Munger did this with
Shakespeare. Wilder applied the same formula: "Even where the Christian heritage
is not involved in any overt way, the artist is characteristically a voice against the
dehumanizations all about us." By this, Wilder meant that the writer stood for "compassion and responsibility." This was often enough for Wilder to claim the Christian
heritage was at work, if not overtly, then covertly. He acknowledged that "we can-

not, of course, connect all the creative impulses in the arts today with Christianity." But he could "connect" many. His humanitarian alembic transformed writers who were indifferent or even hostile to Christianity into the unconscious carriers of a Christian message. Thus, Wallace Stevens fell into line here; even Ezra Pound carried a Christian message.[51]

None of this, however, carried Wilder very far. As with Munger's assertions about humanity, Wilder's humanitarianism did not help him to make sense of the details in a writer's work, for not every bit of romantic ambivalence in an author's work could be explained away as a protest against inhumanity. The problem became especially acute when writers considered Christian subjects. The irony here is that this forced Wilder into arguing with the very authors who were relying most on the Christian tradition. But the problem was that they were not relying on it as Wilder assumed they should. That is, they were not using it to inform their greater sense of humanity but were struggling with it and trying to make sense of it in terms of their romantic ambivalence toward God. But none of this made sense with Wilder's liberal assumptions. In the end he ascribed to God a neoclassical and sentimental character.

Thus, Wilder ended up gently correcting authors for misunderstanding Christianity. For instance, in 1952 Wilder thought that T. S. Eliot's "Four Quartets" was too pessimistic. "Is not the way of victorious renunciation practicable in the world?," Wilder asked rhetorically.[52] In 1958, Wilder similarly handled Robinson Jeffers's poem on the crucifixion, "Dear Judas." In common romantic fashion, Jeffers's treatment of the crucifixion was profoundly ambivalent; the power of the cross both fascinated and repulsed him. Much of Wilder's reading of the poem, however, came down to chiding Jeffers for making the scene "morbid." Wilder suggested that Jeffers's own differences with his Presbyterian father prevented him from appreciating the real meaning of Christianity, that the "secret of the suffering of the Christian is that it is indissolubly merged with joy."[53]

Wilder's treatment of "Dear Judas" is worth spending some time on, for it shows the neoclassical and sentimental assumptions in Wilder's theology. The point here is not that Jeffers was right and Wilder was wrong. It is a question of which literary assumptions each writer brought to the Gospels. If, as Wilder claimed, the Christian's suffering is "indissolubly merged with joy," then there is little room for ambivalence. But this is what Jeffers was after in his depiction of Jesus. To this end, Jeffers drew on a range of details in the Gospels. In this, at least, Jeffers's meditation on the crucifixion was more substantial than Wilder's for Jeffers made use of the Gospels more fully. And he respected their complexity. But Wilder was not interested in this complexity in the Gospels or in Jeffers's poem.

The emotional complexity of Jesus was at the center of "Dear Judas." The fascination with violence in the poem did not exclude other emotions. The cross provoked an uneasy mixture of feelings. And this mixture was concentrated in the character of Jesus. The poem has several subplots, but the major story is a sympathetic account of how Judas came to betray Jesus. The plot is basically a complication of the sentimental life of Christ plot. Recall that in this plot Jesus' followers misunderstand him and believe he may lead a revolution against the Romans. Some of his followers want this, some do not, but all are confused by him and most are worried by the direction he is taking. Stowe had sympathetically depicted Mary wanting to steer Jesus off the path that led to the cross. Jeffers did the same with Judas but carried the plot further.

In "Dear Judas," Judas betrayed Jesus to save him, to save his followers, and, ultimately, to save the Jewish people. Judas was a follower of Jesus because of his message of forgiveness and charity to the poor. But in his provocative trip to Jerusalem, Jesus seemed to have gotten new and strange ideas into his head. Judas feared that Jesus was toying with the notion of leading the people into a revolution. Judas recognized that this would be a failure and lead to the massacre of many and most likely the death of Jesus. But Judas did not think that Jesus was deeply committed to this idea any more than the people were. So, by having Jesus detained, Judas believed he would be giving everyone a cooling-off period. Judas assumed that Jesus would be released in a few days, when he would return to preaching his doctrines of forgiveness and charity. So Judas did not anticipate the crucifixion. Jesus did, however. He made use of his arrest to drive the authorities to kill him—in part, he explained to Judas, because nothing so appealed to the masses as a bloody martyr.

This is what Wilder took as the "thesis" of the poem: that Jesus' fame rested on a morbid fascination with violence. Wilder acknowledged in the beginning of his analysis of the poem that this was just "one particular slant which the poet gives to the Gospel story." But within two sentences Wilder called this a "preoccupation" of Jeffers and then went on to call it a common "heresy" and an "obsession" that modern psychology interpreted as sadomasochism. Wilder remarked that Jeffers was not alone in his "mistaken view" of the cross and that much in modern culture and Christian tradition contributed to this view. But the point is that Wilder took this as the significant point of the poem.[54]

But was it? This is only one of Jesus' views of crucifixion in the poem. It is not clear what we are to make of Jesus here. He says many things, many of which are contradictory. This seems to be the point of his character. It is difficult to know what to make of Jesus; he is not even sure what to make of himself. Indeed, what he says of the crucifixion seems not so much a glorification of violence as dismissive of the masses who find so much in it. If Jesus is unclear about his significance, so is Judas. Perhaps the central theme of the poem is Judas trying to make sense of Jesus. This is not easy, for since Jesus came to Jerusalem, he has been strangely and dangerously erratic. As Judas says:

> Oh, he has changed and changed. But I, what shall I do? His mind is dreadfully exalted and bitter,
> And divided. I cannot understand what he suffers but I see what he does ...
> ... He has the shining power a few moments
> And then stands brooding dumb, or suddenly through the old sweetness a jet of poison. I have begged and prayed to him,
> On my knees, with tears, to return down from the city. He looked across me with haggard eyes and answered
> That he was God, and would never go down. But then I heard that he has begun to despair.[55]

Jeffers used a great deal of material in the Gospels to support this depiction of Jesus. For instance, Jeffers incorporated into the poem Jesus' apparent dismissal of his mother and family in the crowd scene, his rage against the money changers, his exultation at raising up the temple in three days, his calm at the last supper, his apparent indifference toward the poor in allowing a woman to wash his feet with expensive oil, his despair in the Garden of Gethsemane. Of course, we may not agree with how Jeffers's Judas interpreted these scenes. But it is not clear that we are supposed to agree with Judas here. For that matter, it is not clear that Jeffers was putting forth any single view of Jesus that we are supposed to accept or reject. Rather, in common romantic fashion, Jeffers was laying out the complexity of Jesus' character.

Wilder, however, was not interested in this complexity—either in the Gospels or in Jeffers's poem. This is because his assumptions about God and Jesus' character came from neoclassicism and sentimentalism. Given this, it is no wonder that Wilder had little interest in how Jeffers had depicted Jesus. It was easy to latch on to the most sensational view of the crucifixion in the poem, claim that this was the point of the poem, and chide Jeffers for being morbid. As an attack on romantic characterization, the polemic was long established in American theology. Back in 1855, the writer of "Is Effective Writing Necessarily 'Volcanic'?" had dismissed romanticism, saying that "we are so much more struck by violence than the calm on-going of real power." In 1958, Wilder turned this polemic against "volcanic" romanticism onto Jeffers. He had already done so in 1940: "Christianity meets the particular need of men of today [by] the overcoming of that dissociation which we have seen to be general . . . [by] forcing them to accept the role of responsible selfhood. . . . Here all evasions into the cult of the unconscious and the irrational, however sophisticated, are forbidden. Aesthetic solution of conflict whether in the exquisite forms of Yeats' 'Byzantium' or the more violent forms of Jeffers are precluded. The artist must not win his excitement and power cheaply by abandonment of himself to the volcanic but anarchic forces of the soul."[56]

In his analysis of Jeffers's poem, Wilder offered his own explanation of the Gospels. Wilder's God and Jesus had a combination of neoclassical and sentimental traits. Like his nineteenth-century liberal forebears, Wilder sustained these characterizations of Jesus in spite of certain details in the Gospels. Like Channing a hundred years earlier, Wilder believed that there was an unhealthy and morbid interest in Jesus' sufferings. Channing had chalked this up to Protestant and Catholic traditions, not to the Gospels. Wilder proceeded similarly. He acknowledged that there were strains in Protestant, Roman Catholic, and Eastern Orthodox traditions that fixated on Jesus' sufferings. These were especially strong, he noted, in Latin American and Spanish Catholicism. But wherever they were found, they were "excrescences," according to Wilder; "most often they represent survivals of pre-Christian patterns, outcroppings of primitive legacies, or corruptions of Christian piety occasioned by contemporary cultural factors."[57]

This was a remarkable statement. It was especially so given all that Wilder had said about preserving the Christian heritage and the importance of myth and modern culture. Evidently, Wilder did not consider the "Christian heritage" a great resource if it conflicted with his neoclassical and sentimental assumptions about Jesus. Nor were primitive myth and modern culture profound if they interfered with these assumptions. Indeed, to Wilder's mind interest in Christ's sufferings—whether primitive, traditional, or modern—merely served morbid ends: to "feed men's regressive impulses towards excitement and self mortification."[58]

So Wilder strove to wipe away these "excrescences" and reveal the true Gospel. To do this, he armed himself with formidable critical tools. This allowed him to downplay disturbing details about Jesus' suffering, much as his nineteenth-century forebears had done. For instance, the crown of thorns did not really contain thorns: "Our best understanding of *koine* Greek usage today makes it doubtful whether the plant in question, the *ankantha*, had any sharp spines." The scholarly point might be taken, but the question is what one did with it. Wilder's theological agenda was to move attention away from Christ's sufferings. In this vein, Wilder continued: the flagellation of Jesus, Wilder pointed out, was "mentioned only in a passing phrase." Thus, it was not important; its likely significance was as a marker of fulfilled prophecy. In much the same way, nineteenth-century liberals wrote off Jesus' cry, "My God, my God, why hast thou forsaken me?" as only a recital of the Psalms to fulfill prophecy and show Jesus' familiarity with the scriptures. Wilder passed over this whole episode.[59]

Astonishingly, he even dismissed interest in Jesus' character: "What is important here is not the subjective suffering of Christ, but the objective intervention of God in the whole drama of death and victory."[60] It might be thought that if anyone should have been interested in the "subjective suffering of Christ," it would be a theologian who claimed to draw on modernist literature. But in the end, Wilder was not receptive to literature if it threatened to displace his neoclassical and sentimental characterizations of Jesus. Again, the strategy came right out of the nineteenth century. Park and Shedd (in his neoclassical phase) had also warned against speculating about Jesus' mental, or "subjective," sufferings. But they had also assumed that these sufferings came directly from God ("a stroke delivered by a divine person," Shedd called it). But this was not part of Wilder's agenda. In Wilder's theology, Jesus suffered because people had persecuted him; God's involvement in this was confined to turning the cross into a "victory."

What Wilder meant by "the objective intervention of God" (in contrast to Jesus' merely "subjective" sufferings) is not clear, especially since God is barely depicted in the Gospels. Wilder seems to have meant the intent of the Gospel writers. Claiming to know this, he again dismissed attention to the drama of Christ's character. "They portray a divine transaction whose import far transcends the feelings of the protagonist," he declared. "What is important for the Evangelists is the revelation mediated— the operation of God in the event—not the poignancies of the occasion."[61]

Yet once around the gospel details, Wilder was willing to celebrate the emotional force of the cross. This was his answer to Jeffers. The meaning of the crucifixion was to be found "in the operation of God in the event." Wilder's interpretation of the atonement, however, had little to do with the "Christian heritage." The greater part of this heritage was the juristic tradition, which attributed Christ's sufferings to God's wrath against sin. But again, Wilder was not interested in this if it did not support his own liberal view. According to Wilder, God had sustained Jesus and turned his death into victory. So to understand the Christian message, one had to focus on the strength of Jesus rather than his suffering. Over a hundred years earlier, Channing had claimed that the Gospels presented an unambiguous portrait of a victorious, dignified Christ. Once a few troubling details were put in scholarly perspective, Wilder agreed. In his characterizations of Jesus, Wilder was part of the same liberal tradition as Channing. Despite the fact that both men had an interest in romantic literature, this interest had little influence on their characterizations of Jesus. To Wilder's mind, the Gospels were as clear as they were to Channing, and this is what Jeffers and other modern poets needed to learn. "Thus our primary Christian sources show the way," Wilder declared. "The cross of Christ should be a fountain of health and not of morbidity."[62]

❧

CHAPTER NINE

The Social Gospel and Its Critics

Walter Rauschenbusch, Reinhold Niebuhr, and J. Gresham Machen

The greatest innovation in twentieth-century cosmopolitan theology was complete by the second decade of the century. This was the liberal social gospel movement. Its leading theologian was Walter Rauschenbusch. The meaning of the social gospel was found in its name: salvation was social, not just for the individual but for society. This was what Jesus had meant by the kingdom of God. Not just a heavenly afterlife but a better life for everyone here and now. Jesus was a social reformer. What made him special was that he knew that reform came through the power of God. God was immanent in history and spread throughout humanity; thus he could drive history forward and bring people together. Indeed, this was the meaning of the incarnation. First manifest in Jesus, God could become manifest in all of humanity. Humanity integrated into a harmonious whole would be the final incarnation of God.

This was an exciting vision, but it also testified to how little was left to God's character. He could hardly be represented in his own right; so general had his neoclassical and sentimental traits become that they were suited to describing a collective mass rather than a distinctive character.

There were two major influences behind the social gospel. First was the new humanitarianism of utopian writers such as Edward Bellamy, who absorbed evolution and industrialism into a vision of historical progress unifying all of humanity. The more profound influence was the historical criticism of the New Testament coming out of Germany combined with the liberal German theological attempt to find new footing for the message of Christianity in secular history. Biblical criticism, church history, and theology here were of a piece, for this biblical criticism undermined the supernatural claims of the New Testament and grounded Jesus' life and death in secular history. But for that very reason, liberal theologians in Germany, from Albrecht Ritschl to Wilhelm Hermann and Adolph von Harnack, embraced history as the sounding board for trumpeting Jesus' humanitarian accomplishments. But this was not easy. Such accomplishments were difficult to find. Neither the New Testament nor the history of the church offered much in the way of evidence. Indeed, many liberals thought that the church in its nearly 2,000 year history had sought power and privilege more than social justice.[1]

So liberals looked to the future. The social tensions in society coming out of industrialism were seen to make up the world crisis that Jesus' message could solve. If this dismissed the relevance of much of church history, it made the present very exciting, for social gospel theologians imagined that they were on the brink of a major historical development. Christianity was finally coming into its own. The authentic message of Jesus had been rediscovered and (as if by providence) not a moment too soon. In bringing Christ's social teaching to bear on the industrial conflict of the day, theologians could help to avert cataclysmic class war and usher in what Jesus had first proclaimed as the kingdom of God.

This emphasis on present politics made the social gospel seem new. And the scenarios were new. Not the individual but society; not a transcendent God but an immanent God; not heaven but history. But a longer view shows that less had changed than first appeared. The scenarios had changed, but the character of God remained the same. The neoclassical God was made immanent in history. The scope of the sentimental Jesus was expanded from the family to humanity. But God was still defined by neoclassicism and sentimentalism. Indeed, in this sense the social gospel was not so much an innovation as a holding operation.

This was the problem of liberal theology in the twentieth century. Its effort was to make God relevant for modern society, but this did not lead liberals to adapt the character of God to the romanticism of modern society. Rather, liberals tried to give some new power to neoclassicism and sentimentalism. But there was really only one way to do this: make God political. Only in politics did neoclassical and sentimental characterizations continue to carry substantial authority in the twentieth century. So liberals played their best card in the social gospel.

The rest of the century was given to criticizing it and reviving it again. It was easy to criticize, for social gospel theologians had staked many of their claims on their ability to interpret history and influence politics. They did not make good on either claim. Even their grounding in the Gospels was weak. Much of the intellectual support for the social gospel had run out by the 1920s. Yet the social gospel (in various forms) persisted through the end of the twentieth century because there was nothing to replace it with. That is, nothing unless theologians developed a romantic characterization of God, but none did this.

This was not because the social gospel did not have its critics. In fact, criticizing the social gospel became a kind of growth industry in twentieth-century theology. Within liberalism, the neo-orthodox critique of the social gospel emerged in the 1920s and remained strong through the 1960s. One of its greatest writers was Reinhold Niebuhr. Conservative theologians also sustained themselves through the early twentieth century by denouncing the social gospel. Their leading writer was J. Gresham Machen. Both Niebuhr and Machen, from different theological stances, emphasized the transcendence of God, the otherworldly peculiarity of Jesus, and the depth of human sin. In theory, these were strong appeals. But in the end Niebuhr and Machen could say more about human beings than they could about God. The reason was simple: both theologians, having rejected the social gospel, were basically committed to nineteenth-century forms of neoclassical theism and sentimental incarnationalism. This did not make their arguments very strong. When they pointed to gospel details that did not make sense with the social gospel, they could not make much sense of them. When they invoked the solemn mysteries of a transcendent God, their appeals went flat, for they had to rely on the familiar formulations from the nineteenth century. If God seemed especially mysterious now, it was partly because he had become so vague. This was the very reason some liberals had been drawn to the social gospel in the first place; as the century went on, it was one reason some conservatives were drawn to fundamentalism.

Walter Rauschenbusch

Walter Rauschenbusch was born in 1861. Men in his family had been ministers for six generations. There was little doubt that he would be the seventh. He was the only surviving son of August Rauschenbusch, who had immigrated from Germany to America in 1846. After serving in parishes in the Midwest before the Civil War, August Rauschenbusch settled down as professor of divinity and German in the Baptist Rochester Theological Seminary in upstate New York. He made sure that his son received the best education. He sent him to secondary school in Germany and urged him to stay on and attend lectures by Adolph von Harnack, the great liberal church historian. But Walter Rauschenbusch was also equipped to adapt this education to American conditions. From 1886 to 1897, he was minister near an impoverished part of New York City and saw firsthand the urban squalor of modern industrialism. At the same time, he was reading American social visionaries such as Edward Bellamy. This helped him absorb the spirit of America's progressive vision.[2]

But Rauschenbusch also had a sense of crisis looming in American history. The date of his birth—1861—was significant. So was his father's experience: he had come east to Rochester in the first place because while a minister to the German community in Missouri in the 1850s he had gotten into trouble (and his family had even been threatened) because he refused to serve communion to slaveholders. When Walter Rauschenbusch wrote *Christianity and the Social Crisis* in 1907, he intimated that America was on the verge of another Civil War—a class war. Ministers, however, by preaching the social gospel, could avert this catastrophe and usher in the new era of equality, the kingdom of God.[3]

But there remained unresolved tensions in Rauschenbusch's work. If he had a commanding vision of God's sweep through history, the details of the Gospels continued to trip him up. For one thing, Jesus did not always appear concerned about the poor.[4] More troubling was the meaning of the crucifixion. This was an issue that Rauschenbusch could never easily fit into his overall vision. When he tried, he usually fell back on the common explanations of nineteenth-century neoclassical theism and sentimental incarnationalism.

Still, there was much that was new. For one thing, there was a more positive assessment of the Old Testament, particularly the later prophets. Social gospel theologians claimed that the Old Testament prophets had been the first to glimpse the idea that God was concerned about social justice for all people. This did not mean, however, that the social gospel theologians gave up on the polemic against the juristic tradition and the primitivization of the Old Testament. Rather, the polemic was pushed back to earlier portions of the Old Testament. Indeed, social gospel theologians pictured the prophets doing what liberal theologians themselves had been doing during the nineteenth century—replacing the juristic God with the God of philanthropism. So, from being wrathful, God became loving; from being a nationalistic God, he was expanded into a God of humanity. The Hebrew prophets, according to Rauschenbusch, "repudiated the idea of favoritism in divine government" and argued instead that "God moves on a plane of universal and ethical law."[5]

Jesus was also a prophet, but he was special. This was because he recognized something that the earlier prophets had not fully appreciated: because God was immanent in history, he was, in some sense, in everyone. But for God's presence to become manifest, people needed to become conscious of God in themselves. Jesus had arrived at this consciousness of God in himself. Because of this, it made sense to say that God was incarnate in Christ. But the point was that God could be incarnate in everyone. In fact, that was what God was working for in history. He was gradually bringing about the day when everyone could become aware of God in themselves. In that day, there would be no more division among people. The human race would become fully integrated. That was the final incarnation, when God would be incarnate in humanity.

But all of this had to start somewhere in history. So it started with Jesus. As an individual, he was a harbinger of the final incarnation of God in humanity. He was also, in this respect, a revelation of God. Because Jesus was conscious of God in himself, he took on the character of God—which, for Rauschenbusch, meant a neoclassical character. This showed how much greater Jesus was than all of the previous prophets. "In the poise and calm of his mind and manner," Rauschenbusch declared, "and in the love of his heart, he was infinitely above them all."[6]

Unfortunately, he was also so far above his contemporaries that they turned against him. Or it would be more accurate to say that in his historical vision he was far ahead of his contemporaries. Either way, the Jewish people turned against him. The problem, according to the social gospel theologians, was that the Jewish people were still tied to their nationalistic, juristic conception of God. So their understanding of history was primitive. They were given to apocalyptic fantasies. They looked for a God who would swoop down into history from his perch in eternity and vanquish the Romans and restore the Jewish state. But Jesus had a different view. He saw God as immanent in history. Therefore, God worked gradually through historical processes to establish the kingdom of God—an era of justice for all peoples. But the Jewish people did not go along with Jesus here. According to Rauschenbusch, "The people had the impatience which did not see processes, but clamors for big results, big thunderous, miraculous results. Jesus had the scientific insight which comes to most men by training but to the elect few by divine gift. He was seeking to displace the misleading catastrophic conceptions by a saner theory of the coming of the Kingdom." And for this Jesus was rejected by the people and turned over to the Romans to be crucified.[7]

Among other things, this was a neat twist on the sentimental life of Christ. This plot had depended on depicting Jesus' followers as mistakenly believing he was a political messiah. One of the reasons they had turned against him was that they discovered he was not. Now the roles were nearly reversed. Jesus was a political reformer, but the people wanted more of a divine messiah (though one who would still give them an earthly rather than a heavenly kingdom). But this raised another problem. The nineteenth-century sentimental incarnationalists had a good point when they claimed that Jesus preached a heavenly, not an earthly kingdom. In the Gospel of John, Pilate, the Roman magistrate who oversaw the sentencing of Jesus, asked him why, if he was the leader of the Jews, they had handed him over to the Romans to be executed. Jesus answered: "My kingdom is not of this world; if my kingdom were of this world, then my servants would fight." These sorts of passages were troubling for the social gospel theologians.[8]

But here is where their New Testament criticism helped. They claimed that these passages (and much of the Gospel of John) were not authentic; that is, they did not represent what the historical Jesus would actually have said; rather, they were sayings that the early church had ascribed to Jesus to make him into a supernatural and otherworldly being. But if this was the case, then how were theologians to know what Jesus had actually meant by the "kingdom of God"? Theologians must rely on the historical method, Rauschenbusch explained. That is, they must try to gather the meaning of the phrase from its historical context. Jesus must have never precisely defined the phrase, Rauschenbusch surmised, because everyone knew what he meant by it. What did his followers think he meant by it? An earthly kingdom, Rauschenbusch answered. Here again was another reversal of the life of Christ. Whereas Jesus' followers had once been blind, now they could see; they had become the authorities on the historical Jesus.[9]

The implications for the history of Christianity were intoxicating. This was the real kicker of the social gospel. Liberal theologians were suggesting that prior to themselves the church had not really understood Jesus. For nearly two thousand years the church had gotten him wrong. More so, the church had substituted for Jesus' vision an etherealized mishmash of the deluded hopes of those Jews who had persecuted Jesus. From the very beginning, the church had mistakenly linked Jesus to the pre-prophetic, Jewish juristic God and Jewish apocalyptic visions. This was a gutsy charge for social gospel theologians to make.

They had the confidence to make it because they were drawing on prestigious liberal German church history and biblical criticism. This did to the New Testament depiction of Jesus what earlier biblical criticism had done to the Old Testament depiction of God. That is, just as critics of the Old Testament had primitivized anthropomorphism, so critics of the New Testament primitivized the supernatural attributes of Jesus. Then, just as Old Testament critics claimed to find a theistic God behind the primitive overlay, New Testament critics claimed to find the social gospel Jesus behind the supernaturalistic overlay. Once this was done, it was relatively easy to claim that the church had misunderstood Jesus until now.[10]

But why now? The answer was to be found in Rauschenbusch's characterization of Jesus. It was only now, at the beginning of the twentieth century, that enough people had the "scientific training" to understand what Jesus had understood by "divine gift."

The excitement that this vision generated is understandable, for this recovery of Jesus' social message seemed providential. Given the current industrial problems and the growing tensions between classes, the world seemed to need Jesus' vision of the kingdom now more than ever. It was as if God had been moving history to just this point. All of this made the social gospel very exciting in the early twentieth century.

But it was still difficult to know what to make of the crucifixion. The problem was not to explain why Jesus was crucified. This was easy enough. The social gospel theologians updated the old explanation of the moral theology: people had crucified Jesus because they rejected his message. But did the cross mean anything? Did it have any spiritual significance? In the moral theology of the nineteenth century, the cross did. It testified to the boundlessness of Jesus' (and God's) forgiving love. The cross, in short, said that no matter how bad people were, God could still forgive them. But now in the social gospel this was no longer enough. Not just forgiveness but social reform was wanted. Something tangible in history was wanted. But what was the meaning of the cross for social reform? It looked like a testament to Jesus' failure—or, to put a better spin on it, a testimony to how backward people had been in Jesus' day. Still, it seemed to social gospel theologians that the cross must mean something more than this.

But what it meant was difficult to say. In 1907, in *Christianity and the Social Crisis*, Rauschenbusch found it hard to make much of the crucifixion. At most, he could take it as a testimony to Jesus' altruism: "The tone of sadness in his later ministry was not due simply to the approach of his personal death, but to the consciousness that his purpose for his nation had failed." But if this preserved some of the neoclassical resilience of Jesus' character, it still did not give the crucifixion itself much significance, for it amounted to saying that the crucifixion was a symbol of failure. Rauschenbusch could not settle for this. He declared that Jesus had looked to the future and had a "faith that rose triumphant over death." Here was the appeal to the future. It had become common in liberalism, in both the social gospel and modernism. But, as was often the case, this appeal to the future was a way to glide over problems rather than address them.[11]

Ten years later in 1916, Rauschenbusch, in his last work, *A Theology for the Social Gospel*, found a way to make the crucifixion central. It is true that in this work Rauschenbusch also paid more attention to the depth of human sin. This makes sense. For the two—sin and the cross—can go together: more attention to the problem of sin may lead to more consideration of the cross as the solution to sin. Indeed, Rauschenbusch structured his work in this way. The middle chapters dealt with sin; the concluding chapter dealt with the cross. This was one of the major points of the work. "To countless Christian minds," Rauschenbusch wrote, "the doctrine of the atonement has been the marrow of theology." Indeed, to write a *Theology for the Social Gospel* meant to give the social gospel a theology of the cross.[12]

This being said, however, Rauschenbusch had little to say for the cross that was new. He did intriguingly speculate about how it might have moved God. But two other interpretations were more central. One was the governmental theology: the cross publicized the depth of sin. The other was the moral theology: Jesus, by his bearing, revealed the character of God. Once again, this was a neoclassical God. "Jesus had to live out the Father's mind and spirit," Rauschenbusch declared. "He did it in the combination of steadfastness and patience. The most striking thing in his bearing is his silence." With this Rauschenbusch avoided having to deal with Jesus' outcries in the Garden of Gethsemane and on the cross. Indeed, Rauschenbusch's Jesus here rivals Channing's as an expression of neoclassical fortitude. "Even on the cross he fought," Rauschenbusch exclaimed, "but not with fist or stick or a physical level of brute force, but by the quietness which maddens and disarms." It might be wondered how this squares with the gospel depiction of Jesus on the cross. Rauschenbusch handled this much as Channing had. He overlooked the details in the Gospels and declared that Christian tradition had falsely depicted Jesus as anguished. "Christian art has misrepresented him when it makes him suffer with head down," Rauschenbusch declared. "His head was up and he was in command of the situation."[13]

Reinhold Niebuhr

Members of the next generation of liberal theologians were not so sure about Jesus being "in command of the situation." These were liberal critics of the social gospel who emerged in the 1920s. They are usually referred to as neo-orthodox theologians, though this is somewhat of a misnomer. It is easier to keep the name, however, because it has become common. But one thing should be kept in mind: the American neo-orthodox theologians were still liberals. They kept the earlier social gospel focus on humanity and history. The major difference was that they were not as optimistic as the social gospel theologians. The most prominent spokesman for neo-orthodoxy was Reinhold Niebuhr.

Niebuhr may well be the most famous American theologian of the twentieth century. He once rejected the title of theologian and called himself a teacher of "Christian Social Ethics" and a kind of "circuit rider in the colleges and universities." *Time* magazine, when they put him on its cover in 1948, got it about half right: "An intellectual's intellectual, he nevertheless lectures and preaches with the angular armswinging of a revivalist." He was not deeply learned and often relied on simplistic summaries of Christian theology and secular thought. But he was an extremely gifted speaker and a trenchant writer. He was one of the rare ministers who was respected in cosmopolitan culture in the twentieth century.[14]

His background enabled him to be something of a revivalist for university audiences. His father was an evangelical Lutheran minister in Missouri and Illinois. Unlike Rauschenbusch's father, Niebuhr's father, Gustav, had little patience for von Harnack and German liberals who undercut the supernatural character of Jesus while trying to uphold him as a moral teacher. When Niebuhr came east to Yale Divinity School in 1913, he tried to shed much of his midwestern background, but he retained his father's skepticism about liberalism. Subsequent events made this come in handy. World War I undermined some of the liberal faith in evolutionary humanitarianism. During the 1920s, Niebuhr held a parish in a middle-class Detroit suburb, where he observed the labor and racial conflict in the auto industry. This also provided material for him to criticize the social gospel. He developed a sharp polemic that criticized the social gospel for being too "sentimental," meaning too glib about overcoming labor and racial problems. As a polemic, this had become almost traditional. Among liberals, this polemic appeared every time they revised their stances. The problems might change—they might be sin or social inequality—but the caricature of sentimentalism remained the same. A generation earlier, social gospel theologians had lobbed similar charges at sentimental incarnationalists who, in the mid-nineteenth century, had faced similar charges from neoclassical theists. But still, these charges were given some new content. Politically, Niebuhr outflanked the social gospel on both its left and its right, sometimes taking a more leftist stance, sometimes a more moderate one. Theologically, he was all over the map. But he became the popular voice for some important theological trends.[15]

Once again liberalism was revising itself, and once again the theological initiative came from Germany. By the early twentieth century, liberal German theologians were criticizing the earlier generation of liberals, such as Hermann and von Harnack. This criticism came from a number of directions, not all of them in agreement with each other. In biblical criticism, the otherworldly interpretation of Jesus' phrase "the kingdom of God" was now considered authentic after all. In social theology, the German theologian Ernst Troeltsch criticized the earlier liberals and warned that their optimism might be an indication that they were the captives of society rather than its alert moral guardians. From a more conservative perspective, the German theologian Karl Barth denounced much of the historical and social project of liberalism and stressed instead the otherworldly, transcendent nature of God, Christ, and the biblical revelation. Reinhold Niebuhr, much aided by his more scholarly brother, H. Richard Niebuhr, absorbed elements from these and other critiques of liberalism and layered them into his charges against the social gospel. This gave his polemic some theological authority.[16]

By the mid-1920s, Reinhold Niebuhr was a rising star in the lecture circuit of the liberal Christian student movement. In 1928, Union Seminary in New York City snatched him up. This became his platform for the next thirty-two years. It gave him the security of a liberal seminary post to chastise the social gospel for its self-righteousness and lack of political realism. His most severe critique was his 1932 work, *Moral Man and Immoral Society*, which made even his backers at Union balk. But liberals were in the mood for such rebuking. And Niebuhr never questioned the basic political outlook of the social gospel. He just wanted liberals to wrestle more seriously with the depth of sin and the transcendence of God. Besides this, Niebuhr gained a substantial secular, cosmopolitan audience. After World War I, the Great Depression, World War II, and the Cold War, educated Americans were ready to hear about sin from a theologian who chastised other theologians for their self-righteousness and said relatively little about God.

But this was Niebuhr's problem. Could he say anything about God? His emphasis on sin seemed to call for it—what, after all, was God's solution to sin? And Niebuhr's polemic against the social gospel called for it—what did Niebuhr have to say about Christ and a transcendent God?

Niebuhr groped his way forward during the 1930s. The opportunity fell in his lap when he was invited to give the prestigious Gifford lectures in Edinburgh, Scotland. Out of this came Niebuhr's major work, his two-volume *Nature and Destiny of Man*, published in 1941 and 1943. The title was significant. As in *Moral Man and Immoral Society*, Niebuhr was more confident pronouncing on human beings than on God. This had made up the most effective part of his polemic against the social gospel. In his Gifford lectures, Niebuhr extended this polemic over all of Western civilization, finding fault with classicism, rationalism, and romanticism for being too optimistic (and, in reaction, too negative) about human nature. But could Niebuhr say anything about God? Could he provide an alternative to the social gospel? This is what liberalism needed: a compelling characterization of God to replace the social gospel's characterization. Niebuhr was not a deeply learned or nuanced thinker, but this was not the most important requirement for the task. What was needed was a strong writer with some prestige and a lot of nerve. No other liberal in the mid-twentieth century fit the bill like Niebuhr. Yet he fell back on the common forms of nineteenth-century neoclassical theism and sentimental incarnationalism. To understand why, we need to begin with his critique of the social gospel.

As we have noted, Niebuhr's basic charge against the social gospel was that it was too optimistic. This charge, in turn, influenced Niebuhr's ideas of humanity, history, and, to some extent, even God. Let's start with the idea of humanity. Niebuhr did not believe that individuals could ever be harmoniously integrated into a greater whole—humanity. This was because of the intractability of human sin. The basic point here was expressed in the title of Niebuhr's 1932 work, *Moral Man and Immoral Society*. The great mistake of the social gospel theologians, Niebuhr charged, was that they had thought they could expand the vision of individual salvation to humanity. This, however, overlooked the nature of sin. According to Niebuhr, sin got worse as its scope got larger. Sin was already bad enough in individuals; it was worse in social groups. So whatever salvation there might be for the individual, there was no final salvation for society.[17]

This, in turn, influenced the neo-orthodox vision of history. If there was no salvation for humanity, then there was no reason for God to be immanent in history. He might as well go back up to eternity. This is where neo-orthodox theologians put him. So God was transcendent rather than immanent. This being said, however, neo-orthodox theologians still mostly depicted God working through history. This was because to the minds of many neo-orthodox theologians God's transcendent character was virtually incomprehensible. There was little to be said about him in his transcendent state. Something could be said, however, about his operation in history. So neo-orthodox theologians wrote about God expressing himself through history, or within history, to the extent that God was represented in Jesus, who was within history and therefore subject to the laws and limitations of history. For all practical purposes of discussion, therefore, the neo-orthodox God was still a God of history, or at least a God who depended on the medium of history to express himself to humans.

But what did history express about God? In large measure, it expressed God's judgment of humankind. Here, in some respects, the neo-orthodox depiction of God differed from the social gospel.

But it was not all that different. Neo-orthodox theologians were still committed to basically the same liberal agenda as the social gospel. That is, they believed that in order for Christianity to be relevant to cosmopolitan culture, it must address social problems. Likewise, they also believed that Jesus was important because of his social teachings. This might seem hard to reconcile with the neo-orthodox criticism of the social gospel. It is easy to think that the apparent pessimism of neo-orthodoxy was designed to make people give up on social justice. But this was not the neo-orthodox intention at all. In fact, it was the opposite. Neo-orthodox theologians hoped to rally people to work even more toward social justice. But to do this, they thought that liberalism needed to be rid of the false optimism of the social gospel. They believed that this optimism had been detrimental for a number of reasons: it had caused liberals to underestimate social problems; it had made some liberals lazy, believing that history would take care of itself; and the optimism of the social gospel showed that it was the captive of society, not the alert moral guardian it should be. This last charge was crucial, for central to the entire neo-orthodox revision of the social gospel was the notion that often the people who most needed to be reminded of God's judgment were his righteous Christian servants.[18]

So neo-orthodox theologians continually came back to the crucial point of God's judgment. It might be thought that this would lead neo-orthodox theologians back toward the complexity of God in the juristic tradition and the Old Testament. And it did, to some extent. Neo-orthodox theologians were the first liberal theologians in over a hundred years to drop the caricatures of the juristic God and the primitivization of Old Testament anthropomorphism. Indeed, they even praised some aspects of these depictions of God. In particular, they claimed to admire what they called the "mythic paradoxes" of these models of God, by which they meant the complexity involved in the fact that God could be both loving and wrathful. But despite this praise, neo-orthodox theologians did not use these models much because in the end they rarely depicted God as a distinct character. His character was mostly expressed in history or was constrained by history to the point that there was little to say about him. In the few places that any distinct characterizations of God emerged, they were couched in the common forms of nineteenth-century neoclassical theism and sentimental incarnationalism.

Consider how Niebuhr depicted God in *The Nature and Destiny of Man*. As the title indicates, much of the work was given to Niebuhr's pronouncements on human sin. But now Niebuhr did recognize the need to say something more about God's solution to sin in the atonement. Niebuhr claimed that the crucifixion was a symbol of God's perpetual judgment of human history and yet also a symbol of his mercy for sinners. Niebuhr declared that in order to understand God here one had to struggle with the paradox of a wrathful and loving God. He claimed that Old Testament anthropomorphic imagery was a profound guide. But when Niebuhr himself came to depicting God, he did not rely on this anthropomorphism. Instead, he did what nineteenth-century American theologians had commonly done. That is, he did not actually ascribe wrath to God. "The wrath of God," Niebuhr declared, "is the world in its essential order reacting against the sinful corruptions of that structure." Niebuhr, like so many nineteenth-century theologians before him, exteriorized God's wrath. Niebuhr made it an expression of the law, history, or order of the world. And Niebuhr made it largely automatic. This distanced God from his wrath. And it saved Niebuhr from having to consider any emotional complexity within God.[19]

This, in turn, allowed Niebuhr to claim that God's essential nature was love. Still, Niebuhr suggested that he was wrestling with a paradox: how a God of love could still be a judge. But in fact there was no paradox here. Rather, there was a dilemma between God's love for humans and the demands of the law that they be punished. It was not difficult, though, for Niebuhr to resolve this dilemma. He resolved it the same way that moderate, liberal theologians in America had for 150 years—the same way

Park did: Niebuhr relied on the governmental theology. Thus, repeating the basic governmental formula, Niebuhr declared that God could be merciful; he did have "freedom over his own law"—"yet this freedom is not capricious." Rather, Niebuhr continued, "it is paradoxically related to God's law, to the structure of the world." Again, however, there was really no paradox. The relation of the law to God's love was the relation of means to an end. God had to show how hateful sin was before he could pardon sinners; or, as Niebuhr put it, "divine mercy cannot be effective until the seriousness of sin is fully known."[20]

If this is how God expressed himself through history, there was also the question of how he expressed himself from within history. This is where Niebuhr considered Jesus. Niebuhr took him as the Christian symbol of God's participation in history. As such, Jesus demonstrated two things: the limitations that history and human sin imposed on God and that God was willing to take these limitations on himself in the form of suffering in order to melt the hearts of sinners.

The first point took Niebuhr in some interesting directions, for it was here that he sought to check the optimism of the social gospel by saying that even Jesus, the symbol of perfection, had been constrained by history. In making this point, Niebuhr considered some of the more difficult passages in the Gospels. These were passages that had troubled sentimental incarnationalists in the nineteenth century and social gospel theologians in the early twentieth century, such as those in which Jesus had not always been a good son and seemed insensitive to people. Niebuhr, however, did not use these details to suggest that there was any complexity in Jesus. Rather, he used them to say that Jesus' ethic could not be taken as a practical social guide. In some sense, Jesus did not fit into the world. And this, according to Niebuhr, was an important part of his message: Jesus was not trying to fit in. This was because he was not trying to join any side—even the side of the righteous. His message was that there was ultimately no salvation in history. Even the righteous had to recognize this. In fact, according to Niebuhr, it was especially the righteous who needed to recognize this, for their very goodness sometimes blinded them to their own sins and their need for God's mercy.

All of this was rather ingenious of Niebuhr. On one level, it allowed him to incorporate his polemic against the social gospel into his characterization of Jesus. Who else but the social gospel theologians had been so righteous as to work for social justice in history but also had been so blinded by their righteousness that they came to believe they could achieve their goals? Niebuhr's polemic also allowed Niebuhr to turn Jesus' apparent inconsistencies around so that they looked like consistencies. That is, the fact that Jesus sometimes seemed insensitive to the legitimate demands of good people was really part of his consistent refusal to give ultimate sanction to anyone's earthly agenda. "It is impossible to symbolize the divine goodness in history in any other way," Niebuhr declared in *The Nature and Destiny of Man*, "than by complete powerlessness, or rather by the consistent refusal to use power in the rivalries of history."[21]

This returned Jesus to a kind of neoclassical austerity. It was the flip side to Niebuhr's depiction of God's wrath. This wrath was not really in him but in history. By the same token, God's goodness was really in him; therefore it was transcendent and so could not be fully depicted in history. This explained Jesus' apparent inconsistencies—now turned into a "consistent refusal" to take sides. The fact that Jesus did not always appear to be the model moral man was not because he was complex but because there were inevitable limitations on the expression of God's goodness in history.

Niebuhr's Jesus also expressed God's goodness in history through suffering. In depicting this, Niebuhr relied on the most common forms of the moral theology and nineteenth-century sentimental incarnationalism. There is some irony in this, for Niebuhr denounced the social gospel as "sentimental," in the polemical sense of the word, meaning given to unrealistic, wishful thinking.[22] But having undermined the social gospel, Niebuhr had to fall back on the very sentimental incarnationalism that had preceded it. This was the basic problem with neo-orthodoxy. It contained compelling criticisms of the social gospel but could offer little in its place.

Niebuhr, as usual, put the best face on his efforts. He gave the impression that he was struggling with strange and complex characterizations of God. And it would have been interesting if he had done this. But apparently it was too difficult for even someone of Niebuhr's stature to attribute much complexity to God. So again Niebuhr relied on nineteenth-century formulas. For instance, in sermons published shortly after *The Nature and Destiny of Man*, Niebuhr suggested that he had a special sensitivity to the necessary "paradoxes" and "mythic" forms of the religious imagination. "The wise men of the world have always pictured God as dwelling in a supernal serenity, in an Olympian equanimity, untouched by the sorrows of the world and undisturbed by its tumults. The God who is revealed in Christ is not so easily understood," Niebuhr intoned. This was in a sermon entitled "The Peace of God." Niebuhr continued: "There is indeed peace in Him and with Him. He is the calm source from which all life springs and the serene end in which all life finds its fulfillment. But strangely and paradoxically there is also sorrow and suffering."[23]

Actually, this was not strange. When Niebuhr worked out the difference between God's "serenity" and his "sorrow and suffering," this turned out to be the difference between neoclassicism and sentimentalism. Nor was the "sorrow and suffering" of the sentimental characterization of God "paradoxical." The moral theory of the atonement provided the explanation for God's suffering, and nineteenth-century sentimental incarnationalism provided the imagery. By suffering for humans, God melted their hearts. In "The Peace of God," Niebuhr likened God's suffering to an "anxious mother keeping a night watch over the bed of a sick child." In another sermon, "The Power and Weakness of God," Niebuhr repeated the common sentimental formula for the moral theology: only a display of Jesus' suffering sympathy could melt the heart of a sinner. Nothing else could "reach the heart of the rebel"; nothing else could "reach the final source of his defiance"; "it is the weakness of love which touches the heart of the offender." The obvious example of this was the "love of parents" breaking down the "recalcitrance" of a naughty child.[24]

So little had changed in the liberal character of God by the middle of the twentieth century. Whatever the changing scenarios of God's relationship to history in the social gospel and neo-orthodoxy, the character of God remained much the same. He was still the God of neoclassical theism and sentimental incarnationalism.

J. Gresham Machen

Conservatives in the first half of the twentieth century emphasized God's transcendence and separation from history. This served as a useful contrast with liberalism. J. Gresham Machen was the conservative theologian in the early twentieth century who made this point most powerfully. The title of his 1923 work, *Christianity and Liberalism*, expressed his basic charge: liberals were not Christians. The reason was their belief in God's immanence. Liberals, Machen claimed, saw God as basically at home in the world. This, for all practical purposes, was paganism, according to Machen. By contrast, Christians (by which Machen meant conservatives) saw God as transcendent.

This was a shrewd polemic. It allowed Machen to claim that the conservative God was really more interesting than the liberal God. If God was at home in the world, then it was easy (Machen charged) for liberals to picture God as being simply loving and good. But, among other things, this was boring. "For the truth is," Machen declared, "the God of modern preaching, though he perhaps be very good, is rather uninteresting. Nothing is so insipid as indiscriminate good humor."[25]

Machen had a good point—one that even got the attention of leading secular social critics in the 1920s, such as Walter Lippmann.[26] But the problem was that Machen offered little in the way of an alternative to the liberal God. The best alternative would have been an emotionally complex God. But instead Machen simply went tit for tat against the liberals. If the liberal God was immanent, the conservative God was transcendent. If the liberal Jesus was only an inspired man, the conservative Jesus was the divine God-man. Of course, all of these were basic conservative doctrines. But Machen did little more than list them. It was becoming enough just to contrast the conservative God with the liberal. Machen never made a strong case for the conservative God in his own right. His background helps to explain why.

Machen was born in Baltimore in 1881. His parents were transplanted southerners, his father from Virginia and his mother from Georgia. Both had been supporters of the Confederacy, and Machen was raised with deep respect for the Old South. If Rauschenbusch's and Niebuhr's background made them especially good American interpreters of liberal German theology, Machen's southern background gave to his theology a strong political vision. He deeply distrusted the federal government, especially its influence through public education. His vision here was truly ominous. To his mind, both political and theological liberalism were motivated by a heartless utilitarianism that sought collectivism at all costs and threatened to snuff out learning, individuality, and local autonomy. The public school system, he charged, was a more insidious instrument of mind control than the Roman Catholic inquisition. Up to his death in 1937, he likened the growing federal bureaucracy in the United States to fascism and communism. Such views were hardly unique to Machen. But he gave them pointed expression.[27]

Machen, however, did not make his political views an integral part of his theology. He expressed them as passing shots, often in the introductions and conclusions of his works. In this, both his southern background and his conservative Presbyterianism may also have influenced him. Since the days of the divisive debates over slavery during the antebellum era, many conservative Presbyterians had claimed that the church should stay out of politics. The idea persisted that theologians should keep their eyes focused on eternity, not worldly affairs. Conservatives, however, often did not honor this themselves but used it to denounce liberals.

This was Machen's approach. In the conclusion to *Christianity and Liberalism*, Machen decried "the sinister extension of state control" and then denounced liberal ministers for preaching not on the cross but on "the social problems of the hour." Memories of the Civil War were still alive here, for Machen went on to scold ministers for closing their services with "one of those hymns breathing out the angry passions of 1861." Machen's charges against liberalism were full of such discrepancies. He charged liberals with homogenizing the nation into "one huge Main Street," and he charged them with fomenting civil strife (as he suggested they had done in the years leading to the Civil War). "Is there no place," Machen exclaimed, "where two or three can gather in Jesus's name to forget for a moment all those things that divide nation from nation and race from race, to forget human pride, to forget the passions of war, to forget the puzzling problems of industrial strife, and to unite in overflowing gratitude at the foot of the Cross?" Machen wanted the conservative church to provide such a place. But he too kept bringing political issues into the margins of his theology.[28]

So there was this tension in Machen's work: whether to counter the liberal political theology on a political level or on a more strictly theological level. Whether to argue politics or argue for a transcendent God in whose eyes politics mattered little compared to the eternal ramifications of sin. Machen opted for the latter, but his theology was on the verge of becoming distinctly political.

Machen was the last in a long line of dutiful sons that sprang from Archibald Alexander, carried on to Charles Hodge, Archibald Alexander Hodge, and Benjamin Breckinridge Warfield (Machen's teacher), and ended with Machen himself. After being educated at Princeton Seminary, he taught there from 1906 to 1929. That year the stock market crashed, and so did conservativism at Princeton. The seminary gave way to liberalism, and Machen left to found Westminster Seminary near Philadelphia. As a young man, he had known what it was like to have doubts about conservative theology. These had troubled him while studying at Princeton and became worse when he went to the University of Marburg in Germany and heard the moving lectures of Wilhelm Hermann, one of the great liberal German theologians. When Machen returned to teach at Princeton Seminary, he regained his confidence in conservative doctrines and wanted to help other young men keep to them as well. For Machen, this meant holding fast to the style of Princeton. Now that he was teaching, he came to appreciate this style even more. As a student, Machen had chafed against Warfield and what Machen called "the real or supposed rigidities of the Reformed system." But later he recognized his "youthful folly." "Warfield was entirely right," Machen declared; "consistent Christianity is the easiest Christianity to defend."[29]

Machen defended a "consistent" theology for the rest of his life. Among other things, this meant attributing a consistent, neoclassical character to Jesus and God. This, however, was easier to do in the nineteenth century than in the twentieth century. Even if Machen had wanted to make his neoclassical characterization of God as distinct as Charles Hodge's, it would have been extremely difficult. In the nineteenth century, Hodge had been able to fill out his neoclassical character of God with an elaborate scholastic legal terminology and the occasional reference to the order of the enlightenment universe. But by the early twentieth century, all of this had come to sound archaic. Machen's neoclassical theism had very little support, which made a bad situation worse. As it was, Hodge's characterization of God had been fairly austere. By the time it was passed down to Machen, it had become simply vague. Machen, however, did the best he could with this. If his characterization of God was vague, he tried to make up for it with crisp, clear prose.

This can be seen in his treatment of Jesus. The point that Machen made repeatedly about Jesus was that he was a supernatural being. As far as attacking liberals went, this point made sense, for this is what liberals downplayed or even denied about Jesus. Machen tried to show that Jesus' own words were crazy if he was simply the inspired moralist that liberals proclaimed. In doing this, Machen cited some of the same passages that Reinhold Niebuhr used in his criticism of the social gospel and that had given sentimental incarnationalists so much trouble in the nineteenth century. In *Christianity and Liberalism*, Machen asked how liberals could make Jesus out to be a teacher of social ethics when he said such things as, "If a man comes to me and does not hate his father and mother . . . he cannot be my disciple," and, "Let the dead bury the dead." "Coming from the mere prophet constructed by modern liberalism," Machen declared, "these words would be monstrous; coming from the real Jesus they are sublime."[30]

The point was well taken. But Machen only took it so far. Why were these words "sublime"? Machen did not explore the matter; he only added exclamations to it. In the end, the most that Machen could say about Jesus was that he was divine and he was accomplishing the work spelled out in the penal theory of the atonement. What Jesus felt—what he was like—Machen could not say. The few times he tried, all he could offer were the bare bones of neoclassical theism.

In imposing these neoclassical traits on Jesus, Machen was vulnerable to the same charges he leveled at liberals. They, he charged, "manufactured" a character for Jesus and ignored difficult details in the Gospels. But Machen also passed over difficult details. For instance, he glided over Jesus' anxiety in the Garden of Gethsemane— "If the One to whom all power was given needed strengthening and refreshment in prayer, we more." This was an easy way out. No one denied that humans suffered from anxiety and needed comfort in prayer. The question was why Jesus suffered from such anxiety. Why did "the One to whom all power was given" need to pray? Especially if he, as Machen insisted, was the Son of God? But Machen was quick to dismiss details and impose his neoclassical characterization on Jesus. "More effective, too, than all the detail is the indefinable impression of the whole," Machen declared. "Jesus is felt to be far greater than any of his individual words or deeds. His calmness, unselfishness and strength have been the wonder of the ages."[31]

True, Jesus' serene moments have been the "wonder of ages." But it also true that his anxious moments have caused theologians to wonder. They had caused Calvin to wonder. And they had even caused Machen's teacher at Princeton, Benjamin Breckinridge Warfield, to wonder. Warfield ultimately resolved these difficulties and ascribed the same neoclassical character to Jesus as Machen would. But at least Warfield had called attention to such passages, even though he knew that liberals used them to claim that Jesus was only a man. If this was risky, Warfield met some of the challenges head on. This had given Warfield's Jesus some complexity.[32] But Machen left no room for this. For him it was enough just to assert the divinity of Jesus.

Machen depicted God along the same lines developed by Charles Hodge. All of God's attributes were resolved into one trait, holiness. This was the single serene source of both God's love and his wrath. Moreover, this love and wrath could be distanced from God according to their distribution system. Hodge had worked this out using such scholastic and legal terms as "imputation" and the "federal headship" of Adam and Christ. Machen simplified this and wrote starkly of God's absence and presence. But despite this simplification, the result was still the same. Emphasizing God's relationship to humanity allowed Machen to distance God from his expressions of wrath.[33]

According to Machen, God's response to sin was to separate himself from the world. This absence was felt by the sinner as God's wrath. In this way, Machen fended off the liberal caricature of the juristic God. "They speak with horror of the doctrine of an 'alienated' or an 'angry' God," Machen declared. "The truth is that the modern rejection of God's wrath proceeds from a light view of sin." There was some truth to this; but it was also true that the modern rejection of God's wrath proceeded directly from the idea that God could not feel wrath. Machen did not meet this point head on.[34]

Perhaps this was because he did not actually ascribe wrath to God either. Rather, all that Machen claimed was that God (and Jesus) were separate from sinners. In this, there was neither much action nor emotion in God. The drama in Machen's writing was centered on people's realization of their separation from God. Now, as a matter of doctrine, the origin of this realization could be ascribed to the action of the Holy Ghost; but it was still the sinner's feelings and actions, not God's, that got all the attention in Machen's writing. Simply put, Machen did not depict God feeling or doing much of anything. All of the drama was given to human beings. What made God interesting was how people saw him. "Without the conviction of sin," Machen declared, "there can be no appreciation of the uniqueness of Jesus; it is only when we contrast our sinfulness with His holiness that we appreciate the gulf which separates Him from the rest of the children of men." The convicted sinner, in turn, feels this "gulf" as an expression of God's wrath. The "Holy one," Machen exclaimed, "is separate from sinners; there is no room for joy, but only a certain fearful looking for judgment and fiery indignation."[35]

This was as close as Machen came to ascribing "fiery indignation" to God. It was always qualified as something that the sinner felt about God, not something that God himself felt. Moreover, it was something that one felt about God in his absence. This distanced him even further from humans.

The other side of the coin was God's presence. This is how Machen wrote about God's love. It might be thought that in considering God's presence, Machen would have ascribed more emotion and activity to God. Even Hodge had done this, but Machen did not. Machen's God remained opaque and inert. All of the emotion and activity—all of the drama—remained confined to the human being (now a redeemed sinner). It is true that Machen claimed that the redeemed felt complex emotions on being admitted into God's presence. "It is a joy akin to fear," Machen declared.

Moreover, it was more exciting than anything the liberals could offer. Given that the liberal God was immanent and characterized solely by his love, admission into the liberal God's presence was safe and easy. "Were we not safer with a God of our own devising—love and only love, a Father and nothing else, one before whom we could stand in our own merit without fear?," Machen asked rhetorically. If safer, such a God was also much less exciting. "Let him who will, be satisfied with such a God," Machen declared, "but we, God help us—sinful as we are, we would see Jehovah. Despairing, hoping, trembling, half-doubting and half-believing, trusting all to Jesus, we venture into the very presence of the very God. And in His presence we live."[36]

This is a powerful passage. But again it shows Machen's limitations. All of the emotion and activity comes from humans. It is they who "venture" toward God (albeit because of Jesus, but we have already seen how Machen handled Jesus). Moreover, all of the emotion—all of the excitement of the passage—was attributed to humans, not to God. Machen rarely depicted God doing or feeling anything. This was a far cry from Shedd's God, whose vitality penetrated and energized human beings.

The wonder here is that Machen did not turn to anthropomorphism. After all, in the passage above he referred to God as "Jehovah." Moreover, what better way to emphasize the difference between the conservative God and what Machen called the "insipid" liberal God than to draw on anthropomorphism? Even Walter Lippmann, the secular social critic of the 1920s, recognized the power of biblical anthropomorphism over the vague liberal God.[37]

But Machen did not take this route. Part of the reason was that he was so concerned to refute liberals on their own terms that he virtually adopted their criteria for evaluating what was significant in the Bible. By the early twentieth century, this meant the historical accuracy and textual integrity of the New Testament. The job of the biblical critic was to distinguish between passages that were older and so could be claimed to be more authentic and those that had been inserted into the text at a later date. Liberals tried to show that many of the passages ascribing supernatural powers and divine status to Jesus were later insertions. Machen devoted himself to showing the opposite. His two major scholarly works of biblical criticism, *The Origin of Paul's Religion* (1923) and *The Virgin Birth of Christ* (1930), framed Jesus' life. One dealt with his miraculous entry into the world; the other dealt with his miraculous exit, as it were, in Christ's revelation to Paul on the road to Damascus. So in both works Machen, with impressive erudition and cogency, argued this point against liberals: as far as could be determined, the New Testament writers had always thought of Jesus as a miraculous, supernatural person. But again, Machen did not take this point very far. It was enough to refute liberals. He did little with the biblical characters of Mary, Jesus, and Paul themselves. He steered around Jesus's life altogether, and his depiction of Mary was confined to a simple sentimentalism. More striking, Machen passed up the opportunity to explore in detail the character of Christ in his manifestation to Paul, even though Machen claimed this must have been an extremely personal encounter.[38]

But Machen continually passed up such opportunities, as he did in his essay "My Idea of God." This appeared in a collection of essays by leading American theologians on the same topic: "my idea of God." The majority of those participating in the symposium were liberals. Machen was one of the token conservatives. He recognized his position and came out swinging. His opening gambit was shrewd: if "his idea of God" was really just "his," then it would be worthless. What mattered was what God had revealed about himself in the Bible. Having immediately undercut the liberal assumption of the symposium, Machen was in a strong position to move on and examine the biblical depiction of God. But he did not do this. Instead, he continued his polemic and then retreated into his own abstract theism. Again, this exposed his own argument to the charges he had leveled against liberals. Compared to the "feeble and hesitant theism which the highest philosophy" and "the unaided conscience" has to offer, Machen declared, "one feels that in the Bible a veil has been removed from the eyes of man." Yet half a page further, Machen was citing the German theologian Rudolph Otto and mystifying the biblical depiction of God: "God has gently pulled aside the curtain which veils His Being from the gaze of men, but the look thus granted beyond only reveals anew the vastness of the unknown." So Machen fell back on his common formula: the contrast between the immanence of the liberal God and the transcendence of the conservative God. "We cannot love a God of whom we are parts," Machen declared, meaning that we cannot love a God who is part of this sinful world. "Thus, I for my part, cling with all my heart to what are called the metaphysical attributes of God—His infinity and omnipotence and creatorhood."[39]

He also clung to this abstract God as a matter of taste. This had been Hodge's preference as well. "The highest language of emotion is generally simple," Hodge had declared in 1850. Therefore, the "emotions of terror and sublimity," requiring "visible and tangible" images, need not be classed as profound religious feelings. This attitude helped him to translate biblical anthropomorphism into neoclassical theism. This, of course, was not the only view in conservative theology at the time. In 1863, Shedd denounced the "over-refinement of the age" that allowed theologians to overlook the "biblical representation of God" as "an emotional person, or in Scripture phrase, the 'living God.'" "Let, then, these two specific personal qualities—the divine wrath and the divine love," Shedd had declared, "be smitten, driven, hurled like javelins into the consciousness of the nations." But Machen, like most conservatives, shared Hodge's taste in this matter. Machen assumed that biblical anthropomorphism did not substantially reflect on God's character. Rather, it was a pedagogical device. "Such anthropomorphic language," Machen acknowledged, "sets forth an important truth. It teaches us that God deals with us as a living person deals with us." But there was a limit to this. Both "common sense" and the Holy Ghost should be our guides, Machen explained. Both taught a theistic view of God. This was as it should be. For a "literal interpretation" of biblical anthropomorphism "is a very heinous exhibition of misunderstanding and bad taste." What, then, did the Bible reveal about God's true character? It revealed that God was guided by one single, mysterious, unchanging purpose.[40]

This last point was crucial for another reason besides keeping anthropomorphism at bay. It helped Machen to distinguish between the Calvinism of conservatives and the premillennialism of fundamentalists. Machen's God worked according to plans, but these plans were inscrutable. Fundamentalists, by contrast, believed that God's precise plans for history could be ferreted out of such books in the Bible as Daniel and Revelation. So it was important for Machen to emphasize God's mystery. Fundamentalist theology was growing rapidly in the early twentieth century. It had almost no appeal in American cosmopolitan culture at large, but it was becoming appealing to conservatives. Many of them were fed up with cosmopolitan culture. It seemed too liberal and too secular. We have seen Machen's attitude toward the federal government. Fundamentalists shared these fears. They too interpreted the growth of the federal government as a kind of creeping secular totalitarianism with ominous implications for the future of Christianity in America. But fundamentalists could do one thing that conservatives could not: they could address these fears directly in their theology. The evil they saw in cosmopolitan culture could be ascribed to the devil. But Satan was not in control. All of the changes in recent history—the rise of romanticism and Darwinism, their own alienation from cosmopolitan society, the world war and the rise of fascism and communism abroad—could be interpreted as part of God's plan laid out in the Bible.[41]

Here was one of fundamentalism's temptations for conservatives. Fundamentalists could depict God in terms of history. This gave God's character a little more clarity. He was still a transcendent God, and he was still the God whose revelation was in the Bible, but fundamentalists interpreted biblical prophecy as predicting with scientific accuracy what God was doing in history. Therefore, historical events reflected on his character. And these events seemed increasingly dramatic. Given what was happening in American cosmopolitan culture and in the world at large, the end of the world seemed at hand. Christ would come again, take the Christians to heaven, restore the state of Israel to the Jews, and fight Satan and his human minions and then cast them into hell.[42]

This was an exciting historical vision. But it was dramatic more for its scenarios than for its characterization of God. The fundamentalist God and Christ remained mostly neoclassical characters. Like the neoclassical God of the enlightenment, the fundamentalist God was a God of orderly plans. The difference was that these plans now included a regular series of cataclysms. The fundamentalist account of creation, while rejecting Darwinian evolution, did take into account mass extinctions and prehistorical geological catastrophes—all according to God's plans.[43] Such a penchant for cataclysmic plans carried over into God's rule over human history. God divided history into neat epochs, or dispensations, of trial and punishment. If this provided some drama, however, fundamentalists also tended to make it pretty dry. Their insistence on the scientific accuracy of the Bible carried over into their own writing, which was often given to logic chopping. Moreover, the primary biblical material they relied on did not allow much character depth. The Books of Daniel and Revelation were full of fantastic creatures with almost no personality (unlike the more complex characterizations of God in Genesis and Exodus and of Jesus in the Gospels, which had provided juristic theologians with such rich material).

Like conservatives, fundamentalists maintained the penal theory of the atonement in the abstract, but they granted that Christ had come the first time around preaching mainly love and forgiveness. But in the second coming Christ came in judgment. Thus, fundamentalists paid their dues to philanthropism while opening up a new field for dramatic conflict between God and sinners—and now Satan. This, however, did not lead to complex characterization of God's emotions, for fundamentalists tended to separate God's love and anger according to the start and finish of dispensations. God's love was revealed in the first coming and his judgment in the second coming.

Emphasis on the second coming, however, gave Christ something dramatic to do: he could battle Satan.

The drama of the fundamentalist vision of history was analogous in many ways to the social gospel vision. For both, contemporary history became the site of momentous divine action. The Bible became a paradigmatic model for all of this. The Gospels only represented the first round in the contest with evil—and at that, the battle had been incomplete. Now the final fight was to begin. Social gospel theologians looked for the kingdom of God; fundamentalists looked for the second coming. Fundamentaiism and the social gospel, of course, appealed to very different constituencies. The social gospel sustained itself to some extent in cosmopolitan culture by appealing (however superficially) to evolutionary theories and liberal politics. Fundamentalists rejected much of this and were scorned by cosmopolitan people. But as theological visions go, the right and left wings of twentieth-century American theology mirrored each other. If the drama of the social gospel drew in many liberals, fundamentalism offered a powerful temptation for conservatives.

But many conservative theologians resisted this temptation—at least in the first half of the twentieth century. Machen spelled out the crucial difference between the two camps. He acknowledged that fundamentalists and conservatives had much in common. But Machen disagreed with a key fundamentalist claim: that the Bible contained precise historical prophecies. Machen also warned against looking for divine intervention in history. It is true, Machen conceded, that special events recorded in the Bible and in the history of the church (as in the Reformation) showed God at work. "In these great moments of history the hand of God was revealed," Machen declared. But he immediately added, "Alas, the thing is not always so plain." Great people of God, Machen noted, from Elisha to Luther, had been confused about God's purpose for history. Modern people were not more enlightened on this score. This did not mean that they should stop working for what they believed were God's purposes for history. "These are lofty desires," Machen wrote. "But there is one desire that is loftier still. It is the desire for God himself."[44]

This was a defining claim of conservative theology in the first half of the twentieth century. It distinguished conservative theology from the historical visions of the social gospel and fundamentalism. Conservatives tried to look beyond the earthly work of God and "desire . . . God himself." There was a problem with this, however. The desire might be there, but the object of this desire had become vague. Conservatives clung to neoclassical theism and so could depict God with little detail or drama. This took its toll as the century went on.

☙

CHAPTER TEN

The Limitations of Political Theology

Carl Henry, Harvey Cox,
and Martin Luther King, Jr.

*B*y the second half of the twentieth century, God was being swallowed up into history and disappearing as a distinctive character in cosmopolitan theology. The most sensational reflection on this trend was Harvey Cox's 1965 work, *The Secular City*. Cox concluded his book by reflecting on Exodus 3:14. Eighty years earlier, the most Theodore Munger had been able to pick out of this verse was the personal identity implied in the word "I." Now, even this was dropped. So little did God's character signify that emphasis shifted to the verb.

This was the focus of Cox's interpretation of the passage. Cox put the verb tense in the future and made it active: "I will do what I will do." Following the social gospel from half a century earlier, Cox also put the passage in a historical context of political liberation. Here, according to Cox, was the meaning of the passage. Moses asked who was sending him on his mission to liberate the Jews from Egypt. God's answer was "terse and evasive"; it was "not very comforting." God simply said that future events would reveal his identity.[1]

Modern humans were in the same position, Cox explained. We could no longer say who God was. The old names and identities for God would no longer do. This was the meaning of secularization. But secularization was also a liberating movement, for new identities for God would be found in history: "Our transition today from the age of Christendom to the new era of urban secularity will be no less shaking. Rather than clinging stubbornly to antiquated appellations or anxiously synthesizing new ones, perhaps like Moses, we must simply take up the work of liberating the captives, confident that we will be granted a new name by events of the future."[2]

Much in Cox's work was controversial, but others were also coming to interpret Exodus 3:14 by the verb. Even conservative theologians were doing this. Carl Henry thought it significant that "Hebrew verbs have no clearly stipulated tense." The implication was that in declaring "I am," God was also saying that he was and will be. This variability in verb tense did not mean that God was variable, Henry argued, but did suggest that God worked in history. God's declaration of himself as "I am" thus had an "eschatological bearing." It pointed to the second coming. Like Machen, Henry disagreed with fundamentalists that the Bible contained God's precise plans for history. But more so than Machen, Henry read history as a reflection on God's work and character. "The goal of history," Henry declared, is to be found "in the being and precedence of Yahweh whose kingship is vindicated in the sweep and direction of historical events." From the opposite end of the theological spectrum, Cox emphasized an analogous point in the social gospel. "Our present task," Cox declared, is "discerning the evidences of the Kingdom in the secular turmoil of the times."[3]

Now, of course, Cox and Henry were coming at this from different angles. Cox's God was the immanent partner of humanity in an updated version of the social gospel; Henry's God was the transcendent king of the conservative penal theology. Cox read the Bible as a record of ethical progress; Henry read it as the inerrant revelation of God. And, of course, they differed in politics. But they were still coming to this same point: emphasizing the verb in Exodus 3:14. Neither conservatives nor liberals could fill in the "I."

Moreover, what content remained in God's character, if only dimly, was familiar. Cox might dismiss "clinging stubbornly to antiquated appellations or anxiously synthesizing new ones," but the character traits he ascribed to God and Jesus were basically the same ones that liberals had worked with for 200 years. Similarly, Henry might invoke the awful mystery of a transcendent God, but this was still the familiar God of neoclassical theism. By now, however, these characterizations of God had become so vague that the case for God's importance had come down to interpreting the verb in Exodus 3:14. The action rather than the actor took precedence. So little of interest could be said about God's character that theologians needed now more than ever to emphasize what God could do for people politically.

Of course, it might be said that the great political events of the twentieth century were forcing theologians to focus on history. But a hundred years earlier, in the midst of the Civil War, Shedd, Bushnell, and Archibald Alexander Hodge, among others, had concentrated on the atonement. In 1862, according to one contemporary, the atonement remained "almost the only vital and really contested battleground in the domain of theology."[4] By no means did theologians ignore the war, but God's character remained of interest in its own right. This is because in the nineteenth century God had a compelling character and the atonement remained a complex doctrine embedded in the rich material of the Bible. Much of this was lost over the course of the twentieth century. Theologians across the doctrinal spectrum treated the Bible as historical data and spread the meaning of the atonement out over history. Liberals looked for its resolution in the "kingdom of God." Conservatives, drawn in by fundamentalists, looked for the second coming.

The only thing that had not substantially changed since the nineteenth century was the character of God. But this was why he had become so vague. In the nineteenth century, neoclassical and sentimental characterizations of God resonated with cosmopolitan literature and enlightenment science. These supports were gone by the twentieth century. The most these styles could signify was some political authority, inflated by theologians to span all of history. No wonder God's character had become so vague.

But the contrast with the nineteenth century was even more striking. A hundred years before Cox and Henry wrote, Shedd and Bushnell among others had experimented with romantic characterizations of God. This was in the middle of the nineteenth century, when romanticism in America remained a marginal and suspect literary style. But in the twentieth century, despite the fact that romanticism had become assimilated into cosmopolitan culture, theologians clung to the familiar shells of neoclassicism and sentimentalism.

It was difficult to sustain this God. In conservativism, the character of Satan threatened to upstage him. It was not that conservative theologians did not devise futuristic scenarios in which Christ roundly defeated Satan. It was that Satan was stealing the show. He was becoming a more interesting character than Christ. Liberal theology faced an analogous threat in the form of criminal characters. They too were upstaging the political actors with whom liberals identified the spirit of God in history. Again, the problem was not that good was threatened by evil but that good characters had become dull compared to evil characters. This was more of a threat to the imagination than to morality. Theologians had lost their hold on the imagination by letting God's character become so vague.

Carl F. H. Henry

In 1978, Carl Henry looked back over the past quarter-century and declared that conservatives had produced little theology of substance on Christ. Henry was in a position to know. That same year *Time* magazine crowned him the "leading theologian" of conservativism. Born in 1919 in New York City, Henry had his ambitions set on a career in journalism when in 1939 a conversion experience changed his life. In the next ten years, Henry attended seminary, was ordained in the Baptist church, completed a doctorate in philosophy at Boston University, and began teaching at Fuller Theological Seminary in Pasadena, California.[5]

In 1947, he wrote his first major work, *The Uneasy Conscience of Modern Fundamentalism*. It caused something of a sensation among conservatives. The "uneasy conscience" of the title was not worried about conservative doctrines. What worried Henry was the the failure of conservatives to apply their doctrines to solving social problems. Reinhold Niebuhr (among others) had long criticized conservatives for this. Henry's essay was a response to such criticism. He claimed that these charges were not entirely true and cited Machen's political concerns. But Henry wanted to make these political concerns a central part of conservative theology. Unlike Machen, Henry emphasized the importance of plotting God's activity in history. Henry was bringing Machen's transcendent God a little closer to earth. "He works in history as well as above history," Henry declared. This had relevance not only for the interpretation of history but also for the interpretation of God: "He discloses himself in the tragedies as well as the triumphs of history."[6]

Henry recognized some of the pitfalls here, but mainly on his left, not on his right. Conservatives, he declared, needed to avoid "the error of yesterday's liberalism." But Henry was less concerned about fundamentalism. As a Baptist, he was less inclined than Machen to find God inscrutable and suppose that sin totally separated human beings from God. Still, like Machen, Henry insisted that the atonement must be kept central and that the Bible did not provide precise dates for the second coming. Moreover, Henry claimed that he was not changing doctrines, just emphasizing their application. But this inevitably influenced doctrines. Emphasizing God's work in history and the social responsibilities of conservatives became a major part of Henry's message. And soon he had a large forum in which to express this.[7]

In 1956, he became the editor of *Christianity Today*. During the next twelve years, he built this fortnightly magazine up into the leading conservative journal. But when he left in 1968, he was frustrated. He felt that the theological and political content of the magazine was being compromised for the sake of mass appeal. So he devoted himself to lecturing, researching, and writing his six-volume *God, Revelation, and Authority*, published between 1976 and 1983. One of the goals Henry had set for himself was to reverse the decline in conservative theology.

So Henry was speaking from a position of authority in 1978 when he declared that there was little substantial conservative work on Christ. Henry and other conservatives blamed some of this on the priority given to evangelism and missions rather than theology. In other words, too much emphasis had been put on advertising rather than content. There was some truth to this charge. But it begged a crucial question: was there any substantial content left to conservative theology? Conservatives, of course, could list their doctrinal differences with liberals. But the problem was that conservative theology had become little more than this by the late twentieth century. This was already evident in Machen's work, and it was becoming clearer in Henry's work. Indeed, sometimes it was enough for Henry simply to cite Machen when running down the list of familiar complaints against liberals. Henry's Christ, like Machen's, was mostly a name followed by a list of superlative traits.[8]

Unlike Machen, however, Henry emphasized God's work in history. This helped Henry to ascribe some veneer of power to God. Consider the following passage in which Henry summed up God's work in history from the creation to the second coming: "The Living God of Genesis, who through the days of creation patiently shaped a universe in which *homo sapiens* bears his divine image, in the day of redemption fashioned the lifespan in which the incarnate Logos mirrored the perfections of Godhead in the flesh, and moves even now toward that coming moment in history when all the godly host of faithful men and women will be conformed wholly to the likeness of Jesus Christ."[9]

The power of this passage is in its historical sweep. This gives God some grandeur. But God himself is still not given a distinctive character. We are told that God fashioned human beings in his image and that Christ, in turn, reflected the image of God. But in the midst of all of this image making, Henry did not actually say what the image of God was. It is the image making rather than the image that got the attention. But what is this image? What is the "likeness of Jesus Christ"? What Henry claimed about God's character was mostly confined to enumerating "the perfections of the Godhead." These were the familiar theistic, neoclassical traits—love, holiness, omniscience, omnipotence, and so on. This was a long way from the treatment of the Trinity in nineteenth-century romantic anthropomorphism. In Henry's work, there was little interest in probing the fellowship of the Trinity. But this is what had made the writing of Thornwell, Griffin, and Baird so compelling. Rather, Henry's way of handling the perfections of the Trinity was to list them.

Moreover, in depicting God's activity in history, conservatives still limited the scope of his feelings. As evident in the above passage, Henry was willing to picture

God actively (if vaguely) doing things that expressed his love. But conservatives still avoided picturing God expressing his anger. Even in the late twentieth century, the liberal caricature of the juristic God as a God of wrath still made conservatives defensive. Yet by then they had learned to put this polemic in historical perspective. This should have made it less threatening. Henry laid this out in *God, Revelation, and Authority* in 1983. He noted the historical background to this caricature: its immediate origins were in eighteenth-century liberal theology, but it could be traced back to Marcion in the third century. Moreover, it expressed Greek philosophical attitudes foreign to the Old Testament. Yet despite this, Henry still remained defensive about the caricature. He still carried the burden of the liberal charge that the Old Testament depictions of God were unethical.

So Henry bent over backward to translate Old Testament anthropomorphism into the familiar neoclassical theism of nineteenth-century conservative theology. Henry was hardly alone here. He cited the conservative biblical scholar G. O. Griffith: "The Hebrew prophets, when they spoke of the 'wrath of God' . . . ethicized the idea of anger so that it meant the absolute implacable hostility of the Divine Holiness to every form of moral evil." The point may well be true that the ancient Hebrews saw no ethical problem with God's anger. But they still depicted God anthropomorphically. So why did Griffith and Henry translate the Old Testament language into neoclassical theism? Biblical anthropomorphism was so much more powerful than neoclassical theism; why strip the Old Testament language of its power if there was no ethical charge against it?[10]

The answer was that Henry, Griffith, and other conservatives remained committed to the neoclassical theism of Machen and Hodge, not the anthropomorphism of the ancient Hebrew writers. Thus, Henry translated most expressions of God's wrath into the term "holiness." He used the term much as Hodge and Machen had. Henry used it to comprehend both God's love and his anger, but he gave the nod to God's serene love. God's mercy, Henry noted, was optional, while God's anger was a necessary expression of his holiness. This made God's mercy a more intimate expression of his character because, being optional, mercy involved God's active choice. Anger, on the other hand, being invariable, could more easily be pictured as automatic. This helped Henry, as it had helped Hodge and Machen, to distance God from his punitive acts. In fact, Henry distanced God so far from these acts that it began to look as if sinners were punishing themselves. Channing and other liberals had pioneered this sort of language in the early nineteenth century. Conservatives also found it useful, for it helped them to avoid characterizing God by his anger.[11]

It must be remembered here that we are examining styles of writing. Hodge, Machen, and Henry all claimed that God punished sin. But despite this, they still wrote about God in ways that distanced him from this punishment. This enabled them to avoid depicting God feeling anger. For instance, in *God, Revelation, and Authority*, Henry claimed to honor Old Testament depictions of God's wrath. Henry warned against "depersonalizing divine wrath" and imposing "impersonal causal factors" on the "highly personal nature of divine anger." Yet on the very same page Henry did just what he warned against. "The holy God is already present in the proleptic judgement in the wrathful Jesus of Nazareth who declared the divine anger is operative already in earthly history." Henry's grammar helped him a great deal in this passage. His reliance on the verb "to be" and on passive rather than active verbs distanced God from his anger. It is true that anger of a sort was attributed to the "holy God" and was more directly attributed to "the wrathful Jesus." But it is significant that neither of them are said to be acting on this anger. Rather, over the course of the sentence, "divine anger" became disembodied, until at the end of the sentence it was merely "operative . . . in earthly history." Indeed, the only activity of God or Jesus here was to announce this anger—as if it was a force operating automatically in history.[12]

From here, the act of punishment was handed off once again. This time it was passed on from history to the subjects of punishment themselves. This happened in the very next sentence: "Paul enunciates the same theme: God's wrath is already evident in the adverse fortunes of the Gentiles and in the abysmal wickedness of the world. Pagan rulers and people, as well as Satan, implement divine wrath even while they consciously war against the people of God." So once again Paul, like Jesus, announces the wrath. But from there, its actual functioning was handed off to history and then handed off once again to Satan and sinners. God's anger had become a hot potato. In the end, it was Satan and sinners who "implement divine wrath"—they punish themselves.[13]

If there was continuity here with Hodge, there was also a new development. Conservativism had come closer to fundamentalism. The emphasis on God's intervention in history was a sign of this. Even more so was Satan's prominence. This reliance on Satan was a major change from the nineteenth century, but it makes sense. If conservatives were no longer picturing God punishing sinners, then they had to picture someone doing it. Some of this burden fell on sinners, who were increasingly depicted punishing themselves. But given the importance conservatives attached to the punishment of sin, they could not put all of the responsibility for this on sinners. So the job increasingly fell on Satan's shoulders. God's loss was Satan's gain. Conservatives stripped God of a crucial activity—the punishment of sin—making his character less complex and Satan's more dramatic. Not only did Satan war against God, but he perversely brought punishment down on his own head. Some of this was in nineteenth-century conservative theology. But still, Satan's role in cosmopolitan theology in the nineteenth century was relatively small. In the second half of the twentieth century, however, he began to make a comeback. As a more active and complex character, he began to edge God off the stage of conservative theology.[14]

This, in turn, influenced conservative doctrine in the second half of the twentieth century. But conservatives were not equipped to deal with this return of Satan. They did not have the historical scenarios for him, so they had to borrow them from fundamentalism and incorporate into conservative theology futuristic scenarios about the second coming and how Christ would battle the anti-Christ. This gave conservative theology a jolt of drama. But the atonement began to diminish by contrast. The second coming upstaged the first. More important, the anti-Christ began to upstage Christ. In 1978, Carl Henry observed with chagrin: "Even evangelical Bible and preaching conferences, it is often said, will draw twice the audience for a message on anti-Christ than a message on the God-man."[15]

No wonder; compared to Satan, God had become inert and Christ was largely reduced to a speaking part. Some of this stemmed from the fact that Henry and other conservatives had tried to make conservative theology into a commentary on history and contemporary politics. This was supposed to make conservative theology more relevant. Setting the God of neoclassical theism within the sweep of history did give him a veneer of power. But much of this came from the vision of history rather than from compelling character traits within God himself. In fact, God had few distinctive or compelling traits. He had become a vague historical force for holiness, while his perverse nemesis, Satan, became more and more intriguing.

Liberals faced some of the same problems in the late twentieth century. They also let their God get swallowed up into history, and this made evil characters more distinct and interesting by contrast. This can be seen in the work of one of the most prominent liberal theologians in the late twentieth century, Harvey Cox.

Harvey Cox

Born in eastern Pennsylvania in 1929, Cox studied history as an undergraduate at the University of Pennsylvania and received his divinity degree from Yale in 1955 and his doctorate from Harvard in 1963. Within two years, he was back at Harvard—on the faculty. In the intervening time, he worked briefly at Oberlin University, studied in Berlin, and wrote *The Secular City*. Though he wrote many books since then, this remains his most famous. Indeed, *The Secular City* might well be the most famous American theological work written in the second half of the twentieth century. Among other ideas in the work was the thought that God as a distinct character was no longer necessary. This was part of the "secular theology" of the time, owing something to the speculations of the German Dietrich Bonhoeffer, who was executed by the Nazis in 1945. If Cox's secular thesis was not entirely new, it was provocative, and Cox wrote with an engaging style that put it before American culture at large.[16]

It is only with some distance that similarities with conservative theology are beginning to emerge. Both liberal and conservative theologians were struggling with the declining significance of God's character. Exploring the implications of the verb rather than the pronoun in Exodus 3:14 was an example of this. But there are other ways to understand Cox's project. In trying to sustain neoclassical and sentimental characterizations of God (even in his disappearance), Cox was also drawing on the liberal theological tradition. It was recognized in 1965 how much *The Secular City* owed to the social gospel. Indeed, Cox traced his work back to the social gospel.[17] But the continuities go back even further into the nineteenth century.

Let's begin, however, with the social gospel. Consider Cox's point that the disappearance of God was a good thing for religion. He claimed that there was a historical process at work. This process was not so much making the character of God disappear as it was making the concept of God so diffuse that it was becoming one with humanity. All of this was happening, Cox explained, because humans, over the course of history, were becoming more mature, responsible, and adult, all of which Cox considered characteristics of secular, urban people. Cox's concept of the secular was much like Rauschenbusch's concept of the social. The secular, like the social, was a higher stage of human solidarity toward which history was pointing.

And it was where God was leading. Or, as Cox put it in *The Secular City*, God and humans were "partners" in historical progress. This had been a key concept in the social gospel.[18] As in the social gospel also, Cox claimed that the seeds for his vision could be found in the Old Testament. There, according to Cox, the idea began to emerge that God and people were involved in a partnership to achieve social justice. Jesus had enunciated this vision most clearly. Like the social gospel Jesus, however, Cox's Jesus had to struggle against the narrow, parochial views of his time. Just as the social gospel Jesus tried to free people from their supposedly narrow, "nationalistic," juristic, supernaturalistic conception of the divine, so Cox's Jesus tried to deliver people from their "tribal," juristic, and supernaturalistic delusions. For instance, Cox declared that Jesus "confronted demonic images and legalistic compulsions in such a way that people were liberated from both into clearheaded and productive ways of life."[19]

Jesus, however, did not complete this work. But again, as in the social gospel, what Jesus did not finish in his life, history could accomplish for him. Social gospel theologians looked to industrialization. Cox looked to secularization and urbanization. It is true that social gospel theologians expected industrialism to bring on a great crisis, but they also expected the social gospel to steer through this crisis and achieve human solidarity. Cox predicted an easier path. Without this sense of crisis, secularization and urbanization would lead to human solidarity. Urban, secular life, Cox declared, liberated people from their narrow, superstitious, familial, and ethnic loyalties and promoted a larger, more comprehensive idea of humanity. Again, there was much in common here with the social gospel. Rauschenbusch wrote of humanity as the final incarnation of God in history, as if God and humanity in the end would be the same. Cox made a similar point. This was the meaning of secularization for him. In the future, people would not look for God as a distinct character. There would be no need for such particularity in the concept of God. Rather, the free interaction of people for social justice and equality would be God—God diffused throughout humanity.

Yet God was never so diffused that he disappeared entirely. His character traits, though dim, were still evident. Indeed, much of Cox's effort was to carry on the social gospel task of making God immanent in history. And this, of course, also made him political, given that he was revealed more through society than through the individual. This, however, did not involve a significant change in God's character. The sphere of his action changed, but his character remained the same. Cox's God, in short, was the God of neoclassical theism, softened with a bit of sentimentalism. Of course, most of the attention went to heralding the change in God's sphere of activity. Thus, Cox declared the "death of the God of metaphysical theism." Yet Cox also recovered this God in history and politics. "In secular society," he announced, "politics does what metaphysics once did. It brings unity and meaning to human life and thought." This was the "unity and meaning" of a harmonious and benevolent neoclassical character. Rauschenbusch had characterized Jesus by his sanity, his scientific insight, and his "poise and calm" compared to others of his time. Likewise, Cox's Jesus stood out because he was "clearheaded and productive." God was part of the power in history that was spreading these traits more widely, making people responsible, neoclassical figures. "We speak of God politically," Cox declared, "when we give occasion to our neighbor to become a responsible, adult agent."[20]

If the character of God was not new, however, there were some new ways to justify the moral authority of this character. The notion of maturity was key. Some of this came by way of Bonhoeffer, but there were also other, older sources. Cox's basic humanitarian vision was updated with the language of psychological health. Neoclassical serenity and altruism were celebrated as psychological integrity and maturity. We have seen how Munger, Wilder, and Rauschenbusch also emphasized these traits and tied them to historical development. But now the association between historical progress and character type was justified on more distinctly psychological grounds. "The maturation process in cultures and individuals is analogous," Cox exclaimed, going on to cite Freud. But the reference to Freud was not deep, for Cox was not interested in the complexity of human psychology. He relied on Freud mainly to dismiss psychological complexity as infantile or primitive.[21]

Perhaps the most striking continuity with the past in Cox's work, however, was his polemic against the idea of God as a distinct character. There were various aspects to this polemic. Some recalled the social gospel polemic against the domestic focus of sentimental incarnationalism. Some recalled the traditional liberal polemic against the juristic God. But the most striking was Cox's polemic against the notion that God should be a character in his own right. With marvelous confidence, Cox dismissed the whole notion. This is how he put it: "Rather than shutting out the world to delve into each other's depths the way adolescent lovers do, God and man find joy together in doing a common task. . . . God wants man to be interested not in him, but in his fellow man."[22]

We can see in this both the ingenuity of Cox and his continuity with the past. His ingenuity is evident in finding another way to turn the vagueness of the twentieth-century God into an asset. The very vagueness of the liberal God became its recommendation. The implication was that people who wanted more substance in God were emotionally immature and irresponsible. Moral activity was found not in searching the emotional depth of another person but in social activism. Yet here Cox's continuity with American theology is also evident. Cox's polemic was based on an old opposition: humanitarian and neoclassical altruism, on one hand, against romantic emotional complexity and self-absorption, on the other hand. Cox dismissed emotional absorption in much the same way that theologians dismissed romanticism in the nineteenth century. As we have seen, they reduced it to juvenile sensationalism and suggested that more thoughtful (we might say, more mature) readers preferred "the calm on-going of real power." This was the power expressed by neoclassical characters. It was the same power that Cox attributed to the "clearheaded and productive" character of Jesus. The same basic emotional traits were ascribed to God, whether he was figured presiding over the Newtonian universe or immanent in the historical process of secularization.[23]

But if the character of God remained the same, the great changes in American cosmopolitan culture since the middle of the nineteenth century undermined how clearly and dramatically God could be depicted. In the middle of the nineteenth century, neoclassicism was still a distinguished style of characterization that could be recommended by clear and detailed references to enlightenment science, humanitarian reform, and contemporary literature. By the twentieth century, these supports had been lost or shaken. So Cox was forced to defend the value of neoclassical clear-headedness by reference to a very vague God. There is some irony in this, but Cox was hardly alone here. He was struggling with the same problem that conservative and liberal theologians had struggled with throughout the twentieth century. Cox, like other theologians, made a virtue out of vagueness but took it further than most in celebrating the disappearance of God as a distinctive character. And, like other theologians, Cox sustained some of God's authority by giving him a political agenda. But what in the end was the value of this? Rather than making theology more relevant, this politicization of theology helped theologians to ignore the cultural and literary reasons their characterizations of God seemed irrelevant in the first place.

The Lost Generation

The historian Donald Meyer argued that liberal theologians lost touch with American cosmopolitan culture in the early twentieth century because they were too occupied with the politics of the social gospel. In Meyer's judgment, the social gospel offered industrial America little more than vague nineteenth-century humanitarian ideals. This made it especially regrettable that the social gospel so preoccupied theologians. Meyer, like many historians, thought the 1920s were crucial for the emergence of modern American culture. "Perhaps the most poignant of the many forms of isolation from which the [liberals] suffered was their isolation from the real excitement of the decade," wrote Meyer. "This excitement was so often unpolitical, apparently purely literary or esthetic or moral, that it seemed irrelevant." The myopia of the liberals, however, was symptomatic of a larger and increasing isolation suffered by Protestant theologians more generally. "More widely and subtly," Meyer continued, "the whole spirit of the Lost Generation and the Jazz Age, at once passionate and disillusioned, seemed simply to have forsaken the landmarks of the past, whether liberal or orthodox, progressive or conservative. Protestantism had never been more profoundly out of touch with the cultural vanguards."[24]

This is evident in Rauschenbusch. He was a great reader of literature and even something of an amateur poet. But at the start of the twentieth century, his literary tastes were Victorian. Everyone is entitled to their tastes, of course, but Rauschenbusch made a point of criticizing theologians for not being up-to-date and engaging modern culture. He thought this was why the church was losing its authority with cosmopolitan Americans. He tried to reverse this by addressing himself to young, college-educated men. The church, he wrote, "cannot afford to have young men sniff the air as in a stuffy room when they enter the sphere of religious thought." But there was something musty about Rauschenbusch. When he declared in 1907 that "socialism has fully as much claim on the intellect as Robert Browning," it is easy to feel that it would have been better to name a more recent author. Browning, of course, was still widely read and influenced modernists such as Ezra Pound. But much had come along on the literary scene to interest young readers since this Victorian poet. Frank Norris, a Harvard student in 1894–1895, was reading Zola. T. S. Eliot reported that in 1910 Harvard undergraduates were mostly reading "the English poets of the 90s," who had already come to seem a little passé. Worse, among some in the literary avant-garde Browning's name (however unfairly) had become associated with a bygone era of Victorian moralism. Early in the century, George Cram Cook, of the Province-town Players, declared that Nietzsche "saved my soul from Tolstoi, Jesus and Mr. and Mrs. Browning." In *The Modern Temper* in 1929, Joseph Wood Krutch predicted that the emerging modern ethos "will be as different from the spiritual world of, let us say, Robert Browning, as that world is different from the world of Cato the Censor." In this time of rapid cultural change, Rauschenbusch's literary landmarks, as well as his characterizations of God, could easily seem like historical relics.[25]

This was even more the case with Machen. Like Rauschenbusch, Machen was a devoted reader of literature, an interest he shared with his mother. Machen's mother had even written a book of literary criticism: *Browning and the Bible*. Machen shared her tastes and cited Browning in his 1914 ordination sermon. Like hers, his interests were almost scholarly. While in Paris as a YMCA volunteer in 1918–1919, he wrote letters home sharing with her his project of reading up on the great seventeenth-century authors of French neoclassicism, such as Racine and Corneille.[26] Here was the problem in a nutshell. For Machen, Paris in 1919 was the city of the "grand siècle," of Louis XIV and French neoclassicism. For other American servicemen, from Ernest Hemingway to E. E. Cummings, it was the city of modernism. During the 1920s, it would become a home for many American writers who wanted to immerse themselves in the new trends. This has been called the "lost generation." But theirs was clearly the generation of the future; they saw themselves as the cultural vanguard bringing to America advance news of a modernist renaissance. "As Plato came to the ignorance of Europe, so Bernard Shaw comes to us!," Edmund Wilson quipped, reflecting on American culture in his 1922 "Night Thoughts in Paris." This was not a renaissance, however, that would lead to a reformation of American theology in the twentieth century.[27]

Theologians did express views on this cultural and literary transformation. As we have seen, the most sustained effort to make theological sense of these changes came from the liberal modernists such as Munger and Wilder. But other theologians also confronted modern literature from their increasingly entrenched political positions. Machen, for instance, expressed himself on modern literature as perfunctorily as he did in political matters. He tarred it with the same broad brush that he used against the liberal state. According to Machen, a liberal, utilitarian view of human nature was being promulgated insidiously through the public schools of America and Europe and ruining culture. Modern art showed this. The "unprecedented decline in literature and art is only one manifestation of a more far-reaching phenomenon," Machen declared in 1923. "It is only one instance of the narrowing of the range of personality that is going on in the modern world."[28]

We can hardly expect Machen, given his background, to appreciate early twentieth-century modernism. Still, it is hard not to wince when reading this denunciation. Its date—1923—seems particularly unfortunate. R. P. Blackmur was later to call the years 1921–1925 the "*Anni Mirabiles*" in modern literature.[29] Major works by Americans published around this time include T. S. Eliot, *The Waste Land* (1922); Marianne Moore, *Poems* (1922); Wallace Stevens, *Harmonium* (1923); Eugene O'Neill, *Desire under the Elms* (1924); F. Scott Fitzgerald, *The Great Gatsby* (1925); Hilda

Doolittle, *Collected Poems* (1925); John Dos Passos, *Manhattan Transfer* (1925); Gertrude Stein, *The Making of Americans* (1925); Ezra Pound, *Personae: The Collected Poems* (1926); Ernest Hemingway, *The Sun Also Rises* (1926); and Langston Hughes, *The Weary Blues* (1926).

These do not provide the best evidence for an "unprecedented decline in literature." Nor is it easy to argue that these works indicate "a narrowing of the range of personality." If anything, they were bursting the boundaries of the lingering neoclassicism and sentimentalism of America's literary culture. This may have been precisely what disturbed Machen. The point here is not that Machen should have supported literary modernism. Nor was Machen alone in objecting to it; since the start of the century, Irving Babbitt and the "New Humanists" had been battling modernism and tracing it back to what they saw as the emotional excesses of romanticism. But Machen did not make a case for his argument.

His successors tried to; they denounced romanticism as a glorification of the irrational. One of Machen's students, Francis Schaeffer, took this line in the second half of the twentieth century. His most popular work was his survey of Western civilization, entitled *How Should We Then Live?*, published in 1976 (also made into a popular conservative documentary film). Schaeffer walked the reader through the history of Western civilization and dated its decline from the early nineteenth century. This was when art (especially romanticism) focused on the irrational and science (especially Darwinism) turned materialistic. The upshot of both movements was the same: the destruction of reason, failure to recognize the natural order, the loss of a sense of humanity, the glorification of the animal and irrational in human beings, and the plunging of Western civilization into moral and emotional confusion that led to hedonism and eventually totalitarianism.[30]

Most liberals did not go this far, but a few came close. In his 1943 work, *The Nature and Destiny of Man*, Reinhold Niebuhr also took his readers through a survey of Western civilization. Niebuhr found tensions throughout this history, but he also thought that modern civilization had come to a particular impasse, and some of this had to do with romanticism. It is true that Niebuhr praised romanticism to the extent that it checked the enlightenment faith in reason. But Niebuhr, like Schaeffer, also labeled romanticism a glorification of the irrational and beastly that led to hedonism and totalitarianism.[31]

Strains of this attitude are evident in Cox's work. The complex characterization of human beings in modern literature surfaced like the devil had in late twentieth-century conservative theology. Modern literary characters were perverse figures who threatened to upstage Cox's vision of mature competence in *The Secular City*. In this work, Cox, like his Harvard colleague Amos Wilder, tried to identify his literary heroes with his political heroes. This enabled both theologians to praise modern writers for their humanitarian altruism and neoclassical fortitude. But Cox tried to make the connection between politics and literature even closer. For instance, he saw "John Kennedy and Albert Camus as personifications of the buoyant reasonableness and calm sense of assurance which characterizes the best in our epoch."[32] It is hard to see how the French existentialist novelist Camus fits in here. Existentialism is not known as a philosophy of "buoyant reasonableness and calm sense of assurance." Indeed, Cox himself dismissed existentialism as "immature" because of its focus on human anguish. Yet Camus, Cox suggested, outgrew his existentialism. He "lost the stridency of his early novel, *The Stranger*." He "refused" to become "forlorn or crestfallen. . . . Instead, he celebrated the joy of what he called, 'the invincible summer' within, the sheer beatitude of human reciprocity." But this is hard to see, even in the later works of Camus.[33]

Cox's characterization of Kennedy was also thin. To back it up, Cox referred to a remark attributed to Kennedy's aide Walt Rostow that Kennedy was a "pragmatist." If this seems weak (what successful politician is not a "pragmatist"?), we must also remember that *The Secular City* was published in 1965. The Kennedy mystique was still in high gear. Many saw Kennedy as the PT boat war hero, the Pulitzer Prize winning author of *Profiles in Courage*, the charming, self-deprecating, urbane host of the Camelot White House, and the commander-in-chief whose steady nerves had guided America through the Cuban missile crisis. In the last quarter of the twentieth century, a fuller, more complex picture of Kennedy emerged.[34] But there were reasons in 1965 to take Kennedy's political image with a grain of salt. There were also some fairly shrewd profiles of Kennedy at the time, such as Norman Mailer's 1960 portrait, "Superman Comes to the Supermarket." Mailer's piece could have added some complexity to Cox's portrait. But evidently Cox was not interested in this sort of complexity. If his characterization of Kennedy had some political resonance, it had almost no deeper literary resonance.[35]

This led to some problems. Kennedy and Camus did have one thing in common by 1965: the violent manner of their deaths. Cox published *The Secular City* just five years after Camus died and two years after Kennedy died. How could Cox hold these two men up as exemplars of modern humanity's calm participation in history given that Kennedy was assassinated and Camus died by driving his car into a tree? Cox acknowledged the problem; he acknowledged the "irony" of it: that these "reasonable," "calm" men were "dashed into oblivion by eruptions of irrationality." Cox wondered whether this called into question "the notions of adulthood and reasoning responsibility they championed?" No was his answer.

Yet here Cox ran up against a conflicting vision of character, the vision of character that emerged in romanticism, where irrationality is given some free play. Cox, however, quickly marginalized this literary vision to outlaw figures. Still, Cox had to admit that this literary vision threatened to displace his own celebration of Kennedy. In fact, it was threatening to do so in the very person of Kennedy's assassin, Lee Harvey Oswald. But Cox beat the specter back. Though Kennedy's "alleged assassin," Cox wrote, "seems a character from the pages of a Dostoyevski novel, it is still the spirit of Kennedy that triumphs."[36] No doubt Cox was right on a political level. But on a literary level it would have been a better bet to go with Oswald. In fact, the year that Cox published *The Secular City* was ominous in this respect. That was the same year that Truman Capote published *In Cold Blood*, the story of two ordinary murderers in the Midwest. It was a literary sensation, the parallel in literature to what *The Secular City* was in theology. Capote's work was also influential. In both form and content, it prepared ground for some of the most important nonfiction novels in the last quarter of the twentieth century: the 1979 Pulitzer Prize–winning nonfiction novel about the life of the murderer Gary Gilmore by Norman Mailer and Don Delillo's 1988 nonfiction novel *Libra* about the life of Oswald.

The point here is not that theologians should give to Jesus (or Kennedy) the traits of a Dostoyevsky-type criminal. But short of this, much could be done to bring God's character in touch with the vision of human beings in cosmopolitan literature. Some interest in emotional depth and complexity would be a start. This need not be written off as "adolescent." Such an attitude seems especially strange in the work of Harvey Cox, for he claimed to admire much in modern, secular culture. It is odd, therefore, that he was so dismissive of the literary style at the center of this culture.[37]

If odd, however, it was not uncommon. This was the response of most liberal and conservative theologians in the twentieth century. Meyer was right: the politicization of theology enabled theologians to miss out on modern literature; but this seems to have been a kind of avoidance as much as inadvertence. The roots of this avoidance went deep, for the political orientation of twentieth-century theology served to sustain (however ineffectively) the neoclassical and sentimental characterizations of God that liberal and conservative theologians carried over from the nineteenth century. Assertions about tradition or innovation meant little here. Conservatives declared themselves traditionalists and claimed to derive their characterization of God from the Bible; liberals declared themselves modernists and claimed to derive their characterization of God from the felt needs of contemporary society. Neither was as traditional or as modern as they claimed. Their characterizations of God owed much to early nineteenth-century literary styles. But so ingrained had these styles become in theology that theologians could not imagine alternatives to them.

The most striking example of this is feminist theology. Feminist theologians, more than any other, tried to develop new characterizations of God. Their interest in more bodily and emotional depictions of God led some to reject the abstractions of neoclassical theism and reconsider anthropomorphism.[38] But none of this went very far. Feminist theologians quickly fell into an old theological rut. In a number of ways, they ended up replaying the mid-nineteenth-century rebellion against neoclassical theism by sentimental incarnationalists. They relied on a similar polemic. An abstract, distant, wrathful, legalistic God was contrasted with an emotional, intimate, loving, familial God. But now the terms "male" and "female" were added to this roster of contrasts. Polemics, of course, serve their purposes. But if too deeply ingrained in a theological stance, they can influence the theologian's own characterization of God. The God advocated becomes simply the opposite of the caricature. So in feminist theology there was a tendency to make God simply good (and simply female—however construed) in contrast to simplistic caricatures of earlier male depictions of God. This was not a good formula for making complex characterizations of God.

But it was a staple formula for feminists through the twentieth century. Consider Charlotte Perkins Gilman, a leading feminist in the late nineteenth and early twentieth century. Like Rauschenbusch, she was much influenced by Edward Bellamy. She also relied on the common liberal caricatures of the juristic tradition and Old Testament anthropomorphism. In her 1917 utopian novel *Herland*, Gilman contrasted the "ancient Hebrew God"—"that God of Battles . . . that jealous God, that Vengeance-is-mine God"—with a progressive vision of a maternal God, or really a maternal principle of "diffused and competent love." "We are not accustomed to horrible ideas," one of the utopian women explained. "Our mothers are not angry with us—why should God be?"[39]

The clash of such simple dichotomies echoed through the century. Mary Daly, in her 1973 work, *Beyond God the Father*, drew similar contrasts between the juristic God and the feminist God. Like liberal theologians from the beginning of the nineteenth century, Daly relied on the polarization of emotions to dismiss the juristic God. She claimed that the juristic God was really two incompatible beings rather than a depiction of one complex God. "There has been a basic ambivalence in the depiction of the heavenly patriarch—a split between a God of love and the jealous God," she declared. Like most liberal theologians in the two centuries preceding her, she denounced this ambivalence. Like Cox, she relied on the terminology of mental health to dismiss emotional complexity. Emotional harmony was her political norm. This was why she considered the ambivalent characterization of God so dangerous. Like Niebuhr and Francis Schaeffer, Daly was quick to inflate what did not fit her theological and political agenda into something of totalitarian proportions. Patriarchy, she charged, was an omnipresent and insidious social system that sustained itself and squashed dissent by reducing the oppressed into "contradictory, divided beings." A process of "healing," on the other hand, would lead to "the self-esteem that comes with affirming an undivided self." There was a similar litany of opposites throughout Daly's work. What was caricatured as simply bad was contrasted with what was simply good.[40]

The upshot of this was that the God of feminist theology usually had a sentimental character. This was not because feminist theologians wrote about God as female. Sentimental characters can be male as well as female (it is only in the caricature of sentimentalism that these characters are "effeminate"). Rather, the feminist God tended to be sentimental because she was often created to contrast with the God of neoclassical theism. Feminist theologians were not able to escape the notion that God's character must be either neoclassical or sentimental. So if neoclassicism was associated with male depictions of God, sentimentalism became associated with female characterizations.

Even theologians who were conscious of this tendency toward sentimentalism were unable to avoid it. This can be seen in Sallie McFague's characterization of God in her 1987 work, *Models of God: Theology for an Ecological, Nuclear Age.* "The metaphor of God as mother which we have been considering," McFague wrote, "is built not upon stereotypes of maternal tenderness, softness, pity and sentimentality, but upon the female experience of gestation, birth and lactation. This experience in most animals, including human beings, engenders not attributes of weakness and passivity, but qualities contributing to the active defense of the young so that they may not only exist but be nourished and grow."[41]

The denial of sentimentalism did not save McFague from it. This is partly because what she denied was only a caricature of sentimentalism, the old caricature that neoclassical theists used in the mid nineteenth century and social gospel and neoorthodox theologians used in the early twentieth century. As a caricature, however, it does not get at the problem of sentimentalism. Sentimental characters are not necessarily "effeminate," nor are they passive, weak, or incapable of defending themselves or their young. Any reader of nineteenth-century sentimental novels knows this. In *Uncle Tom's Cabin*, Eliza defends her child from slave catchers with astonishing physical strength and courage. And as we have seen, Harriet Beecher Stowe's

Mary was no pushover. So by saying her God was strong, McFague was not avoiding sentimentalism. Nor did she avoid it by writing about God in bodily terms—"the experience of gestation, birth and lactation." As we have also seen, Victorians were not necessarily shy of the body, especially when it came to celebrating the power of propagation. The real question about sentimentalism is not whether parents can feel a range of emotions necessary to protect their children but whether parents can feel a range of emotions toward them.[42]

The question is one of emotional complexity. Can a normal mother or a father sometimes feel ambivalent about a child? Of course, is the answer of modern literature. Such feelings hardly make for bad parents; we are simply ascribing to parents the complex range of emotions that we ascribe to everyone. Indeed, we expect parents sometimes to feel ambivalent about their children, given that they feel so strongly about them. In romanticism, after all, strong feelings tend to be ambivalent. Late twentieth-century literary feminists such as Adrienne Rich have explored some of these issues and tried to offer women alternatives to sentimental notions about maternal devotion. But feminist theologians have not allowed their characterizations of God this complexity. This is because they have kept to the same basic characterizations of God that have dominated American theology since the early nineteenth century.[43]

But it may be said that all of this is necessary. Successful political leaders seldom present themselves as profound characters in our democratic politics. This is as it should be. Our political leaders normally strive to depict themselves as centrist, reasonable, principled role models. This is why neoclassical and sentimental styles of characterization still suit our political leaders.[44] So why should our characterizations of God not continue in the same vein? If God is not engaging on a deep emotional and imaginative level, at least he is politically relevant.

But is he? We may well wonder how important the social gospel was for the labor movement; how influential neo-orthodoxy and secular theology were for liberal politics; or how significant feminist theology was for the women's movement. Certainly, for some members of these movements, theology played a role, but did theology play a significant role in any of these movements?[45] Moreover, we can ask what any of this did for liberal churches. Were they helped by the politicization of liberal theology? Of course, we can ask such questions about conservative theology too, given the increasing politicization of its theology and its growing involvement with the religious right.[46] But liberalism has been at this effort longer, so we have more evidence to go on. Let us, therefore, concentrate on liberalism. After a hundred years, has liberalism been helped by its political theology?

Martin Luther King, Jr., and the Difference between Political and Theological Power

Consider the case of the most successful liberal reform movement of the twentieth century, which also had a strong religious element: the civil rights movement. Certainly there were other influences on this movement than liberal theology. The civil rights movement owed much of its religious authority to the traditions of the African

American churches. But still the social gospel and neo-orthodoxy had some influence on the movement in general and on Martin Luther King, Jr., in particular. King had studied Rauschenbusch and Niebuhr. Both at times had suggested that nonviolence could be an effective form of protest.[47] King, of course, put nonviolent protest to great use in the South. King also drew on social gospel and neo-orthodox characterizations of Jesus. Jesus' neoclassical traits are evident in King's writing. King declared that "the inner stability of the man of faith is the chief legacy of Jesus Christ to his disciples." These invocations of neoclassical fortitude served very real practical purposes. They seem to have helped King achieve an "inner calm" (as he called it) when his life was threatened. And such poise and calm were an important part of the self-presentation of the civil rights marchers.[48]

Some of this can be traced back to Rauschenbusch and Niebuhr. King and his followers put into action Rauschenbusch's vision of Jesus on the cross: there Jesus fought against injustice, "but not with fist or stick or a physical level of brute force, but by the quietness which maddens and disarms." King also put into practice Niebuhr's depiction of Jesus, who "symbolized divine goodness . . . by the consistent refusal to use power in the rivalries of history." For instance, King was careful in his opposition to segregation not to condemn whites; instead, he emphasized the common sinfulness as well as the brotherhood of all peoples. All of this contributed to the extraordinary stature of King. He may be the most admired American political figure of the twentieth century. It makes sense that he (even more than Cox's Kennedy) should be the exemplar of the neoclassical character in its political power.[49]

This being said, however, we may question how much religious power there is here. Granted, King was an inspiring political and civic leader, but it is not clear that he was a great religious leader. When reading his works or listening to him on recordings, it does not seem to be the religious element that is most moving. This is not to say that the religious element was incidental to the movement or that King himself can be understood without it. But King's religious vision did not translate well beyond his movement.

His characterizations of Jesus show this. However inspiring these characterizations of Jesus were for King and for participants in the movement, outside of their political context, these depictions of Jesus do not have much substance. King wrote and spoke much about how serene and good Jesus was, but little else. In his 1963 "Letter from the Birmingham Jail," King wrote that "Jesus Christ was an extremist for love, truth and goodness, and thereby rose above his environment." We can trace such characterizations of Jesus back to Channing, who wrote of Jesus serenely holding fast to his ideals. In the early nineteenth century, this was a powerful way to depict Jesus, for it resonated with literature and science as well as politics. By the twentieth century, this characterization of Jesus had little resonance beyond its political context.[50]

Of course, it may well be said that this is unfair to King because he did not have the luxury to develop more complex characterizations of Jesus. Rather, King needed to rally his nonviolent army. But as we have seen, other liberal theologians did have the leisure to reflect on Jesus's character, and they came up with similar characterizations. This is just the point. If liberal theology is supposed to rally people to political activity, then all of this makes sense. And King may be the best measure of the effectiveness of liberal theology here. But if liberal theology was sometimes effective as politics in the twentieth century, it was much less effective as religion.

The concern with religion is not incidental. It is true that liberal theologians did try to bring religion and politics together. But they did not want religion to dissolve into politics. To the contrary, many liberals hoped that a more political theology would attract cosmopolitan people back to the church.[51] The fact that attendance in liberal churches seems to have declined over the course of the twentieth century, of course, cannot simply be chalked up to theology. Many factors played a role here, and perhaps a greater role than theology.[52] But it does seem clear that the politicization of theology did not halt or reverse this decline. It did not do what some of its liberal champions hoped. Liberal theology may have had some political success, but it does not appear to have been a great religious success.

This might be taken as a warning to conservative theologians. The political activity of the religious right is not the issue here; the danger is that the religious right will influence conservative theologians to such an extent that they will spend more time sanctioning their political positions than developing their doctrinal traditions.[53] In 1947, Carl Henry warned conservatives against following "yesterday's liberalism," but to some extent that is what Henry and other conservatives did in the second half of the twentieth century. In his 1995 work, *Active Faith*, Ralph Reed, the executive director of the conservative political group, the Christian Coalition, suggested that his organization was following in the footsteps of Rauschenbusch's social gospel movement and King's civil rights movement. In claiming this, Reed seemed indifferent to the substantial theological differences between these liberal movements and the conservative religiosity of the Christian Coalition. Similarly, in 1995 Reed called on members of the Christian Coalition to follow King's ten-point pledge of nonviolent protest. One liberal commentator saw this as a cynical appropriation of King's legacy. There are also theological implications here; the first and third points of the pledge call for participants to "meditate daily on the life and teachings of Jesus" and "walk and talk in the manner of love, for God is love."[54] Absent here, but significant for conservative theology—if not politics—is mention of Christ's death and God's wrath. Like liberals in the social gospel movement in the late nineteenth century, conservatives in the religious right in the late twentieth century may feel that they are finally coming into their own by exerting themselves politically. But political power is not the same thing as theological power. Nor does the politicization of theology appear to have been an effective way to reach cosmopolitan Americans. Why these Americans seem to have lost interest in Protestantism during the twentieth century is a complex question. By its very nature, it involves some speculation. But we can offer two suggestions why the politicization of liberal theology in the twentieth century might have had limited appeal for cosmopolitan Americans.

The first reason concerns the authority of theology itself. We get at it by asking a simple question: given the premium put on expertise in twentieth-century cosmopolitan culture, can we really expect educated people to look to theologians in order to understand the social problems of the day—problems involving complex issues of history, politics, economics, sociology, and so forth? The reasonable answer seems to be no. And there is good reason for this. Liberal theologians did not have a good track record in interpreting history in the twentieth century. Similar to their fundamentalist peers on the right, leading liberal theologians were given to predicting unlikely catastrophes. The word "crisis," in fact, popped up quite a lot in twentieth-century liberal theology.

Take two examples. In his great 1907 work, *Christianity and the Social Crisis*, Rauschenbusch suggested that America was on the verge of a class war. Nearly seventy years later, in 1975, numerous leading liberal theologians in a special issue of the aptly named liberal journal *Christianity and Crisis* declared that Western technological society was on the verge of collapse. In both these instances, liberal theologians addressed serious political issues. But their predictions were off the mark. America was not on the verge of class war in 1907. And, if anything, Western technological society grew even more powerful and more technological in the last quarter of the twentieth century.[55] But not all liberal forecasts have been bad—at least in the sense that they have predicted bad things. Yet even where liberals have been optimistic, they have not been fortunate in their predictions. Take Cox's 1965 *Secular City*. It is poignant to read such a celebration of urban life published in the same year as the Watts riot and during a time of flight to the suburbs and the decay of America's cities. Of course, it is easier to find fault with these liberal forecasts in hindsight. But it would not have taken a seer to find them suspect at the time.[56]

Of course, there are answers to all of this. It could be said that these theologians were not social scientists. But this is the point. The question is, why were they trying to be? It may also be said that accuracy was not what was important here, inspiration was. Perhaps liberal theologians were trying to create inspiring visions of history in order to prod social action. There may be some truth to this, but it also may underestimate the ambitions of these theologians. But even granting this point, we can ask whether liberal theologians should settle for this. Do they really want just to inspire people with dubious historical visions? Do they really want to confine themselves to being the cheerleaders while other experts take the field as the real players? If they do, it is no wonder that educated people look to more serious writers for guidance. Given this, it might be better for theologians to concentrate on a subject for which they can claim some traditional expertise, such as the supernatural and God.[57]

The second reason for the limited appeal of political theology concerns the church. Again we can ask a simple question: why would cosmopolitan people look to the church as a major base for political action? Of course, the church could be one starting point for mobilizing support for an issue. But the point is that there are much more direct levers of power, such as political parties, lobbies, interest groups, unions, the courts, and so on. Of course, not everyone in society has access to these levers of power. This is precisely why the church was so important in the early years of the civil rights movement. The church was one of the few African American institutions in the South. The lesson here is that the church may play a crucial political role for people who have been denied access to the levers of power. But almost by definition these are not cosmopolitan people, for cosmopolitan status, and all that it implies, is a position of privilege. It may be argued that the church should specifically devote itself to those people who have been marginalized in society and denied these cultural and political privileges. This is what liberation theologians have called for. In this respect, their political theology is more practical than much of twentieth-century American liberalism. Leading liberals, from Rauschenbusch to Niebuhr and

Cox, specifically addressed themselves to cosmopolitan people.[58] Yet these are the very people in society who do not need the church for politics. But they may need a church to give them what few other institutions can provide: a place committed to fellowship with God.

Of course, even for cosmopolitan people there is some connection between religion and politics. Rauschenbusch, Niebuhr, and Cox may well have inspired many people to work for social justice. But once inspired, these people have had good reason to look beyond the church to put their ideals into action. When it comes to politics, the church can do little more than inspire; it is not in a position in America's secular, pluralistic, democratic society to follow through into the realm of political action. Few would want to see it in this position. So political theology by its very nature must be limited. Where it is effective, it should inspire people to get involved in organizations other than the church and to read writers other than theologians.

⚘

CHAPTER ELEVEN

Prospects

*T*he relationship between theology and literature, of course, is only one aspect of theological development in the nineteenth and twentieth centuries. A more comprehensive analysis of this development would need to focus more on science, especially the challenges that Darwinism posed to theology during this period. But a historical understanding of how neoclassical and sentimental characterizations of God persisted in the twentieth century may give us insight for future study into the challenge of Darwinism. For instance, we can ask, what was it that made Darwinism such a shock to theology in the late nineteenth century? The harshness of Darwinian nature was certainly a factor; such a vision of nature seemed incompatible with the character of God. But is this because theologians assumed that God must have a neoclassical character, a character suited to the enlightenment vision of nature? An emotionally complex characterization of God might prove more resonant with the complexity we now see in nature.[1]

At the end of the twentieth century, there are some hopeful signs that a more complex characterization of God may emerge from a renewed theological interest in the Bible and literature. In "narrative theology," for instance, biblical and literary stories are examined for their ability to convey epistemological and ethical complexity. This may naturally extend to an exploration of the complexities of character.[2] From another angle, one of the most promising developments in recovering the biblical characterization of God is Jack Miles's 1995 work, *God: A Biography*. Though not a theological study, Miles's work may be helpful to theologians in a number of ways. These cannot be treated thoroughly here, but a few points can be made. The first is that Miles demonstrated in an engaging fashion what—amazingly—seems to have been forgotten in cosmopolitan culture: that the biblical characterization of God is complex and intriguing. "Cultivated people" may find this surprising, noted Frank Kermode in his review of Miles's work. John Barton pointed out that Miles helped to make the Bible "readable" again and showed that it is an "immensely powerful, complex and ambivalent work of art." But the effort to understand this "ambivalence" raises two questions concerning fidelity to the Bible and the role of doctrinal tradition.[3]

Why does the biblical God appear ambivalent to us? Miles pointed to the construction of the text itself in ancient history. According to biblical scholars, the God of the Hebrew scriptures is a patchwork character, created by many ancient authors and editors who stitched together different depictions of God and different elements from a range of gods. These multiple sources do not entirely fit together, so this creates the impression of emotional complexity in God. Knowing this, of course, does not mean that these sources' combined impression is illegitimate; nor does it mean that we must break up God's character into the distinct, historical parts that have been delineated by biblical scholars. We can accept the character that emerges for us from the combination of multiple parts. As Miles put it, "A literary critic . . . may read this objective multiplicity back into the character of the Lord God, as a literary protagonist, turning [the] observed inconsistencies into God's experienced inner conflict."[4]

But there is more to our perception of God's ambivalence than this. Why should we interpret these "inconsistencies" in this way? Why should we play them up as ambivalence rather than downplay them and try to make God's character consistent? The literary assumptions of the reader play a part here. We have seen that for two centuries theologians struggled with the "inconsistencies" in God's character and resolved them in the direction of consistency. Rather than "turning [them] into . . . inner conflict," as Miles did, most theologians turned them into a relatively harmonious character. Moreover, in doing this theologians relied on the same sort of biblical scholarship that Miles referred to. That is, theologians used historical scholarship to separate the different biblical depictions of God. Theologians then added to this their own justifications for dismissing some biblical depictions as primitive while elevating others as progressive or, where the opposite strategy was needed, celebrating some material as authentic while denigrating others as later interpolations. They did this in order to come up with a relatively consistent characterization of God. None of this was necessarily determined by the biblical scholarship itself. What mattered was what theologians did with the scholarship. The point here is that scholarly claims about the origin of the Bible do not determine how it will be read.[5]

Why then was the ambivalence of God so interesting to Miles but not to many American theologians? The answer seems to be that they were influenced by neoclassical and sentimental styles of characterization, while Miles seems to have been influenced by romantic characterization. Miles's frequent references to Hamlet suggest this. Hamlet serves Miles not only because he is a famous literary character but also because he is the most famous ambivalent character. Miles suggested that the biblical God may have been the original for the Elizabethan Hamlet. A case could also be made that the romantic Hamlet was the model for Miles's God. We do not know whether our reading of Hamlet resembles what Shakespeare had in mind. We do know that neoclassical critics would not have appreciated our fascination with Hamlet's ambivalence. This aspect of his character was first distinctly celebrated in the early nineteenth century by such literary critics as Coleridge and Hazlitt. So in some respects, Miles's God may be considered a romantic character. But this raises questions concerning the whole notion of a biblical source for God's character: can we speak of being faithful to the text?[6]

Yes; but faith here, as in other matters, is not a science. It may be closer to an art. In this view, Protestant theologians should use as much biblical detail as they can to fill out Protestant doctrines so that they speak to people on their deepest emotional level. This may sound calculated and instrumental.[7] It is not. At issue here are cultural situations no one can control. Sometimes the best that theologians can do is strive to participate effectively in their culture while struggling to fathom the Bible and make sense of it in terms of their doctrinal tradition. According to this standard, Miles has opened up an important way to read the Bible.

But how are Protestants to make sense of his characterization of God? This is to ask about doctrine. We cannot fully address this here, but we can point in a direction. But first it must be stressed that Miles was writing as a literary critic, not a theologian. Moreover, he was writing on the Hebrew scriptures, which are not the same as the Old Testament, as Protestants construe it; and he did not write on the New Testament. But still we can ask how a Protestant theologian might respond to Miles's characterization of God. "It is certainly not the way a modern theologian would portray him," noted John Barton. And Barton was right about the vast majority of theologians.[8]

But the romantic anthropomorphists of the nineteenth century are a different story. Their characterizations of God resemble Miles's. This is not surprising, for these theologians, like Miles, brought to the Bible a romantic appreciation of character. Exodus 3:14, again, provides a good point of comparison. Miles's interpretation of this passage began like that of other recent theologians but then veered off in a different direction. Like Harvey Cox and other modern interpreters, Miles understood God to be saying, "I am what I shall be," or "You'll find out who I am." But for Cox the import of this statement was that people must discover who God is by doing God's presumed political work. For Miles, however, God himself is trying to discover who he is. In other words, God has a character, not just a political agenda. Moreover, he has a character worth exploring. "It is no exaggeration (and it is certainly not intended to be any insult)," Miles remarked, "to say that God does not know who he is." No insult would be taken from a romantic perspective. "I am many men," asserted D. H. Lawrence; "who are you? How many selves have you? And which of these selves do you want to be?"[9]

In Miles's interpretation, God tries to understand himself through his actions, but this creates new complications. He makes human beings in his image, but this does not simply provide God with a mirror. Things become even more complicated when humans start sexually reproducing. Miles's God becomes ambivalent about human sexuality and yet deeply implicated in it. Here we see some of the similarities between his characterization of God and those of Baird and Bushnell and even Stowe in her speculations about the relationship between Mary and Jesus. Indeed, these nineteenth-century writers rival Miles in depicting a God of powerful emotional complexity.[10]

But they differed from Miles in a crucial respect: they were working in the doctrinal tradition that centered on the atonement. This gave them direction and helped them to sustain this emotional complexity in God. It is an awesome thing to write about an ambivalent God. It is difficult to know what to make of him. Is there any resolution to his conflicted feelings? Miles acknowledged the difficulty of these questions and tried to see how they were resolved in the Hebrew scriptures themselves. As Miles read them, they ended with God's silence. This again suggests a parallel with Hamlet, who leaves with the words, "The rest is silence," and entrusts his legacy to the faithful Horatio. But, of course, the Protestant reading of the Old Testament does not end this way. At most, there is an intermission between the Old and New Testaments. Then God returns, impregnates Mary, and drives their son to the cross.[11]

At least this is how the Gospels were read in the juristic tradition. But however the Gospels are read, Protestant identity depends on making the life and death of Jesus the centerpiece of theology. Theologians could not ask for better material to work with. Furthermore, the Gospels leave room for a strong doctrinal interpretation. The challenge for Christians in interpreting them has always been to describe what God was doing during the life and death of Christ. Until recently, Protestants have interpreted this material at a difficult level by saying that God drove Jesus to the cross.

Theologians should avail themselves of the best in this tradition. They need to recover the doctrine of the atonement as it has been handled by their most compelling writers and develop it further. A complex God calls for complex doctrines. Ethics will not do here. They cannot be a substitute for doctrines any more than a novel can be summed up by its presumed moral. Nor will doctrines be compelling if they are vague. Matthew Arnold, in calling for a vague moralism to replace doctrinal theology, got one thing right: he blamed the difficulties of the doctrine of the atonement on the "licence" of anthropomorphism and the "particularity" of insisting on biblical details. "Nay," Arnold declared; "nearly all the difficulties which torment theology—as the reconciling of God's justice with his mercy and so on—come from this licence and particularity."[12] Strong biblical exegesis depends on this "licence and particularity." And the "difficulties which torment theology," such as the complexity of God's character, go to the heart of theology and the power of the cross.

Notes

Chapter One

1. Walter Lippmann, *A Preface to Morals* (1929; reprint, New Brunswick, N.J.: Transaction Publishers, 1989), p. 97; [Whittaker Chambers], "Faith for a Lenten Age," *Time* 51 (March 8, 1948): 70; Stanley Hauerwas, *Dispatches from the Front: Theological Engagements with the Secular* (Durham, N.C.: Duke University Press, 1994). It should be noted that all of these authors recognized the importance of art and literature for religious expression. Lippmann, for instance, explored the "disappearence of religious painting" and the difficulty of the modern writer working without a religious tradition (*Preface to Morals*, pp. 94–111). Chambers's article contained a reproduction of a William Blake picture of God, and Chambers cited the work of Dostoyevsky ("Faith for a Lenten Age, pp. 70–71). Central to Hauerwas's project has been "narrative theology," a late twentieth-century theological development that examines the ethical and epistemological complexity that can be conveyed through fictional, biblical, and other kinds of narratives. In *Dispatches from the Front*, Hauerwas used novels by Anthony Trollope and Anne Tyler to explore the moral agenda he proposed for theology (pp. 31–88).

2. On the emergence of a secular print culture, see Richard D. Brown, *Knowledge Is Power: The Diffusion of Information in Early America, 1700–1865* (New York: Oxford University Press, 1989); Larzer Ziff, *Writing in the New Nation: Prose, Print, and Politics in the Early United States* (New Haven: Yale University Press, 1991); Cathy N. Davidson, *Revolution and the World: The Rise of the Novel in America* (New York: Oxford University Press, 1986), pp. 15–37; and Lawrence Buell, *New England Literary Culture: From Revolution through Renaissance* (Cambridge: Cambridge University Press, 1986), pp. 56–83. On the appropriation of popular culture for religious ends in the nineteenth century, see Nathan Hatch, *The Democratization of American Christianity* (New Haven: Yale University Press, 1989). Jon Butler sees the efforts of evangelists as less egalitarian than Hatch and sets the process of "Christianizing the American people" in a larger spiritual context, including popular interest in magic. See Jon Butler, *Awash in a Sea of Faith: Christianizing the American People* (Cambridge, Mass.: Harvard University Press, 1990). On the use of popular literature and advertising techniques in popular religion in the nineteenth and twentieth centuries, see R. Laurence Moore, *Selling God: American Religion in the Marketplace of Culture* (New York: Oxford University Press, 1994). In the seventeenth and the early eighteenth century, of course, Puri-

tan ministers also sought to communicate persuasively with their congregations; on changing Puritan sermon styles, see Harry S. Stout, *The New England Soul: Preaching and Religious Culture in Colonial New England* (New York: Oxford University Press, 1986). On the efforts of the clergy to appeal to cosmopolitan Americans, especially by rebuilding and redecorating their churches, see Richard L. Bushman, *The Refinement of America: Persons, Houses, Cities* (New York: Random House, 1992), pp. 313–352. On the stratification of American culture more generally in the late eighteenth and the early nineteenth century, see Bushman, *Refinement of America*; Lawrence W. Levine, *Highbrow/Lowbrow: The Emergence of Cultural Hierarchy in America* (Cambridge, Mass.: Harvard University Press, 1988); and Stanley Elkins and Eric McKitrick, *The Age of Federalism: The Early American Republic, 1788–1800* (New York: Oxford University Press, 1993), pp. 164–169. It should be noted here that "cosmopolitan" does not necessarily mean "metropolitan." Certainly cities served as points of entry for European styles into America, and there was a concentration of cosmopolitan culture in cities, but this does not mean that there were not pockets of cosmopolitan culture in rural areas. Richard Bushman found evidence that even in "tiny villages" there was a market for refined culture (*Refinement of America*, p. 292). As far as seeing cities as the peculiar promoters of literary styles, there does not seem to be substantial evidence for this until the emergence of realism, aestheticism, and modernism in the late nineteenth and the early twentieth century. Even here, however, caution is warranted, for among the great American realists and modernists were Sherwood Anderson, the southern agrarians, and William Faulkner. New York City, however, especially Greenwich Village, seems to have played a distinctive role in nurturing American modernism. On this issue, see chap. 8, n. 36. For the theologians in this study, there seems to be no correlation between their location in urban or rural settings and their use of literary styles.

3. Louise Stevenson has provided a table of subjects covered in the *New Englander* in appendix 4 of her study *Scholarly Means to Evangelical Ends: The New Haven Scholars and the Transformation of Higher Learning in America, 1830–1890* (Baltimore: Johns Hopkins University Press, 1986), p. 164. On the response to novels in early nineteenth-century America, see Nina Baym, *Novels, Readers, and Reviewers: Responses to Fiction in Ante-bellum America* (Ithaca: Cornell University Press, 1984).

4. Historians concentrating on the relationship between American Protestant theology and philosophy and science have tended to focus on Jonathan Edwards as the crucial figure in the development of American theology. In his work, historians have identified the transition from the essentially medieval reasoning of the Puritans to an engagement with the enlightenment philosophy of John Locke and science of Isaac Newton. From there, historians carry the story through the nineteenth century as theologians adapted to enlightenment science and struggled with Darwinism. For a survey of the philosophical and scientific aspects of American Protestant theology from the eighteenth to the late nineteenth century, see Bruce Kuklick, *Churchmen and Philosophers: From Jonathan Edwards to John Dewey* (New Haven: Yale University Press, 1985). The classic study of Jonathan Edwards in this vein is Perry Miller, *Jonathan Edwards* (New York: Meridian Books, 1959). Other important studies on Edwards include Norman Fiering, *Jonathan Edwards's Moral Thought and Its British Context* (Chapel Hill: University of North Carolina Press, 1981); and Nathan O. Hatch and Harry S. Stout, eds., *Jonathan Edwards and the American Experience* (New York: Oxford University Press, 1988). For the theological engagement with enlightenment science and Darwinism in the nineteenth century, see Theodore Dwight Bozeman, *Protestantism in an Age of Science: The Baconian Ideal and Ante-Bellum Religious Thought* (Chapel Hill: University of North Carolina Press, 1977); E. Brooks Holifield, *The Gentlemen Theologians: American Theology in Southern Culture, 1795–1860* (Durham, N.C.: Duke University Press, 1978); James R. Moore, *The Post-Darwinian Controversies: A Study of the Protestant Struggle to Come to Terms with Darwin*

in Great Britain and America, 1870–1900 (New York: Cambridge University Press, 1979); and Jon H. Roberts, *Darwinism and the Divine in America: Protestant Intellectuals and Organic Evolution, 1859–1900* (Madison: University of Wisconsin Press, 1988).

5. Noah Porter, *Books and Reading; Or, What Books Shall I Read and How Shall I Read Them?*, 4th ed. (New York: Scribner, Armstrong, and Co., 1873), p. 106.

6. Francis Lieber, *A Popular Essay on Subjects of Penal Law and Uninterrupted Solitary Confinement* (Philadelphia, 1833), pp. 32–33; W. G. T. Shedd, "The Atonement: A Satisfaction for the Ethical Nature of Both God and Man," in *Theological Essays* (New York: Scribner, Armstrong, and Co., 1877), p. 298. This is an example of what the literary historian David Reynolds has called the "fluidity of genres" in antebellum America; see David Reynolds, *Beneath the American Renaissance: The Subversive Imagination in the Age of Emerson and Melville* (Cambridge, Mass.: Harvard University Press, 1989), p. 16. On the relationship between law and literature in the early nineteenth century, see Robert A. Ferguson, *Law and Letters in American Culture* (Cambridge, Mass.: Harvard University Press, 1984).

7. Robert Lewis Dabney, "Dangerous Reading" (1849), in *Discussions of Robert Lewis Dabney* 4 vols. (1891; reprint, Carlisle, Penn.: Banner of Truth Trust, 1982), 2:159; Solon Bush, "The Shady and Sunny Side of the Ministry," *Christian Examiner* 14 (November 1853): 338.

8. "The Reality of Fiction," *Christian Examiner* 75 (September 1863): 177, 179, 184; Porter, *Books*, pp. 8, 76–78.

9. Porter, *Books*, p. 77. Much of this theological fascination with literary characters echoes what Richard Bushman has found in nineteenth-century American cosmopolitan culture more generally. "Sporadically and partially, to be sure," Bushman noted, "fiction took command of character and imagination as readers stepped from real life into the plot lines of stories" (*Refinement of America*, p. 289).

10. Paulding's remark on Dryden is from his 1819 essay "National Literature," in *Theories of American Literature*, 2 vols., ed. Richard Ruland (New York: E. P. Dutton, 1976), 1:133. For a nuanced study of the mixture of neoclassical, sentimental, and romantic literary styles in antebellum America, see Buell, *New England Literary Culture*.

11. John Dryden, "Preface to *Troilus and Cressida*," in *The Dramatic Works*, 6 vols., ed. Montague Summers (New York: Gordian Press, 1968), 5:19, 24–25; Walter Jackson Bate, *From Classic to Romantic: Premises of Taste in Eighteenth-Century England* (New York: Harper and Row, 1946), pp. 14–15. Neoclassicism is an immense topic; leading works on it include Margaret Ann Doody, *The Daring Muse: Augustan Poetry Reconsidered* (Cambridge: Cambridge University Press, 1985); Paul Fussell, *The Rhetorical World of Augustan Humanism* (Oxford: Clarendon Press, 1965); Felicity Nussbaum and Laura Brown, eds., *The New Eighteenth Century* (New York: Methuen, 1987); and Pat Rogers, *The Augustan Vision* (London: Weidenfeld and Nicholson, 1974). On the increasing emotional complexity and interiority of characterization over the course of the eighteenth century, see Robert Folkenflik, ed., *The English Hero, 1660–1800* (London: Associated University Presses, 1982); and Felicity Nussbaum, "Heteroclites: The Gender of Character in the Scandalous Memoirs," in Nussbaum and Brown, *New Eighteenth Century*, pp. 144–168. Of course, also central to this transition in characterization was the rise of the novel; see Ian Watt, *The Rise of the Novel: Studies in Defoe, Richardson, and Fielding* (Berkeley: University of California Press, 1957).

12. Dryden, "Preface to *Troilus and Cressida*," p. 25.

13. Lionel Trilling, *Matthew Arnold* (1939; reprint, New York: Meridian Books, 1955), p. 115. Leading works on romanticism include M. H. Abrams, *The Mirror and the Lamp: Romantic Theory and the Critical Tradition* (New York: Oxford University Press, 1953), and *Natural Supernaturalism* (New York: Norton, 1971); Harold Bloom, ed., *Romanticism and Consciousness: Essays in Criticism* (New York: W. W. Norton and Co., 1970); Marilyn Butler,

Romantics, Rebels, and Reactionaries: English Literature and Its Background, 1760–1830 (New York: Oxford University Press, 1981); Paul de Man, *The Rhetoric of Romanticism* (New York: Columbia University Press, 1984); Jerome J. McGann, *The Romantic Ideology: A Critical Investigation* (Chicago: University of Chicago Press, 1983); and Mario Praz, *The Romantic Agony*, trans. Angus Davidson (Oxford: Oxford University Press, 1933).

14. Adam Gopnik, "Wonderland: Lewis Carroll and the Loves of His Life," *New Yorker* 71 (October 9, 1995): 82; Harold Bloom, *Agon: Towards a Theory of Revisionism* (New York: Oxford University Press, 1982), p. 16. On the romantics as introspective precursors to Freud, see Peter Gay, *The Naked Heart*, vol. 4 of *The Bourgeois Experience: Victoria to Freud* (New York: W. W. Norton and Co., 1995).

15. Toni Morrison, *Beloved* (New York: Penguin Books, 1987), p. 103.

16. George Gordon, Lord Byron, *Manfred*, act 3, scene 1, lines 159–165.

17. Morse Peckham, "The Dilemma of a Century: The Four Stages of Romanticism," in *Romanticism: The Culture of the Nineteenth Century*, ed. Morse Peckham (New York: George Braziller, 1965), pp. 15–33. For another consideration of the lasting impact of romantic figures, see Camille Paglia, *Sexual Personae: Art and Decadence from Nefertiti to Emily Dickinson* (New Haven: Yale University Press, 1990), esp. chaps. 8–14, 17.

18. On the celebration of authenticity in the twentieth century and its roots in romanticism, see Lionel Trilling, *Sincerity and Authenticity* (Cambridge, Mass.: Harvard University Press, 1971). On the more general issue of twentieth-century literary styles and their assimilation into American cosmopolitan culture, see chapters 8 and 10.

19. Byron, "Lara," lines 371–382.

20. "The Hebrew Language and Literature," *Presbyterian Quarterly Review* 9 (January 1861): 468–469.

21. Samuel Johnson, *Johnson on Shakespeare*, 2 vols., ed. Arthur Sherbo (New Haven: Yale University Press, 1968), 2:990; Gary Taylor, *Reinventing Shakespeare: A Cultural History from the Restoration to the Present* (New York: Weidenfeld and Nicholson, 1989), p. 48. On this point, see also James William Johnson, *The Formation of English Neo-Classical Thought* (Princeton: Princeton University Press, 1967), p. 191.

22. William Hazlitt, *Characters of Shakespeare's Plays* (1817), Prophets of Sensibility: Precursors of Modern Cultural Thought, ed. Harold Bloom (New Haven, Conn.: Chelsea House Publishers, 1983), p. 76.

23. Samuel Taylor Coleridge, "Lectures on Shakespeare and Education" (1813), in *The Collected Works of Samuel Taylor Coleridge*, 16 vols., ed. Kathleen Coburn (Princeton: Princeton University Press, Bollingen Series, 1987), 5:543. Coleridge's remark about having a "smack of Hamlet," comes from *Table Talk*, no. 80, in ibid., 14:543.

24. Ralph Waldo Emerson, "The American Scholar" (1837), in *Selections from Ralph Waldo Emerson*, ed. Stephen Whicher (New York: Houghton Mifflin Co., Riverside Editions, 1957), p. 77; Horace Bushnell, "Training for the Pulpit Manward," in *Building Eras in Religion* (New York: Charles Scribner's Sons, 1881), p. 233; Daniel Walker Howe, "The Social Science of Horace Bushnell," *Journal of American History* 70 (September 1983): 313. On the use of literary characters in the nineteenth century to personify feelings and encourage introspection and how this may have prepared the ground for the development and reception of Freudian analysis, see Peter Brooks, *The Melodramatic Imagination: Balzac, Henry James, Melodrama, and the Mode of Excess* (New Haven: Yale University Press, 1976), p. 202; and Gay, *Naked Heart*. Some have argued that Freud derived his Oedipus theory more from Shakespeare than from Sophocles. For a consideration of Freud's debt to Shakespeare, see Harold Bloom, *The Western Canon: The Books and School of the Ages* (New York: Harcourt, Brace and Co., 1994), chap. 16. For considerations of the significance of Hamlet for psychoanalysis and literature, see Jacques Lacan, "Desire and the Interpretation of Desire in *Ham-*

let," in *Literature and Psychoanalysis: The Question of Reading, Otherwise*, ed. Shoshana Felman (Baltimore: Johns Hopkins University Press, 1989), 11–52; and Daniel Sibony, "*Hamlet*: A Writing Effect," in ibid., pp. 53–93.

25. Porter, *Books*, pp. 86–87, 276.

26. The association of romanticism with the liberal theology of Unitarians and Transcendentalists has been an important feature of studies of the "American renaissance." On this issue, see chapter 5.

27. Protestantism's influence on secular literature is a vast topic. Important issues include the effect of Protestantism on printing, literacy, and the development of introspection and character analysis. For introductions to these issues in their American context, see Moore, *Selling God*, pp. 14–16; Brown, *Knowledge Is Power*, pp. 4–15; and Davidson, *Revolution and the Word*, 3–14. On popular religious literature, see Moore, *Selling God*; David Reynolds, *Faith in Fiction: The Emergence of Religious Literature in America* (Cambridge, Mass.: Harvard University Press, 1981); and Jane Tompkins, *Sensational Designs: The Cultural Work of American Fiction, 1790–1860* (New York: Oxford University Press, 1985).

28. Twentieth-century historians of American theology have mostly taken a dim view of the impact of nineteenth-century American culture in general on theology. Henry F. May, for instance, considered the combined influence of the enlightenment and the "genteel tradition" on nineteenth-century American theology and concluded: "Above all, the religion promoted by either the Unitarians or the increasingly compromising and compromised Calvinists was unsatisfactory; it did not address the realities of human nature, it explained away everything that is profound and interesting in Christianity" (*The Enlightenment in America* [New York: Oxford University Press, 1976], p. 358). This judgment is understandable, but it needs greater historical perspective. What nineteenth-century theologians assumed were "the realities of human nature" and what they believed was "profound and interesting in Christianity" changed with new scientific, moral, and literary views of character. Nineteenth-century theologians, holding to neoclassical and sentimental characterizations of God and humanity, thought they were bringing out what was most profound in Christianity. How this affected the characterization of God can be seen most clearly in the doctrine of the atonement. Twentieth-century theologians and historians have tended to focus, however, on the doctrine of original sin as the crucial issue. By abandoning this doctrine, liberals (a common historical argument goes) trivialized Christianity. This is an argument that conservative theologians made through the nineteenth and twentieth centuries. But it did not get much hearing from historians until the liberal "neo-orthodox" theologians used it in the early twentieth century. From then on, this neo-orthodox critique of nineteenth-century liberalism became a staple of historical judgment. One of the first historians to rely on the emerging neo-orthodox view was Joseph Haroutunian in his 1932 work, *Piety versus Moralism: The Passing of the New England Theology* (New York: Henry Holt and Co., 1932). On the impact of neo-orthodoxy and the historical treatment of American theology, see Henry F. May, "The Recovery of American Religious History" (1964), in *Ideas, Faith, and Feelings: Essays on American Intellectual and Religious History, 1952–1982* (New York: Oxford University Press, 1983), pp. 65–86; and Donald Weber, "The Recovery of Edwards," in Hatch and Stout, *Jonathan Edwards and the American Experience*, pp. 50–70. There is certainly much to these historical charges against liberalism regarding original sin. But this approach tends to make theology more anthropological than theological, more about views of human beings than about views of God (a problem, as we will see in chapter 9, that extends to neo-orthodox theological writing as well). Certainly views of God and humanity reflect each other, but they do so in complex ways. Notions of sin, for example, do bear on the characterization of God. If humanity is deeply sinful, this can justify God's anger against it, but if simply misguided, then God has less reason for anger. But justifying God's anger is not the same thing as ascribing the actual emotion to him. Con-

servatives, for instance, have maintained the doctrine of original sin while developing characterizations of God that downplay his anger. See the discussion on Charles Hodge in chapter 3. For the twentieth-century conservatives J. Gresham Machen and Carl F. H. Henry, see, respectively, chapters 9 and 10. For the neo-orthodox theologian Reinhold Niebuhr, see chapter 9. Most historical considerations of notions about sin in American theology have tended to frame the issue in philosophical terms as involving a debate between the claims of free will and necessity that go back to the work of Jonathan Edwards; major studies here include H. Shelton Smith, *Changing Conceptions of Original Sin: A Study in American Theology since 1750* (New York: Charles Scribner's, 1955); and Allen C. Guelzo, *Edwards on the Will: A Century of American Theological Debate* (Middletown, Conn.: Wesleyan University Press, 1989).

29. Leading studies on the impact of sentimentalism on religious writing and sensibility include Reynolds, *Faith in Fiction*; Ann Douglas, *The Feminization of American Culture* (New York: Alfred A. Knopf, 1978); and Richard Rabinowitz, *The Spiritual Self in Everyday Life: The Transformation of Personal Religious Experience in Nineteenth-Century New England* (Boston: Northeastern University Press, 1989). These studies have made major contributions to our understanding of how sentimentalism influenced American Protestantism. But I argue for a more nuanced consideration of sentimentalism in light of how theologians used other literary styles. Without this consideration, sentimental religious writing may appear to mark a more decisive departure in American theological writing than it actually did. Historians have sometimes given the impression that American Protestant theology was rigorously logical until, for better or worse, the advent of sentimentalism made it more literary and emotional. It is easy to see how this view entered into historical writing. As we will see in chapter 4, neoclassical and sentimental theologians used these kinds of categories in their polemical exchanges with each other. Neoclassical theologians sometimes condemned sentimentalists as being "merely literary" and "effeminate," while sentimentalists sometimes attacked neoclassical theologians for being "dry, cold, hard and logical." Polemical caricatures, however, while revealing in some respects, can also be misleading. In their own way, neoclassical theologians were just as influenced by literature as sentimentalists and just as concerned to ascribe certain kinds of emotions to God.

30. Amos N. Wilder, "Art and Theological Meaning," in *The New Orpheus: Essays toward a Christian Poetic*, ed. Nathan A. Scott (New York: Sheen and Ward, 1964), pp. 414, 418.

Chapter Two

1. Peter Gay, *The Enlightenment: An Interpretation*, vol. 1, *The Rise of Modern Paganism* (New York: W. W. Norton and Co., 1977), p. 218. For the influence of classical literature on the Middle Ages, see Ernst Robert Curtius, *European Literature and the Latin Middle Ages*, trans. Willard R. Trask (Princeton: Princeton University Press, 1953).

2. Perry Miller and Thomas H. Johnson, eds., *The Puritans: A Sourcebook for Their Writings*, 2 vols. (New York: Harper and Row, 1938), 2:545, 685–686.

3. Alexander Pope, in the 1715 preface to his translation of the *Iliad*, confidently dismissed Christian worries about Homer: "His books . . . are not now received for a Rule of Life, but valu'd for those just observations which are dispers'd among them" ("An Essay on Homer," in Alexander Pope, *The Iliad of Homer*, 2 vols., ed Maynard Mack [New Haven: Yale University Press, 1967], 1:65). Samuel Johnson considered *Paradise Lost* "not the greatest of heroic poems, only because it is not the first"—that honor went to the *Iliad*; see Paul Fussell, *The Rhetorical World of Augustan Humanism* (Oxford: Clarendon Press, 1985),

p. 17. On Shakespeare's prestige, see Gary Taylor, *Reinventing Shakespeare: A Cultural History from the Restoration to the Present* (New York: Weidenfeld and Nicholson, 1989), p. 114.

4. On Dwight, see Kenneth Silverman, *Timothy Dwight* (New York: Twayne Publishers, 1969); Lawrence Buell, *New England Literary Culture: From Revolution through Renaissance* (Cambridge: Cambridge University Press, 1986), pp. 169–171. On American neoclassicism more generally, see Lewis P. Simpson, ed., *The Federalist Literary Mind* (Baltimore: J. H. Furst Co.; Baton Rouge: Lousiana State University Press, 1962). For the broader social, political, and intellectual context, see Linda K. Kerber, *Federalists in Dissent: Imagery and Ideology in Jeffersonian America* (Ithaca: Cornell University Press, 1970).

5. Noah Porter, "The New England Meeting House," *New Englander* 42 (May 1883): 323–324. For Porter's negative comments on neoclassicism, see his *Books and Reading; Or, What Books Shall I Read and How Shall I Read Them?*, 4th ed. (New York: Scribner, Armstrong, and Co., 1873), pp. 262–263, 270. On the "country movement" in late eighteenth-century English poetry, see Marilyn Butler, "Romanticism in England," in *Romanticism in National Context*, ed. Roy Porter and Mikulas Teich (Cambridge: Cambridge University Press, 1988), pp. 41–51.

6. James Turner, *Without God, without Creed: The Origins of Unbelief in America* (Baltimore: Johns Hopkins University Press, 1985), p. 72. See also Gordon S. Wood, *The Radicalism of the American Revolution* (New York: Random House, Vintage Books, 1991), pp. 213–228.

7. On the neoclassical consideration of history, see James William Johnson, *The Formation of English Neo-Classical Thought* (Princeton: Princeton University Press, 1967); David Spadafora, *The Idea of Progress in Eighteenth-Century Britain* (New Haven: Yale University Press, 1990).

8. The English theologian is cited in G. J. Barker-Benfield, *The Culture of Sensibility: Sex and Society in Eighteenth-Century Britain* (Chicago: University of Chicago Press, 1992), p. 69; Alexander Pope, "An Essay on Criticism," lines 90–91; Alexander Pope, "An Essay on Man," epistle 2, line 21.

9. Horace Bushnell, "Revelation"(1839), unpublished ms. in Yale Divinity School library, reprinted in appendix B of David Stanley Steward, "Horace Bushnell and Contemporary Christian Education: A Study of Revelation and Nurture," Ph.D. diss., Yale University, 1966; Bushnell's remark about Newton appears in ibid., p. 334; Edwards A. Park, "All the Moral Attributes of God Are Comprehended in His Love," in *Discourses on Some Theological Doctrines as Related to the Religious Character* (Andover, Mass.: Warren F. Draper, 1885), pp. 163, 167.

10. Clarke is cited in R. S. Crane, "Suggestions toward a Genealogy of the 'Man of Feeling,'" *English Literary History* 1 (December 1934): 212. Also on the emergence of humanitarian sensibility, see John K. Sheriff, *The Good-Natured Man: The Evolution of a Moral Idea, 1660–1800* (University: University of Alabama Press, 1982); and Barker-Benfield, *Culture of Sensibility*, chap. 2. On the relationship of humanitarianism and theology, see also Turner, *Without God*, pp. 64–72.

11. Tillotson's remark is cited in Sheriff, *Good-Natured Man*, p. 3. On the wider embrace of humanitarianism outside of Tillotson's liberal religious circles, see Donald Green, "Latitudinarianism and Sensibility: The Genealogy of the 'Man of Feeling' Reconsidered," *Modern Philology* 75 (November 1977): 159–183; and Ernest L. Tuveson, "The Importance of Shaftesbury," *English Literary History* 20 (December 1953): 267–299. On the early reception of Tillotson in America, see Norman Fiering, "The First American Enlightenment: Tillotson, Leverett, and Philosophical Anglicanism," *New England Quarterly* 44 (September 1981): 307–344.

12. On the relationship between capitalism and humanitarianism, see Barker-Benfield, *Culture of Sensibility*, chap. 2; Thomas L. Haskall, "Capitalism and the Origins of the Humanitarian Sensibility," *American Historical Review* 90 (April 1985): 339–361, and 90 (June 1985): 547–566; David Brion Davis, "Reflections on Abolitionism and Ideological Hegemony," *American Historical Review* 92 (October 1987): 797–812; John Ashworth, "The Relationship between Capitalism and Humanitarianism," *American Historical Review* 92 (October 1987): 813–828; and Thomas L. Haskall, "Convention and Hegemonic Interest in the Debate over Antislavery: A Reply to Davis and Ashworth," *American Historical Review* 92 (October 1987): 829–878. On the emergence of humanitarian reform more generally, see Michael Kraus, *The Atlantic Civilization: Eighteenth-Century Origins* (Ithaca: Cornell University Press, 1949), chap. 6. A vast amount of literature exists on religion and humanitarian reform movements in antebellum America; for two general considerations, see Robert H. Abzug, *Cosmos Crumbling: American Reform and the Religious Imagination* (New York: Oxford University Press, 1994); and Turner, *Without God*, pp. 73–113.

13. On the reaction against stoical restraint, see Crane, "Suggestions toward a Genealogy of the 'Man of Feeling'"; Ian Donaldson, "Cato in Tears: Stoical Guises of the Man of Feeling," in *Studies in the Eighteenth Century*, ed. R. F. Brissendon (Toronto: University of Toronto Press, 1973), pp. 377–395; and Norman Fiering, "Irresistible Compassion: An Aspect of Eighteenth-Century Sympathy and Humanitarianism," *Journal of the History of Ideas* 37 (April–May, 1976): 186–203. On the emergence of sentimentalism more generally, see Sheriff, *Good-Natured Man*; Barker-Benfield, *Culture of Sensibility*; and Paul Langford, *A Polite and Commercial People: England, 1727–1783* (New York: Oxford University Press, 1989), chap. 10.

14. On sentimentalism and the family, see Lawrence Stone, *The Family, Sex, and Marriage in England, 1500–1800* (New York: Harper and Row, 1977). On changing child-rearing practices in America, see Philip Greven, *The Protestant Temperament: Patterns of Child-Rearing, Religious Experience, and the Self in Early America* (New York: Alfred A. Knopf, 1977); Jay Fliegelman, *Prodigals and Pilgrims: The American Revolution against Patriarchal Authority, 1750–1800* (Cambridge: Cambridge University Press, 1982); and Richard L. Bushman, *The Refinement of America: Persons, Houses, Cities* (New York: Random House, 1992). Leading works on the sentimental novel in America include Ann Douglas, *The Feminization of American Culture* (New York: Alfred A. Knopf, 1978); Jane Tompkins, *Sensational Designs: The Cultural Work of American Fiction, 1790–1860* (New York: Oxford University Press, 1985); David Reynolds, *Faith in Fiction: The Emergence of Religious Literature in America* (Cambridge, Mass.: Harvard University Press, 1981); and Cathy N. Davidson, *Revolution and the Word: The Rise of the Novel in America* (New York: Oxford University Press, 1986). The relationship between sentimentalism and nineteenth-century American reform politics is a large topic; two works in the field are Shirley Samuels, ed., *The Culture of Sentiment: Race, Gender, and Sentimentality in Nineteenth-Century America* (New York: Oxford University Press, 1992); and Barbara Leslie Epstein, *The Politics of Domesticity: Women, Evangelicalism, and Temperance in Nineteenth-Century America* (Middletown, Conn.: Wesleyan University Press, 1981).

15. Catharine Sedgwick, *Home* (Boston: James Munroe and Co., 1841), pp. 17, 22–23. On the paternal aspects of Dryden's poem, see Larry Carver, "*Absalom and Achitophel* and the Father Hero," in *The English Hero, 1660–1800*, ed. Robert Folkenflik (London: Associated University Presses, 1982), pp. 35–45.

16. Karen Lystra, *Searching the Heart: Women, Men, and Romantic Love in Nineteenth-Century America* (New York: Oxford University Press, 1989), pp. 10–11, 39–40. In the title to her work, Lystra used the word "romantic" in a general sense, not in the more specific literary sense used in this book. On the penetration of literature into life, see also Bushman, *Refinement of America*, chap. 9.

17. John F. Kasson, *Rudeness and Civility: Manners in Nineteenth-Century Urban America* (New York: Hill and Wang, 1990), pp. 150, 157, 161; Frederick Douglass, *Narrative of the Life of Frederick Douglass* (1845; reprint, New York: Signet Books, New American Library, 1968), pp. 48–49. On views of anger in the nineteenth century, see Carol Z. Stearns and Peter Stearns, *Anger: The Struggle for Emotional Control in American History* (Chicago: University of Chicago Press, 1986); Richard H. Broadhead, "Sparing the Rod: Discipline and Fiction in Ante-Bellum America," *Representations* 24 (Winter 1988): 67–96; and Karen Halttunen, "Humanitarianism and the Pornography of Pain in Anglo-American Culture," *American Historical Review* 100 (April 1995): 303–334.

18. "All the truths of God flow into the atonement," wrote Edwards A. Park; "there is more of profound and even abstruse philosophy involved in the specific doctrine of the atonement than in any other doctrine" ("The Prominence of the Atonement," in *Discourses on Some Theological Doctrines*, pp. 55, 59). See also R. W. Brown, "Christ Dying for the Sins of Men: The Foundation of the Christian Superstructure," *New Englander* 21 (July 1862): 491; and Moses Stuart, *Two Discourses on the Atonement* (Andover, Mass.: Flagg and Gould, 1828), p. 40. It must be said, however, that most evangelical and popular theologians paid less attention to the doctrine of the atonement. Reasons for this may have to do with their Arminianism (hence their greater consideration of what people have to do to be saved in addition to what God has done for them); their emphasis on the process of sanctification and the role of the Holy Spirit rather than on justification and the work of Christ; and their tendency to eschew complex theological formulations for more simple and straightforward appeals to conversion and moral improvement. This last point in particular can be seen in the way that Methodist and Baptist reviewers responded to treatises on the atonement by Edwards Park and Horace Bushnell. William Fairfield Warren, a Methodist, reviewing Park's 1859 work, *The Atonement: Discourses and Treatises*, wrote: "The genius of Arminianism is, and ever has been, quite averse to the dogmatic discussion of such abstrusities as the question before us" ("The 'Edwardean' Theory of the Atonement," *Methodist Quarterly Review* 42 [July 1860]: 393, 397). In a similar spirit, a Baptist theologian began his review of Bushnell's second treatise on the atonement, *Forgiveness and Law* (1874), with the comment, "It is not essential to salvation that one believe any theory of the atonement" (L. E. Smith, "Elements Essential to a True Theory of the Atonement," *Baptist Quartery Review* 8 [October 1874]: 379). On the emergence of the atonement as a subject of debate in nineteenth-century theology, see David F. Wells, "The Debate over the Atonement in Nineteenth-Century America," *Bibliotheca Sacra* 144 (April–June 1987): 123–143; 144 (July–September 1987): 243–253; 144 (October–December 1987): 363–376; 145 (January–March 1988): 3–14. For a consideration of how the atonement figured in British social views in the early nineteenth century, see Boyd Hilton, *The Age of Atonement: The Influence of Evangelicalism on Social and Economic Thought, 1795–1865* (New York: Oxford University Press, 1988); also of interest here is: David Nichols, *Deity and Domination: Images of God and the State in the Nineteenth and Twentieth Centuries* (London: Routledge, 1989), pp. 52–60.

19. J. Jay Dana, "The Religion of Geology," *Bibliotheca Sacra* 10 (July 1853): 505; Gardiner Spring, *The Attraction of the Cross* (New York: M. W. Dodd, 1846), p. 34.

20. The best overview of Christian theology on this point is the two-volume work by Alister E. McGrath, *Iustatia Dei: A History of the Christian Doctrine of Justification*, vol. 1, *From the Beginnings to 1500*, and vol. 2, *From 1500 to the Present Day* (Cambridge: Cambridge University Press, 1986). Also helpful here are L. W. Grensted, *A Short History of the Doctrine of the Atonement* (Manchester: Manchester University Press, 1920); Gustaf Aulen, *Christus Victor: An Historical Survey of the Three Main Types of the Idea of the Atonement* (London: Society for the Propagation of Christian Knowledge, 1931); and F. W. Dillistone, *The Christian Understanding of the Atonement* (London: SCM Press, 1984).

21. John Calvin, *Institutes of the Christian Religion*, 2 vols., ed. John T. McNeil, trans. Ford Lewis Battles (Philadelphia: Westminster Press, 1960), bk. II, chap. xvi, sec. 4.

22. This does not mean that the Puritans or early eighteenth-century New England theologians were entirely isolated from cosmopolitan theological currents in Europe. Moreover, social changes occurring in New England encouraged theologians to liberalize some of their doctrines, especially concerning election and church membership. But a major theological reassessment of the character of God does not seem to have gotten under way until the middle decades of the eighteenth century. On the variety of theological thought in Puritan New England, see Philip F. Gura, *A Glimpse of Sion's Glory: Puritan Radicalism in New England, 1620–1860* (Middletown, Conn.: Wesleyan University Press, 1984). The classic work on the theology of the New England Puritans and the liberalization of their theology from the seventeenth to the eighteenth century remains Perry Miller's *The New England Mind in the Seventeenth Century* (Cambridge, Mass.: Harvard University Press, 1939), and *The New England Mind: From Colony to Province* (Cambridge, Mass.: Harvard University Press, 1953).

23. The transition from the juristic tradition to philanthropism in America has been studied mainly as a liberal movement. It certainly was a movement led by liberals, though it substantially influenced conservatives as well. One of the best surveys of American theology to the middle of the nineteenth century remains Frank Hugh Foster's *A Genetic History of New England Theology* (Chicago: University of Chicago Press, 1907). See also Joseph Haroutunian, *Piety versus Moralism: The Passing of the New England Theology* (New York: Henry Holt and Co., 1932). In contrast to Foster, Haroutunian gave a more sympathetic account of the juristic tradition, reflecting here the views of the "neo-orthodox" movement in mid-twentieth-century American liberalism. Unlike Foster also, Haroutunian focused more on the social factors involved in the transition to philanthropism. So did Ann Douglas, who, unlike Haroutunian, concentrated on the role of sentimentalism in these changes (*Feminization of American Culture*, esp. pp. 121–164). Like Douglas, Richard Rabinowitz also concentrated on sentimentalism but gave a more positive estimation of it than Douglas (Richard Rabinowitz, *The Spiritual Self in Everyday Life: The Transformation of Personal Religious Experience in Nineteenth-Century New England* [Boston: Northeastern University Press, 1989]). Foster was a student of Edwards A. Park, one of the major nineteenth-century theological champions of philanthropism. Readers should be aware that in his history Foster relied on some of Park's polemic against the juristic tradition (such as associating the juristic God with a distant and arbitrary God of wrath). As we will see in this chapter, this polemic was very effective. Indeed, it creeps into many histories of American theology, just as does the liberal caricature of conservatives as dry-as-dust logic choppers and the conservative caricature of liberals as Pollyannas and dilettantes. While these polemics tell us a great deal about how theologians saw and caricatured each other, they are not accurate representations of how theologians actually wrote.

24. On the New Divinity movement, see Joseph Conforti, *Samuel Hopkins and the New Divinity Movement: Calvinism, the Congregational Ministry, and Reform in New England between the Great Awakenings* (Grand Rapids, Mich.: Christian University Press and Eerdmans Publishing Co., 1981). The New Divinity theology is also covered in Foster, *New England Theology*, and Haroutunian, *Piety versus Moralism*. The influences of Edwards's work on the atonement for New Divinity theologians is considered in Park's introductory essay, "The Rise of the Edwardean Theory of the Atonement," in *The Atonement: Discourses and Treatises by Edwards, Smalley, Maxcy, Emmons, Griffin, Burge, and Weeks*, ed. Edwards A. Park (Boston: Congregational Board of Publication, 1859), pp. ix–lxxix. Park, of course, was writing to promulgate a particular theological agenda, which needs to be kept in mind when one is reading him or his student, the historian Frank Hugh Foster. Foster carried on Park's historical work, but more than Park he traced Edwards's theory of the atonement back to Grotius.

See Frank Hugh Foster, "The Benevolence Theory of the Atonement," *Bibliotheca Sacra* 47 (October 1890): 567–588; 48 (January 1891): 104–127. See also Foster's introduction to Hugo Grotius, *A Defence of the Catholic Faith concerning the Satisfaction of Christ against Faustus Socinus*, trans. Frank Hugh Foster (Andover, Mass.: W. F. Draper, 1889). On the theological use of Edwards in the nineteenth century, see Joseph A. Conforti, *Jonathan Edwards, Religious Tradition, and American Culture* (Chapel Hill: University of North Carolina Press, 1995); and Allen C. Guelzo, *Edwards on the Will: A Century of American Theological Debate* (Middletown, Conn.: Wesleyan University Press, 1989).

25. On this division in the Presbyterian church, see George Marsden, *The Evangelical Mind and the New School Presbyterian Experience: A Case Study of Thought and Theology in Nineteenth-Century America* (New Haven: Yale University Press, 1970); and Earl A. Pope, "Albert Barnes, 'The Way of Salvation,' and Theological Controversy," *Journal of Presbyterian History* 57 (Spring 1979): 20–32.

26. Brown, "Christ Dying for the Sins of Men," p. 491. Lyman Abbott et al., *The Atonement in Modern Religious Thought: A Theological Symposium* (London: James Clarke and Co., 1900), p. 359.

27. Tompkins, *Sensational Designs*, p. 134. Frederick Douglass alluded to the crucifixion to describe his fight with Mr. Covey, which was triggered when Douglass collapsed from overwork on a Friday afternoon at 3 o'clock (*Narrative of the Life of Frederick Douglass*, pp. 77–83). Stowe ascribed Christlike traits to Uncle Tom throughout her novel, but for those scenes specifically alluding to the crucifixion, see chapter 38 ("The Victory") and 40 ("The Martyr") in Harriet Beecher Stowe, *Uncle Tom's Cabin or, Life among the Lowly* (1852; reprint, New York: Penguin Classics, 1981). Lincoln's second inaugural address, of course, can be found in many sources; the citation here comes from Richard Hofstadter, ed., *Great Issues in American History*, 2 vols. (New York: Random House, Vintage Books, 1958), 1:416. On religious interpretations of the Civil War, see James R. Moorhead, *American Apocalypse: Yankee Protestants and the Civil War, 1860–1869* (New Haven: Yale University Press, 1978); and Charles Reagan Wilson, *Baptized in Blood: The Religion of the Lost Cause, 1865–1920* (Athens: University of Georgia Press, 1980).

28. The comments about Grotius and the "over-refinement of the age" are in [W. G. T. Shedd], "The True Tone in Preaching and the True Temper in Hearing," Princeton Review 35 (July 1863): 425, 438. Shedd later republished this essay as a chapter entitled "Reciprocal Relations of Preachers and Hearers" in his *Homiletics and Pastorial Theology* (New York: Charles Scribner and Co., 1867), pp. 258–295. The comment about the "demon" is from W. G. T. Shedd, "The Atonement: A Satisfaction for the Ethical Nature of Both God and Man," in *Theological Essays* (New York: Scribner, Armstrong, and Co., 1877), pp. 280–281. For religious interest in the Civil War, see Moorhead, *American Apocalypse*, and Wilson, *Baptized in Blood*.

29. Noah Worcester, *The Atoning Sacrifice: A Display of Love Not of Wrath* (Cambridge, Mass.: Hilliard and Brown, 1829), p. 14.

30. Ibid., p. 14.

31. George Rapall Noyes, "The Scripture Doctrine of Sacrifice," *Christian Examiner* 59 (September 1855): 243.

32. "Justice as Satisfied by the Atonement," *Presbyterian Quarterly Review* 8 (January 1860): 437–438. The title to this article might suggest that the author was supporting the juristic tradition. This was not the case; rather, it was a concessionary gesture to the defeated camp. The author's point was that juristic theologians should not worry that their emphasis on God's justice was overlooked in philanthropism. Justice still had a place, the author assured his readers. But the place of justice was still secondary to love. About this, the author left no room for doubt: "The office and place of justice in a virtuous character is not supreme,"

the author declared; "justice is essential but it does not hold the highest place among the attributes of goodness: the supremacy belongs to love" (pp. 437–438).

33. The issue of anthropomorphism is a complex one for Christianity, as well as many religions. For a consideration of anthropomorphism as central to religion in general, see Stewart Guthrie, *Faces in the Clouds: A New Theory of Religion* (New York: Oxford University Press, 1993). Chapter 7 of this work reviews some of the recent Christian theological attitudes toward anthropomorphism. The tension between theistic and anthropomorphic characterizations of God goes back to the start of Christian theology in late antiquity; see Christopher Stead, *Philosophy in Christian Antiquity* (Cambridge: Cambridge University Press, 1994); and James L. Kugel and Rowan A. Greer, *Early Biblical Interpretation* (Philadelphia: Westminster Press, 1986), pp. 122–123, 145–146, 166. Historians have often assumed that theism is necessarily more sophisticated that anthropomorphism. This was the view of one of the founders of the modern historical study of ancient Christianity, Adolph von Harnack. For instance, he noted, "how many shades of belief there were between the crude anthropomorphists and spiritualists" (*History of Dogma*, 7 vols., trans. Neil Buchanan [London: Williams and Norgate, 1984] 3:200). Similar theological assumptions pervade Karen Armstrong's 1993 *History of God*. In the index to her work, under the heading "God," there is the category "man's invention (anthropomorphism)." Much like the nineteenth-century champions of philanthropism, Armstrong saw anthropomorphism as an early stage in the development of Hebrew religion, one that has "the grave liability" of making God into an "idol" who can seem "callous and cruel." Like many nineteenth-century liberals, Armstrong relied on this primitivization of Old Testament anthropomorphism as part of a polemic against contemporary conservatives, in her case fundamentalists. Her preferred characterization of God was one of mystical compassion. See Karen Armstrong, *A History of God: The 4,000–Year Quest of Judaism, Christianity, and Islam* (New York: Ballantine Books, 1993), pp. 87, 210–211, 390–392, 444. Also, see below, chap. 10, n. 3.

34. John Owen, *A Dissertation on Divine Justice*, in *The Works of John Owen*, 12 vols., ed. Thomas Russell (London: Richard Baynes, 1826), 9:400. We must guard, however, against a simplistic view of this. Medieval and Reformation theologians were not simplistic readers of the Bible when it came to anthropomorphism. The contrary was the case. They argued forcefully against taking biblical anthropomorphism literally. John Calvin, for instance, denounced the "boundless barbarism" of those Christians who as "Pagans" did not know any better than to take anthropomorphic depictions of God literally (*Institutes*, bk. IV, chap. vii, sec. 23). John Owen decried the "cursed madness of anthropomorphites" who "cry out the bare word, the letter [and] away with the gloss and interpretation" ("The Death of Death in the Death of Christ," in Russell, *Works*, 5:407). Juristic theologians, then, were not strangers to complex biblical interpretation. They routinely translated anthropomorphic depictions of God into theistic depictions.

35. For Calvin on the difference between the ancient Jews and Christians, see *Institutes*, bk. II, chap. xi, sec. 13. For Calvin on God's condescension as a nurse to children, see ibid., bk. I, chap. xiii, sec. 1. Of course, juristic theologians could also be contemptuous of the limited capacities of the human mind. John Owen, for instance, wrote that God "condescends to the nature and capacities of men, and speaks for the most part to the imagination (further than which few among the sons of men were ever able to raise their cognitions" (*Vindicae Evangelicae; Or, the Mystery of the Gospel Vindicated and Socianism Examined* in Russell, *Works*, 8:154).

36. For the positions of moderate and liberal biblical critics at Andover and Harvard, see Jerry Wayne Brown, *The Rise of Biblical Criticism in America: The New England Scholars* (Middletown, Conn.: Wesleyan University Press, 1969). For conservative approaches to the Bible, see Jack B. Rogers and Donald K. McKim, *The Authority and Interpretation of the*

Bible: An Historical Approach (San Francisco: Harper and Row, 1979), pp. 263–279; and Mark A. Noll, "Introduction," in *The Princeton Defense of Plenary Inspiration*, ed. Mark A. Noll (New York: Garland Publishing, 1988), pp. 1–15. For general considerations of the role of the Bible in American culture, see Nathan O. Hatch and Mark A. Noll, eds., *The Bible in America: Essays in Cultural History* (New York: Oxford University Press, 1982). For a consideration of how eighteenth- and nineteenth-century European biblical criticism distanced the Bible from readers, see Hans Frei, *The Eclipse of Biblical Narrative: A Study of Eighteenth- and Nineteenth-Century Hermeneutics* (New Haven: Yale University Press, 1974). On nineteenth-century European biblical criticism more generally, see John Rogerson, *Old Testament Criticism in the Nineteenth Century* (London: Society for the Propagation of Christian Knowledge, 1984); R. E. Clements, "The Study of the Old Testament," in *Nineteenth Century Religious Thought in the West*, 3 vols., ed. Ninlan Smart, John Clayton, Stephen Katz, and Patrick Sherry (Cambridge: Cambridge University Press, 1985): 3:109–141; and J. C. O'Neill, "The Study of the New Testament," in ibid., 3:143–178.

37. E. C. Wines, "The Hebrew Theocracy," *Biblical Repository and Classical Review* 80 (October 1850): 591.

38. Edwards A. Park, *The Theology of the Intellect and That of the Feelings* (Andover, Mass.: W. F. Draper, 1850), p. 6. Andover Seminary was a center for disseminating liberal European biblical criticism. See also Edwards A. Park, "The Mode of Exhibiting Theological Truth," *American Biblical Repository* 10 (October 1837): 436–478. On Park's essay and the controversy surrounding it, see Robert Whittemore, *The Transformation of New England Theology*, American University Studies, Series 7, Theology and Religion, vol. 23 (New York: Peter Lang, 1973), pp. 296–315; and D. G. Hart, "Divided between Heart and Mind: The Critical Period for Protestant Thought in America," *Journal of Ecclesiastical History* 33 (April 1987): 254–270. Park's essay triggered an extensive debate between Park and Charles Hodge, discussed later in this chapter. In 1853, the leading New School Presbyterian theologian, Albert Barnes, though also a governmental theologian like Park, attacked Park's sermon; see Albert Barnes, "Thoughts on Theology," in *Essays and Reviews*, 2 vols. (New York: Ivison and Phinny, 1855), 2:323–324. The conservative Presbyterian theologian W. G. T. Shedd most likely had Park in mind in his attack on liberal biblical interpretation, "The True Tone in Preaching and the True Temper in Hearing." In 1869, Horace Bushnell was still arguing with Park's sermon; see Bushnell, "Our Gospel, a Gift to the Imagination," in *Building Eras of Religion* (New York: Charles Scribner's Sons, 1881), pp. 269–270.

39. Park drew an analogy between theology and chemistry. If chemists had to use theological terms, it would undermine the authority of their science: "If one acid were figuratively called 'sanctification,' and one alkali were termed 'depravity,' . . . we should weep over the sad results of such a profane style. . . . And on a similar principle, when we read [in theology] of 'the vindictive justice of God,' . . . we mourn over the ruinous impression that will be made" (*Theology of the Intellect*, pp. 10, 15, 44). On the debate among astronomers over the use of mythological names for planets and stars, see Thomas Dick, *The Sidereal Heavens and Other Subjects Connected with Astronomy* (New York: Harper and Bros., 1844), pp. 42–57.

40. Charles Hodge, "The Theology of the Intellect and That of the Feelings," in *Essays and Reviews* (New York: Robert Carter and Bros., 1857), pp. 539–633. Park's responses to Hodge are in Edwards A. Park, "Remarks on the Biblical Repertory and Princeton Review," *Bibliotheca Sacra* 8 (January 1851): 135–180, and "Remarks on the Princeton Review," *Bibliotheca Sacra* 9 (July 1851): 306–347. This exchange between Park and Hodge became a subject of commentary for Unitarians: "The Andover and Princeton Theologies," *Christian Examiner* 52 (May 1852): 309–335.

41. Hodge, *Essays and Reviews*, pp. 543, 548.

42. Ibid., p. 547.

43. For Hodge's defense of the Hebrew practice of animal sacrifice as a harbinger of the atonement, see Hodge, "Beman on the Atonement," in *Essays and Reviews*, pp. 149–150.

44. "Andover and Princeton Theologies," p. 319.

45. Wines, "Hebrew Theocracy," p. 598.

46. Taylor Lewis, "The Spirit of the Old Testament," *Biblical Repository and Classical Review* 77 (January 1850): 3.

47. As Park put it, "A wise preacher would not exhort a Newton and Leibnitz, in the same terms, although he would use the same ideas, which he would employ in addressing little children, or in expostulating with the rudest and coarsest of malefactors" (*Theology of the Intellect*, p. 39).

48. Henry Ward Beecher, *Yale Lectures on Preaching* (New York: J. B. Ford and Co., 1874), p. 82. See also: Beecher, *Yale Lectures on Preaching* (New York: J. B. Ford and Co., 1872), pp. 89–90. For Beecher's more extensive treatment of human evolution and the character of God, see his *Evolution and Religion* (New York: Fords, Howard, and Hulbert, 1885), pp. 25–43.

49. Matthew 3:16–17, 17:5; Mark 1:10–11, 9:7; Luke 3:22, 10:34–35; John 1:32.

50. Owen, "Death of Death in the Death of Christ," 5:385.

51. Matthew 26:38–39, 27:32, 46; Mark 14:31–42, 15:21, 34; Luke 22:39–47, 23:36, 46. To do justice to the complexity and drama of the Gospels seemed to some theologians beyond human capability. As one writer put it in 1860, "The full significance of the facts of the atonement, the incarnation, the temptation, the agony and bloody sweat, the desertion and outcry from the cross, the death and burial of Christ, can neither be explained nor comprehended by man" ("Justice as Satisfied by the Atonement," 450).

52. Owen, "Death of Death in the Death of Christ," 5:245–246.

53. François Turretin, *Turretin on the Atonement*, trans. James R. Wilson (New York: Board of Publication of the Reformed Protestant Dutch Church, 1859), p. 54; Moses Stuart, *Two Discourses on the Atonement* (Andover, Mass.: Mark Newman, 1828), p. 13. Even Calvin was troubled by Christ's behavior. But at least Calvin had a way to explain it. From Calvin's perspective, Christ's behavior made sense, given that he was bearing the infinite wrath of God (see Calvin, *Institutes*, bk. II, chap. xvi, sec. 12). For a discussion of Stuart's biblical criticism, see Brown, *Rise of Biblical Criticism*, pp. 45–59, 94–110.

54. Edward Gibbon, *The Decline and Fall of the Roman Empire*, 2 vols. (New York: Modern Library, 1932), 1:2. As in all of this, of course, writers could take sensible and nuanced views. Samuel Johnson, for instance, while recommending the practical benefits of a pious patience, thought that the ancient Stoics had gone too far in their vision of indifference to pain; see Johnson, "Stoicism," *Rambler*, no. 32 (July 7, 1750), in *Samuel Johnson*, ed. Donald Greene (New York: Oxford University Press, 1984), pp. 186–189.

Chapter Three

1. Edwards A. Park, "All the Moral Attributes of God Are Comprehended in His Love," in *Discourses on Some Theological Doctrines as Related to the Religious Character* (Andover, Mass.: W. F. Draper, 1885), p. 165. Exodus 3:14, of course, has been interpreted in different ways in the history of Christian theology, for different ends. It was especially significant in philosophical speculation about God's nature during the Middle Ages; see Etienne Gilson, *The Spirit of Medieval Philosophy*, trans. A. H. C. Downes (New York: Charles Scribner's Sons, 1940), pp. 50–53, 433–434.

2. James Henley Thornwell, "The Necessity of the Atonement" (1845), in *The Collected Writings of James Henley Thornwell*, 2 vols., ed. John B. Adger (Richmond: Presbyterian Committee of Publication, 1871), 2:257. "His cross became, for the time, the centre of observation of the Universe," declared Albert Barnes in *The Atonement in Its Relations to Law and Moral Government* (Philadelphia: Parry and McMillan, 1860), pp. 256–257. The universe was meant here quite literally. Angels and astronomy went together in nineteenth-century American theology; many theologians believed that other planets were inhabited and that somehow other intelligent creatures there had followed the drama of humanity's fall on earth and its dramatic redemption in the crucifixion. See, for instance, "Are the Planets Inhabited?," *Presbyterian Quarterly Review* 15 (December 1855): 396; and E. F. Burr, "Are the Heavens Inhabited?" *Presbyterian Review* 22 (April 1855): 262–266.

3. For background on Channing, see: Andrew Delbanco, *William Ellery Channing: An Essay on the Liberal Spirit in America* (Cambridge, Mass.: Harvard University Press, 1971). For a broader look at Unitarian thought in antebellum America, see Daniel Walker Howe, *The Unitarian Conscience: The Harvard Moral Philosophers, 1805–1861* (Cambridge, Mass.: Harvard University Press, 1970); and David Robinson, *The Unitarians and the Universalists* (Westport, Conn.: Greenwood Press, 1985).

4. Numerous works discuss antebellum social reform and its relation to liberal Christianity; an intriguing work is Robert H. Abzug, *Cosmos Crumbling: American Reform and the Religious Imagination* (New York: Oxford University Press, 1994). For another intriguing thesis on the relationships among religion, literature, and social reform (and authority) from the Puritans to the antebellum era, see Sacvan Bercovitch, *The American Jeremiad* (Madison: University of Wisconsin Press, 1978). Participants and observers at the time noted the link between liberal Protestantism, especially Unitarianism, and the emergence of American romanticism and what came to be called the "American renaissance." Two classic works on this subject from the early twentieth century are Vernon L. Parrington, *Main Currents in American Thought*, 3 vols. (New York: Harcourt, Brace and Co., 1927), and F. O. Matthiessen, *The American Renaissance: Art and Expression in the Age of Emerson and Whitman* (New York: Oxford University Press, 1941). Other important works on this subject include David S. Reynolds, *Beneath the American Renaissance: The Subversive Imagination in the Age of Emerson and Melville* (Cambridge, Mass.: Harvard University Press, 1989), and Lawrence Buell, *New England Literary Culture: From Revolution through Renaissance* (Cambridge: Cambridge University Press, 1986). See also Buell's essay "The Literary Significance of the Unitarian Movement," in *American Unitarianism, 1805–1865*, ed. Conrad E. Wright (Boston: Massachusetts Historical Society and New England University Press, 1989), pp. 163–179.

5. Despite Emerson's praise (if somewhat backhanded) for Channing as "our bishop," Emerson also wearied of what he called the "pale negations" of Unitarianism; see Matthiessen, *American Renaissance*, p. 12. For Emerson's style in relation to Channing's, see Buell, *New England Literary Culture*, pp. 143–144. For Emerson's assertion of the romantic self against what he saw as the conformity of the social reform movements, see his essays "Self Reliance" and "The Transcendentalist." For Emerson's notions about the divine, see his essays "Compensation" and "The Oversoul." Emerson's "Divinity School Address" expressed some earlier ideas about God's incarnation in Jesus (and all people). Much of Emerson's thought about God is summed up in this 1843 journal entry: "The thinker looks for God in the direction of the consciousness, the churchman out of it. If you ask the former for his definition of God, he would answer 'my possibility,' for his definition of man, 'my actuality'" (see Ralph Waldo Emerson, *Emerson in His Journals*, ed. Joel Porte [Cambridge, Mass.: Harvard University Press, 1982]). On Emerson's vision of God within the self, see: Jeffrey Steele, *The*

Representation of the Self in the American Renaissance (Chapel Hill: University of North Carolina Press, 1987), pp. 14–20.

6. For Channing's view of hell, see William Ellery Channing, "The Evil of Sin," in *The Works of William Ellery Channing* (Boston: American Unitarian Association, 1901), pp. 350–353. For Channing's romantic appreciation of Milton's Satan, see Channing, "Remarks on the Character and Writings of John Milton," in ibid., pp. 500–501.

7. Noah Worcester, *The Atoning Sacrifice: A Display of Love Not of Wrath* (Cambridge, Mass.: Hillard and Brown, 1829), pp. 97–100.

8. William Ellery Channing, "The Perfect Life," in *Works*, p. 972.

9. William Ellery Channing, "Love to Christ," in *Works*, pp. 319, 324–326. On Channing's criticism that the doctrine of the Trinity must necessarily make Christ impassive during the crucifixion, see Channing's "Unitarian Christianity," in ibid., p. 375.

10. William Ellery Channing, "Character of Christ," in *Works*, p. 306; William Ellery Channing, "The Great Purpose of Christianity," in ibid., p. 253.

11. Channing, "Character of Christ," p. 306.

12. Edwards A. Park, "Introductory Essay: The Dignity and Importance of the Preacher's Work," in *The Preacher and the Pastor: Sermons by Fenelon, Herbert, Baxter, and Campbell*, ed. Edwards A. Park (Andover, Mass.: Allen, Morrill, and Wardwell, 1845), p. 18.

13. Ibid., pp. 19, 44–45.

14. Park's remark about his childhood comes from Frank Hugh Foster, *The Life of Edwards Amasa Park* (New York: Fleming H. Revell, 1936), p. 31.

15. Good discussions of Park's work can be found in Robert Whittemore, *The Transformation of New England Theology*, American University Studies, Series 7, Theology and Religion, vol. 23 (New York: Peter Lang, 1973), pp. 291–330; Bruce Kuklick, *Churchmen and Philosophers: From Jonathan Edwards to John Dewey* (New Haven: Yale University Press, 1985), pp. 205–206, 209–213. Also of great use is Anthony C. Cecil, Jr., *The Theological Development of Edwards Amasa Park: Last of the Consistent Calvinists*, Dissertation Series, no. 1 (Missoula, Mont.: Scholar's Press, 1974). Park's historical and biographical sketches of American theologians are copious; in addition to writing long memoirs on Samuel Hopkins, Nathaniel Emmons, and Leonard Woods, Park wrote numerous entries for the *Schaff-Herzog Encyclopedia*, including those on New England theology, Hopkinsianism, Jonathan Edwards (Sr. and Jr.), Joseph Bellamy, Moses Stuart, and Samuel Worcester. For a complete bibliography of writings by and about Park, see Cecil, *Theological Development*, pp. 281–342. Foster's discussion of Park in *Genetic History* as well as in his "Professor Park's Theological System," *Bibliotheca Sacra* 60 (April 1903): 672–697, are also helpful, but it must be recognized that Foster was saluting his recently deceased teacher. For background on Foster, see Walter Horton's "Preface" to Foster's *Life of Edwards Amasa Park*, pp. 7–15.

16. Park, "All the Moral Attributes of God," p. 162.

17. Edwards A. Park, "The Sorrow of the Redeemer in Anticipation of His Death," in *Discourses on Some Theological Doctrines*, pp. 334, 354.

18. Ibid., p. 339.

19. Ibid., p. 349.

20. See Moses Stuart, *Two Discourses on the Atonement* (Andover, Mass.: Mark Newman, 1828), pp. 25–26; Owen, *Vindicae Evangelicae; Or, The Mystery of the Gospel Vindicated and Socinianism Examined*, in *The Works of John Owen*, ed. Thomas Russell (London: Richard Boynes, 1826), 9:118; François Turretin, *Turretin on the Atonement*, trans. James R. Wilson (New York: Board of Publication of the Reformed Protestant Dutch Church, 1859), p. 34.

21. John Dryden, *Absalom and Achitophel*, line 1005. The passage from *Advice to a Young Gentleman* is cited in John F. Kasson, *Rudeness and Civility: Manners in Nineteenth-Century Urban America* (New York: Hill and Wang, 1990), p. 150.

22. Edwards A. Park, "The Rise of the Edwardean Theory of the Atonement," in *The Atonement: Discourses and Treatises by Edwards, Smalley, Maxcy, Emmons, Griffin, Burge, and Weeks*, ed. Edwards A. Park (Boston: Congregational Board of Publication, 1859), pp. xxvii–xxxii.

23. Gardiner Spring, *The Attraction of the Cross* (New York: M. W. Dodd, 1846), p. 10.

24. "Old Orthodoxy, New Divinity, and Unitarianism," *Princeton Review* 29 (October 1857): 587.

25. On Charles Hodge's work, see Paul K. Conkin, *The Uneasy Center: Reformed Christianity in Antebellum America* (Chapel Hill: University of North Carolina Press, 1995), pp. 220–233; Kuklick, *Churchmen and Philosophers*, pp. 66–79; David F. Wells, "Charles Hodge," in *Reformed Theology in America: A History of Its Modern Development*, ed. David F. Wells (Grand Rapids, Mich.: William B. Eerdmans, 1985), pp. 36–59. See also the biography written by his son: Archibald Alexander Hodge, *The Life of Charles Hodge* (New York: Charles Scribner and Sons, 1880). Also of interest here is Charles Cashdollar, "The Pursuit of Piety: Charles Hodge's Diary, 1819–1820," *Journal of Presbyterian History* 55 (Fall 1977): 267–274. A good short summary of Charles Hodge's life and work can also be found in Mark Noll's Introduction to Charles Hodge, *The Way of Life* (1841; reprint, Mahway, N.Y.: Paulist Press, 1987), pp. 1–49. For both of the Hodges, see C. A. Salmond, *Charles and A. A. Hodge with Class and Table Talk of Hodge the Younger* (Edinburgh: Oliphant, Anderson, and Ferrier, 1888).

26. The remark is quoted by A. A. Hodge in *Life of Charles Hodge*, p. 521. Two historians who have seen Hodge's remark as a literal declaration of his theological agenda include Lefferts A. Loetcher, *The Broadening Church: A Study of Theological Issues in the Presbyterian Church since 1869* (Philadelphia: University of Pennsylvania Press, 1954), p. 25; and Perry Miller, *The Life of the Mind in America: From the Revolution to the Civil War* (New York: Harcourt, Brace and World, 1965), p. 17. One historian who has been most sensitive to the nature of Hodge's remark is Robert Whittemore, who wrote: "[Hodge's] most famous aphorism, quoted ad nauseum with glee by his Andover adversaries and by liberals who mistakenly thought it the epitome of fundamentalism, was that Princeton had never originated, nor ever would originate in his lifetime, any new idea. What he meant, of course, and professed lifelong, was the faith of our fathers, living still, in spite of [Jonathan] Edwards, [Samuel] Hopkins and [Edwards] Park" (*Transformation of New England Theology*, p. 300).

27. The story of the walking stick is told by A. A. Hodge in *Life of Charles Hodge*, pp. 519–521. For Charles Hodge's appreciation of Alexander, see Charles Hodge, "Memoir of Dr. Alexander," *Princeton Review* 27 (January 1885): 133–159. The influences of both Hodges lasted a long time at Princeton. Benjamin Breckinridge Warfield took Archibald Alexander Hodge's place. He, in turn, trained his successor, J. Gresham Machen, perhaps the only American conservative theologian whose work received some substantial notice in twentieth-century American cosmopolitan culture. In 1929, Princeton finally fell to liberalism, and Machen founded Westminster Seminary in nearby Philadelphia. But Princeton had held out for a long time, thanks in part to Hodge. At the centennial of the seminary in 1912, Francis Patton proudly claimed that the theology of the seminary "is exactly the same as it was a hundred years ago." Patton's statement is recorded in Ned B. Stonehouse, *J. Gresham Machen* (Grand Rapids, Mich.: William B. Eerdmans, 1954), p. 62. This is the only biography of Machen and contains helpful discussions of Princeton Seminary and the formation of Westminster. On Machen, see also George Marsden, *Understanding Fundamentalism and Evangelicalism* (Grand Rapids, Mich.: William B. Eerdmans, 1991), pp. 182–201. For another analysis of Machen and controversies in the Presbyterian church in the early twentieth century, see Bradley J. Longfeld, *The Presbyterian Controversy: Fundamentalists, Modernists, and Moderates* (New York: Oxford University Press, 1991). On continuity at Princeton

Seminary more generally, see Mark Noll, *Princeton Theology: 1812–1921* (Grand Rapids, Mich.: Baker Book House, 1983); and Andrew W. Hoffecker, *Piety and the Princeton Theologians: Archibald Alexander, Charles Hodge, and Benjamin B. Warfield* (Grand Rapids, Mich.: Baker Book House, 1981). On Princeton and Westminster, see Wells, *Reformed Theology*, pp. 15–134.

28. *Proceedings Connected with the Semi-Centennial Celebration of the Professorship of Charles Hodge in the Theological Seminary at Princeton, New Jersey, April 24, 1872* (New York: D. F. Randolph, 1872), pp. 81–82.

29. Hodge, "God in Christ" (1849), in *Essays and Reviews* (New York: Robert Carter and Bros., 1857), pp. 443, 471.

30. Charles Hodge, "Barnes on the Atonement," *Princeton Review* 31 (July 1859): 488.

31. The remark to his mother about old age comes from A. A. Hodge, *Life of Charles Hodge*, p. 56; the nursery remark comes from Charles Hodge's "Barnes on the Epistle to the Romans," *Princeton Review* 7 (April 1835): 289. For Hodge's claim that the governmental and moral theologies were simply revivals of Socinianism and Grotian theology, see Hodge's "Beman on the Atonement," in *Essays and Reviews*, pp. 140, 161–164.

32. Samuel Hopkins, "The Perfections of God," in *The Works of Samuel Hopkins* 3 vols. (1865; reprint, New York: Garland Publishing Co., 1987), 1:48. On Hopkins, see Joseph A. Conforti, *Samuel Hopkins and the New Divinity Movement: Calvinism, the Congregational Ministry, and Reform in New England between the Great Awakenings* (Grand Rapids, Mich.: William B. Eerdmans, 1981).

33. For the development of Calvin's and Turretin's ideas here, see David A. Weir, *The Origins of the Federal Theology in Sixteenth-Century Reformation Thought* (Oxford: Clarendon Press, 1990).

34. Calvin, Turretin, and American theologians through the nineteenth century from Albert Barnes to W. G. T. Shedd, S. J. Baird, and Horace Bushnell and Robert Lewis Dabney all relied on this passage as a basis to support their wide-ranging characterizations of God. But Hodge, more so than any other theologian of his day, worked this passage over continuously. Hodge's emphasis on reading Romans 5 as a strict parallel was somewhat unusual. Hodge acknowledged this when he wrote in a revised edition to his commentary on Romans that "every theology is a gradual growth," that some points emerge at different times in history in response to different theological debates. Still, he maintained that "this interpretation [of Romans] is old," going back, in its "essential features," to the Reformation as well as the "early Christian fathers." See Hodge, *Commentary on the Epistle to the Romans*, rev. ed. (Philadelphia: James S. Claxton, 1864), pp. 234, 276. Hodge used his interpretation to attack the writings of governmental theologians such as Moses Stuart and Albert Barnes. Reviews of these debates can be found in Wells, *Reformed Theology*, pp. 49–52; Stephen J. Stein, "Stuart and Hodge on Romans 5:12–21: An Exegetical Controversy on Original Sin," *Journal of Presbyterian History* 47 (Winter 1969): 340–508; and Thomas Obricht, "Charles Hodge as American New Testament Interpreter," *Journal of Presbyterian History* 57 (Summer 1979): 117–133. Some of Hodge's conservative colleagues considered his interpretation of Romans 5 to be extreme. See W. G. T. Shedd, *A Critical and Doctrinal Commentary upon the Epistle of St. Paul to the Romans* (New York: Charles Scribner's Sons, 1879), pp. 119–144; and Samuel J. Baird, *The First and Second Adam: The Elohim Revealed in the Creation and Redemption of Man* (Philadelphia: Lindsey and Blakistone, 1860), pp. 370–374, 612. For Hodge's response to Baird, see Hodge, "The First and Second Adam," *Princeton Review* 32 (April 1860): 344–346; for Dabney's criticism of Hodge's theory of imputation, see Robert Lewis Dabney, "Hodge's Systematic Theology," in *Discussions*, 4 vols. (1891; reprint, Carlisle, Penn.: Banner of Truth, 1982), 1:229–281.

35. See, for instance, Robert Lewis Dabney, "God's Indiscriminate Proposals of Mercy, as Related to His Power, Wisdom, and Sincerity," *Princeton Review* 50 (July 1878): 33–67; also in Dabney, *Discussions*, 2:282–313.

36. Charles Hodge, "Bushnell on Vicarious Sacrifice," *Princeton Review* 38 (April 1866): 189; Archibald Alexander Hodge, *The Atonement* (Philadelphia: Presbyterian Board of Publication, 1867), pp. 408–409.

37. Charles Hodge, *Commentary on the Epistle to the Romans*, p. 216.

38. Ibid., pp. 215–216.

39. A. A. Hodge, *Atonement*, p. 51. Hodge also emphasized the automatic nature of the relationship. The purpose was the same: to disengage the depiction of God from his acts of punishment. In these passages, anger might be attributed to God, but then quickly this anger became distanced from him, more like a free-floating trait than something distinctly expressive of God himself. "As God hates sin," A. A. Hodge wrote in *The Atonement*, "because of its intrinsic hatefulness, having in itself the reason for the hatred it excites, so he punishes it because of its intrinsic demerit, having the reason of its punishment in itself." As Hodge developed this idea, "hatred" for sin and "punishment" became increasingly separated from God. He was less and less the one feeling hatred and acting to punish. Rather, sin brought this upon itself, surrounding itself, as it were, in a cloud of disembodied condemnation. "Sin," Hodge finally declared, "can no more exist without punishableness than it can exist without hatefulness" (pp. 52–53).

40. Ibid, p. 168.

Chapter Four

1. The two major interpretations of sentimentalism in American religious life are Ann Douglas, *The Feminization of American Culture* (New York: Alfred A. Knopf, 1978); and Richard Rabinowitz, *The Spiritual Self in Everyday Life: The Tranformation of Personal Religious Experience in Nineteenth-Century New England* (Boston: Northeastern University Press, 1989). For a case study touching on the relationship between revivalism and sentimentalism, see Mary P. Ryan, *Cradle of the Middle Class: The Family in Oneida County, New York, 1790–1865* (Cambridge: Cambridge University Press, 1981). For interpretations of the changing emotional styles associated with sentimentalism, see Philip Greven, *The Protestant Temperament: Patterns of Child-Rearing, Religious Experience, and the Self in Early America* (New York: Alfred A. Knopf, 1977); Barbara Welter, "The Cult of True Womanhood, 1820–1860," *American Quarterly* 18 (Summer 1966): 151–174; and Jan Lewis, "Mother's Love: The Construction of an Emotion in Nineteenth-Century America," in *Social History and Issues in Human Consciousness: Some Interdisciplinary Connections*, ed. Andrew E. Barnes and Peter N. Stearns (New York: New York University Press, 1989), pp. 209–229. On the increasing religious significance of the home in America, see Colleen McDannell, *The Christian Home in Victorian America, 1840–1900* (Bloomington: Indiana University Press, 1986).

2. James I. T. Coolidge, *Jesus the Manifestation of the Father* (Boston: W. M. Crosby and H. P. Nichols, 1848), p. 12.

3. Ibid., p. 14.

4. Edwards A. Park, *The Theology of the Intellect and That of the Feelings* (Andover, Mass.: W. F. Draper, 1850), p. 34. Clarke's comment was on the difference in the audiences of the theological treatises of Edwards Park and Horace Bushnell, on one hand, and the novels of Susan Warner, on the other hand; see James Freeman Clarke, "Bushnell on Vicarious Sacrifice," *Christian Examiner* 79 (May 1866): 360–361.

5. John Owen, *A Dissertation on Divine Justice*, in *The Works of John Owen*, 12 vols., ed. Thomas Russell (London: Richard Baynes, 1826), 9:396; Joseph P. Thompson, *Love and Penalty; Or, Eternal Punishment Consistent with the Fatherhood of God* (New York: Sheldon and Co., 1860), pp. 8–10. Conservative penal theologians, of course, also joined the bashing of sentimental incarnationalists. Taylor Lewis, for instance, denounced the "feeble and effeminate sentimentalists" of his day ("The Sufferings of Christ," *Biblical Repository and Classical Review* 63 [July 1846]: p. 384).

6. Noah Porter, "Review of Dr. Bushnell on 'The Vicarious Sacrifice,'" *New Englander* 25 (April 1866): 232. Conservatives also relied on this polemical distinction between "effeminate" and "manly" literature. See "Dr. Spring and the Power of the Pulpit," *Princeton Review* 20 (July 1848): 467–468, 483.

7. Clarke, "Bushnell on Vicarious Sacrifice," 361. For Hawthorne's remark, see Jane Tompkins, *Sensational Designs: The Cultural Work of American Fiction, 1790–1860* (New York: Oxford University Press, 1985), p. 217, n. 5, p. 220, n. 1. The difficulty Stowe experienced as a woman in establishing herself as a writer is an important theme of Joan D. Hedrick's *Harriet Beecher Stowe: A Life* (New York: Oxford University Press, 1994).

8. See, for instance, Henry Ward Beecher, "The Fatherhood of God," in *Sermons*, 2 vols. (New York: Harper and Brothers, 1869), 1:416.

9. Ibid., p. 418.

10. Park, "All the Moral Attributes of God Are Comprehended in His Love," in *Discourses on Some Theological Doctrines as Related to the Religious Character* (Andover, Mass.: W. F. Draper, 1885), p. 166; Park, "The Sorrow of the Redeemer," in ibid., p. 348. Much of Park's view here relied on the vast scenarios that neoclassical theism encompassed. "Through all time and eternity, do the influences of [God's] government penetrate," Park maintained; "His laws affect all spirits that have been, or are to be" ("All the Moral Attributes of God," pp. 166–167).

11. Mention of this meeting between Stowe and Park is in Hedrick, *Harriet Beecher Stowe*, pp. 284, 451. Park's work in question was "Memoir of the Life and Character of Samuel Hopkins," in *The Works of Samuel Hopkins, D.D.*, 3 vols. (Boston: Doctrinal Book and Tract Society, 1852), 1:v–vii, 1–264. Stowe's brother, Edward Beecher, wrote a review of this publication of Hopkins's *Works* in 1853; see Edward Beecher, "The Works of Samuel Hopkins," *Bibliotheca Sacra* 10 (January 1853): 63–82.

12. Harriet Beecher Stowe, *The Minister's Wooing* (1859), in *The Writings of Harriet Beecher Stowe*, 16 vols. (Boston: Houghton Mifflin, 1896), 5:247. See also Hedrick, *Harriet Beecher Stowe*, pp. 276–285. For Stowe's depiction of Hopkins in the novel, see also Lawrence Buell, "Calvinism Romanticized: Harriet Beecher Stowe, Samuel Hopkins, and *The Minister's Wooing*," in *Critical Essays on Harriet Beecher Stowe*, ed. Elizabeth Ammons (Boston: G. K. Hall, 1980), pp. 259–275.

13. Stowe's reveries about getting all of her brothers together to form a seminary are recorded in Hedrick, *Harriet Beecher Stowe*, p. 370. Also on Stowe, see Charles H. Foster, *The Rungless Ladder: Harriet Beecher Stowe and New England Puritanism* (Durham, N.C.: Duke University Press, 1954). On the Beecher family in general, see Milton Rugoff, *The Beechers: An American Family in the Nineteenth Century* (New York: Harper and Row, 1981); and Marie Caskey, *Chariot of Fire: Religion and the Beecher Family* (New Haven: Yale University Press, 1978).

14. The remark about the millionaires at Beecher's church is noted in William Leach, *True Love and Perfect Union: The Feminist Reform of Sex and Society* (New York: Basic Books, 1980), p. 102. Also on Henry Ward Beecher see William G. McLoughlin, *The Meaning of Henry Ward Beecher: An Essay on the Shifting Values of Mid-Victorian America, 1840–1870* (New York: Alfred A. Knopf, 1970). On Catharine and Edward Beecher, see Kathryn Kish

Sklar, *Catharine Beecher: A Study in American Domesticity* (New York: W. W. Norton, 1976); Robert Merideth, *The Politics of the Universe: Edward Beecher, Abolition, and Orthodoxy* (Nashville, Tenn: Vanderbilt University Press, 1968).

15. Isabella Beecher Hooker's likening of her interest in women's rights to Stowe's interest in antislavery is recorded in Hedrick, *Harriet Beecher Stowe*, p. 353.

16. Woodhull's exclamation and Stowe's rebuke of her are recorded in ibid., pp. 374–375, 377; for an account of the whole episode, see ibid., pp. 353–379. On the Tilton-Beecher episode, see also Leach, *True Love*, pp. 102–105; and Altina L. Waller, *Reverend Beecher and Mrs. Tilton: Sex and Class in Victorian America* (Amherst, Mass.: University of Massachusetts Press, 1982). On the Beechers and women's rights, see Jeanne Boydston, Mary Kelly, and Ann Margolis, *The Limits of Sisterhood: The Beecher Sisters on Women's Rights and Woman's Sphere* (Chapel Hill: University of North Carolina Press, 1988). On tensions in the suffrage movement during this time, see Ellen Carol Dubois, *Feminism and Suffrage: The Emergence of an Independent Women's Movement in America, 1848–1869* (Ithaca: Cornell University Press, 1978).

17. For Stowe's attitude toward her writing, see Hedrick, *Harriet Beecher Stowe*, pp. 331–332; and Harriet Beecher Stowe, "Introductory Note" to *Religious Studies: Sketches and Poems*, in *The Writings of Harriet of Beecher Stowe*, 16 vols. (Boston: Houghton Mifflin Co., 1896), 16:ix.

18. On the literary views of Lyman Beecher and the reading of the Beecher children, see Hedrick, *Harriet Beecher Stowe*, pp. 19–21. On Stowe's treatment of Lady Byron, see ibid., pp. 353–374. For a collection of primary documents and critical essays on Stowe as a writer, see Ammons, *Critical Essays on Harriet Beecher Stowe*.

19. Luke 2:48–49; John 2:4; Mark 3:32–35.

20. There was some critical edge to the sentimental lives as they were used against neoclassical theism. Not having to depict God the Father (as the theists did) presiding over Jesus, the sentimentalists could extoll the simplicity of their approach and thereby their supposed fidelity to the Gospels themselves. For background on this genre, see Daniel J. Pals, *The Victorian "Lives" of Jesus*. For the reaction to Strauss's *Life of Jesus* by Unitarians, see Jerry Wayne Brown, *The Rise of Biblical Criticism in America: The New England Scholars* (Middletown, Conn.: Wesleyan University Press, 1969), pp. 140–152.

21. Henry Ward Beecher, *The Life of Jesus, the Christ* (New York: J. B. Ford, 1871), pp. iv–v, 28, 36.

22. Ibid., pp. 18–20, 22–23.

23. Ibid., pp. 20, 33. Beecher's method of dealing with miracles here was not uncommon in liberal theology; see Lawrence Buell, "The Literary Significance of the Unitarian Movement," in *American Unitarianism: 1805–1865*, ed. Conrad Wright (Boston: Massachusetts Historical Society and Northeastern University Press, 1989), pp. 174–176.

24. Beecher, *Life of Jesus*, pp. 19, 188–191, 395.

25. Ibid., pp. 394–395, n. 1.

26. Cited in Henry Ward Beecher, *The Life of Jesus, the Christ: Later Scenes* (New York: Bromfield, 1891), p. v. When speaking of the "atonement," Beecher preferred to use the word "Christ," by which he meant not just the "historic name" but God's loving, restoring activity among human beings; see the section entitled "The Atonement" in Beecher's "Theological Statement," printed in the appendix to Lyman Abbott, *Henry Ward Beecher* (1903; reprint, New York: Chelsea House, 1980), pp. 442–445. Marie Casky suggested that Beecher's views of the atonement followed along the lines set out by James Barr Walker in his *Philosophy of the Plan of Salvation*, which was also endorsed by Calvin Stowe, who, Casky suggested, influenced Beecher in this thinking about the atonement. Beecher certainly claimed at times that Stowe agreed with him. In his work, Walker emphasized some common ideas of the moral

theology and sentimental incarnationalism, which Beecher may indeed have learned from him. Walker also depicted God as working gradually to educate the ancient Hebrews and lead them away from idolatry to a spiritual conception of God; the atonement, Walker maintained, fit into this overall pattern of education. As we saw in chapter 2, Beecher held a similar view of God. Yet, as we also saw there, this was not an uncommon view at the time. See Casky, *Chariot of Fire*, pp. 231, 239; and James Barr Walker, *Philosophy of the Plan of Salvation*, with an introductory essay by Calvin E. Stowe (Boston: Gould, Kendall, and Lincoln, 1848).

27. The only substantial study I know of that concentrates on these works is Eileen Razzari Elrod, "'Exactly Like My Father': Feminist Hermeneutics in Harriet Beecher Stowe's Non-Fiction," *Journal of the American Academy of Religion* 63 (Winter 1995): 695–719. Elrod's article tends to focus on Stowe's complex relation with her father's religious views and authority.

28. Calvin Stowe, "The Right Interpretation of the Sacred Scriptures: The Helps and the Hindrances," *Bibliotheca Sacra* 10 (January 1853): 50, 60.

29. Henry Ward Beecher, *Yale Lectures on Preaching* (New York: J. B. Ford and Co., 1874), p. 18; Calvin Stowe, "Right Interpretation of the Sacred Scriptures," p. 60. On the possible influence of Calvin Stowe's biblical criticism on Beecher and Harriet Beecher Stowe, see Casky, *Chariot of Fire*, pp. 181–183, 229–231.

30. Harriet Beecher Stowe, introduction to *Bible Heroines: Being Narrative Biographies of Prominent Hebrew Women, Giving Views of Woman in Sacred History* (New York: Fords, Howard, and Hulbert, 1878), pp. 3–4. On biblical heroines at the time, see Mary De Jong, "Dark-Eyed Daughters: Nineteenth-Century Popular Portrayals of Biblical Women," *Women's Studies: An Interdisciplinary Journal* 19, nos. 2–4 (1991): 283–308.

31. Harriet Beecher Stowe, "Mary, the Mother of Jesus," in *Bible Heroines*, p. 3. This being said, Stowe also seemed to affirm the separate-spheres ideology in her characterization of Mary: "Mary never seems to have sought to present herself as a public teacher. . . . Mary is presented to us as the mother, and the mother alone, seeking no other sphere" (ibid., p. 18).

32. Ibid., p. 4.

33. Ibid, pp. 9–10.

34. Ibid, p. 12.

35. Ibid., p. 13.

36. Ibid.

37. Ibid., p. 9.

38. Ibid., p. 15.

39. Ibid., p. 17.

40. Ibid.

41. See Foster, *Rungless Ladder*, pp. 134–144, 232.

42. Stowe, "Mary, the Mother of Jesus," p. 17.

43. Harriet Beecher Stowe, *The Footsteps of the Master*, in *Writings*, 15:39.

44. Ibid., p. 36.

45. Ibid. Elrod, while mostly focusing on the historical context in which Stowe wrote, did see in these passages suggestions of a "matriarchal Christianity, one that anticipates the concerns of twentieth-century Christian feminists" ("'Exactly Like My Father,'" pp. 696, 715–716). While recognizing some general similarities between Stowe's work and twentieth-century feminist theology, I am less convinced that Stowe is well understood in this way. Beyond the general similarity in emphasizing strong female figures, there are differences in the emotional complexity ascribed to these characters. As I note in chapter 10, Stowe's characterizations of Mary and Jesus are more emotionally complex than many depictions of God in twentieth-century feminist theology. I am also leery of the tendency in liberal theology to celebrate earlier writers as precursors of contemporary theology, as, for instance, liberal

modernists did with Bushnell through the twentieth century (on this issue, see chapters 7 and 8). This is not to say that theologians may not learn or take inspiration from past writers—and Stowe's work may provide a helpful example of how complex characterizations of Mary and Jesus may be generated out of the biblical material and framed in a doctrinal tradition. But this being said, Stowe still must be understood in terms of her own time. It is important to recognize here that characterizing Christ in maternal or feminine terms was not unusual in nineteenth-century liberal, cosmopolitan incarnationalism. The emotional complexity that Stowe ascribed to Mary and Jesus was far more unusual than the fact that Stowe celebrated Mary as a strong figure or ascribed feminine traits to Jesus. Catharine Sedgwick, Oliver Wendell Holmes and Theodore Parker, among others, characterized Christ in female terms. See Caskey, *Chariot of Fire*, p. 362. For Parker especially, see Richard A. Grusin, *Transcendentalist Hermeneutics: Institutions, Authority, and the Higher Criticism of the Bible* (Durham, N.C.: Duke University Press, 1991), pp. 115–140. In *Uncle Tom's Cabin*, as many critics have noted, female characters assume Christlike roles, and feminine characteristics are ascribed to Tom; see Tompkins, *Sensational Designs*, pp. 122–146; Jane Silverman Van Buren, *The Modernist Madonna: Semiotics of the Maternal Metaphor* (Bloomington: Indiana University Press, 1989), pp. 64–95; Elizabeth Ammons, "Stowe's Dream of the Mother-Savior: *Uncle Tom's Cabin* and American Women Writers before the 1920s," in *New Essays on "Uncle Tom's Cabin,"* ed. Eric J. Sundquist (Cambridge: Cambridge University Press, 1986), pp. 155–195. On nineteenth-century middle-class visions of motherhood and its religious aspects more generally, see Jan Lewis, "Mother's Love," pp. 209–229.

46. Beecher, *Yale Lectures on Preaching* (1874), p. 186; Stowe, *Footsteps of the Master*, p. 3.

47. Stowe, *Footsteps of the Master*, p. 1.

48. Ibid.

49. Ibid., p. 10.

50. Ibid., pp. 17–18. For the argument that Jesus was citing Psalm 22 on the cross to demonstrate his knowledge of scripture and show how one should conduct oneself while suffering, see David Newton Sheldon, *Sin and Redemption: A Series of Sermons to Which Is added an Oration on Freedom* (New York: Sheldon, Lamport, and Blakeman, 1856), pp. 205–206.

51. Stowe, "Preface," in *Writings*, 15: x; Shakespeare, *Macbeth*, act 5, scene 5, lines 17–27. Stowe also used this image of following in the "footsteps" of Jesus in her polemic against neoclassical theism; in *The Minister's Wooing*, she wrote: "Where theorists and philosophers tread with sublime assurance, woman often follows with bleeding footsteps; women are always turning from the abstract to the individual, and feeling where the philosopher only thinks" (p. 19).

Chapter Five

1. [W. G. T. Shedd], "The True Tone in Preaching and the True Temper in Hearing," *Princeton Review* 35 (July 1863): 421. Shedd later republished this as a chapter entitled "Reciprocal Relations of Preachers and Hearers" in his *Homiletics and Pastoral Theology* (New York: Charles Scribner and Co., 1867), pp. 258–295. Citations come from the original essay.

2. If Hodge could blend the "feelings" and the "intellect" together into a mild mixture, he could also blend anthropomorphism and theism together. In his *Systematic Theology* (1874) Hodge remarked that anthropomorphism was "a word much abused, and often used in the bad sense to express the idea that God is altogether such a one as ourselves, a being of like limitations and passions." Hodge suggested that this was a caricature of anthropomorphism (as indeed it was). But what Hodge claimed was that a proper understanding of anthropomor-

phism for all practical purposes conflated it with theism. Thus, as Hodge laid the matter out, there were only three ways of characterizing God: as a person, as everything, or as nothing. This approach helped him to defend the penal theology against liberalism because he could suggest that liberal doctrines logically led to pantheism or atheism (*Systematic Theology*, 3 vols. [New York: Scribner, Armstrong, and Co., 1874], 1:339).

3. For an account of this split, see George A. Marsden, *The Evangelical Mind and the New School Presbyterian Experience: A Case Study of Thought and Theology in Nineteenth-Century America* (New Haven: Yale University Press, 1970).

4. James Freeman Clarke, "Bushnell on the Vicarious Sacrifice," *Christian Examiner* 80 (May 1866): 371. Leading formulators of the notion of an "American renaissance" shared Clarke's assumption that conservative theological writing was inherently dry and logical; see Octavius Brooks Frothingham, *Transcendentalism in New England* (1876; reprint, Philadelphia: University of Pennsylvania Press, 1959), pp. 186–217; Paul Elmer Moore, *Shelbourne Essays on American Literature*, ed. Daniel Aaron (New York: Harcourt, Brace, and World, 1963), pp. 180–181; Vernon L. Parrington, *Main Currents in American Thought*, 3 vols. (1927; reprint, New York: Harcourt, Brace, and Co., 1954), 1:151–165, 2:313–324, 371–377; Van Wyck Brooks, *The Flowering of New England, 1815–1865* (New York: Modern Library, 1941), pp. 107–110; and F. O. Matthiessen, *American Renaissance: Art and Expression in the Age of Emerson and Whitman* (New York: Oxford University Press, 1968), pp. 13–15, 25, 56, 98.

5. Critics have recognized that Calvinism had a lingering influence on writers of the "American renaissance," especially Hawthorne, Melville, and Dickinson, and that writers drew on Calvinism to critique some of the optimism of liberal theology; see, for instance, William H. Shurr, *Rappaccini's Children: American Writers in a Calvinist Mode* (Lexington: University of Kentucky Press, 1981). Also helpful here is Gene Bluestein, "The Brotherhood of Sinners: Literary Calvinism," *New England Quarterly* 50 (June 1977): 195–213. Sacvan Bercovitch has traced the lingering influence of Puritan notions of the individual and community among the writers of the "American renaissance"; see Sacvan Bercovitch, *The Puritan Origins of the American Self* (New Haven: Yale University Press, 1975), and *The American Jeremiad* (Madison: University of Wisconsin Press, 1978). But this being said, the assumption still remains strong that liberal, not conservative, theology made it possible for writers to explore romanticism and that even the critique of liberal theology was necessarily an in-house critique, similar to the neo-orthodox critique of the social gospel in the mid-twentieth century. But now it is being recognized that Calvinism itself could, in some circumstances, provide a foundation for embracing romanticism. Lawrence Buell has written that "modern literary scholarship has concentrated overwhelmingly on the hegemonic literary culture of eastern Massachusetts liberalism" (e.g., Unitarians and Transcendentalists). But, he continued, there is the "possibility that we shall want one day to envisage an equally complex and even more extensive network of late Calvinist literary culture." See Lawrence Buell, *New England Literary Culture: From Revolution through Renaissance* (Cambridge: Cambridge University Press, 1989), p. 50. Studies that Buell recommended here were Ann Douglas, *The Feminization of American Culture* (New York: Alfred A. Knopf, 1978); and Richard Rabinowitz, *The Spiritual Self in Everyday Life: The Transformtion of Personal Religious Experience in Nineteenth-Century New England* (Boston: Northeastern University Press, 1989). Another critic who has explored religious literature in ways that break some of the molds of the "American renaissance" tradition is David Reynolds. He has written that while the "scholarly consensus" has tended to depict conservatives as opposed to fiction, this does not do justice to the "complexity" of the case. See David Reynolds, *Faith in Fiction: The Emergence of Religious Literature in America* (Cambridge, Mass.: Harvard University Press, 1981), p. 73. His subsequent study of major literary writers in the "American renaissance" uncovered links be-

tween these writers and popular evangelical styles. See David Reynolds, *Beneath the American Renaissance: The Subversive Imagination in the Age of Emerson and Melville* (Cambridge, Mass.: Harvard University Press, 1989). On revived interest in the notion of an "American renaissance," see Michael J. Colacurcio, "The American Renaissance Renaissance," *New England Quarterly* 64 (September 1991): 445–493.

6. Joseph Haroutunian, *Piety versus Moralism: The Passing of the New England Theology* (New York: Henry Holt and Co., 1932); Douglas, *Feminization of American Culture*, pp. 6–7, 121–130; T. J. Jackson Lears, *No Place of Grace: Antimodernism and the Transformation of American Culture, 1880 to 1920* (New York: Pantheon Books, 1981), pp. 42–45; James Turner, *Without God, without Creed: The Origins of Unbelief in America* (Baltimore: Johns Hopkins University Press, 1985), pp. 266–267. Another form of this contrast has been played out in characterizations of theologians and popular revivalists. One side of this debate has it that revivalism stripped American theology of its rigor. Major historians in this tradition include Perry Miller, *The Life of the Mind in America from the Revolution to the Civil War* (New York: Harcourt, Brace, and World, 1965), bks. 1–3; Richard Hofstadter, *Anti-Intellectualism in American Life* (New York: Random House, 1963); and Daniel Calhoun, *The Intelligence of a People* (Princeton: Princeton University Press, 1973). When historians began studying popular religion more sympathetically during the 1970s, the point of this characterization was turned around, and revivalism was portrayed as giving new life to a moribund and boring religious establishment; see Rhys Isaac, *The Transformation of Virginia, 1740–1790* (Chapel Hill: University of North Carolina Press, 1985); and Nathan O. Hatch, *The Democratization of American Christianity* (New Haven: Yale University Press, 1989). The relationship between the work of theologians and popular revivalists needs more study. An important model for such a study may be found in the work of Harry Stout, who has examined how preaching styles developed in seventeenth- and eighteenth-century New England. See Harry S. Stout, *The New England Soul: Preaching and Religious Culture in Colonial New England* (New York: Oxford University Press, 1986).

7. Unfortunately, Shedd has received little historical examination. For a consideration of the influence of Marsh on Shedd's historical vision of Christianity, see Cushing Strout, "Faith and History: The Mind of William G. T. Shedd," *Journal of the History of Ideas* 15 (January 1954): 153–162. For a comparison of the preaching styles of Henry Ward Beecher and Shedd, see Calhoun, *Intelligence of a People*, pp. 274–286. For Shedd's comments on the relationship between theological writing and literature, see his *Homiletics and Pastoral Theology*, pp. 1–37, 245–287, and *Discourses and Essays* (Andover, Mass.: W. F. Draper, 1859), pp. 7–52, 53–87. Also of interest on this point is Shedd's essay "Symbols and Congregationalism," in Theological Essays (New York: Armstrong and Co., 1877), pp. 321–353.

8. W. G. T. Shedd, "The Method and Influence of Theological Studies" (1845), in *Discourses and Essays*, p. 43.

9. John Calvin, *Institutes of the Christian Religion*, 2 vols., ed. John T. McNeil, trans. Ford Lewis Battles (Philadelphia: Westminster Press, 1960), bk. II, chap. xvi, sec. 2.

10. Alexander Pope, "Preface to the *Iliad*," in Alexander Pope, *The Iliad of Homer*, ed. Maynard Mack (New Haven: Yale University Press, 1967), 1:5, 12.

11. John Dryden, *Absalom and Achitophel*, lines 327–328, 381–382, 1000–1006.

12. Susan Warner, *The Wide, Wide World* (1892; reprint, New York: Feminist Press at the City University of New York, 1987), p. 178; Catharine Sedgwick, *Home* (Boston: James Munroe and Co., 1841), pp. 25–26. As another example of the struggle to control anger in the sentimental novel, Marmee tells Jo in *Little Women*: "I am angry nearly every day of my life, Jo; but I have learned not to show it; and I still hope to learn not to feel it, though it may take me another forty years to do so" (Louisa May Alcott, *Little Women* [New York: A. L. Burt, 1911], p. 68). On the "hortatory and instructional" aspect of the sentimental novel and

"the ethic of submission" in Warner's novel, see Jane Tompkins, *Sensational Designs: The Cultural Work of American Fiction, 1790–1860* (New York: Oxford University Press, 1985), pp. 159–161. See also Tompkins's afterword to Warner, *Wide, Wide World*, pp. 596–601. This being said, however, Tompkins also saw women writers as appropriating sentimental norms for their own purposes. Tompkins also ascribed more social power to the sentimental novel than have other critics such as Douglas in *Feminization of American Culture*.

13. Tompkins, *Sensational Designs*, p. 161. On the idea of a prurient side to humanitarianism and sentimentalism, see Karen Halttunen, "Humanitarianism and the Pornography of Pain in Anglo-American Culture," *American Historical Review* 100 (April 1995): 303–334; and Richard H. Brodhead, "Sparing the Rod: Discipline and Fiction in Ante-Bellum America," *Representations* 24 (Winter 1988): 67–96. For a consideration of the subversive aspects of the sentimental novel, see also Jane Silverman Van Buren, *The Modernist Madonna: Semiotics of the Maternal Metaphor* (Bloomington: Indiana University Press, 1989), pp. 64–123. Rebellion against sentimental norms, however, need not lead into an embrace of romanticism. Elaine Showalter suggested that Louisa May Alcott may have been rejecting the romantic model of the tormented individual writer for a larger sense of community; see Elaine Showalter, introduction to Louisa May Alcott, *Little Women* (New York: Penguin Books, 1989), pp. xxiii–xxiv.

14. "Is Effective Writing Necessarily 'Volcanic'?," *Presbyterian Quarterly Review* 3 (June 1855): 135–137, 147–148.

15. Ibid., pp. 135–137.

16. See Murray Roston, *Poet and Prophet: The Bible and the Growth of Romanticism* (Evanston: Northwestern University Press, 1965); and E. S. Schaffer, *"Kubla Khan" and the Fall of Jerusalem: The Mythological School in Biblical Criticism and Secular Literature, 1770–1880* (Cambridge: Cambridge University Press, 1977).

17. "The Hebrew Language and Literature," *Presbyterian Quarterly Review* 9 (January 1861): 469.

18. Ibid., pp. 468–469.

19. Ibid., p. 458.

20. Taylor Lewis, "The Spirit of the Old Testament," *Biblical Repository and Classical Review* 77 (January 1850): 23.

21. Ibid., p. 39.

22. Calvin, *Institutes*, bk. X, chap. xiii, sec. 1; Joseph P. Thompson, *Love and Penalty: Or, Eternal Punishment Consistent with the Fatherhood of God* (New York: Sheldon and Co., 1860), p. 28.

23. Shedd, "True Tone in Preaching," pp. 420–425, 439.

24. Ibid., p. 435; George Rapall Noyes, "The Scripture Doctrine of Sacrifice," *Christian Examiner* 59 (September 1855): 243. For a discussion of Noyes's career as a biblical critic, see Jerry Wayne Brown, *The Rise of Biblical Criticism in America: The New England Scholars* (Middletown, Conn.: Wesleyan University Press, 1969), pp. 125–139.

25. Shedd, "True Tone in Preaching," p. 425.

26. Ibid., pp. 424–425; see also David Hume, "Of Tragedy," in *Essays: Moral, Political, and Literary*, ed. Eugene F. Miller (Indianapolis: Liberty Classics, 1987), pp. 216–226.

27. Shedd, "True Tone in Preaching," p. 424; Shedd, "The Atonement: A Satisfaction for the Ethical Nature of Both God and Man," in *Theological Essays*, p. 275. This essay was originally published in the journal *Bibliotheca Sacra* in 1859. Citations come from the edition in *Theological Essays*.

28. On the erotics of guilt and punishment in romanticism, see Mario Praz, *The Romantic Agony*, trans. Angus Davidson (London: Oxford University Press, 1933). More generally, see also Halttunen, "Humanitarianism and the Pornography of Pain."

29. Shedd, "Atonement," p. 298.

30. W. G. T. Shedd, "The Use of Fear in Religion," in *Sermons to the Natural Man* (New York: Charles Scribner's Sons, 1892), p. 329.

31. Shedd, "Atonement," p. 275, 294.

32. John Keats, "On First Looking into Chapman's Homer," line 14. Shedd cited this poem to describe the "stimulation" man could get from "nature" and from "revelation" (*Homiletics and Pastoral Theology*, p. 10).

33. Shedd, "Atonement," pp. 280–281.

34. Ibid., p. 273.

35. W. G. T. Shedd, *Dogmatic Theology*, 2 vols. (New York: Charles Scribner's Sons, 1888), 2:425–427.

36. Ibid., p. 428.

37. Ibid., p. 393.

Chapter Six

1. Samuel Taylor Coleridge, "Christabel," lines, 412–413.

2. For reevaluations of middle-class styles of affection in the nineteenth-century that question the stereotype of "Victorian" prudery, see Patricia Anderson, *When Passion Reigned: Sex and the Victorians* (New York: Basic Books, 1995); Karen Lystra, *Searching the Heart: Women, Men, and Romantic Love in Nineteenth-Century America* (New York: Oxford University Press, 1989); and Peter Gay, *The Bourgeois Experience: Victoria to Freud*, esp. vol. 1, *Education of the Senses* (New York: Oxford University Press, 1984), and vol. 2, *The Tender Passion* (New York: Oxford University Press, 1986). For a reflection on this historical reassessment of Victorian sexuality, see Richard Jenkyns, "Victoria's Secret," *New York Review of Books*, 42, no. 19 (November 30, 1995): 19–21. On phrenological theories of sex in mid-nineteenth-century America, see David S. Reynolds, *Walt Whitman's America: A Cultural Biography* (New York: Alfred A. Knopf, 1995), pp. 194–234. Leading manuals of the time include Eugene Becklard, *The Physiologist*, trans. Sherman Wharton (Boston: Bella Marsh, 1859); R. T. Trall, *Sexual Physiology* (New York: Miller and Wood, 1867); John Cowan, *The Science of a New Life* (New York: Fowler and Wells, 1869); George Naphys, *The Transmission of Life* (Philadelphia: J. G. Fergus and Co., 1873); and Edward B. Foote, *Plain Home Talk* (New York: Murray Hill Publishing Co., 1886). The appeal of such manuals on personal hygiene, marriage, and child rearing dovetailed with an interest among middle-class Americans to limit family size for spiritual, economic, and social reasons. See Donald H. Parkerson and Jo Ann Parkerson, "Fewer Children of Greater Spiritual Quality: Religion and the Decline of Fertility in Nineteenth-Century America," *Social Science History* 12 (Spring 1988): 49–70. For use of phrenological and eugenic theories about propagation by mid- and late nineteenth-century feminists, see William Leach, *True Love and Perfect Union: The Feminist Reform of Sex and Society* (New York: Basic Books, 1980). For an example of these views in nineteenth- and early twentieth-century thought, see Charlotte Perkins Gilman, *Herland* (1915; reprint, New York: Pantheon Books, 1979), esp. chaps. 5, 6, and 11. For more general surveys of the structure of emotional relationships in the nineteenth-century American middle-class family, see John D'Emillio and Estelle B. Freedman, *Intimate Matters: A History of Sexuality in America* (New York: Harper and Row, 1970), pp. 55–170; and Stephanie Coontz, *The Social Origins of Private Life: A History of American Families, 1600–1900* (New York: Verso Press, 1988), pp. 210–280.

3. Henry Clarke Wright, *Marriage and Parentage* (1855; reprint, New York: Arno Press, 1974). See also Lewis Perry, *Childhood, Marriage, and Reform: Henry Clarke Wright,*

1797–1860 (Chicago: University of Chicago Press, 1980). The relation between American perceptions of sexual and spiritual transport is considered in Peter Gardella, *Innocent Ecstasy: How Christianity Gave America an Ethic of Sexual Pleasure* (New York: Oxford University Press, 1985).

4. John Calvin, *Institutes of the Christian Religion*, 2 vols., ed. John T. McNeil, trans. Ford Lewis Battles (Philadelphia: Westminster Press, 1960), bk. II, chap. xvi, sec. 10.

5. For Calvin on this point, see ibid.; John Owen, *Vindicae Evangelicae: Or the Mystery of the Gospel Vindicated and Socinianism Examined*, in *The Works of John Owen*, 12 vols., ed. Thomas Russell (London: Richard Baynes, 1826), 9:113.

6. John Owen, *The Death of Death in the Death of Christ*, in *Works*, 5:391; John Howe, *Discourse concerning the Redeemer's Dominion over the Invisible World, and the Entrance Thereinto by Death*, in *Works of John Howe*, 2 vols. (New York: Robert Carter and Bros., 1869), 1:318. For Shedd's remark on Howe, see W. G. T. Shedd, "The Method and Influence of Theological Studies," in *Discourses and Essays* (Andover, Mass.: W. F. Draper, 1859), p. 22.

7. The declining theological significance of Satan may be traced through the liberal theological and humanitarian reaction against the doctrine of hell. See Geoffrey Rowell, *Hell and the Victorians: A Study of the Nineteenth-Century Theological Controversies concerning Eternal Punishment and the Future Life* (New York: Oxford University Press, 1974); Daniel Pinckering Walker, *The Decline of Hell: Seventeenth-Century Discussions of Eternal Torments* (London: Routledge, Kegan and Paul, 1964); and Philip C. Almond, *Heaven and Hell in Enlightenment England* (Cambridge: Cambridge University Press, 1994). Enlightenment notions of the natural order also contributed to the declining interest in magic and, hence, in the devil; see Keith Thomas, *Religion and the Decline of Magic* (New York: Charles Scribner's Sons, 1971). On the larger cultural significance of Satan and his modern decline, see Jeffrey Burton Russell, *Mephistopheles: The Devil in the Modern World* (Ithaca: Cornell University Press, 1986); and Andrew Delbanco, *The Death of Satan: How Americans Have Lost the Sense of Evil* (New York: Farrar, Straus, and Giroux, 1995). For a consideration of the disappearance of the devil from a literary point of view, see Paul Fry, "The Possession of the Sublime," *Studies in Romanticism* 26 (Summer 1987): 191–192.

8. It is for this reason that George Boardman preferred Bushnell's depiction of the serpent to Milton's depiction of Satan ("The Genesis of Sin," *Princeton Review* 56 [July 1880]: 51).

9. John Milton, *Paradise Lost*, bk. 2, lines 724–814.

10. On the romantic appreciation of Milton's figure for death, see Steven Knapp, *Personification and the Sublime: Milton to Coleridge* (Cambridge, Mass.: Harvard University Press, 1985), chap. 1; and Thomas Weiskel, *The Romantic Sublime: Studies in the Structure and Psychology of Transcendence* (Baltimore: Johns Hopkins University Press), chap. 4. For Park's use of the "king of terrors," see his "The Sorrow of the Redeemer in Anticipation of His Death," in *Discourses on Some Theological Doctrines as Related to the Religious Character* (Andover, Mass.: W. F. Draper, 1885), pp. 329–330. For literary and religious notions of the sublime more generally at the time, see Samuel H. Monk, *The Sublime: A Study of Critical Theories in Eighteenth-Century England* (1953; reprint, Ann Arbor: University of Michigan Press, 1960); David B. Morris, *The Religious Sublime: Christian Poetry and the Critical Tradition in Eighteenth-Century England* (Lexington: University of Kentucky Press, 1972); Ernst Tuveson, "Space, Deity, and the 'Natural Sublime,'" *Modern Language Quarterly* 12 (1951): 20–38; and Marjorie Nicholson, *Mountain Gloom and Mountain Glory: The Development of the Aesthetics of the Infinite* (Ithaca: Cornell University Press, 1959).

11. For Channing's appreciation of Milton's Satan, see William Ellery Channing, "Remarks on the Character and Writings of John Milton," in *The Works of William Ellery Channing*

(Boston: American Unitarian Association, 1901), pp. 500–501; for Channing's view of hell, see Channing, "The Evil of Sin," in ibid., pp. 350–353.

12. William Ellery Channing, "Unitarian Christianity: Discourse at the Ordination of the Rev. Jared Sparks," in *Works*, pp. 374–375.

13. Calvin, *Institutes*, bk. II, chap. xvi, sec. 11; for the continuing charge that the governmental theology reduced the atonement to a fiction, see George Ellis, *A Half Century of the Unitarian Controversy* (Boston: Crosby, Nichols, and Co., 1857), p. 216.

14. James Murdock, *The Nature of the Atonement* (Andover, Mass.: Flagg and Gould, 1823), pp. 23–24.

15. For background on Thornwell, see Benjamin Morgan Palmer, *The Life and Letters of James Henley Thornwell* (1875; reprint, New York: Arno Press, 1969); James Oscar Farmer, Jr., *The Metaphysical Confederacy: James Henley Thornwell and the Synthesis of Southern Values* (Macon, Ga.: Mercer University Press, 1978); and Luder G. Whitlock, Jr., "James Henley Thornwell," in *Southern Reformed Theology*, ed. David F. Wells (Grand Rapids, Mich.: Baker Book House, 1989), pp. 61–74. In most of his theological writing, Thornwell confined himself to neoclassical theism. He considered ascribing "passions" to God to be on the same low level as ascribing a body to him. "Incalculable mischief" had been done by anthropomorphic reasoning on this level. Still, Thornwell acknowledged that anthropomorphism might serve purposes of "devotion," if not "speculation." This sounded the familiar division that Park had drawn between the "theology of intellect and that of the feelings." But more so than Park or Hodge, Thornwell saw a devotional side, or almost a mystical side, to theism. Thornwell sometimes almost endorsed a negative theology. When trying to imagine God, Thornwell claimed, human beings must strip away as many finite qualities as possible and strive for "the utmost abstraction and purity." The point of this, however, was not just to arrive at a logical theism. Imagining God in this way could certainly give one a "theology of the intellect," to use Park's term; but, for Thornwell, a theistic conception of God was also suited to stir the deepest feelings in people. According to Thornwell, only an abstract God could be vast enough, and mysterious enough, to elicit deep human devotion. "There is no limit upon our affections," Thornwell wrote, "when the object is known to be unlimited in its right and fitness to receive them. The very darkness which shrouds this infinitude reacts upon our worship, and expands our emotions in rapture and adoration." So as a theological writer, Thornwell did his best to invest theism with drama, and t some degree this brought anthropomorphism back into his writing. Thornwell also had a knack for the striking phrase and this also brought in some anthropomorphism. "Man, therefore, sits for the portrait that he sketches of God," Thornwell wrote, acknowledging the inevitability of some degree of anthropomorphism in all attempts to apprehend God. See James Henley Thornwell, "Limits of Our Knowledge of God," in *The Collected Writings of James Henley Thornwell*, 2 vols., ed. John B. Adger (Richmond: Presbyterian Committee of Publication, 1871), 1:112, 120–123, 129, 135. Thornwell was also one of the leading antebellum and wartime defenders of southern slavery; see William H. Freeling, "James Henley Thornwell's Mysterious Anti-Slavery Moment," *Journal of Southern History* 67 (August 1991): 383–406; Elizabeth Fox-Genovese and Eugene D. Genovese, "The Divine Sanction of Social Order: Religious Foundations of the Southern Slaveholders' World View," *Journal of the American Academy of Religion* 55 (Summer 1987): 211–233; and Marilyn J. Westerkamp, "James Henley Thornwell, Pro-Slavery Spokesman within a Calvinist Faith," *South Carolina Historical Magazine* 87 (January 1986): 49–64. On antebellum southern theologians and religion more generally, see E. Brooks Holifield, *The Gentlemen Theologians: American Theology in Southern Culture, 1779–1860* (Durham, N.C.: Duke University Press, 1978); and Anne C. Loveland, *Southern Evangelicals and the Social Order, 1800–1860* (Baton Rouge: Louisiana State University Press, 1980).

16. For Thornwell's comment on Andover, see Palmer, *Life and Letters of Thornwell*, p. 115. On Thornwell's education, see also Farmer, *Metaphysical Confederacy*, pp. 44–52.

17. James Henley Thornwell, "The Necessity of the Atonement," in *Collected Writings*, 2:234–235.

18. Ibid., 2:253, 257.

19. Ibid., 2:257–258.

20. Ibid., 2:258.

21. John R. McDowall, *McDowall's Journal* 2 (May 1834): 67.

22. Biographical information on George Griffin is slim. My information comes from *Appleton's Cyclopedia of American Biography*, ed. James Grant Wilson and John Fiske (New York: D. Appleton and Co., 1888).

23. "The Sufferings of Christ," *Christian Review* 44 (December 1846): 584; Taylor Lewis, "The Sufferings of Christ," *Biblical Repository and Classical Review* 63 (July 1846): 420.

24. Knapp, *Personification and the Sublime*, chap. 1; Weiskel, *Romantic Sublime*, chap. 4.

25. George Griffin, *The Sufferings of Christ* (New York: Harper and Bros., 1852), pp. 144–146.

26. Ibid., pp. 145–146.

27. "Sufferings of Christ," *Christian Review*, p. 585.

28. Milton, *Paradise Lost*, bk. 2, lines 658–659.

29. Baird unfortunately has received even less historical consideration than Shedd. For biographical information on Baird, see Peter Walker, *Biblical Repository and Princeton Review: Index Volume 1825–1868* (Philadelphia: Peter Walker, 1871), pp. 99–101; and Samuel John Baird, *A History of the New School, and of the Questions Involved in the Disruption of the Presbyterian Church in 1838* (Philadelphia: Claxton, Remsen, and Haffelfinger, 1868).

30. Samuel John Baird, *The First Adam and the Second: The Elohim Revealed in the Creation and Redemption of Man* (Philadelphia: Parry and McMillan, 1860), pp. 137–138.

31. Ibid., pp. 138–140.

32. Ibid.

33. Owen, *Death of Death in the Death of Christ*, 5:391.

34. Baird, *First Adam and the Second*, p. 612.

35. Ibid., pp. 612, 615–616.

36. Charles Hodge, "The First and Second Adam," *Princeton Review* 32 (April 1860): 335–376; James Henley Thornwell, "Baird's Elohim Revealed," *Southern Presbyterian Review* 13 (April 1860): 209.

Chapter Seven

1. Horace Bushnell, *Christian Nurture* (1861; reprint, New Haven: Yale University Press, 1967), pp. 173–74.

2. Ibid., p. 174.

3. William Hutchison, *The Modernist Impulse in American Protestantism* (New York: Oxford University Press, 1982), p. 43. For Bushnell's liberal champions, see Theodore Munger, *Horace Bushnell: Preacher and Theologian* (Boston: Houghton Mifflin Co., 1904), and "The Secret of Horace Bushnell," in *Essays for the Day* (Boston: Houghton Mifflin Co., 1904), pp. 157–182. Along these lines, see also Charles E. McKinley et al., *Bushnell Centenary* (Hartford, Conn.: Hartford Press, 1902); Williston Walker, *Great Men of the Christian Church* (Chicago: University of Chicago Press, 1908); Arthur Cushman McGiffert, *The Rise of Modern Religious Ideas* (New York: Macmillan, 1915); and John Wright Buckham, *Pro-*

gressive Religious Thought in America: A Survey of the Enlarging Pilgrim Faith (Boston: Houghton Mifflin Co., 1919), pp. 3–54. For recent introductions to Bushnell's work, see Paul K. Conkin, *The Uneasy Center: Reformed Christianity in Antebellum America* (Chapel Hill: University of North Carolina Press, 1995), pp. 233–249; Bruce Kuklick, *Churchmen and Philosophers: From Jonathan Edwards to John Dewey* (New Haven: Yale University Press, 1985), pp. 161–171; David L. Smith, introduction to *Horace Bushnell: Selected Writings on Language, Religion, and American Culture*, ed. David L. Smith (Chico, Calif.: Scholar's Press, 1984); Claude Welch, *Protestant Thought in the Nineteenth Century*, 2 vols. (New Haven: Yale University Press, 1972), 1:258–268. On Park and Edwards's reputation in the nineteenth century, see Joseph A. Conforti, *Jonathan Edwards, Religious Tradition, and American Culture* (Chapel Hill: University of North Carolina Press, 1995).

4. William James, "Review of Bushnell's Women's Suffrage and J. S. Mill's *The Subjection of Women*," *North American Review* 109 (October 1869): 556. For Isabella Beecher Hooker's communications with Bushnell's spirit, see Kenneth R. Andrews, *Nook Farm: Mark Twain's Hartford Circle* (Cambridge, Mass.: Harvard University Press, 1950), p. 56.

5. Mary Bushnell Cheney, *Life and Letters of Horace Bushnell* (New York: Harper and Brothers, 1880), pp. 2–3.

6. The leading biography of Bushnell is Barbara Cross, *Horace Bushnell: Minister to a Changing America* (Chicago: University of Chicago Press, 1958). Other biographies include Warren Archibald, *Horace Bushnell* (Hartford, Conn.: Edwin Valentine Mitchell, 1930); and William R. Adamson, *Bushnell Rediscovered* (Philadelphia: Fortress Press, 1966). The first major biography of Bushnell following Cheney's *Life and Letters of Horace Bushnell* was Theodore Munger's *Horace Bushnell*.

7. Cheney, *Life and Letters of Horace Bushnell*, pp. 24–27.

8. Ibid., pp. 27–28.

9. Ibid., pp. 32, 40.

10. Ibid., p. 32.

11. Ibid., pp. 31, 33–34, 52.

12. Ibid., p. 118; for Bushnell's use of the phrase "winged words," see ibid., p. 209, and Horace Bushnell, *God in Christ* (1849; reprint, New York: AMS Press, 1972), p. 22.

13. Cheney, *Life and Letters of Horace Bushnell*, p. 171.

14. Mary B. Cheney, MSS note, Learned Collection, Yale University. For another consideration of Bushnell's relationships with his mother and his wife, see Donald Meyer, *Sex and Power: The Rise of Women in America, Russia, Sweden, and Italy* (Middletown, Conn.: Wesleyan University Press, 1987), pp. 316–323.

15. Cheney, *Life and Letters of Horace Bushnell*, pp. 428–429.

16. Ibid., p. 456.

17. Charles Hodge, "God in Christ" (1849), in *Essays and Reviews* (New York: Robert Carter and Bros., 1857), p. 471; Noah Porter, "Horace Bushnell," *New Englander* 36 (January 1877): 158–164; Henry M. Goodwin, "Dr. Bushnell's Sermons for the New Life," *New Englander* 17 (May 1859): 384, 388, and "Horace Bushnell," *New Englander* 39 (January 1881): 32–33, 39.

18. "The Fragmentary Age in Literature," *Presbyterian Quarterly Review* 4 (September 1855): 336–337.

19. Cheney, *Life and Letters of Horace Bushnell*, pp. 98–99. In one of his first published essays, in 1843, Bushnell allied the cause of religion with literature; see Horace Bushnell, "Taste and Fashion," *New Englander* 1 (April 1843): 164.

20. For a transcript of Horace Bushnell's "Revelation" and comments on it, see Stanley Steward, "Horace Bushnell and Contemporary Christian Education," Ph.D diss., Yale University, 1966, pp. 308–335.

21. Munger, *Horace Bushnell*, p. 109; Charles Fiedelson, Jr., *Symbolism and American Literature* (Chicago: University of Chicago Press, 1954), p. 151; Sydney Ahlstrom, ed., *Theology in America* (New York: Bobbs-Merrill Co., 1967), p. 318. The leading historical considerations of *God in Christ* are Philip F. Gura, *The Wisdom of Words: Language, Theology, and Literature in the New England Renaissance* (Middletown, Conn.: Wesleyan University Press, 1981), pp. 51–71; Conrad Cherry, *Nature and Religious Imagination: From Edwards to Bushnell* (Philadelphia: Fortress Press, 1980), pp. 157–190; Donald A. Crosby, *Horace Bushnell's Theory of Language in the Context of Other Nineteenth-Century Philosophies of Language* (The Hague: Mouton, 1975); David L. Smith, *Symbolism and Growth: The Religious Thought of Horace Bushnell* (Chico, Calif.: Scholar's Press, 1981); and James O. Duke, *Horace Bushnell on the Vitality of Biblical Language* (Chico, Calif.: Scholar's Press, 1984).

22. Bushnell, *God in Christ*, pp. 73–74.

23. Bushnell made little more than a passing effort to find support for his assertions and acknowledged that he was hardly a specialist in philology; see ibid., pp. 14, 29–36. Bushnell's "Preliminary Dissertation on Language" received a great deal of attention because the question of the relation between figurative and literal uses of language was in the air, as it had been periodically throughout the history of Christian theology. In this complex debate, Bushnell's theories became something of a straw man. Because Bushnell had a liberal reputation for his interpretations of the atonement and incarnation, conservative theologians lampooned his work as representative of liberal philology. Conservative reviewers took some enjoyment in this; see Enoch Pond, *Review of Dr. Bushnell's "God in Christ"* (Bangor, Maine: E. P. Duren, 1849), pp. 2–3. The question, as even Park and Hodge could agree, was never about whether spiritual language was exclusively figurative or exclusively literal but how these two uses of language interpenetrated and how their different kinds of signification might be understood (Hodge, "God in Christ," pp. 439–445; and David N. Lord, "Dr. Bushnell's Dissertation on Language," *Theological and Literary Journal* [July 1849]: 61–131). It has been suggested that Bushnell's "Dissertation" influenced Park's *The Theology of the Intellect and That of the Feelings*. See Sydney Ahlstrom, *A Religious History of the American People* (New Haven: Yale University Press, 1972), p. 613; and D. G. Hart, "Divided between Heart and Mind: The Critical Period for Protestant Thought in America," *Journal of Ecclesiastical History* 33 (April 1987): 264. This view seems to rely on the assumption that Bushnell introduced New England theologians to speculation on the literal and figurative aspects of language. But Park was considering an issue that was very much in the air before Bushnell had written, and Park's treatment shows no reliance on Bushnell. It is true that contemporaries tried to discredit Park's thought by linking it with Bushnell's; for instance, see Albert Barnes in his 1853 essay, "Thoughts on Theology," in *Essays and Reviews*, 2 vols. (New York: Iviston and Phinny, 1855), 2:323–324. Barnes, however, grossly misrepresented Park's ideas in *The Theology of the Intellect and That of the Feelings*. This was part of Barnes's effort to supplant Park and become the leading governmental theologian in the North. More intellectually honest opponents of Park than Barnes refused to do this. The Southern Presbyterian Thomas E. Peck, for instance, though an opponent of Park's, recognized that it was unfair to condemn Park's work simply by associating it with Bushnell's; see Thomas E. Peck, "God in Christ," *Southern Presbyterian Review* 6 (April 1851): 560.

24. Horace Bushnell, *Nature and the Supernatural* (New York: Charles Scribner's, 1858), pp. 167–174, 198–199, 206. Bushnell's later champions presented *Nature and the Supernatural* as a deliberation on the relationship between the natural sciences and religion and even suggested that Bushnell anticipated an "evolutionary philosophy" (Munger, *Horace Bushnell*, pp. 212, 216, and "Secret of Horace Bushnell," p. 179; see also H. Shelton Smith, ed., *Horace Bushnell* [New York: Oxford University Press, 1965], pp. 129–131; and William Alexander

Johnson, *Nature and the Supernatural in the Theology of Horace Bushnell* [Lund: Gleerup, 1963]). It was recognized at the time it was written, however, that *Nature and the Supernatural* took in very little serious science. As Noah Porter gently put it, Bushnell was "scarcely a neophyte" in the sciences. When James L. Dana, a geologist at Yale, reviewed *Nature and the Supernatural*, he scratched his head over it, remarking that though passages were "sublime," they had little to do with current scientific theories. Porter and Dana were right. As in *God in Christ*, in *Nature and the Supernatural* Bushnell's conception of nature was far more literary than scientific (Porter, "Horace Bushnell," *New Englander* 36 [January 1877]: 64; Dana, "Anticipations of Man in Nature," *New Englander* 17 [May 1859]: 299).

25. Bushnell, *Nature and the Supernatural*, pp. 198–199, 206.

26. Ibid., p. 161.

27. Ibid.

28. Bushnell, *Christian Nurture*, pp. 70–71.

29. For Munger's interest in finding an American precursor in Bushnell in contrast to German liberal theology, see Munger, *Horace Bushnell*, p. 271, and "Secret of Horace Bushnell," pp. 156, 160–161, 179. For another effort, see George B. Stevens, "Horace Bushnell and Albrecht Ritschl: A Comparison," *American Journal of Theology* 6 (January 1902): 35–56. The question of whether Bushnell had been influenced by the early nineteenth-century German liberal theologian Friedrich Schleiermacher was also raised. Munger alternately suggested that Bushnell "discovered for himself" ideas associated with Schleiermacher and yet was "influenced" by him (*Horace Bushnell*, pp. 46, 119, 209–210). In "Secret of Horace Bushnell" (p. 159), Munger dismissed the notion that Bushnell owed much to Schleiermacher. Late twentieth-century historians, however, have seen Schleiermacher's influence, as well as that of Samuel Coleridge and Frederick Denison Maurice. See, for example, Ahlstrom, *Religious History*, p. 610; Smith, *Horace Bushnell*, pp. 6–7; Cross, *Horace Bushnell*, pp. 69, 102–103, 141; and Gura, *Wisdom of Words*, p. 53.

30. Luther Weigle, introduction to Bushnell, *Christian Nurture*, p. xxxi. McGiffert wrote, "Bushnell's epoch-making book on Christian Nurture (1846 [*sic*], 1861) . . . did perhaps more than any other single agency to break down the extreme individualism of the old Puritan theology of America" (*Rise of Modern Religious Ideas*, p. 277). For similar evaluations of the work, see Charles Howard Hopkins, *The Rise of the Social Gospel in American Protestantism, 1865–1915* (New Haven: Yale University Press, 1940), p. 5; and Henry F. May, *Protestant Churches in Industrial America* (New York: Harper and Brothers, 1949), pp. 84–85. The 1916 edition of *Christian Nurture* included some minor editing of the 1861 version, but nothing was excluded that is germane to this discussion. See Weigle, Introduction, p. xxxix. For considerations of the historical significance of the work in influencing attitudes about children, see Peter Gregg Slater, *Children in the New England Mind in Death and Life* (Hamden, Conn.: Archon Books, 1977), pp. 152–157; on the significance of the work for theological interpretations of the doctrine of original sin, see H. Shelton Smith, *Changing Conceptions of Original Sin: A Study in American Theology since 1750* (New York: Charles Scribner's, 1955), pp. 144–149. For an assessment of Bushnell's ideas in terms of modern sociology and psychology, see Daniel Walker Howe, "The Social Science of Horace Bushnell," *Journal of American History* 70 (September 1983): 305–322. Studies of early nineteenth-century views of child rearing have shown that Bushnell's ideas about family religiosity were less original and pioneering than previously thought. See Philip Greven, *The Protestant Temperament: Patterns of Child-Rearing, Religious Experience, and the Self in Early America* (New York: Alfred A. Knopf, 1977), p. 173; and Mary P. Ryan, *Cradle of the Middle Class: The Family in Oneida County, New York, 1790–1865* (Cambridge: Cambridge University Press, 1981), p. 100.

31. Weigle, Introduction, p. xxxvi.

32. After relying on phrenological concepts in his 1847 edition of *Christian Nurture* to suggest that humanity might overcome original sin, Bushnell turned around two years later and rejected the whole notion. In his "Preliminary Discourse" (1849), Bushnell ridiculed phrenologists for believing that they could produce "dictionary men," meaning people whose emotions were neatly labeled and defined. Sin made this an impossiblity. Therefore, phrenology could never replace literature as the way to understand human nature. This was why Bushnell declared, "Poets are the true metaphysicians," echoing Shelley's famous line from *A Defence of Poetry,* "Poets are the unacknowledged legislators of the world" (Bushnell, *God in Christ,* p. 73; Percy Bysshe Shelley, *A Defence of Poetry,* in *English Romantic Writers,* ed. David Perkins [New York: Harcourt, Brace, and World, 1967], p. 1087).

33. On nineteenth-century phrenological notions about sexuality, see chap. 6, n. 2.

34. Bushnell, *Christian Nurture,* pp. 7, 94, 172–175. The "post-natal" sphere carried the brunt of Bushnell's anti-Catholicism. "Busy, worldly" fathers and "vain, irritable, captious and fashion-loving mothers" made families into little "popedoms." "Monks" became "cruel" because they did not have the company of children to soften them, and the same would happen to men and women—but most likely to women—who did not devote themselves to their children (ibid., pp. 46, 61, 99). The year before Bushnell published *Christian Nurture,* he was in Europe and visited Italy. In London, he attended the anti-Catholic Evangelical Alliance conference. He published at that time a "Letter to the Pope." After printing it, Bushnell wondered if he had been "perhaps a little too hard on the old gentleman." But Mary Bushnell Cheney commented in her biography of her father that his letter was "one of the most characteristic things which Horace Bushnell ever did" (*Life and Letters of Horace Bushnell,* pp. 168, 172). On attitudes toward Catholicism among antebellum Protestants, see Jenny Franchot, *Roads to Rome: The Antebellum Protestant Encounter with Catholicism* (Berkeley: University of California Press, 1994).

35. Bushnell, *Christian Nurture,* pp. 175, 180–181. See also Horace Bushnell, "The Kingdom of God as a Grain of Mustard Seed," *New Englander* 2 (October 1844): 600–619, and "On the Principles of National Greatness" (1837), reprinted as "The True Wealth and Weal of Nations," in *Work and Play* (New York: Charles Scribner's Sons, 1864), pp. 44–73.

36. Bushnell, *Christian Nurture,* p. 181.

37. Ibid., p. 175.

38. Ibid., pp. 173–174.

39. Horace Bushnell, "Our Obligations to the Dead" (1865), in *Building Eras in Religion* (New York: Charles Scribner's Sons, 1881), pp. 337–338.

40. On Christ in heaven, see Bushnell, "Our Relation to Christ in the Afterlife," in *Sermons on Living Subjects* (New York: Scribner, Armstrong, and Co., 1892), p. 447. The line about "God's last metaphor" is from Horace Bushnell, "The Gospel: A Gift to the Imagination" (1869), in *Building Eras in Religion,* p. 259. In the introduction to *The Vicarious Sacrifice,* Bushnell referred to God as the author of the "incarnate biography," making Jesus a character whom God had created to represent himself (*The Vicarious Sacrifice: Grounded in Principles of Universal Obligation* [1866; reprint, Hicksville, N.Y.: Regina Press, 1975], p. 31). Of course, Bushnell's liberal theological champions stressed the opposite of this: Bushnell's incarnationalism. See Munger, *Horace Bushnell;* Buckham, *Progressive Religious Thought in America,* pp. 6–32; and H. Shelton Smith, who wrote in 1965: "All his theological works are Christocentric. Bushnell's ultimate center, to be sure, was God; but it was God as revealed in Jesus Christ. . . . Thus it cannot be too strongly emphasized that Christ was the magnetic center of the thought and ministry of Horace Bushnell" (in Smith, *Horace Bushnell,* p. 26). The association between Bushnell and Sabellianism hangs to some extent on a passing reference Bushnell made to Moses Stuart's translation of Schleiermacher's "On the Discrepancy between the Sabellian and Athanasian Method of Repre-

senting the Trinity," *Biblical Repository* (April 1835): 265–353, (July 1835): 1–116. Bushnell vaguely claimed that the article coincided with some of his own views, which in themselves were hardly formulated at the time; see Bushnell, *God in Christ*, pp. 11–12. This is not to say that Bushnell's views of God (which were never consistent) do not have Sabellian traits, but Bushnell's depictions of God are hardly comprehended by this label. In Sabellianism, God himself is beyond human comprehension, an idea Bushnell tried out in *God in Christ* but then gave up in his later anthropomorphic works. See Bushnell, *God in Christ*, pp. 137–139.

41. Horace Bushnell, *Reverses Needed: A Discourse Delivered on Sunday after the Disaster of Bull Run* (Hartford, Conn.: L. E. Hunt, 1861), pp. 12–13, 23–24. The remark about David and Jonathan is recorded in Cheney, *Life and Letters of Horace Bushnell*, p. 482. On Bushnell's enthusiasm for the fighting, see Henry Clay Trumbull, *My Four Religious Teachers* (Philadelphia: Sunday School Times, 1903), pp. 80–83.

42. Bushnell, *Vicarious Sacrifice*, p. 516.

43. George Rapall Noyes, "The Scripture Doctrine of Sacrifice," *Christian Examiner* 59 (September 1855): 237. Noyes also cited with some approval and some disapproval Bushnell's remarks on sacrifices from earlier works; see ibid., pp. 261–262, 267, 270; Bushnell, *Vicarious Sacrifice*, p. 64.

44. Bushnell, *Vicarious Sacrifice*, p. 67. Bushnell scorned the liberal primitivization of the Old Testament: "Affecting great admiration of Christianity, they declare that the God of the Old Testament is a lower being and not the same [as the God of the New Testament]; a barbarian's God, a figment evidently of barbarism itself" (ibid., p. 63).

45. Ibid., p. 67.

46. Ibid., pp. 67–68, 69. Indeed, Bushnell downplayed Christ's sufferings even further. "God," Bushnell wrote, "has in fact put nothing of his pain upon him [Christ]; he only takes it on himself, and there is really no more reason to be troubled about the severity of his lot than there is here in the retributions of this life" (ibid., p. 345). In another ironic twist, Bushnell drew on a common caricature of the juristic atonement to diminish Christ's importance. "Does he then intercede for us," Bushnell wrote of Christ, "in the sense that he goes before God in a plea to gain him over to us, showing God his wounds and the print of his nails to soften him towards us?" Like the champions of philanthropism, Bushnell used this caricature of the suffering Christ to argue that God did not need to be appeased in his wrath against sin; but unlike other liberals, Bushnell also used this caricature to suggest that Christ's sufferings were not that significant compared to God's (ibid., pp. 71–72).

47. Ibid., p. 73.

48. Ibid., pp. 285–286.

49. Ibid., p. 31. In the midst of the war in 1864, Bushnell celebrated God's power in terms of a canon: "Oh, it is religion, it is God. Every drumbeat is a hymn, the canon thunder God" ("Popular Government by Divine Right" [1864], in *Building Eras in Religion*, p. 316).

50. Bushnell, *Vicarious Sacrifice*, pp. 347, 362–363. Bushnell's use of the word "Kosmos" was not uncommon in mid-nineteenth-century America. The word had been popularized by Alexander von Humboldt in his *Cosmos: A Sketch of the Physical Description of the Universe*, which had been translated into English in 1850. Like Walt Whitman, Bushnell used the German spelling of the word—"Kosmos"—for affect. It should be noted, however, that Humboldt subscribed to a more neoclassical and harmonious view of creation than Bushnell. On Humboldt's work in America and Whitman's use of it, see David Reynolds, *Walt Whitman's America: A Cultural Biography* (New York: Alfred A. Knopf, 1995), p. 244.

51. Bushnell, *Vicarious Sacrifice*, pp. 345–347.

52. W. G. T. Shedd, "Bushnell on the Atonement," *American Theological Review* 8 (January 1866): 167, 169.

53. Charles Hodge, "Bushnell on Vicarious Sacrifice," *Princeton Review* 38 (April 1866): 161–194.

54. James Freeman Clarke, "Bushnell on Vicarious Sacrifice," *Christian Examiner* 80 (May 1866): 372–373; Edwards A. Park, "Review of Horace Bushnell on Vicarious Sacrifice," *Bibliotheca Sacra* 23 (April 1866): 345. See also Noah Porter, "Review of Dr. Bushnell on the Vicarious Sacrifice," *New Englander* 25 (April 1866): 228–282.

55. E. C. Towne, "The Vicarious Sacrifice," *Christian Examiner* 80 (March 1866): 276–280.

56. Henry James, Sr., "Bushnell on Vicarious Sacrifice," *North American Review* 102 (April 1866): 564.

57. Horace Bushnell, "Training for the Pulpit Manward" (1866), in *Building Eras in Religion*, p. 233. For wider historical considerations of this passage, see chap. 1, n. 24.

58. Horace Bushnell, *Forgiveness and Law: Grounded in Principles Interpreted by Human Analogies* (1874; reprint, Hicksville, N.Y.: Regina Press, 1975), p. 9.

59. Ibid., pp. 77–78.

60. Bushnell, *Vicarious Sacrifice*, p. 378; Bushnell, *Forgiveness and Law*, p. 58.

61. Bushnell, *Forgiveness and Law*, pp. 54, 62; Edwards A. Park, "All the Moral Attributes of God Are Comprehended in His Love," in *Discourses on Some Theological Doctrines as Related to the Religious Character* (Andover, Mass.: W. F. Draper, 1885), p. 165.

62. Bushnell, *Forgiveness and Law*, pp. 39–41, 53–54.

63. Ibid., pp. 55, 71.

64. Munger, *Horace Bushnell*, p. 267; the rest of the quotation indicates Munger's method of interpreting Bushnell: the idea that God became more loving by propitiating man "savors of the schools and the schemes rather than of the simple human love that overspreads the life of Christ. This, indeed, Bushnell would have, and fills pages with protests against regarding it in any other light, but he fails to remove the impression." Why had Bushnell "fail[ed] to remove the impression" that his book gives? Why (in Munger's construction) had a theologian supposedly devoted to sentimental incarnationalism finished his career with a book such as *Forgiveness and Law*? Munger's answer was that Bushnell had tried to translate his theory into the language of conservative theology so that conservatives would understand it; but in doing this, Bushnell's theory got so tangled in this conservative language that it began to sound conservative. As Munger put it: "[Bushnell] thought it was necessary to enter the world of legalism in order to deliver the doctrine [of the atonement] out of it. It must also be said that he himself had not fully escaped from it." Because of progress since Bushnell's day, Munger considered that Bushnell's failed effort in *Forgiveness and Law* could be forgotten: "The thought of the coming age would itself have eliminated the legalism left in the doctrine, and saved a discussion that could not do the work of time and growth" (*Horace Bushnell*, pp. 251–252). On this point, see also Munger, "Secret of Horace Bushnell," p. 178. Of course, it might well be wondered how Munger could construe *The Vicarious Sacrifice* to suit his sentimental incarnationalism; see the next chapter.

Chapter Eight

1. Theodore T. Munger, *The Freedom of Faith* (Boston: Houghton Mifflin Co., 1883), p. 116.

2. Matthew Arnold, *Literature and Dogma: An Essay Towards a Better Understanding of the Bible* (New York: Macmillan, 1883), pp. 27, 30, 36, 42–43, 79. For a summary of Arnold's religious views, see Lionel Trilling, *Matthew Arnold* (New York: Meridian Books,

1955), pp. 289–336; Basil Wiley, "Arnold and Religion," in *Matthew Arnold*, ed. Kenneth Allott, (London: G. Bell and Sons, 1975), pp. 236–258. Others have seen Arnold's religious thought as more profound: Nathan Scott, Jr., "Arnold's Version of Transcendence—The *Via Poetica*," *Journal of Religion* 59 (July 1979): 261–284; and Ruth Roberts, *Arnold and God* (Berkeley: University of California Press, 1983). Arnold had reservations about the emerging aesthetic movement. He found the erotic and ambivalent elements in Keats and Shelley disturbing. For similar reasons, Arnold also denounced distasteful trends in contemporary French literature. See Trilling, *Matthew Arnold*, pp. 314–315. For a consideration of Arnold's influence in America, see John Henry Raleigh, *Matthew Arnold and American Culture* (Berkeley: University of California Press, 1961).

3. Munger, *Freedom of Faith*, p. 116.

4. On these adjustments in moral philosophy and political theory, see John L. Thomas, *Alternative America: Henry George, Edward Bellamy, Henry Demarest Lloyd, and the Adversary Tradition* (Cambridge, Mass.: Harvard University Press, 1983); James T. Kloppenberg, *Uncertain Victory: Social Democracy and Progressivism in European and American Thought, 1870–1920* (New York: Oxford University Press, 1986). Also helpful here more generally are George Cotkin, *Reluctant Modernism: American Thought and Culture, 1880–1900* (New York: Twayne Publishers, 1992); Alan Trachtenberg, *The Incorporation of America: Culture and Society in the Gilded Age* (New York: Hill and Wang, 1982); Robert H. Wiebe, *The Search for Order, 1877–1920* (New York: Hill and Wang, 1967); and Richard Hofstadter, *Social Darwinism in American Thought*, rev. ed. (Boston: Beacon Press, 1955).

5. *National Cyclopedia of Biography*, 31:339–340. For Munger's role in the modernist movement, see William Hutchison, *The Modernist Impulse in American Protestantism* (New York: Oxford University Press, 1982).

6. See Susan Curtis, *A Consuming Faith: The Social Gospel and Modern American Culture* (Baltimore: Johns Hopkins University Press, 1991), pp. 81–82.

7. Munger, *Freedom of Faith*, pp. 123–124.

8. Ibid., p. 121.

9. Ibid., pp. 131–132.

10. Charles Allen Dinsmore, foreword, to Ernest G. Guthrie, Percy H. Epler, and Willard B. Thorpe, *The Significance of the Personality of Christ for the Minister of To-day: Three Addresses* (Boston: Pilgrim Press, 1907), pp. vii–viii.

11. Munger, *Freedom of Faith*, p. 116.

12. On modernism, see Hutchison, *Modernist Impulse*. On the social gospel, see Curtis, *Consuming Faith*; William McGuire King, "An Enthusiasm for Humanity: The Social Emphasis in Religion and Its Accommodation in Protestant Theology," in *Religion and Twentieth-Century American Intellectual Life*, ed. Michael J. Lacey (Cambridge: Cambridge University Press and Woodrow Wilson International Center for Scholars, 1991), pp. 49–77; Paul Boyer, *Urban Masses and Moral Order in America, 1820–1920* (Cambridge, Mass.: Harvard University Press, 1978); Charles Howard Hopkins and Robert C. White, Jr., eds., *The Social Gospel* (Philadelphia: Temple University Press, 1976); William R. Hutchison, "The Americanness of the Social Gospel," *Church History* 44 (September 1975): 367–381; Donald Meyer, *The Protestant Search for Political Realism, 1919–1941*, 2d ed. (Middletown, Conn.: Wesleyan University Press, 1988); Henry F. May, *Protestant Churches and Industrial America* (New York: Harper and Row, 1949); and Charles Howard Hopkins, *The Rise of the Social Gospel in American Protestantism, 1865–1915* (New Haven: Yale University Press, 1940). For introductions to nineteenth- and early twentieth-century German liberal theology, see Alister E. McGrath, *The Making of Modern German Christology: From the Enlightenment to Pannenberg* (London: Blackwell, 1986); Gerald Parsons, "Reforming the Tradition: A Forgotten

Dimension of Liberal Protestantism," *Religion* 13 (July 1983): 257–271; and George Rupp, *Culture Protestantism: German Liberal Theology at the Turn of the Century* (Missoula, Mont.: Scholar's Press, 1977).

13. Lyman Abbott et al., *The Atonement in Modern Religious Thought: A Theological Symposium* (London: James Clarke, 1990), pp. 92–93.

14. Ibid., pp. 357, 370.

15. Theodore Munger, "The Secret of Horace Bushnell," in *Essays for the Day* (Boston: Houghton Mifflin Co., 1904), pp. 157, 175, 179.

16. It is understandable how Bushnell's anthropomorphism could be read as lessening the difference between God and humans and thus as a kind of move toward conceiving God as immanent in the world. Some contemporaries of Bushnell had charged him with this. They also read the subtitle of *The Vicarious Sacrifice* as suggesting that Bushnell was effacing the difference between God and humans. See W. G. T. Shedd, "Bushnell on the Atonement," *American Theological Review* 8 (January 1866): 166. But Bushnell had tried to correct this misinterpretation. He later suggested that by "the principles of universal obligation" he did not mean to conflate God and humanity. All he had meant was that there was some basis on which to draw analogies between God's character and that of people. These analogies, Bushnell acknowledged, must be highly inaccurate. But given the limitations of human knowledge, these analogies might be the best the human race could hope for in trying to appreciate God's character. This point was clarified in *Forgiveness and Law* and later editions of *The Vicarious Sacrifice*, as Munger acknowledged. Munger, however, was not deterred. He overrode Bushnell's effort at clarification. Munger claimed that Bushnell was right the first time (that is, when his meaning was unclear): God and humanity were both guided by "universal" principles because God was in humanity and this was revealed in Jesus's love for humanity (*Horace Bushnell*, pp. 243, 250–251).

17. Munger, *Horace Bushnell*, p. 400.

18. Munger, "Secret of Horace Bushnell," pp. 179–180.

19. The development of realism (or naturalism) in the nineteenth- and twentieth-century novel is a vast topic. For some considerations of this field, see George Levine, ed., *Realism and Representation: Essays on the Problem of Realism in Relation to Science, Literature, and Culture* (Madison: University of Wisconsin Press, 1993); Lilian R. Furst, ed., *Realism* (New York: Longman, 1992); and Henry Harris, *Hippolyte's Club Foot: The Medical Roots of Realism in Modern European Literature* (Oxford: Clarendon Press, 1993). On American realism, important works include Alfred Kazin, *On Native Grounds: A Study of American Prose Literature from 1890 to the Present* (New York: Harcourt, Brace and Co., 1942); Malcolm Cowley, ed., *After the Genteel Tradition* (Carbondale: Southern Illinois University Press, 1964); Donald Pizer, ed., *The Cambridge Companion to American Realism and Naturalism* (New York: Cambridge University Press, 1995); Philip Fisher, *Hard Facts: Setting and Form in the American Novel* (New York: Oxford University Press, 1985); Edwin H. Cady, *The Light of Common Day: Realism in American Fiction* (Bloomington: Indiana University Press, 1971); and Alfred Habegger, *Gender, Fantasy, and Realism in American Literature* (New York: Columbia University Press, 1982). On the aesthetic movement, see Leon Chai, *Aestheticism: The Religion of Art in Post-Romantic Literature* (New York: Columbia University Press, 1990); Carl Woodring, *Nature in Art: Cultural Transformation in the Nineteenth Century* (Cambridge, Mass: Harvard University Press, 1989); and Hilary Fraser, *Beauty and Belief: Aesthetics and Religion in Victorian Literature* (Cambridge: Cambridge University Press, 1986). For two considerations of the ongoing impact of late nineteenth-century aestheticism, see Camille Paglia, *Sexual Personae: Art and Decadence from Nefertiti to Emily Dickinson* (New Haven: Yale University Press, 1990), chaps. 16, 18–21; and Elaine Showalter, *Sexual Anarchy: Gender and Culture at the Fin de Siècle* (New York: Viking Penguin, 1990).

20. Theodore W. Hunt, "Modern Aestheticism," *Princeton Review* 58 (March 1882): 148–163.

21. For the condemnation of modern literature by two prominent conservatives, see J. Gresham Machen, *Christianity and Liberalism* (New York: Macmillan, 1923), p. 10; and Francis Schaeffer, *How Should We Then Live?: The Rise and Decline of Western Thought and Culture* (Old Tappan, N.J.: Fleming H. Revell Co., 1976). Machen's work is discussed in more detail in chapter 9; and his and Schaeffer's attitudes toward modern literature are also considered in chapter 10. There have been some conservative attempts to deal with modern literature, but these have not constituted a sustained movement in conservative theology and have not sought to integrate theology and modern literature on a substantive level. Most of these works are confined to the appreciation and moral evaluation of modern literature and literary theory. One of the more prolific conservatives in the twentieth century on this subject has been Leland Ryken; see his *Triumphs of the Imagination* (Downer's Grove, Ill.: Inter-Varsity Press, 1979), and *Windows to the World: Literature in Christian Perspective* (1985; reprint, Dallas: Word Publishers, 1990). A summary of his views can be found in Leland Ryken, "Literature and Christian Perspective," in *God and Culture: Essays in Honor of Carl F. H. Henry* ed. D. A. Carson and John D. Woodbridge (Grand Rapids, Mich.: Eerdmans Publishing Co., 1993), pp. 215–234. For a more wide-ranging conservative take on the arts, see Edmund P. Clowney, "Living Art: Christian Experience and the Arts," in Carson and Woodbridge, *God and Culture*, pp. 235–253.

22. Noah Porter, *Books and Reading; Or, What Books Shall I Read and How Shall I Read Them?*, 4th ed. (New York: Scribner, Armstrong, and Co., 1873), p. 92.

23. Munger, *Freedom of Faith*, p. 88.

24. Ibid.

25. Horace Bushnell, "Training for the Pulpit Manward," in *Buiding Eras in Religion* (New York: Charles Scribner's Sons, 1881), p. 233; Munger, *Freedom of Faith*, p. 88.

26. Theodore Munger, "The Interplay of Christianity and Literature," in *Essays for the Day*, pp. 98–99.

27. Ibid., pp. 77–78; Charles Allen Dinsmore, *Atonement in Literature and Life* (Boston: Houghton Mifflin Co., 1906), pp. ix, 187, 243–244.

28. Munger, "Interplay of Christianity and Literature," p. 92.

29. Ibid., pp. 92–96.

30. Ibid., p. 65.

31. Ibid., p. 75.

32. Ibid., p. 100. Dinsmore also relied on this polemic; see his *Atonement*, p. viii.

33. Munger, "Secret of Horace Bushnell," pp. 179–180. Munger, however, did not consider Bushnell a man of the future when it came to his last work, *Forgiveness and Law*. In language similar to his treatment of Goethe in "The Interplay of Christianity and Literature," Munger tried to make the best he could of Bushnell but had to acknowledge that this aspect of Bushnell's work was not progressive: "If this [his atonement theory in *Forgiveness and Law*] takes him into the temple of ancient orthodoxy, he stands in the outer court, and with eyes turned toward the broad fields of life and not the altars of sacrifice. . . . [Bushnell's theory] has, however, made no headway as a phase of the atonement. Thought is not moving in that direction, but rather away from it, and is grounding itself more and more on the 'moral view,' which accords so well with the great duties and capacities of humanity" ("Secret of Horace Bushnell," pp. 178–179).

34. Munger, "Interplay of Christianity and Literature," pp. 79, 84–85. It was not unusual for theologians in the nineteenth century to claim inspiration from Goethe; Bushnell and von Harnack did. So, in a general sense, Munger was in good company in saluting Goethe. For Bushnell on Goethe, see Bushnell's *God in Christ* (1849; reprint, New York: AMS Press,

1972), pp. 67–71; for von Harnack on Goethe, see Adolph von Harnack, *What Is Christianity?*, trans. Thomas Bailey Saunders (New York: Harper and Brothers, 1957), p. 4; and Ernest Troeltsch, "Adolph von Harnack and Ferdinand Christian Bauer, 1921," in William Pauck, *Harnack and Troeltsch: Two Historical Theologians* (New York: Oxford University Press, 1968), pp. 103–113. By the logic of his argument, however, Munger had nearly forced himself to claim Goethe and Arnold for Christianity. God had given them their talent, after all. Therefore, they must be serving his purposes. Besides, history was moving toward the fusion of Christianity and literature. So these writers must be part of that process. In the case of Goethe, Munger wrote, "it would be a misfortune, indeed, if he could not be regarded as an interpreter of Christianity,—not because the Divine order needs the help of such a name, but because it would seem as though Providence had defeated itself in so richly endowing a human mind and then suffering it to appear on the wrong side." Munger suggested that God had been using their writing as toxic solvents to wash off the false doctrines that conservatives had affixed to Christianity ("Interplay of Christianity and Literature," p. 78).

35. Munger, "Interplay of Christianity and Literature," pp. 89–90.

36. T. S. Eliot, "Ezra Pound," in *Ezra Pound: A Collection of Essays*, ed. Peter Russell (London: Peter Neville, 1950), p. 25. The development of literary modernism is a huge topic. One of the best single volumes on Pound, Eliot, and Joyce is Hugh Kenner, *The Pound Era* (Berkeley: University of California Press, 1971). See also M. H. Levenson, *A Genealogy of Modernism: A Study of English Literary Doctrine, 1908–1922* (Cambridge: Cambridge University Press, 1984). On the development of modernism in New York and its assimilation into American cosmopolitan culture at large, see Ann Douglas, *Terrible Honesty: Mongrel Manhattan in the 1920s* (New York: Farrar, Straus, and Giroux, 1995); and William R. Taylor, *In Pursuit of Gotham: Culture and Commerce in New York* (New York: Oxford University Press, 1992), esp. chaps. 7–9. For more general considerations of modernism and its assimilation into American society, see Adele Heller and Lois Rudnick, eds., *1915—The Cultural Moment: The New Politics, the New Woman, the New Psychology, the New Art, and the New Theatre in America* (New Brunswick, N.J.: Rutgers University Press, 1991); and Stanley Coben, *Rebellion against Victorianism: The Impetus for Cultural Change in 1920s America* (New York: Oxford University Press, 1991).

37. John Crowe Ransom, *God without Thunder: An Unorthodox Defence of Orthodoxy* (New York: Harcourt, Brace and Co., 1930); Douglas, *Terrible Honesty*, p. 243.

38. Virginia Woolf, "Mr. Bennet and Mr. Brown" (1924), in *The Captain's Death Bed and Other Essays* (London: Hogarth Press, 1950), pp. 91, 108. Important in changing notions of morality here were new views of psychology and sexuality; on these topics, see Douglas, *Terrible Honesty*; Heller and Rudnick, 1915; and Coben, *Rebellion*. Also of significance here is the increasing emphasis on consumerism in America. For intriguing essays linking consumer values with changes in popular and cosmopolitan culture, see Warren I. Susman, *Culture as History: The Transformation of American Society in the Twentieth Century* (New York: Pantheon Books, 1984), esp. chaps. 7, 11, 14. Also helpful here, though more focused on popular culture, is William Leach, *Land of Desire: Merchants, Power, and the Rise of a New American Culture* (New York: Pantheon Books, 1993). Leach also considers the impact of consumer values on what he calls "liberal evangelicals," particularly John Wanamaker. Leach, however, sometimes gives the impression that Walter Rauschenbusch's criticism of materialism and consumer values was unusual in liberal American Protestantism. Whether the social gospel was widely preached from American pulpits is an interesting question needing further research. But as a theological position, Rauschenbusch's social gospel represented the mainstream of cosmopolitan American liberal theology from the late nineteenth century through the twentieth century. Indeed, Leach's criticism of consumerism seems

to echo this central argument in American liberal theology; see Leach, *Land of Desire*, chap. 7. Whether or not the social gospel itself was compromised by American consumerism is another question, one that Susan Curtis considered in *Consuming Faith*. For another criticism of the morality of both consumerism and modernism, see James Lincoln Collier, *The Rise of Selfishness in America* (New York: Oxford University Press, 1991), chap. 11.

39. Carl Van Doren, "Toward a New Canon," *Nation* 134 (April 13, 1932): 429–430. On the changing canon, see also Jay B. Hubbell, *Who Are the Major American Writers? A Study of the Changing Literary Canon* (Durham, N.C.: Duke University Press, 1972). For the academic context of changes in the canon, see Kermit Vanderbilt, *American Literature and the Academy: The Roots, Growth, and Maturity of a Profession* (Philadelphia: University of Pennsylvania Press, 1986).

40. On Wilder, see John Dominic Crossan, *A Fragile Craft: The Work of Amos Niven Wilder* (Chico, Calif.: Scholar's Press, 1981).

41. The remark about Dinsmore is from Amos N. Wilder, *Theology and Modern Literature* (Cambridge, Mass.: Harvard University Press, 1958), p. 49. The references to "Christian idealists" comes from Amos N. Wilder, *Modern Poetry and the Christian Tradition: A Study in the Relation of Christianity to Culture* (New York: Charles Scribner's Sons, 1952), pp. 18, 22, 47. For the remark about the "post-Victorians," see Amos N. Wilder, *The Bible and the Literary Critic* (Minneapolis: Fortress Press, 1991), p. 38. In 1940, Wilder, writing about modernist literature, noted: "these new moods are not solely 'post war.' They grew out of conditions which have been partially present for a century in Western culture, but it is only recently that they have extended themselves to a wide strata of society" (*The Spiritual Aspects of the New Poetry* [New York: Harper and Brothers], pp. 217–218).

42. Wilder, *Theology and Modern Literature*, p. 50. Not only religion but also Western civilization seemed to be caught in the crisis. So there was a political cast to this. "The Cross is one thing, and the Swastika is another," Wilder declared; "The 'Battle Hymn of the Republic' speaks one faith and the 'Internationale' another. The Lincoln Memorial and the tomb of Lenin nourish mutually exclusive images of mankind" (ibid., p. 50).

43. Wilder, *Spiritual Aspects*, p. 222.

44. See, for instance, Wilder's references to Tillich in *Modern Poetry*, pp. xiv, 208, 258; and to Niebuhr and neo-orthodoxy, in ibid, pp. 67, 212, 261, 270. For another consideration of Tillich's influence on the "theology and literature" movement, see David H. Hesla, "Religion and Literature: The Second Stage," *Journal of the American Academy of Religion* 46 (June 1978): 181–192. For Tillich's "method of correlation," see Paul Tillich, *Systematic Theology*, vol. 1, *Reason and Revelation; Being and God* (Chicago: University of Chicago Press, 1951).

45. Wilder, *Spiritual Aspects*, pp. 61, 220.

46. Amos N. Wilder, "Art and Theological Meaning," in *The New Orpheus: Essays Toward a Christian Poetic*, ed. Nathan A. Scott, Jr. (New York: Sheed and Ward, 1964), pp. 414–415.

47. Ibid., p. 418.

48. Ibid.

49. Wilder, *Spiritual Aspects*, pp. 220, 221, 223, 226. In his judgment about Proust and Joyce, Wilder cited Edmund Wilson and appears to have been relying on his work *Axel's Castle: A Study of the Imaginative Literature of 1870–1930* (New York: Charles Scribner's Sons, 1931). Wilder seems to have read Wilson as suggesting that modernism was more of a spent force than he actually claimed. It is true that Wilson saw much of modernist literature as an outgrowth of late nineteenth-century French neosymbolism, and to some extent Wilson saw that the significance of this influence was at an end. Wilson also suggested that modernist literature risked becoming too effete and esoteric to command a wide cosmopolitan audi-

ence. It was these aspects of Wilson's critique that Wilder seems to have latched on to. But Wilson also saw modernism as still a strong and productive movement in literature.

50. Wilder, *Modern Poetry*, p. 52. See also Crossan's treatment of this theme in *Fragile Craft*, p. 35.

51. Wilder, *Modern Poetry*, pp. 266–267.

52. Ibid., p. 277.

53. Wilder, *Theology and Modern Literature*, pp. 99–100, 106, 108.

54. Ibid., pp. 95–96.

55. Robinson Jeffers, "Dear Judas," in *The Collected Poetry of Robinson Jeffers*, 3 vols., ed. Tim Hunt (Stanford: Stanford University Press, 1989), 2:18–20.

56. "Is Effective Writing Necessarily 'Volcanic'?" *Presbyterian Quarterly Review* 3 (June 1855): 135–137, 147–148; Wilder, *Spiritual Aspects*, p. 226.

57. Wilder, *Theology and Modern Literature*, p. 107.

58. Ibid., p. 109. Yet Wilder also complained that since the 1960s appreciation for the Christian tradition had declined as younger people became interested in Eastern religions. He suggested that the high point for the appreciation of the Christian past was the 1940s and 1950s. The "carnival of the sixties," according to Wilder, led theologians to turn their attention to more exotic subjects—Eastern religions, Jungian psychology, dreams. He acknowledged that there was something to be said for the spirit of pluralism. But it came at a cost. The specifically Western Christian heritage risked being lost. "The proclaimed pluralism of the alienated," he wrote, "reflects a contemporary spirituality which has failed to wrestle with its antecedents and with its stubborn empirical context" ("Theology and Literature," in *Bible and the Literary Critic*, p. 40).

59. Wilder, *Theology and Modern Literature*, pp. 107, 109. For an example of the nineteenth-century effort to account for Christ's outcries as mainly a fulfillment of prophecy and an honoring of scripture, see David Newton Sheldon, *Sin and Redemption: A Series of Sermons to Which Is Added an Oration on Moral Freedom* (New York: Sheldon, Lamport, and Blakeman, 1856), pp. 205–206.

60. Wilder, *Theology and Modern Literature*, p. 110.

61. Ibid., p. 109

62. Ibid.

Chapter Nine

1. For studies on the social gospel, see chap. 8, n. 12. On Bellamy and late nineteenth-century humanitarian reform, see chap. 8, n. 2. On biblical criticism and the social gospel, see William McGuire King, "The Biblical Base of the Social Gospel," in *The Bible and Social Reform*, ed. Ernest R. Sandeen (Chico, Calif.: Scholar's Press and Society of Biblical Literature, 1982), pp. 59–84. On the liberal biblical criticism more generally that was the foundation for the social gospel, see chap. 2, n. 36. For introductions to Ritschl and Hermann, see Claude Welch, *Protestant Thought in the Nineteenth Century*, 2 vols. (New Haven: Yale University Press, 1972), 2:1–54. On Ritschl see also Alister E. McGrath, *Iustitia Dei: A History of the Christian Doctrine of Justification from 1500 to the Present* (Cambridge: Cambridge University Press, 1986), pp. 159–170. For an introduction to von Harnack, see Martin Rumscheidt, Harnack's Liberalism in Theology: A Struggle for the Freedom of Theology," in Adolph von Harnack, *Adolph von Harnack: Liberal Theology at Its Height*, ed. Martin Rumscheidt (Minneapolis: Fortress Press, 1991), pp. 9–41; and Wilhelm Pauck, "The Significance of Adolph von Harnack among Church Historians," *Union Theological Seminary Quarterly*, special issue (January 1954): 13–24.

2. For Rauschenbusch's relationship with his father, see Susan Curtis, *A Consuming Faith: The Social Gospel and Modern American Culture* (Baltimore: Johns Hopkins University Press, 1991), pp. 101–113; for Rasuchenbusch's reading of Bellamy, see Dores Sharpe, *Walter Rauschenbusch* (New York: Macmillan, 1942), p. 83. Sharpe's biography remains one of the most informative about Rauschenbusch; see also Paul H. Minus, *Walter Rauschenbusch: American Reformer* (New York: Macmillan, 1980).

3. Walter Rauschenbusch, *Christianity and the Social Crisis* (1907; reprint, Louisville, Ky.: Westminster/John Knox Press, 1991), pp. xxxvi–xxxvii, 368–369.

4. See, for instance, the parable of the unjust steward in Luke 16:1–9 and Rauschenbusch's treatment of it in *Christianity and the Social Crisis*, pp. 77–79.

5. Rauschenbusch, *Christianity and the Social Crisis*, p. 25.

6. Ibid., p. 53.

7. Ibid., p. 59.

8. John 18:36.

9. Rauschenbusch, *Christianity and the Social Crisis*, p. 57. This sort of interpretation was common in the social gospel movement; see King, "Biblical Base of the Social Gospel," pp. 59–84. For Rauschenbusch's account of how this meaning of the kingdom of God came to him and the "new security" it gave his "social impulses," see: Sharpe, *Rauschenbusch*, p. 69. For background on the critical debate over the Gospel of John, see J. C. O'Neill, "The Study of the New Testament," in *Nineteenth Century Religious Thought in the West*, 3 vols., ed. Ninian Smart, John Clayton, Stephen Katz, and Patrick Sherry (Cambridge: Cambridge University Press, 1985), 3:153–164.

10. See King, "Biblical Base of the Social Gospel," pp. 59–84.

11. Rauschenbusch, *Christianity and the Social Crisis*, p. 66.

12. Walter Rauschenbusch, *A Theology for the Social Gospel* (New York: Macmillan, 1917), p. 240.

13. Ibid., pp. 263, 268–269. Rauschenbusch did note "the struggle in the garden." But this was in passing and served to emphasize that it was a struggle that Jesus met and overcame. Indeed, it all served to highlight "the dramatic expression of his personality, the consistent assertion of the purpose and law which had ruled and formed him" (ibid., p. 261).

14. For Niebuhr's remarks about being a teacher of "Christian social ethics" and a "circuit rider," see Reinhold Niebuhr, "Intellectual Autobiography," in *Reinhold Niebuhr: His Religious, Social and Political Thought*, ed. Charles W. Kegley (New York: Pilgrim Press, 1984), p. 3. This book also contains helpful essays on Niebuhr's life, religious thought, and politics. *Time* 51 (March 8, 1948): 76. On Niebuhr's stature, see William R. Hutchison, "Protestantism as Establishment," in *Between the Times: The Travail of the Protestant Establishment in America, 1900–1960*, ed. William R. Hutchison (Cambridge: Cambridge University Press, 1989), pp. 7–9.

15. On Gustav Niebuhr and von Harnack, see Richard Wightman Fox, *Reinhold Niebuhr: A Biography* (New York: Pantheon Books, 1985). This is the best biography of Reinhold Niebuhr.

16. Richard Wightman Fox, "The Niebuhr Brothers and the Liberal Protestant Heritage," in *Religion and Twentieth-Century American Intellectual Life*, ed. Michael J. Lacey (Cambridge: Cambridge University Press, 1989), pp. 94–115. Also of interest here on H. Richard Niebuhr is Hans W. Frei, "Niebuhr's Theological Background," in *Faith and Ethics: The Theology of H. Richard Niebuhr*, ed. Paul Ramsey (New York: Harper and Row, 1957). On the changing critical understanding of the phrase "kingdom of God," see King, "Biblical Base of the Social Gospel," pp. 69–70. For introductions to Troeltsch, see Welch, *Protestant Thought*, 2:266–301; S. Coakley, *Christ without Absolutes: A Study of the Christology of Ernst Troeltsch* (New York: Oxford University Press, 1988); J. P. Clayton, ed., *Ernst Troeltsch*

and the Future of Theology (Cambridge: Cambridge University Press, 1976); and Wilhelm Pauck, *Harnack and Troeltsch: Two Historical Theologians* (New York: Oxford University Press, 1968). For introductions to Barth, see Robert W. Jenson, "Karl Barth," in *The Modern Theologians: An Introduction to Christian Theology in the Twentieth Century*, 2 vols., ed. David F. Ford (London: Blackwell, 1989), 1:23–49; McGrath, *Iustitia Dei: From 1500 to the Present*, pp. 170–184; and Clifford Green, "Introduction: Karl Barth's Life and Theology," in Karl Barth, *Karl Barth: Theologian of Freedom*, ed. Clifford Green (Minneapolis: Fortress Press, 1991), pp. 11–35.

17. Reinhold Niebuhr, *Moral Man and Immoral Society* (New York: Charles Scribner's Sons, 1932), pp. xxi–xxiii, 272. See also Richard Fox, "Reinhold Niebuhr's Revolution," in *Wilson Quarterly* 8 (Autumn 1984): 90. See also Niebuhr's essay "The Kingdom Not of This World," in Reinhold Niebuhr, *Beyond Tragedy: Essays on the Christian Interpretation of History* (New York: Charles Scribner's Sons, 1937), pp. 271–286.

18. Niebuhr made the argument that an optimistic vision of history leads to moral complacency in *Does Civilization Need Religion?: A Study in the Social Resources and Limitations of Religion in Modern Life* (New York: Macmillan, 1928), p. 216. His idea that the righteous need to be reminded of their innevitable failings forms the center of his work, *An Interpretation of Christian Ethics* (New York: Harper and Bros., 1935), p. 138. Neibuhr also relied on Jesus' parable of the sheep and the goats to argue that Jesus' message was in some measure directed at informing the righteous that they still needed God's mercy; see Niebuhr, *The Nature and Destiny of Man*, 2 vols. (New York: Charles Scribner's Sons, 1944), 2:43, and *Justice and Mercy*, ed. Ursula Niebuhr (Louisville, Ky.: Westminster/John Knox Press, 1974), p. 93.

19. Niebuhr, *Nature and Destiny of Man*, 2:56.

20. Ibid., pp. 56, 67.

21. Ibid., p. 72. For Niebuhr's consideration of the difficult gospel passages in which Jesus appears insensitive, see Niebuhr, *Interpretation of Christian Ethics*, p. 31. On this page, Niebuhr acknowledged Karl Barth's more severe observation along these lines, but Niebuhr also backed away from this and insisted on retaining some social relevance for Jesus' teaching.

22. See Niebuhr, *Moral Man and Immoral Society*, pp. 81–82; *Nature and Destiny of Man*, 2:48; and *Justice and Mercy*, p. 91.

23. Reinhold Niebuhr, *Discerning the Signs of the Times* (New York: Charles Scribner's Sons, 1946), p. 177.

24. Ibid., pp. 145–147, 184.

25. J. Gresham Machen, *Christianity and Liberalism* (New York: Macmillan, 1922), p. 133. For Machen's links between liberalism and paganism, see ibid., pp. 2, 65, 78.

26. Walter Lippmann, *A Preface to Morals* (1929; reprint, New Brunswick, N.J.: Transaction Publications, 1989), pp. 32–33.

27. For Machen's political views, see Machen, *Christianity and Liberalism*, pp. 10–16, 174–180, and "Christianity in Conflict," *Contemporary American Theologians: Theological Autobiographies*, 2 vols., ed. Vergilius Ferm (New York: Round Table Press, 1932), 1: 271–273. The latter work is a helpful introduction to Machen's life and work as he saw them. For an informative biography of Machen by a colleague and friend, see Ned B. Stonehouse, *J. Gresham Machen: A Biographical Memoir* (Grand Rapids, Mich.: Eerdmans Publishing Co., 1954). Other examinations of Machen's life and thought include W. Stanford Reid, "J. Gresham Machen," in *Reformed Theology in America: A History of Its Modern Development*, ed. David F. Wells (Grand Rapids, Mich.: Eerdmans Publishing Co., 1985), pp. 102–108; George Marsden, *Understanding Fundamentalism and Evangelicalism* (Grand Rapids, Mich.: Eerdmans Publishing Co., 1991), pp. 182–201; and Bradley J. Longfeld, *The Presbyterian*

Controversy: Fundamentalists, Modernists, and Moderates (New York: Oxford University Press, 1991), pp. 28–53.

28. Machen, *Christianity and Liberalism*, pp. 15, 176, 180. On the tensions between the spiritual and political conceptions of the church in Southern Presbyterianism, see the example of Thornwell, chap. 6, n. 15.

29. Machen, "Christianity in Conflict," p. 254. For another expression by Machen of his debt to Princeton, and Hodge and Warfield in particular, see J. Gresham Machen, *The Christian View of Man* (New York: Macmillan, 1937), pp. v, 274.

30. Machen, *Christianity and Liberalism*, p. 95. This was a point that Machen made over and over again; see Machen, "Christianity in Conflict," p. 256; Machen, *The Origin of Paul's Religion* (New York: Macmillan, 1923), p. 158. He also made the same point about the liberal treatment of Mary; see Machen, *The Virgin Birth of Christ* (New York: Harper and Bros., 1930), p. 132.

31. Machen, *Christianity and Liberalism*, pp. 93–94.

32. Benjamin Breckinridge Warfield, "On the Emotional Life of Our Lord," in *Biblical and Theological Studies*, ed. Benjamin Breckinridge Warfield et al. (New York: Charles Scribner's Sons, 1922), pp. 35–90. For background on Warfield, see W. Andrew Hoffecker, "Benjamin B. Warfield," in Wells, *Reformed Theology*, pp. 60–88.

33. See Machen, *Christianity and Liberalism*, p. 65; J. Gresham Machen, *What Is Faith?* (New York: Macmillan, 1925), p. 65; J. Gresham Machen, "My Idea of God," in *My Idea of God: A Symposium of Faith*, ed. Joseph Fort Newton (Boston: Little Brown, 1926), p. 46. For Machen's simplification of Hodge's language about relationship to one about presences, see Machen, *Christianity and Liberalism*, p. 135.

34. Machen, *Christianity and Liberalism*, p. 131; see also p. 64.

35. Ibid., pp. 105, 134.

36. Ibid., p. 135.

37. Lippmann, *Preface to Morals*, pp. 28, 33. Indeed, Lippmann remarked on Machen's strong defense of the Bible but failed to note that Machen himself did not make use of the anthropomorphism that Lippmann recognized was so important for depicting God powerfully.

38. Machen, *Origin of Paul's Religion*, pp. 67–68; Machen, *Virgin Birth of Christ*, pp. 132–134. Machen's failure to develop his own views was noted in Everett F. Harrison, "The New Testament," in *Contemporary Evangelical Thought*, ed. Carl F. H. Henry (New York: Harper and Bros., 1957), p. 59.

39. Machen, "My Idea of God," pp. 45–46. The work that Machen had in mind here was Rudolph Otto, *The Idea of the Holy*, trans. John W. Harvey (1923; reprint, New York: Oxford University Press, 1972). On this point, see also J. Gresham Machen, "The Modern Use of the Bible," *Princeton Theological Review* 23 (January 1925): 66–81. This essay is reprinted in the helpful collection edited by Mark Noll, *The Princeton Defense of Plenary Inspiration* (New York: Garland Publishers, 1988), pp. 233–248.

40. Charles Hodge, "The Theology of the Intellect and That of the Feelings" (1850), in *Essays and Reviews* (New York: Robert Carter and Bros., 1857), p. 547. W. G. T. Shedd, "The True Tone in Preaching and the True Temper in Hearing," Princeton Review 35 (July 1863): 420, 439; Machen, *Christian View of Man*, pp. 24–28.

41. Machen, *Christianity and Liberalism*, pp. 13–15; Machen, "Christianity in Conflict," p. 271.

42. On the premillennialist theology of fundamentalism, see Ernest R. Sandeen, *The Roots of Fundamentalism: British and American Millenarianism, 1800–1930* (Chicago: University of Chicago Press, 1970); George M. Marsden, *Fundamentalism and American Culture: The Shaping of Twentieth-Century Evangelicalism, 1870–1925* (New York: Oxford University

Press, 1980), and Paul Boyer, *When Time Shall Be No More: Prophecy Belief in Modern American Culture* (Cambridge: Harvard University Press, 1992).

43. On creationism, see Ronald L. Numbers, *The Creationists: The Evolution of Scientific Creationism* (Berkeley: University of California Press, 1992); Marsden, *Understanding Fundamentalism and Evangelicalism*, pp. 122–181; George Marsden, "Evangelicals and the Scientific Culture: An Overview," in Lacey, *Religion and Twentieth-Century American Intellectual Life*, pp. 23–47. For a good sourcebook on the controversies over evolution in the 1920s, especially the famous Scopes trial, see Willard B. Gatewood, Jr., ed., *Controversy in the Twenties: Fundamentalism, Modernism, and Evolution* (Nashville, Tenn.: Vanderbilt University Press, 1969).

44. Machen, *What Is Faith?*, pp. 67, 73, and *Christianity and Liberalism*, p. 49.

Chapter Ten

1. Harvey Cox, *The Secular City*, 25th anniversary ed. (New York: Collier Books, 1990), p. 235. For criticism of Cox's interpretation of Exodus 3:14, see Steven S. Schwarzschild, "A Little Bit of Revolution?" in *The Secular City Debate*, ed. Daniel Callahan (New York: Macmillan, 1966), p. 150; for Cox's response to this criticism, see ibid., p. 184.

2. Cox, *Secular City*, p. 235.

3. Carl F. H. Henry, *God, Revelation, and Authority*, 6 vols. (Waco, Tex.: Word Books, 1983), 6:493; Harvey G. Cox, *On Not Leaving It to the Snake* (Toronto: Macmillan, 1964), p. 91. On the interpretation of Exodus 3:14, see Harold B. Kuhn, "God: His Names and Nature," in *Fundamentals of the Faith*, ed. Carl F. H. Henry (Grand Rapids, Mich.: Zondervan Publishers, 1968), p. 46; Brevard S. Childs, *Biblical Theology of the Old and New Testaments: Theological Reflections on the Christian Bible* (Minneapolis: Fortress Press, 1993), p. 355; and Karen Armstrong, *A History of God: The 4000-Year-Old Quest of Judaism, Christianity, and Islam* (New York: Ballantine Books, 1993), pp. 21–22. Like Cox, Armstrong interpreted God as saying, "I shall be that which I shall be." Like Cox also, she stressed God's "deliberate vagueness," though he "promised that he would participate in the history of his people," and this engendered "hope for the future." Like the early twentieth-century popular liberal minister Harry Emerson Fosdick, Armstrong also claimed that the deliberate vagueness of God was important for teaching the ancient Hebrews that they could not manipulate God as pagans tried to do with their idols; see Harry Emerson Fosdick, *A Guide to Understanding the Bible: The Development of Ideas within the Old and New Testaments* (New York: Harper and Bros., 1938), pp. 10, 248–249. On the liberal theological association between anthropomorphism and idol worship, see chapter 2. For literary uses of the interpretation of Exodus 3:14 along these lines, see Northrop Frye, *The Great Code: The Bible and Literature* (New York: Harcourt, Brace, Jovanovich, 1982), p. 17; for environmentalist uses, see Max Oelschlaeger, *Caring for Creation: An Ecumenical Approach to the Environmental Crisis* (New Haven: Yale University Press, 1994), p. 182. On what C. T. McIntire called "the renewal of the Christian view of history in the twentieth century, especially since 1939," see C. T. McIntire, *God, History, and Historians: An Anthology of Modern Chrisian Views of History* (New York: Oxford University Press, 1977).

4. R. W. Brown, "Christ Dying for the Sins of Men: The Foundation for the Christian Superstructure," *New Englander* 21 (July 1862): 491.

5. Carl F. H. Henry, "Christological Neglect by a Mission-Minded Church," in *Scripture, Tradition, and Interpretation*, ed. W. Ward Gasque and William Sanford LaSor (Grand Rapids, Mich.: Eerdmans Publishing Co., 1978), p. 226. For similar complaints by late twentieth-century conservatives, see David F. Wells, *No Place for Truth: Or Whatever Happened to*

Evangelical Theology? (Grand Rapids, Mich.: Eerdmans Publishing Co., 1993); and John R. W. Stott, *The Cross of Christ* (Downer's Grove, Ill.: InterVarsity University Press, 1986), p. 11. For background on Henry, see his autobiography: *Confessions of a Theologian: An Autobiography* (Waco, Tex.: Word Books, 1986). See also Henry's essay "American Evangelicals at a Turning Point," in *Theologians in Transition: The Christian Century*, "How My Mind Has Changed" Series, ed. James M. Wall (New York: Crossroad, 1981), pp. 41–52. For introductions to Henry's life and work, see John D. Woodbridge, "Carl F. H. Henry: Spokesperson for American Evangelicalism," in *God and Culture: Essays in Honor of Carl F. H. Henry*, ed. D. A. Carlson and John D. Woodbridge (Grand Rapids, Mich.: Eerdmans Publishing Co., 1993), pp. 378–393; and Ray S. Anderson, "Evangelical Theology," in *The Modern Theologians: An Introduction to Christian Theology in the Twentieth Century*, 2 vols., ed. David F. Ford (London: Blackwell, 1989), 2:141–145. For the larger political and social context in which Henry wrote, see Robert Booth Fowler, *A New Engagement: Evangelical Political Thought, 1966–1976* (Grand Rapids, Mich.: Erdmans Publishing Co., 1982), esp. chap. 5; George Marsden, *Reforming Fundamentalism: Fuller Seminary and the New Evangelicalism* (Grand Rapids, Mich.: Eerdmans Publishing Co., 1987); Mark Silk, "The Rise of the 'New Evangelicalism': Shock and Adjustment," in *Between the Times: The Travail of the Protestant Establishment in America, 1900–1960*, ed. William R. Hutchison (Cambridge: Cambridge University Press, 1989), pp. 278–300; Robert Wuthnow, *The Restructuring of American Religion* (Princeton: Princeton University Press, 1988); Randall Balmer, *Mine Eyes Have Seen the Glory: A Journey into the Evangelical Subculture* (New York: Oxford University Press, 1989); and James Davison Hunter, *American Evangelicalism: Conservative Religion and the Quandry of Modernity* (New Brunswick, N.J.: Rutgers University Press, 1983).

6. Carl F. H. Henry, *The Uneasy Conscience of Modern Fundamentalism* (1947), in *Two Reformers of Fundamentalism: Harold John Ockenga and Carl F. H. Henry*, ed. Joel A. Carpenter (New York: Garland Publishers, 1988), pp. 19, 84, 85.

7. Ibid., pp. 84–85. It is easy to confuse the terms "conservative," "evangelical," and "fundamentalist." As I use these terms, "conservative" comprehends "evangelical" but not "fundamentalist," which I define more narrowly as those theologians focusing on biblical prophecy, the second coming, and premillennialism. On the uses of these terms, see George M. Marsden, *Understanding Fundamentalism and Evangelicalism* (Grand Rapids, Mich.: Eerdmans Publishing Co., 1991), pp. 1–6.

8. Henry, "Christological Neglect," p. 223. Late twentieth-century conservatives relied not just on Machen but also on other precursors, such as the late nineteenth, early twentieth-century Princeton theologian, Benjamin Breckinridge Warfield; see Stott, *Cross of Christ*, pp. 73–74.

9. Henry, "Christological Neglect," p. 229.

10. Henry, *God, Revelation, and Authority*, 6:328–329.

11. Ibid., p. 349. See also the emphasis on God's holiness in Wells, *No Place for Truth*, pp. 299–300.

12. Henry, *God, Revelation, and Authority*, 6:332.

13. Ibid.

14. On the fundamentalist focus on Satan and the anti-Christ, see Paul Boyer, *When Time Shall Be No More: Prophecy Belief in Modern American Culture* (Cambridge, Mass.: Harvard University Press, 1992); and Robert Fuller, *Naming the Antichrist: The History of an American Obsession* (New York: Oxford University Press, 1995). For wider, modern cultural views of Satan, see chap. 6, n. 7.

15. Henry, "Christological Neglect," p. 226.

16. For reactions to *The Secular City*, see Callahan, *Secular City Debate*. The two key works here by Dietrich Bonhoeffer were his *Ethics* (New York: Macmillan, 1955) and *Let-*

ters and Papers from Prison (New York: Macmillan, 1962). Before Cox, John A. T. Robinson popularized some of Bonhoeffer's ideas in *Honest to God* (Philadelphia: Westminster Press, 1963). Also of importance here is Paul van Buren, *The Secular Meaning of the Gospel* (New York: Macmillan, 1963). See also R. Laurence Moore, "Secularization: Religion and the Social Sciences," in Hutchison, *Between the Times*, pp. 233–252.

17. David Little, "The Social Gospel Revisited," in Callahan, *Secular City Debate*, pp. 69–74; George D. Younger, "Does *The Secular City* Revisit the Social Gospel," in Callahan, *Secular City Debate*, pp. 77–80; for Cox's response to Little's observation, see ibid., pp. 87–88; Cox, *On Not Leaving It to the Snake*, p. 133. See also Cox's reference to the social gospel in *Secular City*, p. 96.

18. Cox, *Secular City*, pp. 38–42, 68, 72, 97, 187. Social gospel theologians believed that God was working through humanity for the kingdom of God and so wrote of God and people as "co-workers" in history. See Edward Scrivner Ames, "My Conception of God," in Newton, *My Idea of God*, p. 242.

19. Cox, *Secular City*, p. 133. On freeing people from their tribal and familial conceptions of God, see ibid., p. 239. Cox, citing Amos Wilder, used this point about moving beyond family ties to make sense of Jesus' remark that the dead should bury the dead; see ibid., p. 97. This was a remarkable twist on Munger's contention that Jesus expands human love from the family to humanity.

20. Ibid., pp. 70, 223.

21. Ibid., p. 133.

22. Ibid., p. 232.

23. "Is Effective Writing Necessarily 'Volcanic'?," *Presbyterian Quarterly Review* 3 (June 1855): 135–137, 147–148.

24. Donald Meyer, *The Protestant Search for Political Realism: 1919–1941*, 2d ed. (Middletown, Conn.: Wesleyan University Press, 1988), p. 117.

25. Walter Rauschenbusch, *Christianity and the Social Crisis* (1907; reprint, Louisville, Ky.: Westminster/John Knox Press, 1991), pp. 339, 362. On Norris, see Willard E. Martin, Jr., "Frank Norris's Reading at Harvard College," *American Literature* 7 (May 1935): 203–204; James D. Hart, introduction to Frank Norris, *A Novelist in the Making: A Collection of Student Themes and the Novels "Blix" and "Vandover and the Brute,"* ed. James D. Hart (Cambridge, Mass.: Harvard University Press, Belknap Press, 1970), pp. 1–54. For Eliot's remark, see T. S. Eliot, "Ezra Pound," in *Ezra Pound: A Collection of Essays*, ed. Peter Russell (New York: Peter Nevill, 1950), p. 25. Cook's remark is cited by Fred Matthews in "The New Psychology and American Drama," in *1915—The Cultural Moment: The New Politics, the New Woman, the New Psychology, the New Art, and the New Theatre in America*, ed. Adele Heller and Lois Rudnick (New Brunswick, N.J.: Rutgers University Press, 1991), p. 149. For Krutch's remark, see Joseph Wood Krutch, *The Modern Temper* (New York: Harcourt, Brace and Co., 1929), p. 26.

26. Ned B. Stonehouse, *J. Gresham Machen: A Biographical Memoir* (Grand Rapids, Mich.: Eerdmans Publishing Co., 1954), pp. 198, 293–295.

27. Edmund Wilson, "Night Thoughts in Paris," *New Republic* 30 (March 15, 1922): 76. On American writers in Paris, see Malcolm Cowley, *Exiles Return: A Literary Odyssey of the 1920s* (1951; reprint, New York: Penguin, 1979).

28. J. Gresham Machen, *Christianity and Liberalism* (New York: Macmillan, 1922), p. 10.

29. R. P. Blackmur, *Anni Mirabiles, 1921–1925: Reason in the Madness of Letters* (Washington, D.C.: Library of Congress, 1956).

30. Francis A. Schaeffer, *How Should We Then Live?: The Rise and Decline of Western Thought and Culture* (Old Tappan, N.J.: Fleming H. Revell, 1976). On Schaeffer, see Fowler,

New Engagement, chap. 4; and Garry Wills, *Under God: Religion and American Politics* (New York: Simon and Schuster, 1990), chap. 28.

31. Reinhold Niebuhr, *The Nature and Destiny of Man*, 2 vols. (New York: Charles Scribner's Sons, 1944), 1:29–53, 81–92, 105, 121. A decade earlier, Niebuhr had opposed literature to psychiatry but had trouble with this, for it made literature seem "sentimental." See Reinhold Niebuhr, "Religion and Poetry" (1930), in *Young Reinhold Niebuhr*, ed. William G. Chrystal (New York: Pilgrim Press, 1977), pp. 220–226.

32. Cox, *Secular City*, p. 68.

33. Ibid., pp. 61, 221. Camus has been used by many theologians, but few have found him as "buoyant" as Cox. For two of Cox's contemporaries who saw a bleaker but still interesting Camus, see Richard L. Rubenstein, "Cox's Vision of the Secular City," in Callahan, *Secular City Debate*, pp. 140–141; and Nathan A. Scott, Jr., *The Broken Center: Studies in the Theological Horizon of Modern Literature* (New Haven: Yale University Press, 1966), pp. 150–152.

34. Cox, *Secular City*, p. 64.

35. Norman Mailer, "Superman Comes to the Supermarket" (1960), in *The Presidential Papers* (New York: G. P. Putnam's Sons, 1963).

36. Cox, *Secular City*, pp. 67–68.

37. For instance, while applauding the drama of Eugene O'Neill, Cox could dismiss Tennessee Williams's *Cat on a Hot Tin Roof* as shallow in its sexual anguish. "We cannot emerge cleansed and quickened from the ritual of drama if we have gone no deeper than between the sheets of the post-Victorian couch," Cox declared. By "deeper," Cox meant getting to "the universal dimension in man." It is easy to feel, given what we have seen, that what Cox had in mind here was the neoclassical and sentimental in human beings—and God. Like Munger and Wilder, Cox thought that modern literature, when it was profound, was inevitably a reflection on Christianity. In Cox's view, the "puzzled existence" and "irony" of modern humanity spoke to the absence of Christianity—"the pathos of the post-Christian plot unfolds itself on a stage constructed with another Drama in mind." But this was the problem: the life and death of Christ had lost much of its drama in the hands of theologians. ("Theological Reflections on the Cinema," in *The New Orpheus: Essays Towards a Christian Poetics*, ed. Nathan A. Scott, Jr. [New York: Sheen and Ward, 1964], pp. 351–352, 354–355). In his 1969 work, *The Feast of Fools*, Cox tried to come to grips with some aspects of cosmopolitan culture at the time, especially the counterculture. This led him to consider a "profound truth about man—his capacity to hold two or more seemingly contradictory ideas or emotions at once." The problem today, Cox continued, was "how to reconcile a high degree of critical self-consciousness with a burning desire for experience, which is not spoiled by too much self-analysis" (*The Feast of Fools: A Theological Essay on Festivity and Fantasy* [Cambridge, Mass.: Harvard University Press, 1969], pp. 143–144). Cox's formulation, however, did not really deal with emotional ambivalence on a romantic level. As Cox laid out the problem, it was more of an intellectual and emotional split, similar to the division that Park in 1850 drew between the theology of the intellect nd that of the feelings. In *The Feast of Fools*, Cox put less emphasis on the "clearheadedness" of Jesus than Cox had ascribed to him in *The Secular City*. But this was more a matter of Jesus' style of conveying his message, for in considering "Christ the harlequin," what was important for Cox was that the message be conveyed through winsome wit, "the combination of merriment and seriousness." In this respect, Cox's Christ resembled the shrewd, comic characters, often African American servants, in nineteenth-century sentimental novels, such as Candace in Stowe's *The Minister's Wooing*. These characters were depicted as being less inhibited in their religious feelings than their more educated employers, who were given to fruitless theological analysis.

38. For a positive estimation of anthropomorphism, see Sallie McFague, *Models of God: Theology for an Ecological, Nuclear Age* (Philadelphia: Fortress Press, 1988). McFague's attitude here seems to be informed by her appreciation of what she called the "reckless flamboyance" of the biblical characterization of God (Sallie McFague, *The Body of God: An Ecological Theology* [Minneapolis: Augsburg Fortress Press, 1993], p. 131). Not all feminist theologians, however, have supported anthropomorphism; see Mary Daly, *Beyond God the Father: Towards a Philosophy of Woman's Liberation* (1973; reprint, Boston: Beacon Press, 1985), pp. 33–34.

39. Charlotte Perkins Gilman, *Herland* (1915; reprint, New York: Pantheon Books, 1979), pp. 110–117. On Gilman's reading of Bellamy and her relation to the social gospel movement and religious views more generally, see Mary A. Hill, *Charlotte Perkins Gilman: The Making of a Radical Feminist, 1860–1896* (Philadelphia: Temple University Press, 1980), pp. 168–174, 230, 262–264.

40. For Daly's consideration of the juristic God, see *Beyond God the Father*, p. 16. To back up her assertion about the juristic God being two incompatible characterizations of God, Daly relied on Arnold Toynbee, *Christianity among the Religions of the World* (New York: Charles Scribner's Sons, 1957), p. 19. This charge, deriving from old theological polemics, had become common in twentieth-century historical writing; see, for instance, Arthur O. Lovejoy, *The Great Chain of Being: A Study of the History of an Idea* (1936; reprint, New York: Harper and Row, Harper Torchbooks, 1967), p. 43. Late twentieth-century feminist notions of patriarchy were much informed by the Cold War model of totalitarianism; for examples of Daly's use of it, see *Beyond God the Father*, pp. 103–107. For her psychological formulations of oppression and health, see ibid., pp. 48, 52. There is a similar play of opposites throughout Daly's work. Consider her treatment of the doctrine of the fall. In the juristic tradition, this was a complex doctrine; if it was a great evil, the fall in a larger context also provided the opportunity for God to bring good out of evil, which led to the redemption of humans. But again, for purposes of easy contrast, Daly stripped the doctrine of its complexity and so stripped her own interpretation of complexity. The fall, she declared, "is divested of its negativity and becomes positive and healing" (ibid., p. 67). See also Sallie McFague, who wrote, "The monarchical model [of God] implies that the crucial divine activity is the redemption of rebellious humanity, which is loved in spite of its unloveableness, whereas our models [of God] suggest that the crucial divine activity is the creation of the world, which is loved passionately to the limit of God's very being" (*Models of God*, p. 93). In this statement, the notion that the "monarchical God" could be less than entirely loving toward humans is dismissed and contrasted with an entirely loving God. This leaves no room for emotional complexity. Daly's background, it should be noted, is in Roman Catholicism, which raises the question of how much Daly inherited her polemic and her assumptions about God's character from Roman Catholic theology; this, in turn, raises the important question for future study of whether Roman Catholic theology was also informed by neoclassical and sentimental styles of depicting God. It should also be noted, however, that Daly, like many liberal theologians in the twentieth century, viewed herself as radically breaking away from common theological characterizations of God. For her view of herself, see Mary Daly, "Sin Big," *New Yorker* 72 (February 26 and March 4, 1996): 76–84.

41. McFague, *Models of God*, p. 113.

42. For Stowe's depiction of Eliza, see Harriet Beecher Stowe, *Uncle Tom's Cabin, or Life among the Lowly* (1852; reprint, New York: Penguin, 1987), chaps. 7–8, "The Mother's Struggle" and "Eliza's Escape."

43. See Adrienne Rich, *Of Woman Born: Motherhood as Experience and Institution*, 10th anniversary ed. (New York: W. W. Norton and Co., 1986), esp. chaps. 1 and 10, "Anger and Tenderness" and "Violence: The Heart of Maternal Darkness."

44. Note the neoclassical assumptions in the following passage. "Bush has a style problem," observed Elizabeth Drew during the presidential campaign in 1988. "When he tries to
show that he is tough . . . he often gets it wrong, and too often the dignity goes. . . . He looks
frantic. . . . What Bush doesn't seem to understand, or perhaps understands but hasn't assimilated, is that in most cases tough equals calm: Clint Eastwood, Gary Cooper, Ronald
Reagan" ("Letter from Washington," *New Yorker* 64 [July 4, 1988]: 76). American movie
heroes often contain neoclassical and sentimental traits, and as Drew noted, these are often
reflected in politics. For a celebration of Reagan's traits in this regard, see Peggy Noonan,
What I Saw at the Revolution: A Political Life of the Reagan Era (New York: Ballantine Books,
1990), esp. chap. 8, "Who Was That Masked Man?" Certainly the strong response to the
possible presidential candidacy of Colin Powell in late 1995 was partly due to the fact that he
seemed to embody traditional American political neoclassical and sentimental traits. On the
question of character, Bill Clinton, by contrast, often provokes "ambivalence," even among
his supporters, as his best biographer to date admits; see David Maranis, *First in His Class:
A Biography of Bill Clinton* (New York: Simon and Schuster, 1995). If politically troublesome for Clinton, this ambivalence about his character makes him, like Kennedy and Nixon,
ripe for literary treatment.

45. As we have seen, Donald Meyer concluded that the social gospel had relatively little
political impact, but he did rate Reinhold Niebuhr as an effective critic of the social gospel;
see Meyer, *Protestant Search for Political Realism*. Niebuhr, of course, was celebrated in
cosmopolitan circles; for a consideration of his impact, see Richard Wightman Fox, "Reinhold
Niebuhr's 'Revolution,'" *Wilson Quarterly* 8 (Autumn 1984): 82–93. For a fuller treatment,
see Fox's *Reinhold Niebuhr: A Biography* (New York: Pantheon Books, 1955). For Cox's
assessment of the impact of *The Secular City*, see below, n. 56. The role of religion in the
women's rights movement seems to have been significant in the nineteenth century, though
more research needs to be done here; see, for instance, Maureen Fitzgerald, foreword to Elizabeth Cady Stanton, *The Woman's Bible* (1895; reprint, Boston: Northeastern University Press,
1993), vii–xxxiv; Sally Roesch Wagner, introduction to Matilda Joslyn Gage, *Woman, Church,
and State* (1893; reprint, Watertown, Mass.: Persephone Press, 1980), pp. xv–xxxix; Ann
Braude, *Radical Spirits: Spiritualism and Women's Rights in Nineteenth-Century America*
(Boston: Beacon Press, 1989); and Elizabeth B. Clark, "Religion, Rights, and Difference in
the Early Woman's Rights Movement," *Wisconsin Women's Law Journal* 3 (September, 1987):
29–58. Historical considerations of the role of religion and feminist theology in late twentieth-
century feminism remain to be explored. One survey of some of the most radical developments in late twentieth-century feminism does not give much attention to feminist theology;
see Alice Echols, *Daring to Be Bad: Radical Feminism in America, 1967–1975* (Minneapolis:
University of Minnesota Press, 1989).

46. On the growing political mobilization of fundamentalists and conservatives, see Leo
P. Ribuffo, "God and Contemporary Politics," *Journal of American History* 79 (March 1993):
1515–1533; Robert Wuthnow, *The Struggle for America's Soul: Evangelicals, Liberals, and
Secularism* (Grand Rapids, Mich.: Eerdmans Publishing Co., 1989); Hunter, *American Evan-
gelicalism*; James Davison Hunter, *Culture Wars: The Struggle to Define America* (New York:
Basic Books, 1991); Fowler, *A New Engagement*; Gary Wills, *Under God*; and Stephen L.
Carter, *The Culture of Disbelief: How American Law and Politics Trivialize Devotion* (New
York: Doubleday, 1993). The question I am raising here is not whether religious conservatives should be involved in politics; that, of course, is their right, and it is to be expected that
their beliefs will inform their politics. Rather, the question is whether they should make their
theology distinctly political. Evidence does suggest that at the end of the twentieth century
conservative churches have been more successful in attracting and keeping members than
liberal churches. This may have more to do with the appeal of conservative theological doc-

trines—or at least otherwordly doctrines—and conservative morality than with a distinctively conservative political program. See Roger Finke and Rodney Stark, *The Churching of America, 1776–1990: Winners and Losers in Our Religious Economy* (New Brunswick, N.J.: Rutgers University Press, 1992). In 1973, Robert Wuthnow found that no correlation could be drawn between strong religious participation and commitment to conservative politics ("Religious Commitment and Conservativism: In Search of an Elusive Relationship," in *Religion in Sociological Perspective*, ed. Charles Y. Glock (Belmont, Calif.: Wadsworth Publishing Co., 1973).

47. Walter Rauschenbusch, *A Theology for the Social Gospel* (New York: Macmillan, 1917), pp. 263, 269. In *Moral Man and Immoral Society* (New York: Charles Scribner's Sons, 1932), Niebuhr, relying on common racialist views, suggested that Asians and Africans might make better candidates for nonviolent protest than Westerners: "The Occident may be incapable of this kind of non-violent social conflict, because the white man is a fiercer beast of prey than the oriental" (p. 255). In later works, Niebuhr remained cautious about how much non-violence could achieve; see Niebuhr, *An Interpretation of Christian Ethics* (New York: Harper and Bros., 1935), p. 28, and *Nature and Destiny of Man*, 2:72.

48. Martin Luther King, Jr., *The Strength to Love*, in *A Testament of Hope: The Essential Writings of Martin Luther King, Jr.*, ed. James M. Washington (New York: HarperCollins, 1991), pp. 508–509. On King's religious background and stature, see Ralph E. Luker, *The Social Gospel in Black and White: American Racial Reform, 1885–1912* (Chapel Hill: University of North Carolina Press, 1991), chap. 11; James H. Cone, *Martin and Malcolm: A Dream or a Nightmare* (Maryknoll, N.Y.: Orbis Books, 1991); Christopher Lasch, *The True and Only Heaven: Progress and Its Critics* (New York: W. W. Norton and Co., 1991), pp. 369–407; John J. Ansbro, *Martin Luther King, Jr.: The Making of a Mind* (Maryknoll, N.Y.: Orbis Books, 1982); Frederick L. Downing, *To See the Promised Land: The Faith Pilgrimage of Martin Luther King, Jr.* (Macon, Ga.: Mercer University Press, 1988); and Adam Fairclough, *To Redeem the Soul of America: The Southern Christian Leadership Conference and Martin Luther King, Jr.* (Athens: University of Georgia Press, 1987). Studies that focus more on the political aspects of King and the civil rights movement include Harvard Sitkoff, *The Struggle for Black Equality, 1954–1992*, rev. ed. (New York: Hill and Wang, 1993); Taylor Branch, *Parting the Waters: America in the King Years, 1954–1963* (New York: Simon and Schuster, 1988); and David J. Garrow, *Bearing the Cross: Martin Luther King, Jr., and the Southern Christian Leadership Conference* (New York: Morrow, 1986). For considerations of King's significance in American history, see "A Round Table on Martin Luther King, Jr.," *Journal of American History* 74 (September 1987): 436–481.

49. Rauschenbusch, *Theology and the Social Gospel*, p. 269; Niebuhr, *Nature and Destiny of Man*, 2:72. The importance that King attached to the self-presentation of the nonviolent marchers, and King's effort not to blame individuals for racism, can be seen in Martin Luther King, Jr., *Why We Can't Wait* (1963; reprint, New York: Penguin, 1986), pp. 30, 38, 63. King's great political stature is evident in the fact that he is the only twentieth-century American whose birthday was made into a federal holiday, putting him in the ranks of George Washington and Abraham Lincoln. Some historians have worried that this celebration of King could flatten his image. "He must not be transformed into a simplistic image designed to offend no one—a black counterpart to the static, heroic myths that have embalmed George Washington as the Father of his country and Abraham Lincoln as the Great Emancipator," wrote Clayborne Carson in "Martin Luther King, Jr.: Charismatic Leadership in a Mass Struggle," *Journal of American History* 74 (September 1987): 448. Carson is certainly right that it is the duty of the historian to explore the complexity of historical figures, whether King, Lincoln, or Washington. But part of this exploration must include the point that King is not simply the victim of this image. He crafted his persona in his writings and actions according to liberal theological and political notions of character. Likewise, George Washington fash-

ioned his image according to neoclassical notions of character in classical republicanism, such as the legend of Cincinnatus. This, of course, need not be a bad thing; King and Washington recognized the importance of their images for the success of their agendas. For Washington on this point, see Gordon S. Wood, *The Radicalism of the American Revolution* (New York: Random House, Vintage Books, 1993), pp. 198, 205–208; and Paul K. Longmore, *The Invention of George Washington* (Berkeley: University of California Press, 1988).

50. King, *Why We Can't Wait*, p. 89.

51. Walter Rauschenbusch, *Christianity and the Social Crisis* (1907; reprint, Louisville, Ky.: Westminster/John Knox Press, 1991), p. 340; Niebuhr, *Moral Man and Immoral Society*, p. 81.

52. See Finke and Stark, *Churching of America, 1776–1990*. For more focused studies on the "mainline" denominations in the late twentieth century, see Wade Clark Roof and William McKinney, *American Mainline Religion: Its Changing Shape and Future* (New Brunswick, N.J.: Rutgers University Press, 1987); and Dean R. Hoge, Benton Johnson, and Donald A. Luidens, *Vanishing Boundaries: The Religion of Mainline Protestant Baby Boomers* (Louisville, Ky.: Westminster/John Knox Press, 1994). The latter work calls for an approach opposite to mine; Hoge, Johnson, and Luidens conclude that in order to draw "Protestant baby boomers" back to the mainline churches, ministers should emphasize the church's "moral authority," not its "doctrinal authority." The authors came to this conclusion, it seems, because their surveys suggested that the moral views supported by mainline churches were mostly uncontroversial, whereas doctrinal issues were. The analysis of Finke and Starke, however, suggests that controversial religious views may attract and sustain church membership. Hoge, Johnson and Luidens, on the other hand, seem to support theological positions because they echo widely held moral and political views. For instance, "The mainline churches may find a new voice of authority among baby boomers," they write, by developing a "theology centering on ecological responsibility" (ibid., p. 209). This, however, runs the risk of making blandness the basis of theological appeal—who could be opposed to "ecological responsibility"? Attention to details, also, is apt to puncture the vague formulations around which there seems to be a moral consensus. This is evident in the work of Hoge, Johnson, and Luidens when they declare that Archbishop Desmond Tutu and ex-President Jimmy Carter have "charismatic" moral authority; "anyone observing them or listening to them feels their moral power"(ibid., p. 210) The question of Archbishop Tutu aside, certainly many Americans—even many politically liberal Americans—would question if not the sincerity, then the charisma and sometimes the moral acuity of Carter.

53. Calvin, of course, and the Puritans believed that the governance of society should be a significant concern of theologians. How American conservative theologians moved away from this position and focused primarily on salvation, without ignoring social concerns, is a subject that needs more research. One place to begin is Fred Hood's study, *Reformed America: The Middle and Southern States, 1783–1837* (University: University of Alabama Press, 1980).

54. Henry, *Uneasy Conscience*, p. 85; Ralph Reed, *Active Faith: How Christians Are Changing the Soul of American Politics* (New York: Free Press, 1996), pp. 40–51, 56–65, 255–256. For King's ten-point pledge, see King, *Why We Can't Wait*, pp. 63–64. Reed presented a truncated and edited copy of King's pledge at the end of *Active Faith*, pp. 280–281. Reed's reading of King's pledge was reported by Christopher Hitchens in "Minority Report," *Nation* 26 (October 8, 1995): 375.

55. Rauschenbusch, *Christianity and the Social Crisis*, p. 369; "Whatever Happened to Theology?," *Christianity and Crisis* 35 (May 12, 1975): 106–120. On this point, it is interesting to contrast the titles of two works by McFague: her 1987 study, *Models of God: Theology for an Ecological, Nuclear Age*, and her 1993 work, *The Body of God: An Ecological Theology*. During the intervening six years, the Cold War ended, perhaps accounting for the

disappearance of the word "nuclear" from the later work's title, a point McFague suggests in the opening of her later book: "Earlier this century we faced the possibility of nuclear extinction and now, ecological deterioration" (*The Body of God: An Ecological Theology* [Minneapolis: Fortress Press, 1993], p. 1). The question could be raised, why, if theology contributed so little in the intervening six years to the diminishment of the nuclear threat, should people concerned about environmental pollution think that theology can substantially contribute here? This, of course, is not to say that nuclear and ecological concerns are not important. To the contrary, it is because they are so important that anyone who really wants to address them should do so in ways that are actually effective. It is hard to see how theology can be a substantial help here, either in terms of the scientific aspects or in terms of the political aspects of these problems.

56. In a 1995 introductory essay to *The Secular City*, Cox defended his vision. He acknowledged that since 1965, "instead of contributing to the liberative process, many cities have become sprawling concentrations of human misery, wracked with racial, religious and class animosity." Given this, "one is sometimes tempted to give up on the city." But Cox made the indisputable point that this would be a mistake. One of the reasons he had written his book in 1965 was "to challenge the anti-urban bias that infects American religion." The implication was that this was more necessary in 1995 than it had been in 1965 because cities had become so much worse. This associated the misfortunes of the cities with "bias" against them and replaced his 1965 historical and sociological argument for the liberating power of the cities with the indisputable point that the problems of the cities should not be ignored. In a larger sense, Cox thought his work was a success in terms of future developments—if not in America, then around the world. He suggested that *The Secular City* played a part in the emergence of Latin American liberation theology and the overthrow of Soviet communism in Eastern Europe (given that, according to Cox, some Eastern European theologians who had protested Soviet rule had been influenced by Latin American liberation theology, which supposedly had been influenced by Cox). *The Secular City*, according to Cox, was also important for future trends in America. For instance, because he had criticized *Playboy* magazine in *The Secular City*, he thought of himself as a "protofeminist. Not on par with current feminist cultural criticism, but not too bad for twenty-five years ago, and for a man." Also, according to Cox, "*The Secular City* may well have marked the end of the unchallenged reign of clerical and academic elitism in theology" See Harvey Cox, "The Secular City: Twenty-Five Years Later," in *Secular City*, pp. xv–xxii. For Cox's most recent views of the future of religion, see his *Fire from Heaven: The Rise of Pentecostal Spirituality and the Reshaping of Religion in the Twenty-first Century* (Reading, Mass.: Addison-Wesley, 1995). The future of liberal theology, however, as Cox sees it, resembles the past. "The public role of religion," Cox wrote in 1996, "will require that the connections between philosophy, theology, ethics and politics—once so precious to liberals—be reclaimed." This appeared in an article that began with Cox recalling being introduced as a young man to the theology of Reinhold Niebuhr by a minister who had worked with Rauschenbusch. See Harvey Cox, "Rethinking the Transcendent," *Nation* 262 (January 1, 1996): 20.

57. In *Moral Man and Immoral Society*, Reinhold Niebuhr wrote about the need for "illusions" to inspire people, but there is no indication that Niebuhr thought his pronouncements on contemporary politics or his vast generalizations about human history were simply inspiring "illusions." See Niebuhr, *Moral Man and Immoral Society*, p. 277.

58. Rauschenbusch, *Christianity and the Social Crisis*, pp. 339–401; Niebuhr, *Moral Man and Immoral Society*, pp. 81, 276. In his essay on the twenty-fifth anniversary of *The Secular City*, Cox acknowledged that "the perspective from which I had written *The Secular City* was that of a relatively privileged urbanite." He also admitted that he had largely ignored African Americans in the city. But in his own defense, he noted that he had "started a friend-

ship" with Martin Luther King, Jr., and had participated in the civil rights movement, was "jailed briefly" because of this, and lived with his family for some time in "Roxbury, the predominantly African American section of Boston." Also, as we have noted, Cox believed that "the next logical step after *The Secular City* was liberation theology." See Cox, "*The Secular City*: Twenty-five Years Later," pp. xv, xvii–xviii. On Cox's reflections about "a theology for the elite," see his essay "Theology: What Is It? Who Does It? How Is It Done?," in Wall, *Theologians in Transition*, pp. 151–160. For considerations of these issues, see also William McGuire King, "The Reform Establishment and the Ambiguities of Influence," in Hutchison, *Between the Times*, pp. 122–140; and David W. Wills, "An Enduring Distance: Black Americans and the Establishment," in ibid., pp. 168–192.

Chapter Eleven

1. William James, for one, found that the Darwinian view of nature was largely incompatible with his notions of God's character; see James, "Is Life Worth Living" (1896), in *The Will to Believe and Other Essays in Popular Philosophy and Human Immortality* (New York: Dover Publications, 1956), pp. 41–42. James, of course, was not a theologian, but his assumptions about God's character owed a great deal to nineteenth-century liberal theology, and he saluted Unitarians, in particular, for their "departure from our orthodox ancestral Calvinism [with its] God who gives so little scope to love" (see James, "Reflex Action and Theism" [1881] in ibid., pp. 126, 133. Work on James is immense; good places to begin to consider the relationship between James's religious and scientific views are Gerald E. Myers, *William James: His Life and Thought* (New Haven: Yale University Press, 1986), chap. 14; and Paul Jerome Croce, *Science and Religion in the Era of William James*, vol. 1, *Eclipse of Certainty, 1820–1880* (Chapel Hill: University of North Carolina Press, 1995). I have considered James's religious views about Darwinian nature in a paper entitled "William James on Animal Suffering and God," presented at the conference of the American Academy of Religion, November 1996. James R. Moore suggested that initially some Calvinists, such as George Frederick Wright, were better able than liberals to accept the harshness of Darwinian nature. Moore attributed this to Calvinist views of providence. Another factor may have been the complexity of God's character in Calvinism. George Frederick Wright, for instance, in trying to make sense of the carnage of Darwinian evolution, wrote, "The universe is a compromise in which subordinate ends are but imperfectly realized. Justice and mercy are not the only principles which coalesce with difficulty." This being said, however, Wright's major object of attack seems to have been sentimental characterizations of God, and his own depiction of God seems to have been more neoclassical than romantic; see George Frederick Wright, *Studies in Science and Religion* (Andover, Mass.: W. F. Draper, 1882), p. 189. On Wright, see James R. Moore, *The Post-Darwinian Controversies* (Cambridge: Cambridge University Press, 1979), pp. 334–335; and Ronald L. Numbers, *The Creationists: The Evolution of Scientific Creationism* (Berkeley: University of California Press, 1993), chap. 2.

2. "Narrative theology" is a term that is used to group together a number of theological strategies in the late twentieth century. To one extent or another, all of these strategies use theories of literature, literary genres, and especially narrative to examine a range of fields, from the Bible and imaginative fiction to epistemology, ethics, personal identity, the traditions of religious communities, and even the nature of human experience. For an introduction to this diverse theological approach, see Stanley Hauerwas and L. Gregory Jones, *Why Narrative?: Readings in Narrative Theology* (Grand Rapids, Mich.: Eerdmans Publishing Co.,

1989). An important American work that preceded the emergence of narrative theology but has been taken as a foundation text for this approach is H. Richard Niebuhr's *The Meaning of Revelation* (New York: Macmillan, 1941), esp. chap. 2, "The Story of Our Lives." Chapter 4, "The Deity of God," also suggests some of the limitations of this approach if God is mainly conceived of as the unifier of narrative, whether in life or in texts. For instance, H. Richard Niebuhr, while claiming that God surprises all human expectations about goodness and unity, also implies that in the Gospels God ultimately makes the twists and turns of life coherent in ways not expected. A risk in narrative theology is that ultimate, if unexpected, coherence will be taken as the measure of narrative strength or fulfillment, and quirks and tensions in characterization will receive little elaboration beyond the effort to make the point that God's ways are not those of human beings. There is also the risk that the examination of literary character in narrative theology will follow mainly in the liberal modernist tradition of seeking to confirm a broad humanitarian ethic in literature and claim it for Christianity. But as Stanley Hauerwas and L. Gregory Jones warn readers in the introduction to *Why Narrative?*, "While Niebuhr's essay is important for understanding some of the origins of the rediscovery of narrative, it should not be assumed that his proposals establish the parameters of debate" (p. 6). For a recent and provocative work that, among other things, complains that God has become "boring" in American Christianity, see Stanley Hauerwas, *Dispatches from the Front: Theological Engagements with the Secular* (Durham, N.C.: Duke University Press, 1994).

3. Frank Kermode, "World of Our Father," *New Republic* 212 (June 26, 1995): 29; John Barton, "A God's Life," *New York Review of Books* 42, no. 19 (November 30, 1995): 9.

4. Jack Miles, *God: A Biography* (New York: Alfred A. Knopf, 1995), p. 21.

5. Miles himself illustrates a similar point about what can happen when the biblical God is broken up into his diverse historical antecedents. "As each of the several gods mentioned is reduced to a signature trait or two, the narrative acquires, notwithstanding the turbulence of the action, a certain underlying calm. . . . Diffuse anxiety, by contrast, is more characteristic of [the composite characterization of God]. . . . Clarity disappears beneath the welter of personalities and functions that are gathered into him" (ibid., p. 401). This resembles the difference in characterization between neoclassicism and romanticism. In the former, "one signature trait" is emphasized and the goal for theologians is to assign to God "a certain underlying calm." Romantic characterization, by contrast, mixes this up and produces emotional complexity and intense activity. In order for theologians to come up with these characterizations, of course, more was involved than just seeing the biblical God whole or in parts; but still we get a sense of how differences between these two modes of interpretation help to set up a neoclassical or a romantic characterization of God.

6. For instance, in order to distinguish Greek tragedy from *Hamlet*, Miles stressed the "conflict within Hamlet's own character" (ibid., 398). For Miles's suggestion that the biblical God may have been the model for the Elizabethan Hamlet, see ibid., p. 407. Miles's reading of God's character is also similar in some respects to Harold Bloom's. Bloom is a critic who has focused on romantic ambivalence throughout his career and has applied this to one of the characterizations of God in the Hebrew scriptures; see Harold Bloom, *The Book of J* (New York: Grove Weidenfeld, 1990).

7. This, of course, also raises theological questions about the divine inspiration of the Bible. This is not an issue discussed in this book primarily for reasons of space. But it is a very important topic. It was a key point of debate between liberal and conservative Protestants in the nineteenth and twentieth centuries. It also is a topic that bears on the characterization of God through the third person of the Trinity, the Holy Ghost, which Protestants have seen as the major agent for inspiration. In this, however, Protestants have usually not ascribed to the Holy Ghost the array of personal character traits that they have ascribed to God the Father and Christ.

8. Barton, "God's Life," p. 7.

9. Miles, *God*, p. 99. Lawrence is cited by Walter Jackson Bate to contrast a modernist from a neoclassical view of character; see Walter Jackson Bate, *From Classic to Romantic: Premises of Taste in Eighteenth-Century England* (1946; reprint, New York: Harper and Row, 1961), p. 12.

10. For Miles's view of God's ambivalence about sexuality, see Miles, *God*, pp. 42, 52, 57, 67. Miles made the point that God's restrictions on sexuality are more a matter of "power" than "morality"—and power for Miles's God is tied up with his identity and efforts at self-understanding; see ibid., p. 57.

11. On the apparent silence of God at the end of the Hebrew scriptures, Miles suggested a number of interpretations ranging from the tragic to the comic and the pious. The potential for tragedy was that in seeing himself reflected in Job, God ended his quest, in a sense, and perhaps even lost interest in himself. But Miles also suggested a certain comic resolution in God's encounter with a secular, or "feminine," element, characterized, according to Miles, in The Song of Songs as "playfulness, physical exuberance, and joy." This "diffuses an otherwise fatal intensity" in God. In another respect, God, as a distinct character, seems to be succeeded by religious piety on the part of humans, so that he becomes "a motivating force rather than an actor." For Miles's summary of these views, see ibid., pp. 402–408. At the beginning of his work, Miles also suggested that God's biography followed a pattern in human biographies. "Not always, but often, that stage of interior division and quest ends in a life's work that permits the double or multiple personalities coexisting in a given immature character to find simultaneous expression and so to fuse in a mature and dynamic identity" (ibid., p. 23).

12. Matthew Arnold, *Literature and Dogma: An Essay towards a Better Apprehension of the Bible* (1873; reprint, New York: Macmillan, 1908), p. 53.

Abbott, Lyman, 143, 225n.26
Addison, Joseph, 20–21, 43, 85
Aestheticism, 9, 96, 139, 144–146, 149–150
Alcott, Louisa May, 229n.12
Alexander, Archibald, 49, 52, 173
American renaissance, 7, 43, 82, 151, 228nn.4, 5
Angels, 39–40, 109–110, 219n.2
Annunciation to Mary, 65, 72, 113, 123, 125–128
Anselm, St. (archbishop of Canterbury), 26
Anthropomorphism
    and conservative neoclassical theism, 34–35, 54, 80, 176–177, 184, 227n.2
    defined and contrasted with theism, 31, 216n.33
    and feminist theology, 193, 254n.38
    and juristic tradition, 31–32, 216n.34
    liberal primitivization of, 32–38, 56, 65, 125, 164, 216n.33, 250n.3
    and neo-orthodox theology, 169
    and romanticism, 80, 85–92, 96, 106, 110, 119–120, 144, 203, 242n.16
Antislavery movement, 23, 25, 61
Armstrong, Karen, 216n.33, 250n.3
Arnold, Matthew, 137–139, 146–149, 154, 203, 240n.2
Astronomy, 22, 24, 33–34, 50, 60, 217n.39

Atonement, doctrine of, 14, 25–30, 133, 158, 165, 202–203
    governmental theory, 27, 44–49, 51, 59, 60, 84, 88, 96, 102–104, 107, 127, 130, 165, 170, 214n.24
    moral influence theory, 26–27, 41–42, 58, 102, 114, 127, 165, 171
    penal substitute theory, 26, 48–55, 60, 89, 92, 96, 102–103, 174, 178
    ransom theory, 98
Augustine, St. (bishop of Hippo), 19, 26, 49, 148

Babbitt, Irving, 191
Baird, Samuel John, 80, 97, 99, 109–112, 124, 202, 222n.34
Baptists, 5, 27, 162, 182, 213n.18
Barnes, Albert, 51, 217n.38, 222n.34, 236n.23
Barth, Karl, 167, 248n.21
Barton, John, 200, 202
Bate, Walter Jackson, 7
Beecher, Catharine, 61
Beecher, Edward, 61, 224n.11
Beecher, Henry Ward, 59, 60–67, 72, 118, 143
    and antislavery, 61
    on the atonement, 225n.26
    background, 60–63, 122
    criticism of governmental theology, 59–60

Beecher, Henry Ward (*continued*)
  Life of Jesus, the Christ, 64–67
  and literature, 62–63
  on Old Testament, 36, 67, 72
  sentimental characterizations of Jesus
    and Mary, 64–67
  and women's rights, 62, 115
Beecher, Lyman, 60–63
Bellamy, Edward, 160, 162, 193
Bellamy, Joseph, 27
Biblical criticism
  and character of Jesus, 13–14, 36–38,
    40–43, 45–48, 56, 63–75, 93–94, 111,
    127, 238n.40. *See also* Sentimental
    incarnationalism
  and complexity of God's character, 19,
    30, 201–202
  and divine inspiration of the Bible, 260n.7
  and God's anger, 13–14, 19, 30–37,
    49–55, 80, 88–90, 99, 175, 184–185
  and God's love, 30, 33, 93–94, 99, 111,
    113
  the "higher criticism," 47, 143, 160, 164,
    167
  and humanitarianism, 32, 87–88
  interpretations of Exodus 3:14, 39–40,
    56, 79, 137–138, 180–181, 186, 202,
    218n.1, 250n.3
  and literary styles, 11, 13–14, 201–202
  New Testament, 52–53, 113, 142–143, 167,
    170, 176, 218n.51, 222n.34, 225n.20
  Old Testament, 30–36, 65, 85–90, 111,
    123, 126, 138, 142–143, 180–181, 187
  See also Anthropomorphism;
    Atonement, doctrine of; God
Blackmur, R. P., 190
Bloom, Harold, 9, 260n.6
Bonhoeffer, Dietrich, 186, 188
Brooks, Cleanth, 154
Browning, Robert, 7, 147, 152, 189–190
Bryant, William Cullen, 7, 151
Buell, Lawrence, 228n.5
Burke, Edmund, 100
Burns, Robert, 6
Bush, Solon, 6
Bushman, Richard, 5
Bushnell, Horace, 13–14, 22, 59, 101, 113–
  133, 181, 202, 222n.34
  and anthropomorphism, 119–121, 124–
    127, 239n.44, 242n.16

  background, 114–121
  Christian Nurture, 97, 113–114, 121–
    124, 238n.32
  contemporary views of, 50, 116, 118,
    129–130, 213n.18, 236n.23
  Forgiveness and Law, 114, 130–133
  and gender, 115, 128
  God in Christ, 50, 114, 118–122, 125–
    133, 236n.23, 238n.32, 239n.44
  historical reputation, 14, 79–80, 114,
    116, 121–124, 133, 143–144,
    236nn.23, 24, 237nn.29, 30, 238n.40,
    240n.64, 243n.33
  and Milton, 118, 120–121
  Nature and the Supernatural, 114, 120–
    121, 132, 144, 236n.24
  romantic characterization of God, 119,
    124–133, 239n.44
  and Shakespeare, 13, 118–121, 128, 131,
    146
  The Vicarious Sacrifice, 113–114, 125–
    132, 144
  and W. G. T. Shedd, 129, 131
Butler, Jon, 5
Byron, George Gordon, Lord, 7, 9–10, 13,
  62, 85–86, 91

Calvin, John, 26, 83, 98, 102, 174,
  218n.53, 257n.53, 259n.1
  on biblical anthropomorphism, 32, 87,
    216n.34
Calvinism, 44, 48–49, 51–52, 177, 209n.28
  in American literary history, 14, 81–82,
    150, 228nn.4, 5, 6
  and romantic characterization of God,
    14, 79–112
Camus, Albert, 191–192, 253n.33
Capitalism, 8, 23. *See also* Consumer
  culture; Industrialization; Social gospel
Capote, Truman, 192
Carson, Clayborne, 256n.49
Catholicism, 71, 254n.40
  anti-Catholicism, 66, 70, 117, 122, 172,
    238n.34
Chambers, Whittaker, 4
Channing, William Ellery, 29, 40–44, 48,
  51, 54–56, 121, 159, 184
  background, 40–41
  criticism of Trinitarian doctrine, 42,
    101–102

on hell, 41, 101
and literature, 40–41, 101
neoclassical characterization of Christ,
   41–43, 101–102, 120, 157, 184, 196
Character, literary depiction of, 6–15, 20–
   30, 57, 95, 144–145, 149–151, 190–
   191. *See also* Neoclassicism;
   Romanticism; Sentimentalism
Cheney, Mary Bushnell, 115–118, 238n.34
Christian Coalition, 197. *See also* Religious
   right
Civil rights movement, 195–196, 198
Civil War, 28, 121, 125, 128, 162, 173,
   180, 239n.49
Clarke, James Freeman, 58–59, 82, 130,
   223n.4
Clarke, Samuel, 23
Cold War, 152, 167, 245n.42, 257n.55,
   258n.56
Coleridge, Samuel Taylor, 6–7, 12–13, 82,
   86, 91, 95, 100, 118–119, 201
Congregationalists, 5, 27, 58, 114
Consumer culture, 10, 244n.38
Cook, George Cram, 190
Coolidge, James, 56–57
"Cosmopolitan," use of term, 4, 205n.2
Cowper, William, 43
Cox, Harvey, 180–181, 186–189, 191–194,
   198–199, 202, 258n.56
   background, 186
   The Feast of Fools, 253n.37
   and literature, 146, 191–192, 253n.37
   neoclassical and sentimental
      characterization of God, 181, 187–188
   and nineteenth-century objections to
      romanticism, 188
   The Secular City, 180, 186–189, 191–
      192, 198, 258n.56, 258–259n.58
   and social gospel, 101, 181, 186–188,
      258n.56

Dabney, Robert Lewis, 6, 222n.34,
   223n.35
Daly, Mary, 194, 254nn.38, 40
Dana, James L., 236n.24
Darwinism
   as challenge to neoclassical and
      sentimental characterization of God, 4,
      22–23, 28, 138, 143–145, 178, 191,
      200, 206n.4, 259n.1

and literary realism, 9, 144, 150
and romantic characterization, 10, 200,
   259n.1
Deism, 22, 90
Delillo, Don, 192
Dickens, Charles, 6, 121
Dickinson, Emily, 43, 151
Dinsmore, Charles Allan, 140, 142, 147, 152
Dostoyevski, Fyodor, 192–193
Douglas, Ann, 150, 210n.29, 214n.23
Douglass, Frederick, 25, 215n.27
Drew, Elizabeth, 225n.44
Dryden, John, 7, 20–21, 24, 35, 43, 46, 83–
   84
Dwight, Timothy, 7, 20–21

Edwards, Jonathan, 27, 44, 47, 49, 72, 114,
   221n.26
   in American religious history, 114,
      206n.4, 209n.28
Edwards, Jonathan, Jr., 106
Eliot, T. S., 150, 154–155, 189
Elrod, Eileen Razzari, 226nn.27, 45
Emerson, Ralph Waldo, 7, 12, 41, 118–
   119, 151, 219n.5
Enlightenment, 21–23
   and fundamentalism, 178
   and neoclassical characterization, 21, 49,
      58, 138, 174, 188, 200, 209n.28
   and views of historical progress, 30, 80
   and views of nature, 4, 8, 21–22, 144,
      174, 200, 206n.4
   See also Humanitarianism;
      Neoclassicism; Sentimentalism
Environmentalism, 250n.3, 257nn.52, 55
Episcopalians, 5
Ethics, 4, 150, 182, 203
Eugenics, 97, 122

Feminist theology, 193–195, 226n.45,
   254nn.38, 40, 258n.56. *See also*
   Women's rights, nineteenth-century
Fosdick, Harry Emerson, 250n.3
Foster, Frank Hugh, 44, 115, 214nn.23, 24
Freud, Sigmund, and Freudianism, 9, 10,
   13, 96, 150, 188
Fundamentalism, 161, 177–179, 185, 197–
   198, 255n.46
   distinguished from conservative
      theology, 177–179, 251n.7

Genteel tradition, 7, 85, 139, 151, 209n.28
Gibbon, Edward, 21, 38
Gilman, Charlotte Perkins, 193
God
  atonement as doctrine most revealing of
    character of, 14, 25–30, 165,
    181–182, 185, 203, 213n.18,
    215n.27, 218n.51
  conservative emphasis on transcendence
    in twentieth century, 139, 161–162,
    167–168, 172, 181, 183
  and emotional complexity. *See* Juristic
    tradition; Romantic anthropomorphism
  and emotional singularity. *See*
    Neoclassical theism; Philanthropism;
    Sentimental incarnationalism
  Holy Ghost, 65, 95–96, 100, 104, 110,
    175, 177, 260n.7
  liberal emphasis on immanence in
    twentieth century, 139, 141–142, 160,
    163, 168, 172, 176, 181, 187
  political characterization in twentieth
    century, 15, 160–161, 180–199, 202,
    257nn.52, 53, 55. *See also* Politics and
    theology
  vagueness in twentieth century, 15, 137–
    139, 142, 160–162, 168–169, 174,
    176–182, 186, 189
  See also Anthropomorphism;
    Atonement, doctrine of; Biblical
    criticism; Sexuality and
    characterizations of God; Trinity
Goethe, Johann Wolfgang von, 12–13, 149,
  243n.34
Goodwin, Henry, 118
Gopnik, Adam, 9
Gray, Thomas, 21, 43
Griffin, George, 80, 98, 100, 103, 106–
  109
Griffith, G. O., 185
Grotius, Hugo, 26–28, 44, 88, 214n.24
Guthrie, Stewart, 216n.33

Harnack, Adolph von, 143, 160, 162, 166–
  167, 216n.33
Hatch, Nathan, 5
Hauerwas, Stanley, 4, 259n.2
Hawthorne, Nathaniel, 7, 59, 150–151
Hazlitt, William, 12, 201
Heinroth, Johann, 6, 91

Henry, Carl F. H.
  on the anti-Christ, 185
  background, 182
  on biblical anthropomorphism, 184
  and Charles Hodge, 184–185
  God, Revelation, and Authority,
    183–185
  and J. Gresham Machen, 180–183
  neoclassical characterization of God,
    183–184
  politicization of conservative theology,
    182–183, 186, 197
  and social gospel, 182, 197
  *The Uneasy Conscience of Modern
    Fundamentalism,* 182
Hermann, Wilhelm, 160, 167, 173
Hodge, Archibald Alexander, 40, 50–55,
  93, 115, 173, 181
  The Atonement, 53–55, 223n.39
  neoclassical characterization of God, 54–
    55, 223n.39
Hodge, Charles, 40, 48–55, 92–93, 103,
  115, 118, 145, 221n.26
  on anthropomorphism, 227n.5
  background, 40, 49–51
  biblical criticism, 34–35, 52–54,
    222n.34
  and Carl Henry, 184–185
  *Commentary on the Epistle to the
    Romans,* 52–54, 222n.34
  and Horace Bushnell, 50, 118, 121,
    129
  and J. Gresham Machen, 173, 175,
    177
  and literature, 49–51
  neoclassical characterization of God,
    52–54, 131
  and romantic anthropomorphism,
    80–81
  and Samuel John Baird, 110–111
  Systematic Theology, 50, 227n.5
Hoge, Dean R., 257n.52
Holmes, Oliver Wendell, 7, 85, 151,
  226n.45
Homer, 19–20, 83
Hooker, Isabella Beecher, 62, 115
Hopkins, Samuel, 27, 41, 49, 52, 60,
  221n.26
  in Stowe's *Minister's Wooing,* 60
Howe, Daniel Walker, 13

Howe, John, 99, 108
Humanitarianism, 23–25
  and biblical criticism, 32, 87–88
  and characterization of God in
    theological modernism and social
    gospel, 140–144, 154–155, 160, 188–
    189
  and child-rearing practices, 23–24, 32,
    87–88, 122
  and neoclassical and sentimental
    characterization, 8, 23–25, 49, 58, 95,
    138–139
  tensions with romanticism, 41, 124
  and views of historical progress, 30, 32
Humboldt, Alexander von, 239n.50
Hume, David, 89
Hunt, Theodore, 145
Hutchison, William, 114

Industrialization, 138, 160–162, 187

James, Henry, Sr., 113, 130
James, William, 115, 259n.1
Jeffers, Robinson, 155–159
Jesus, characterization of. *See* Biblical
    criticism; God; Neoclassical theism;
    Romantic anthropomorphism;
    Sentimental incarnationalism; Trinity
Jews and Judaism, Protestant attitudes
    toward, 31, 68, 88, 90, 109, 123, 126,
    143, 163–164, 178
Johnson, Benton, 257n.52
Johnson, Samuel, 12–13, 20, 210n.3,
    218n.54
Jones, L. Gregory, 259n.2
Juristic tradition, 26–30, 44–45, 54, 87,
    111, 114, 128, 133, 158, 203
  caricature of, 28–30, 51, 83, 148, 163,
    169, 184, 194, 214n.23, 228n.4
  caricature of philanthropism, 45, 58
  characterization of God, 26, 29–30, 36–
    37, 83, 96–99, 203
  historical treatment of decline, 214n.23
  and New Testament, 36–38, 203
  and Old Testament, 30–36, 68, 70, 88,
    119–120
  and the Trinity, 96–100

Keats, John, 7, 92
Kennedy, John F., 191–192

Kermode, Frank, 200
King, Martin Luther, Jr., 195–196,
    258n.58
  and neoclassical traits, 196, 256n.49
  and social gospel and neo-orthodoxy, 196
Krutch, Joseph Wood, 190

Lawrence, D. H., 202
Leach, William, 244n.38
Lewis, Taylor, 36, 86–87, 106, 224n.5
Liberation theology, 198, 258nn.56, 58
Lieber, Francis, 6
Lincoln, Abraham, 28
Lippmann, Walter, 4, 172, 176, 249n.37
Literature, theological views of
  in nineteenth century, 5–7, 19–30
  prior to nineteenth century, 19–20
  by twentieth-century conservatives, 15,
    145, 190–191, 243n.21
  by twentieth-century liberals, 15, 137–
    159, 189–193, 200, 203
Locke, John, 21, 206n.4
Longfellow, Henry Wadsworth, 7, 85, 151
Lowell, James Russell, 7, 85, 151
Lowth, Richard, 86
Luidens, Donald A., 257n.52
Luther, Martin, 12–13, 179
Lystra, Karen, 24

Macaulay, Thomas, 86
Machen, J. Gresham, 161–162, 172–179
  background, 172–173, 221n.27
  on biblical anthropomorphism, 176–177
  and Carl Henry, 182–183
  and Charles Hodge, 173, 175, 177
  Christianity and Liberalism, 172, 174
  and fundamentalism, 177–179
  and literature, 190
  neoclassical characterization of God,
    174–179
  The Origin of Paul's Religion, 176
  and politics, 173, 190
  and Reinhold Niebuhr, 161, 174
  and social gospel, 161, 173
  The Virgin Birth of Christ, 176
Mailer, Norman, 192
Mainstream churches, decline of, 197–199,
    257n.52
Marsden, George, 251n.7
Marsh, James, 82

Mary, mother of Jesus, characterization of, 57, 63–75, 113, 123, 126–127, 142, 155, 176, 226nn.31, 45. *See also* Annunciation to Mary; Sentimental incarnationalism
Mather, Cotton, 20, 145
May, Henry F., 209n.28
McDowall, John, 105
McFague, Sallie, 194–195, 254nn.38, 40, 257n.55
McGiffert, Arthur Cushman, 237n.30
Melville, Herman, 7, 150–151
Methodists, 5, 27, 213n.18
Meyer, Donald, 189, 193
Miles, Jack, 200–203
    and biblical criticism, 201, 260n.5
    romantic characterization of God, 201–202, 260n.5, 261nn.10, 11
Miller, Perry, 20
Milton, John, 6, 11, 20–21, 35, 63, 72, 86, 108, 118, 120, 145
    depiction of Satan, 63, 100–101, 107, 120
    personification of sin and death, 100, 103, 105, 107–108
Miracles, 65, 225n.23
Modernism
    the liberal theological movement, 114, 139–159
    the literary movement, 9, 150–151, 190
Moore, James R., 259n.1
Moore, R. Laurence, 5
Morrison, Toni, 9
Munger, Theodore, 27, 137–153, 180
    background, 139–140
    The Freedom of Faith, 137, 140
    and Horace Bushnell, 114, 133, 140, 143–144, 149, 240n.64, 242n.16, 243n.33
    "The Interplay of Christianity and Literature," 140, 147–149
    and literature, 144–151, 243n.34, 253n.37
    and Matthew Arnold, 137–138, 148–149
    neoclassical and sentimental characterization of God, 133, 137, 140–144
Murdock, James, 45, 102–103

Narrative theology, 200, 259n.2
Neoclassical theism, 32, 39–55, 79, 114, 140–144, 161, 224n.10, 260n.5
    and biblical depiction of God's anger, 13, 19, 30–37, 49–55, 169–170, 176–177, 184–185
    and biblical depiction of Jesus, 13, 37–38, 40–48, 142, 158–159, 164–166, 170–171, 174
    and caricature of juristic tradition, 28–29, 254n.40
    in liberal modernism, neo-orthodoxy, and social gospel, 140–144, 160–161, 171
    and New Testament, 36–38
    and Old Testament, 30–36
    tensions with sentimental incarnationalism, 53, 57–60, 140, 166, 210n.29, 224n.5, 227n.51
Neoclassicism, 7–8, 12, 19–25, 49–50, 58, 181, 191
    celebration of serenity, 8, 25, 32, 38–39, 46–47, 53–55, 57, 92, 105, 255n.44. *See also* Stoicism
    depiction of anger, 8, 24–25, 38, 83–84
    depiction of love, 8, 21, 23, 39, 57, 95, 130
    polarization of emotions, 7, 23–24, 28–30, 57–58, 84, 87, 93, 95, 105, 181
    and political styles, 8, 23, 195–196, 225n.44, 256n.49
Neo-orthodoxy, 150, 152, 154, 161, 166–171
    influence on historiography, 209n.28
    and social gospel, 152, 166, 168–169, 171
    See also Niebuhr, Reinhold
New divinity theologians, 27, 49
Newton, Sir Isaac, and Newtonian astronomy, 22, 24, 50, 60, 85, 142, 188, 206n.4
Niebuhr, H. Richard, 167, 259n.2
Niebuhr, Reinhold, 161–162, 166–171, 182, 198–199
    background, 166, 172
    biblical anthropomorphism, 169
    and civil rights movement, 196
    governmental and moral theories of the atonement, 169–171

and literature, 191, 253n.31
Moral Man and Immoral Society, 167–168, 256n.47, 258n.57
The Nature and Destiny of Man, 167, 169–171, 191
neoclassical and sentimental characterization of God, 169–171
as polemicist, 166–167
racialism, 256n.47
reputation, 166–167
Norris, Frank, 189
Noyes, George Rapall, 30, 89, 126, 239n.43
Nuclear war, threat of, 257n.55

Otto, Rudolph, 177
Owen, John, 36–37, 46, 58, 98–99, 111
on biblical anthropomorphism, 31, 216nn.34, 35

Paganism and literature, 19–20, 145, 149, 157
Park, Edwards, 43–49, 51, 54–55, 100, 115, 170, 213n.18, 221n.26
background, 43–44, 103
biblical criticism, 33–36, 87–88, 217n.38, 236n.23, 253n.37
and Harriet Beecher Stowe, 56, 59–60, 67
and literature, 43–44
neoclassical characterization of God, 22, 39–40, 44–48, 56, 93–94, 98, 102, 104, 127, 130, 132, 142, 158, 217n.39, 218n.47, 224n.10
"The Rise of the Edwardean Theory of the Atonement," 47–48, 214n.24
and sentimental incarnationalism, 58–60
The Theology of the Intellect and That of the Feelings, 33–36, 46, 58, 87–88, 106, 125–126, 217nn.38, 39, 218n.47, 236n.23, 253n.37
Parker, Theodore, 226n.45
Patton, Francis, 221n.27
Paulding, James Kirk, 7
Philanthropism, 26–38
caricature of, 58, 129
characterization or God, 26–30, 32–38, 59, 83, 215n.32
historical treatment of, 209n.28, 214n.23

and Old Testament criticism, 30–36, 68, 88
and New Testament criticism, 36–38
and the Trinity, 96, 100–103
Phrenology, 97, 122, 238n.32
Politics and theology, 15, 139, 142, 153, 168, 172–173, 180–199, 255n.45, 257nn.52, 55
See also Civil rights movement; Environmentalism; Feminist theology; Fundamentalism; God; Neoclassicism; Religious right; Social gospel
Pope, Alexander, 21–22, 43, 83, 85, 210n.3
Popular religion, 4–5, 213n.18, 229n.6
Porter, Noah, 5, 11, 13–14, 21, 43, 58
on aestheticism, 145
on Bushnell, 118
Postmodernism, 9
Presbyterians, 5, 27, 40, 58, 80–82, 109
Psychology
and nineteenth-century literature, 6, 12–13
and twentieth-century literature, 9, 150–151
and twentieth-century theology, 146, 150, 156, 188, 190–192, 253nn.31, 37, 254n.40
See also Freud, Sigmund, and Freudianism
Puritans, 5, 20, 26, 214n.22, 257n.53
Pynchon, Thomas, 9

Rabinowitz, Richard, 210n.29, 214n.23
Racism, 122–123
Ransom, John Crowe, 150
Rauschenbusch, Walter, 160, 162–166, 186, 198–199
background, 162, 172
Christianity and the Social Crisis, 162–165
and civil rights movement, 196
governmental and moral theories of the atonement, 165–166
and literature, 189–190
neoclassical and sentimental characterization of God, 163–166, 247n.13
New Testament criticism, 164
Old Testament criticism, 162–163

Rauschenbusch, Walter (*continued*)
  and Ralph Reed, 197
  A Theology for the Social Gospel, 165–
    166, 196
  warning of class warfare, 162, 198
Realism, 9, 96, 139, 144–145, 149
Reed, Ralph, 197
Reformation, 19, 26, 148, 179
Religious right, 195, 197, 225n.46
Revivalism, 5, 121, 123
Reynolds, David, 210n.29, 228n.5
Rich, Adrienne, 195
Ritschl, Albrecht, 143
Romantic anthropomorphism, 79–133,
    183, 202, 260n.5
  revival of anthropomorphism, 85–90
Romanticism, 8–13, 124, 146, 182, 191
  depiction of ambivalence, 8, 25, 41,
    82, 95, 105, 130, 132–133, 144,
    152–153, 155–157, 195, 201,
    253n.37
  depiction of anger, 8–11, 25, 80, 82,
    84–85, 90–92
  depiction of guilt, 90, 132
  depiction of love, 8–11, 25, 82, 95,
    130
  theological criticism of, 13, 84–85,
    157, 188, 191

Satan, 6, 63, 69, 98, 178, 182, 185–186.
    See also Milton, John
Schaeffer, Francis, 191, 194
Schleiermacher, Friedrich, 237n.29,
    238n.40
Scott, Sir Walter, 6, 21, 62
Sedgwick, Catharine, 24, 84, 226n.45
Sentimental incarnationalism, 56–75, 79–
    80, 114
  and biblical depiction of Jesus, 38, 42,
    63–64, 142, 158–159, 163–166, 170–
    171, 174, 225n.20
  and caricature of juristic tradition, 28–
    29, 193
  and feminist theology, 193–195
  in liberal modernism, neo-orthodoxy,
    and social gospel, 140–144, 160–161,
    171
  tensions with neoclassical theism, 58–60,
    140, 166, 193–194, 210n.29, 224n.5,
    227n.51

Sentimentalism, 7–8, 24–25, 49, 57
  bodily expression, 24–25, 57, 181, 191
  depiction of anger, 8, 24–25, 84
  depiction of love, 8, 24, 57, 95–96, 121,
    130
  and gender, 57–59, 68, 84, 115, 226n.45
  polarization of emotions, 7, 24, 28–30,
    57–58, 84, 87, 93, 95
Sexuality, Victorian and modern views of,
    96–97, 195
Sexuality and characterizations of God
  and annunciation, 65, 72
  in Harriet Beecher Stowe's work, 72
  in Horace Bushnell's work, 113, 121–129
  in Jack Miles's work, 202, 261n.10
  in Samuel John Baird's work, 109–112
  and the Trinity, 96–100, 113
Shakespeare, William, 6, 11–13, 20–21,
    88–90, 154
  Hamlet, 12–13, 107, 146, 201, 203,
    260n.6
  and Horace Bushnell, 13, 119–121, 128,
    131
  Macbeth, 74–75, 90, 121
Shedd, W. G. T., 6, 14, 28, 79–94, 99, 145,
    181
  "The Atonement: A Satisfaction for the
    Ethical Nature of Both God and Man,"
    28, 91–93, 131
  background, 82, 104
  on biblical anthropomorphism, 88–90, 119
  and Charles Hodge, 92–93, 222n.34
  Dogmatic Theology, 93–94
  and Horace Bushnell, 119, 127, 129, 131
  and literature, 82–83
  romantic and neoclassical
    characterization of God, 79, 88–94,
    127, 158, 176–177
  "The True Tone in Preaching and the
    True Temper in Hearing," 28, 88–90
Sheldon, David Newton, 227n.50, 246n.59
Shelley, Percy Bysshe, 7, 91, 119,
    238n.32
Sin, doctrines of
  in histories of American theology,
    209n.28
  in nineteenth-century theology, 99,
    123–124, 128, 161, 165–168, 175
  in twentieth-century theology, 146, 150,
    152, 173, 185

Smith, H. Shelton, 238n.40

Social gospel, 15, 114, 145, 160–171, 189, 244n.38
  and civil rights movement, 196
  criticism of, 161–162, 166–179, 189
  and fundamentalism, 179
  and Harvey Cox's secularization thesis, 101, 181, 186–188, 258n.56
  neoclassical and sentimental traits of God, 140–144, 161
  and religious right, 197

Socinus, Faustus, 26–27

Spring, Gardiner, 26, 48

Stanton, Elizabeth Cady, 62

Stevens, Wallace, 153, 155

Stoicism, 20, 23–24, 218n.54

Stowe, Calvin, 67–68, 225n.26

Stowe, Harriet Beecher, 7, 28, 56, 67–75, 116, 194
  antislavery, 61
  background, 60–63
  and Edwards Park, 56, 59–60, 67
  Footsteps of the Master, 71–76
  and literature, 62–63
  Minister's Wooing, 59–60, 227n.51, 253n.37
  sentimental characterizations of Mary and Jesus, 67–75, 123, 125, 155, 195, 226n.45
  Uncle Tom's Cabin, 28, 59, 62, 194, 215n.27, 226n.45
  Woman in Sacred History, 67–71
  and women's rights, 62, 68, 226n.31

Stuart, Moses, 37, 46, 238n.40

Swift, Jonathan, 105

Swinburne, Algernon, 145, 149–150

Tappan, Lewis, 117

Taylor, Gary, 12

Temperance movement, 23

Tennyson, Alfred, Lord, 7, 147, 152

"Theism," contrasted with "anthropomorphism," 31, 86–87

Thompson, Joseph, 58, 88

Thornwell, James Henley, 40, 98, 100, 102–109, 233n.15
  on Samuel John Baird, 112

Tillich, Paul, 152

Tillotson, John, 23, 43

Tompkins, Jane, 28, 229n.12

Towne, E. C., 130

Transcendentalism, 81

Trilling, Lionel, 9

Trinity, 37, 56, 95–112, 183
  in George Griffin's work, 98, 106–108
  in Horace Bushnell's work, 113, 125, 127, 131, 238n.40
  in James Henley Thornwell's work, 98, 104–106
  in juristic tradition, 48, 96, 98–99
  in philanthropism, 100–103
  in romantic anthropomorphism, 95–100
  in Samuel John Baird's work, 98, 109–112
  Satan, sin, and death as an anti-Trinity, 98–100, 108
  in W. G. T. Shedd's work, 93–94, 131
  in William Ellery Channing's work, 41–42, 101–102
  See also God

Troeltsch, Ernst, 167

Turner, James, 21

Turretin, François, 37, 46, 52

Unitarians, 5, 27, 37–38, 40–41, 44–45, 48, 81, 96, 102, 209n.28, 219n.5

Van Doren, Carl, 151

Virgil, 19–20, 83

Walker, James Barr, 225n.26

Warfield, Benjamin Breckinridge, 173–174, 221n.27, 251n.8

Warner, Susan, 7, 59, 84

Watts, Isaac, 72

Weigle, Luther, 122

Whitman, Walt, 7, 122, 151, 239n.50

Whittemore, Robert, 221n.26

Whittier, John Greenleaf, 7, 140, 151

Wilder, Amos, 15, 145, 151–159, 246n.58
  "Art and Theological Meaning," 152–153
  background, 151–152
  and Harvey Cox, 191
  and literature, 146, 152–159, 245nn.41, 42, 49, 253n.37
  Modern Poetry and the Christian Tradition, 154

Wilder, Amos (*continued*)
  neoclassical and sentimental
    characterization of Christ, 158–159
  and nineteenth-century objections to
    romanticism, 157–159
  on Robinson Jeffers's "Dear Judas,"
    155–159
  The Spiritual Aspects of the New Poetry,
    152–153
  and Theodore Munger, 152–155
  Theology and Modern Literature, 155–
    159
Wilder, Thornton, 151
Wilson, Edmund, 190, 245n.49
Wimsatt, William, 154
Wines, E. C., 33

Women's rights, nineteenth-century,
    61–62, 84, 97, 115, 225n.45, 226n.31.
    See also Feminist theology
Woodhull, Victoria, 62
Woolf, Virginia, 150–151
Woolsey, Theodore Dwight, 66
Worcester, Noah, 29–30, 35–36, 42, 48,
    80, 130
Wordsworth, William, 7, 21, 43, 145
World War I, 152, 166–167
World War II, 152, 167
Wright, George Frederick, 259n.1
Wright, Henry Clarke, 97
Wuthnow, Robert, 255n.46

Zola, Emile, 189